The Manhattan Family Guide to Private Schools and Selective Public Schools

The Manhattan Family Guide to Private Schools

and Selective Public Schools

Victoria Goldman

Published by
Soho Press, Inc.
853 Broadway
New York, NY 10003

Library of Congress Cataloging-in-Publication Data

Goldman, Victoria, 1958–
The Manhattan family guide to private schools and selective public schools /
Victoria Goldman
ISBN 978-1-56947-641-3
Sixth Edition

Printed in the United States of America

10 9 8 7 6 5 4 3 2

This edition, the sixth, is dedicated to the memory of Laura Hruska, editor extraordinaire. Laura's guidance, vision, support and keen interest in this book and my career, as well as in education, will always provide an invaluable source of inspiration and encouragement.

Acknowledgments

This book could not have been written without the help of countless people in the independent school community: the parents, students and alumni who answered extensive questionnaires and shared their experiences, and the nursery school directors, heads of schools, admissions and development office personnel, educators and psychologists who offered their expertise, updates, and insights. For rolling up their sleeves and pitching in, a hearty thank you to Mickey Napolitano and her assistant, Janet Hart. And, of course, Laura Hruska, whom I thank for her partnership, patience, guidance (and red pencil).

Authors' Note

When I underwent the nursery school and kindergarten admissions process and found it daunting, I vowed that something had to be done to make the process more humane, or at least easier. I was overwhelmed by the number of applications that had to be completed for my children and found myself confused by the number of choices and ultimately intimidated by the admissions process. I hardly thought then that my research would lead to an educational consulting business (Education First, *infra* p. 35), an independent career as a journalist, countless columns, articles, and books, culminating in six editions of this book.

Touring schools and scrutinizing brochures, annual reports, handbooks, curriculum guides and student publications has become routine for me and I interview admissions directors, heads of schools, educators, IQ test administrators, child psychologists, students, alumni and parents. Originally, a letter and questionnaire was mailed to all of the heads of schools describing the project. Now, updated information is requested and, in most cases, promptly sent; when appropriate, school visits and revisits are made.

It should not surprise parents that the schools that were most open to questions are also the most secure about their missions and the directions in which they are moving, and are the most welcoming to parents in general. While it is easy to understand the reluctance of the schools to disclose the inner workings of their admissions decision-making processes, many heads of schools, admissions directors and administrators continue to be very generous with their time and advice and I thank them for their cheerful cooperation.

Victoria Goldman
www.VictoriaGoldman.net

Table of Contents

EVERYTHING YOU SHOULD KNOW ABOUT PRIVATE SCHOOL BUT ARE AFRAID TO ASK

INTRODUCTION

The "private"° school admissions season begins the day after Labor Day when New York City parents start to drag their children, through four months of touring and testing, then wait in a state of suspended animation until the middle of that bleak wintry day in February or March when a thick or thin envelope arrives in the mail. (Typically, thick envelopes contain a contract; thin, a non-acceptance letter). Parental egos are either elated or deflated, but for those who are disappointed, it's still not too late to go house hunting.

There are over seventy independent schools in the New York City area; these include some of the best schools in the nation. There are schools with religious affiliations, schools for children with learning disabilities, Montessori Schools and a Waldorf School: There really is an independent school for everyone, but it just might not be the one you have your heart set on. Applying to New York City's independent schools has not gotten less stressful over the years; the city's demographics significantly impact the admissions game. Although fifteen years ago just under 2,000 children were applicants for prekindergarten and kindergarten places, today, despite the economy and rising tuition rates, over 3,300 children were tested by the Educational Records Bureau (ERB) for these openings recently.

What Is an Independent School?

All of the member schools of the Independent Schools Admissions Association of Greater New York (ISAAGNY) are not-for-profit, racially nondiscriminatory, have their own board of trustees, are chartered by the New York State Board of Regents and accredited by the New York State Association of Independent Schools or the Middle-States Association of Colleges and Schools. Independent schools have six basic characteristics: 1) self-governance, 2) self-support, 3) self-defined curriculum, 4) self-selected students, 5) self-selected faculty, 6) small size.°° Private schools, on the other hand, are owned by indi-

°In New York City most "private" schools are either "independent" (nonprofit) or privately owned and operated for profit. Most of the schools discussed in this book are actually independent schools.
°°*Independent Schools, Independent Thinkers,* edited by Pearl Rock Kane (Jossey-Bass Publishers, San Francisco, 1992), pp. 6–17.

viduals who may derive profits or incur losses from school operations.[*]

Teachers in these schools do not need to be certified by the state. They are, however, likely to be experts in their fields. For example, a historian teaching history courses or a drama department head who is a playwright and director when he's not teaching. There is a good side to this; the teacher is likely to be a true enthusiast who will be able to convey the excitement of his subject. The downside is that without an appreciation for the child's time and learning level, the expert may demand collegiate or graduate school level work from a twelve-year-old. For example, one recent holder of a doctorate in French demanded that the eighth graders at one top private school read Pascal's philosophy in French because without mastering Pascal, "an appreciation of French culture was not possible." Most independent school kindergarten teachers do have a master's in early childhood education.

Perhaps the most important difference between independent and public schools is that the formers' "fundamental freedom from state and local governments' regulation has allowed independent schools to develop outside of the ferment that has rocked the public schools."[**] And, of course, public schools do not charge tuition and every child is entitled to placement in such a school (subject to residence requirements and other such prerequisites).

Each school has its own unique character, with a board of trustees that appoints the head of school, who ensures that the school fulfills its educational mission. The headmaster (in conjunction with the development office) assumes the role of CEO and major fund-raiser. Every independent school has its own philosophy of education, its "statement of mission" (the primary aims of the school). This mission statement is always included in the school's literature, but you sometimes have to read between the lines to find it. Each independent school is accountable to its students and their parents; if the parents are not happy with the fulfillment of the school's mission they can remove their children and find another that suits them better. If enough parents do so, the school will fail.

A good reputation is so vital to independent schools that although some myths about a school such as "having the brightest kids" or

[*]"Independent School Myths and Realities," a newsletter published by NAIS (National Association of Independent Schools), revised March 1994.
[**]*Independent Schools, Independent Thinkers, supra.*

admitting "only the most terrific families" or "getting the most kids into the top Ivy League colleges" are misleading and often false, they do attract applicants. And some school admissions personnel, perhaps inadvertently, help perpetuate these "positive" myths. (Increasingly, independent schools have created a position for a "communications director" or a director of public relations to deal with the media and to shape their public profiles.) The fact is, independent schools are much more mixed than anyone admits. (I find that siblings and legacies are often the great equalizers, but even so, they must measure up to the school's standards.) As the *New York State Association of Independent Schools Guide to Choosing a School* states, while SAT scores and college admissions records are "good indicators of the quality of the student body, not necessarily of the school . . . the schools of worth are those whose students, facile or not, are helped to realize their highest potential, develop a lifelong love of learning and forge good character."*

The level of work, the pressure, pace of learning and challenge, hours of homework and amount of remedial support provided by the school all contribute to designation as "very selective." The qualities a child needs to get in and stay in one of these schools are strong academic potential, an outgoing nature, intensity, good self-esteem, independence, maturity and perseverance. A less competitive, more nurturing school would be better for a child with an average IQ, a known learning disability, a very creative or artistic nature or a nonconformist or shy personality. A desire not to subject a child to externally imposed requirements at an early age and a belief in a child's innate abilities, which, given time to flower, will lead him to a happier, more fulfilling life militate against the choice of a highly pressured school experience.

There truly is a school for your child, but it is not true that if you can pay, your child can go to the school of your choice. The apparent arbitrariness of admissions decisions is hard for many successful, ambitious and influential Manhattan parents to accept. Said one admissions director: "After all, they got into an Ivy League school, joined the sorority/fraternity of their choice, landed the job of their dreams and they expect the same for their child too." Despite the economy, admissions at all levels to the most selective schools remains very competitive. Some schools have expanded their enrollments,

*"Choosing a School—A Guide For Parents," a pamphlet published by the New York State Association of Independent Schools (NYSAIS), *infra* pp. 507–508.

added an extra kindergarten or first grade class that continue up through the school. And, new schools have opened since the last edition of this book. But, the bottom line is: seats are limited even though tuition costs roughly $30,000 or more a year.

In the past few years, schools that give preference to siblings and legacies (descendants of former students) have often had more applicants than places, and have been forced to make some difficult decisions. Your child's year might be a year in which many siblings apply at the school of your choice but take heart: If your child doesn't get into your first-choice school in kindergarten, you might try again in a few years, by which time attrition will probably have occurred due to divorce and families relocating to other cities and the suburbs. Because more families are now staying in the city, fewer places may be available in the earliest years. Places do become available in sixth and ninth grades at many schools that go through twelfth grade.

Changes in School Services

Gone are the days when women volunteers devoted their time exclusively to serving on school committees, chaperoning field trips and organizing fund-raisers. The two-career family is now the norm (and you are as likely to see a fifty-year-old father attending the school play or walking afternoon safety patrol as a mother). There is an increased need for after-school, vacation and summer programs, and working parents are often happiest if those programs are located at their children's own schools. Most schools now have after-school programs. Caedmon School was the first to introduce "child-minding" until 6:00 P.M. Even the Collegiate School and The Brearley School added their own after-school programs, recognizing that working families depend on these services and if they want all types of diversity in their schools they have to provide support for them. (Parents are continually scheduling after-school activities such as sports, music and religious instruction, in addition to playdates, for younger children while older children often stay at school until five-forty-five or later and then have hours of homework, as well as other lessons or activities. Some of our children work longer days than their parents!

One outcome of working parents' desire to have their children in school for longer hours is that the Guild of New York Independent Schools agreed to extend the independent school year from 160 days to 170 days (still ten days or more short of the public school schedule). Schools also agreed to open their doors earlier in the fall, closer to the Labor Day holiday weekend, and extend school days through mid-June like Riverdale Country School where recently five to seven more school days were added to the school's academic calendar. A handful of schools still give "travel days" on either side of spring break, a vestige of the era in which families routinely packed a trunk for Europe. Now some of these families travel to snow country in Utah or Colorado.

Financial Pressures

The question of the affordability of private school education is becoming more acute as a result of a turbulent economy, and tuition for Manhattan day schools, which doubled in the past decade, continues to rise. Now parents can expect to pay at least $30,000 or more for third-grade tuition. In addition, the gap between income generated by tuition, rising operating costs, and capital improvements has widened and all schools count upon voluntary giving and annual fundraising revenues. Schools are under more pressure for outside fundraising from any place they can find it, but more often than not, it comes from parents. The pressure to give can be especially intense when the class representative tells you they are hoping for 100% participation. What most parents don't realize is that there is no threshold for annual giving. Parents are asked to give whatever they can; contributions within a given class may range from $5.00 to $25,000. Of course only a contribution of $25,000 or more will earn you inclusion in "The Headmaster's Circle", almost always an extremely elite group.

While many independent schools took advantage of the economic boom around the turn of the millennium to make capital improvements and raise the bar academically; tuitions have steadily increased as have endowments since the late 90's. Touring schools for this edition shows the fruits of the past. There are bright, new state-of-the-art buildings with greenhouses, science labs, music and art studios, theaters, playing fields, pools and more. Now, in the face of a deep recession, many school's finances have become strained and improvements revaluated or stalled as the need for financial aid increases. (However, parents who are concerned about the financial health of a prospective school should not ask for the annual report until after their child has been accepted.) A healthy endowment shouldn't be the only reason to pick a school. But, unless a school has a substantial endowment, current parents will be the school's prime source of revenue.

Many parents do not know that tuition covers only about 80 percent of a school's operating expenses and budget, much of this going toward teacher salaries and other benefits. Capital improvements, new technology and science labs, and improvements and repairs to existing facilities, are necessary to keep the schools competitive. Adding to this pressure is the increased need for tuition assistance of parents whose children are already in the schools.°Thus it doesn't hurt to have families who manage charitable foundations in the parent body. As one admissions director confided, "We are a business, you know."

There is increased concern about socioeconomic stratification within school populations as many middle and upper middle income families find that they are unable or unwilling to pay approximately $400,000 for thirteen years of private school tuition. Most schools are seeing an increase in families with high income levels applying for financial aid. According to the Director of Financial Aid Services at NAIS, "Families may well have financial need from their perspective, but does the school have the financial aid available to meet the needs of all families applying?" Schools are being forced to make tough decisions about which families to support. "The decisions they make illustrate the school's attitude toward socioeconomic diversity and their desire to have it."

Following the national trend in public schools towards eliminating junior high schools in favor of middle schools (serving grades six through eight), Community School Districts 2 and 3 on the Upper East and West sides of Manhattan decided to end their elementary schools at fifth grade. A number of very bright and highly motivated fifth grade public school students now apply to the private schools for entrance at sixth grade. Many of the top private schools are making space for them, while at the same time, reserving places for kids in various scholarship programs who enter at sixth, seventh or ninth grade. Some schools surveyed, such as Trinity School, say that because of the way their schools are structured and/or because of space restraints, openings in sixth grade at those schools would depend upon attrition and reorganization. Others, including The Brearley School, Horace Mann, Riverdale Country, Fieldston, and The Dalton School

°See "Applying for Financial Aid," p. 49, *infra*.

8

have already expanded their sixth grades to accommodate public school applicants.

As tuitions climb and the competition for places in the most exclusive schools remain intense, the private schools face growing resentment from full-tuition paying families who find that their hard earned tuition dollars are subsidizing increasing numbers of scholarship students. However, typically, the numbers of students receiving full scholarship is markedly lower than those who receive partial aid. Schools find it is more cost effective to support two families on partial assistance (each paying $6,000 or more toward tuition, for example) thus achieving a greater diversity of families for the same investment. In another instance of how elementary and secondary private school admissions parallel admissions at the college level, some middle class families of color, Hispanic and Asian families, (all of whom are historically underrepresented in private schools), cognizant of their marketability, find that they are able to shop around for the best deal.

Parents should keep in mind that there is a significant difference between applying for financial assistance at the elementary and secondary levels and applying at the college level where federal assistance is available in addition to a wide variety of institutional assistance. Parents of elementary and secondary school age children also have another viable option—public school. More middle and upper middle class parents are considering select city public schools for a portion of their child's education. Although Hunter Elementary is under the aegis of Hunter College of the City of New York, acceptance to this highly selective tuition-free school is often considered as desirable as acceptance to the most prestigious private school. The specialized high schools such as Stuyvesant, Bronx Science and Brooklyn Tech are still magnets for many private school students beginning in ninth grade.

Technology

To remain competitive and up-to-the-minute, schools are under increasing pressure to spend more of their budgets on technology and related programs. In addition, many schools are running "computer initiative" capital campaigns to further augment their technology programs. One school hosted a "cybercarnival" to give the school's technology program a boost.

Upgrading hardware, adding high speed wireless connections to the Internet and buying the latest software is just a part of the expense. The best technology in the world is useless without people; almost every comprehensive independent school now has a Director of Technology. Many schools also find it essential to have a full-time "network administrator" to maintain the system.

And that's not all. A good educational technology program requires trained faculty to integrate all this "stuff" into the curriculum in meaningful ways. Staff training, whether through an outside workshop or an "in-house" technology coordinator, is fundamental—and expensive.

According to one technology seer, the day when "machines are the hand-maiden of cognition in the classroom" is not far off. Now, many lower school classrooms have the latest technology. Students at most schools tote laptops to and from school in their backpacks and use the computer in every subject class as a "transparent tool"—as they would use pencil and paper. Students at most schools already have access to a school "intranet" or internal website that allows students to access homework assignments, read school notices, join in school conferences, communicate with faculty and send in their homework via e-mail.

The Internet has become a primary research tool and nearly every school library is now on-line. Schools subscribe to several services that allow students to search an extensive database of full-text articles from thousands of periodicals, including The New York Times and many magazines. For example, an English teacher at York Prep uses the Internet to look up the lyrics of Bob Dylan's songs for a course on the oral tradition, and for a recent physics class at Riverdale Country School, homework assignments were downloaded through the University of Texas's website.

Desktop publishing gives students "ownership" of the publication process. For instance, The Brearley School offers desktop publishing workshops and an interactive design class for aspiring student editors. Students in their own Student Publications Office also produce a literary magazine and The Brearley School Yearbook.

At Convent of the Sacred Heart a young woman in a biology class used special motion, temperature, pH and pressure probes attached to a laptop computer to record and graph laboratory data, allowing her to fine-tune her experiment.

Learning literally "comes alive" when students create multi-media projects. It is not enough that students acquire basic computing skills such as word-processing, computer graphics, desktop publishing, databases and simulation. "Computer literacy means knowing how to use the computer as a tool to help create and think; to manage information, to solve problems, to express ideas and to communicate with others."*

Parents looking at a prospective school should discreetly find out:

- Does the school have a Technology Mission Statement?
- How much of the technology budget is devoted to faculty support and training?
- How is technology integrated into all subject areas, not just the obvious ones?

An educational technology consultant suggested parents look at how the computer is used. Does the school use the computer as an "electronic playbook" or as a creative tool involving high level thinking? Do students spend computer time visiting the computer lab to play games or do they create something of their own?

In the most developed programs, the classroom teacher initiates projects using different applications to solve problems, so students think in new ways. One fifth grade homeroom teacher at Little Red School House and Elisabeth Irwin High School asserts, "All the hardware in the world can't beat a good curriculum idea." For a unit on the study of ancient civilizations, he created a project that looks at the problems faced by archeologists in the interpretation of artifacts. The project integrates science, math, writing, computer, history and art and culminates in the creation of a classroom museum of artifacts as well as a "computer museum."

For students who do not have access to a home computer, and/or may not have the latest software applications or a connection to the Internet, schools have become increasingly accommodating by devising their own solutions to this issue of equity. Some have purchased computers for scholarship students, others are keeping their computer labs open and staffed until late afternoon. Some independent schools bridge the gap by opening the school to public school students on Saturdays. Most NYC public libraries provide Internet access free of charge.

Ibid.

Faculty

In addition to the composition of the student body, another essential component in measuring the quality of a school is the caliber of the faculty. Teachers in the independent schools do not have the bargaining power of a union and can be hired and fired at the will of the administration. However, teachers in independent schools do have the ability to design the curriculum and have flexibility in their choice of approach to their subject, books, grades, and materials. The advantage for schools is that they can handpick teachers who conform to the school's philosophy and style.

In some cases, independent school teachers receive pay parity with public school teachers; in other cases they are paid significantly less. For instance, the head of the English department at an independent school told us that she earns about $10,000 less than her suburban public school counterpart. The exact figures vary from school to school. Heads of schools contend that it is health and other benefits for staff that really eat into the budget. Still, in order to keep the best teachers, schools are under constant pressure to offer faculty inducements such as housing and stipends for study and travel. Many schools have named scholarship funds earmarked for this purpose.

Multiculturalism and Diversity

Since, New York City is one of the most multicultural cities in the country, many parents and educators believe that its independent schools should reflect that "metropolitan mix" in their student bodies. Despite programs such as Early Steps, a program that promotes diversity at the kindergarten and first grade levels, the lower schools (kindergarten through fifth grade) have remained remarkably homogeneous. Prep for Prep prepares talented junior high school students of color for entrance into New York City's independent upper schools where there is more abundant scholarship money. The so-called "progressive" schools have always been in the vanguard of new thinking, while more "traditional" schools adapt at their own pace, especially regarding the thorny issues of diversity and multiculturalism. Schools such as The Ethical Culture Fieldston Schools, Friends Seminary and United Nations International School have always welcomed and encouraged a diverse student body. Some of the older, more traditional schools did not always do so but many of these schools now actively seek cultural diversity.

The pace of change is likely to become more rapid for several reasons. Among them, the changing college admissions profile—bright and able students of color and other minorities have fared particularly well in gaining admissions to the elite Ivy League colleges and universities; since a large part of an independent school's status derives from the number of students they feed to the Ivy League, this trend has inevitably trickled down to kindergarten admissions. And, the schools do not want to seem elitist.

A faculty commitment to diversity is also important. Diversity training for faculty is on the rise and many independent school teachers spend time at anti-bias retreats and conferences related to these themes. The parent body also influences the pace of change. Many of the independent schools have a parent committee on diversity. Some parents prefer to have their children in a more homogeneous setting and therefore may choose a different sort of school.

Students at New York City's independent schools, along with the rest of the nation, are struggling with the issues of race and ethnicity and the meaning of "difference." Active recruiting and competition for children of color makes some educators uneasy, fanning fears of tokenism and concern for the schools' sensitivity to these students' needs once they are enrolled. A former Parents Association president illustrated this attitude by saying "We want to see our kids in a school with a healthy scholarship program, but of course, we will bring them up to our level." Support groups for families of color and students of color (some adopted students of color are not from families of color) abound. In addition, many schools now have anti-bias groups, Cultural Awareness Days and clubs such as Students Aware of Multicultural Ethics (S.A.M.E.). There is an Interschool Multicultural Coalition. Yet even in schools with diverse student bodies there are problems. For example, younger children who commute from Upper Manhattan and the boroughs find it difficult to reciprocate playdates. In some instances parents have been mistaken for baby sitters. In the upper grades are "scholarship cliques" and tensions have been aired in school assemblies or focus groups.

The independent schools, particularly the girls' schools, are also concerned about gender issues. A 1992 study commissioned by the American Association of University Women (AAUW) carried out by the Wellesley College Center for Research on Women, entitled *How*

Schools Shortchange Girls documented the subtle gender bias in schools and how girls are steered away from pursuing careers in math, science and technology. The AAUW report showed that young women were not receiving the "same quality or quantity of education as their brothers."[*]

The AAUW issued a new report in 1998 which took a critical look at the value of single-sex education for girls and found no evidence that girls were better off in separate schools: "What the research shows is that separating by sex is not the solution to gender inequity in education. When elements of a good education are present, girls and boys succeed." A press release from the AAUW states, "No learning environment, single-sex or coed, provides a sure escape from sexism. Sound teacher training is key to reducing sex stereotyping in both the coed and single-sex programs." Ninety-five per cent of America's schoolchildren attend coed public schools. The press release also states that there is debate about whether the benefits of some single-sex programs (such as a heightened regard for math and science among girls) derive from factors unique to single-sex programs or factors that promote good education such as small classes and schools, intensive academic curriculum and a disciplined environment.

On the other hand, it has been contended that schools as they are organized require skills and behavior favoring girls. The difference in diagnosis of both Attention Deficit Disorder (ADD) and dyslexia is skewed heavily toward boys. It is possible that boys' schools cope better with the need for physical activity and with their differing pace of development. It would be eye-opening to ascertain the percentage of first, second, and third grade boys at selective co-educational schools who are privately tutored to keep up with the school's expectations. This is an extra expense to the parents, of course. (See also AAUW, *infra* pp. 504–505).

Some independent schools have special programs to deal with gender bias. For example, The Dalton School has a parent-sponsored committee that reviews sex-equity issues in the school. The Berkeley Carroll School has a faculty sex-equity study group that meets regularly; Manhattan Country School received a five-year "gender equity grant" for $100,000 from a private family foundation in Washington; The Riverdale Country School holds a series of parent education evenings on gender issues.

---

[*]*The AAUW Report: How Schools Shortchange Girls*, the AAUW Educational Foundation and the National Education Association, Washington, D.C., 1992 (p. v.).

In response to gender equity concerns, many schools have reevaluated their curricula, either adding or revising courses that include other perspectives including electives such as "Africa in America: an Examination of the Literature of the Men and Women Who Shaped Contemporary Black American Culture" and "Reform Movements: The Advent of Feminism, Black History and Civil Rights." Certainly there are still some schools where the DWEM (Dead White European Males) curriculum predominates, and for some parents a classic curriculum in a traditional setting is just fine. That's what freedom of choice is about.

In recent years, single-sex, established, traditional schools (many of which have ample endowments) once again became very attractive to many well-to-do parents. Even though both parents might have high-powered careers, these "new traditionalists" are reassured by structured classrooms, the old-fashioned values and a traditional curriculum, as well as the status that acceptance into these schools still confers. But today even the so-called traditional schools are sometimes hard to tell apart from the progressive schools.° Some schools have a unique educational philosophy such as Bank Street School for Children, Fieldston Lower School, The Dalton School, The Rudolf Steiner School and City & Country School; many traditional schools have incorporated what were once considered "progressive" approaches to elementary education into their curricula. Schools are moving away from teacher-directed classrooms and toward encouraging classrooms where collaborative learning is stressed and where different learning styles and different rates of development are accommodated. There is increased integration of subject matter; most elementary programs favor using the experiential or hands-on approach to learning for everything from science to social studies. Parents should be aware that it is at the middle and upper levels that the schools are most different from one another. When they look at a kindergarten they should look at the upper school as well.

New York City's independent schools are not the ivory towers they once were. Although still exclusionary financially, certain schools are more inclusive in the makeup of their student bodies than they ever have been. When schools renovate, they must now make accommodations for the disabled. But as a former associate director of the

°I have noted the schools where uniforms are prescribed. This is often a clue for parents: it can be argued that uniforms diminish dress competition but usually coed progressive schools do not require them.

Educational Records Bureau reminded us, "Private school education is still a privilege, not an entitlement." The private, independent schools of New York City are still distinguished by their ability to select . . . and exclude.

SELECTING A SCHOOL

Choosing an independent school in New York City is like dating. As one admissions director said, "The chemistry has to be right on both sides." Respect the judgment of the admissions personnel; they really know which children will be successful in their type of program. In making the final decision, a former Parents League president and leader of a toddler group advises, "There should be a commonality between home and school" and, in the final decision, "Use your gut feeling. The decision should be ninety-eight percent stomach and heart and two percent head." Through it all remember that your child is unique. And be wary of the Trophy Child Syndrome. As David Elkind writes in *Miseducation: Preschoolers at Risk*, "The social pressure on contemporary parents to use their children as symbols of economic surplus and status is powerful, even if parents are not fully aware of it." Misguided parents believe that "a successful child is the ultimate proof of one's own success."° As one Director of Admissions advised us, "Consider your child's comfort level" when selecting a school.

Factors to consider

1. **Location: City or "Campus"**
   Note that a campus school (located outside of Manhattan) may require busing or other transportation, which can cost up to $4,000 annually. The child attending a school far from his immediate neighborhood spends many hours in travel over the course of his education. Parents of young children may choose a campus school so that they can experience a clean outdoor environment for relaxation and recreation daily, and so that, when they are older, they may enjoy grassy playing fields and tree-shaded quads. There is

°*Miseducation: Preschoolers at Risk,* by David Elkind (Knopf, New York, 1987), p. 78

always a late bus to accommodate children enrolled in after-school activities. But for some children there may be better uses for this time. Many adjust with no problem, even in the early years; others find the extra travel draining.

2. **Single Sex or Coed°**

   In the younger grades, many children do not seem to value friend-ships with members of the opposite sex. Later, this changes drasti-cally. Parents sometimes prefer a single-sex school where girls may feel more encouraged to be leaders and where their competitive instincts may be less fettered or where boys' needs for physical activity and differing rate of academic development are accommo-dated.

3. **Philosophy of School (Educational Practices and Values)**

   A school's goals are spelled out in its mission statement. Look at the history of the school, at its founder and his or her philosophy of education. Is the parents association active and inclusive? Does the school strive for a diverse student body? Are multicultural per-spectives included in the curriculum? Are classes formal or informal? How much homework is given? How much support is provided to students who are struggling? Is there enrichment for those who need it? Is community service required (or incorpo-rated into the curriculum)? Perhaps the most important question parents of a kindergarten applicant can ask is "How are develop-mental differences handled in the early years?" Ask your nursery school teacher about your child's learning style to determine what type of learning environment would be best for him or her.

4. **Religious Affiliation**

   Is the school presently affiliated with a religious institution? Many schools were founded in church buildings and later became inde-pendent entities, although they may retain the name of the church. In some cases, a representative of the church continues to serve on the board of trustees. Some Jewish schools are associ-ated with a congregation. Is there mandatory prayer or chapel attendance? Which religious holidays are recognized on the school calendar?

°Brearley, Browning, Chapin, Collegiate, Dalton, Nightingale-Bamford, Spence and Trinity are members of the coeducational Interschool Program. Students from member schools can participate in after-school activities, academic courses, intramural sports, community service projects and other activities and clubs. Weekend and holiday dances are an adjunct to single-sex schooling.

5. **Parent Body**

How well will you fit in? Remember that you have to live with these people for the next eight or more years and their children will form your child's peer group.

6. **Size of School**

Consider your child's "comfort level." Will he or she fare better in a smaller, more nurturing environment? Are there programs a larger school may be able to offer that will be important to your child's fulfillment?

7. **After-School Programs, Early Bird Programs, Vacation Programs and Child Minding**

These programs are of particular interest to many parents, those who work as well as those who don't.

8. **Grade at Which School Ends (sixth, eighth, ninth or twelfth)**

Pick the school that will be right for your child at the outset. Schools without a high school may put more emphasis on the lower grades and offer more leadership opportunities at an earlier age, such as student council president or editorship of the yearbook. Students say that exposure to the behavior of older adolescents, with the concomitant possibilities of experimentation with sex, drugs and alcohol, is more limited at a school without a high school. On the other hand, a parent may breathe a sigh of relief when his kindergartner begins at a school that continues through twelfth grade. But bear in mind that while the child may complete his or her education at this school that is not always the case. Further school applications may still lie in wait.

9. **Pace and Expectations of the Academic Program**

How academic is the kindergarten? Certain New York City schools such as Horace Mann, Dalton, Trinity, Fieldston, Collegiate, Chapin, Brearley and Spence are considered the most demanding of their students and are often categorized as "very selective." However, parents should note that the pace and expectations vary greatly amongst the lower schools at these "top tier" institutions. But a child develops at his or her own pace. Not every child who enters such a school is happy as it becomes more academically demanding; yet many who are not "ready" at the age of five blossom in the later years.

10. **Consider Your Own Family Pattern**

If your family enjoys ski weekends be aware that some schools require more work on weekends and vacations than others. On the other hand, if your academic expectations are traditional you won't be comfortable waiting until your child wants to learn a subject you feel is important.

11. **Birthday Cut-Off**

It's important to know whether your child is the appropriate age for entrance to the school.

Feeder Schools

Many New York City parents are concerned about getting their children onto the "Harvard Track"; they believe that if a child is accepted into the right nursery school, then he/she will get into the right ongoing school and will eventually be accepted at a prestigious Ivy League college. A "feeder school" is a nursery school that channels its graduates into specific ongoing schools. Twenty or more years ago, certain schools preselected their applicant bodies. When parents called a nursery school for an application, they would have a "chat" with the admissions director after which an application might or might not be forwarded.

Today, the reality is that each season, certain nursery schools have a large number of applicants to certain ongoing schools but acceptances are narrowing. Some are siblings of the students already enrolled, some live nearby, some are following the fashion at that nursery school. And, over the years, certain nursery school directors have developed relationships with the admissions directors at the ongoing schools. They can communicate to those schools whether or not certain children would be good candidates for their programs. There is absolutely no guarantee that even at the "right" nursery school, your child will get into your number-one choice ongoing school. An educational consultant and former admissions director told us: "Kindergarten admissions have become terribly arbitrary over the past couple of years."

Even the most traditional schools, which used to take children predominantly from the Upper East Side or Upper West Side, now accept children from all parts of New York City. Admissions directors are having to go farther and farther afield to look at candidates these days. Commonly, in a class of forty-four children at Collegiate School, roughly twenty-five or more different preschool programs are represented. One year, The Chapin School had applicants from sixty nursery schools and enrolled children from at least twenty.

At nursery schools with a large number of applicants to a particular ongoing school, the director of admissions or a member of the admissions department of an ongoing school will go and observe the applicants in their nursery-school environment. This is an advantage because a child is more relaxed and natural when interacting with his peers in his own familiar classroom. (Most ongoing schools, however, still require that a parent bring the child in for additional testing at the school interview.)

Keep in mind that some ongoing schools have their own nursery or pre-K programs, most of which were originally set up as a service for the children of alumni. Now, these pre-K programs predominantly serve siblings and the children of faculty members. But Friends Seminary and Dalton dropped their pre-K programs, and Horace Mann dropped its youngest twos, in response to limitations on classroom space and the recognition that it is too difficult to pick a two- or three-year old who will ultimately succeed in a demanding academic environment.

The bottom line is, select a nursery school program based on proximity to your home, philosophy and schedule.

THE APPLICATION

Parents of kindergarten applicants should telephone to request school applications immediately after Labor Day of the year their child is four years old (applicants to the upper grades can wait a little longer). Typically, applications should be filed no later than the first week of December. This deadine is getting earlier and earlier due to the huge number of applications that the schools have to process. Most New York City independent schools have a birthday cutoff date of September 1 (your child must turn five before entering kindergarten). But since the first step in the application process is to make tentative selections of the schools to which you may apply by consulting your nursery school director and other sources, you must start thinking about school far earlier, perhaps the spring before you are going to apply. Some schools give spring tours.

If your child is in a nursery school program, the school's director will usually set up a meeting with each family to discuss proposed choices for further schooling. If you need more information than you have been able to obtain about a school or its suitability for your child, you should request a meeting with the director to further discuss ongoing schools.

In early fall, the Parents League sponsors Independent School Day. Most of the New York City independent schools attend, staff a table and set out their literature. Usually a school's admissions director is there to answer brief questions. Be prepared: It's a little like Saks Fifth Avenue at Christmastime. But going, picking up brochures and asking questions will save you a lot of time and phone calls.

Try to be organized. I recommend starting a file (some parents use Excel spreadsheets), with each school in a separate folder, to keep track of correspondence and appointments. Have some nice wallet-size photos on hand because some applications require a photograph. (Although one family that sent a nude photo of their toddler to a crusty but prestigious school received an acceptance.)

Type or write your application legibly, neatly and gramatically. The sooner you return your application, the sooner you will get your appointments for tours and/or interviews. It's a good idea to seek an early appointment; in case your child is ill the day of the interview, you will still have time to reschedule.

Some applications, like those for Dalton and Friends, contain essay questions. Read the school catalog very carefully and be familiar with the program before you write your essay. But remember that the essay is about your child, not about your many accomplishments or great expectations. For some parents, the most difficult part of the entire admissions process can be this essay, as it requires a real knowledge of your child, objectivity and verbal ability.

Don't send anything with the application except a letter(s) of recommendation if requested by the school. And if the school doesn't ask for an essay or photograph, don't send one unless you are a genuinely talented writer or photographer.

Early Notification

At most schools, if your family is connected to a school (that is, if there is a sibling already enrolled, or if the child is a "legacy") then you are eligible for the Early Notification Program. In the interest of creating a more equitable admissions process some schools have dropped their Early Notification Programs. Riverdale Country School recently dropped theirs. Under Early Notification, families will be notified approximately a month earlier than others not so connected. If your child is accepted and you accept the school, then you are required to withdraw your application to all other schools. You may wait until you have heard from all of the other schools on the regular ISAAGNY reply date, but you are not then guaranteed a place at the school that offered early admission.

A word of advice to parents of boys and some girls with spring or summer birthdays: There is a mistaken assumption that these children are immature. As a result, many parents hold their children back a year, so that quite a few turn seven during the kindergarten year. Discuss with your nursery school director whether or not it would be best to hold your child back. If you think your child is ready, trust your instincts.

THE INTERVIEW

After the school receives your application you will be contacted to set up an appointment for your child's interview. Independent schools like to see both parents at tours and parent interviews as a demonstration of their commitment to their child's education. Parents usually meet with the head of school or the director of admissions. The requirements are different for every school so be sure to read the instructions on your admissions packet carefully.

Most schools, but the single-sex schools in particular, like to meet with both parents together though at some schools, school personnel only meet parents as members of a tour group. Does this mean they are looking more carefully at the parents at some schools than others? Absolutely. Be prepared to talk in detail about your child. One mother was asked the following sequence of questions at a prestigious school, "When did you wean? When did he walk? When did he talk? Where do you go on weekends?" One admission director simply asks, "Tell me about your child." Parents have asked if it matters whether they are interviewed by the admissions director or a junior staff member or even a parent. The schools say it makes no difference who conducts the interview, the important thing is open and honest communication.

Nursery school and admissions directors say, "Dress your child comfortably" for the interview. If your child is fussing with his suspenders or playing with her hair it will detract from the interview. Long hair should be pulled back and off the child's face. And keep in the mind the style of the school—that is, whether or not there is a uniform or dress code. For example, when applying to Dalton, Ethical Culture, Riverdale, Friends Seminary, Village Community School or

Calhoun, where most of the students will be casually dressed, play clothes are quite acceptable for your child. However, at Buckley, Chapin, St. Bernard's, Spence, or Convent of the Sacred Heart, children will be dressed more formally, and your child should be too: boys in a cardigan, collared shirt, slacks and shoes; girls in a not too fancy dress. Parents should also consider the style of the school and dress accordingly.

For kindergarten admissions, the interview may be conducted individually or in a group. The interview might be conducted by one of the following: the kindergarten teachers, the head of the lower school or the director of admissions, who will record their observations of your child at play. At some schools your child will be asked to complete specific tasks, or take the school's own age-appropriate test. Children are frequently asked to draw a picture and we found that it does help if he/she can recognize and write his/her name.

You can form an idea about whether or not the school is child-centered during the admissions process, says one educational consultant. "Who is the admissions director focusing on, you or your child? Is your child addressed by name? Are they really getting down to the child's level? After the interview is over do they give you any feedback about your child? Some admissions directors give parents a few minutes after the interview," she says.

How to Prepare Your Child For the Interview

The day or night before your child's interview is enough advance notice to give him or her. Don't communicate your anxiety to the child. Tell your child as specifically as possible what to expect; for example, if he or she will be accompanying you on a tour or will be joining a group, or will be meeting with a member of the admissions staff alone. The nature of the interview is usually described in the admissions packet but if you are not sure, call the school and ask so that you can prepare your child.

If your child wakes up with a runny nose, looking under the weather, it's a judgment call whether or not to cancel your interview. Some schools are so booked that you might not get another chance. But never miss your appointment without calling the school to notify them!

If you notice during the interview that your child is really feeling and behaving oddly, and later that day the child is diagnosed with a double ear infection, call the school and let them know. They might either invite you back or take it into consideration. These are teachers; they can tell when children are not up to par.

To Bribe or Not to Bribe

Parents who are desperate to get their child to perform well at an important interview may be tempted to use bribes. This can backfire. According to an early-childhood consultant, if you really want to offer an inducement to cooperate, promise your child quality time, such as playtime in the park with you, lunch with daddy or mommy or grandpa at the office or a visit to grandma's, rather than a material reward like a trip to the toy store or that expensive toy car he's always wanted.

What if your child won't separate? We observed a fair amount of leg hanging and weeping at interviews. Please don't feel bad if your child won't go off willingly with a stranger, even though you've explained that it's a teacher. Remember he/she won't be going to kindergarten for another full year. How the school handles the separation is a good indicator of how much independence and maturity will be expected during the following year. For example, at one very selective school we were told if your child doesn't separate easily "it doesn't bode well." At other schools parents were invited to come and sit with their children during the group interview.

You should of course encourage and reassure your child that he or she is able to go with the teacher and that you'll be waiting right there for him or her to come back. The separation at the interview can be the most anxiety-producing part of the touring/interviewing process. And don't pay attention to other parents who boast about their child's easy separation. This is only one of many factors, and I know plenty of leg hangers who went on to all of the best schools.

Letters of Recommendation/
Thank You Notes/First Choice Letters

Directors of admissions at nearly every school advise me that letters of recommendation should be written by someone who really knows the family and the child. One admissions director said she could wallpaper her office with letters from celebrities and politicians. The most valuable recommendation comes from a parent of a child already in the school who knows you well. Never send more than two letters. But bear in mind, things can and do get lost in the shuffle. Always keep a copy on hand just in case.

If you know a trustee at the school, now may be the moment to let him know you have an applicant, but be advised that if your child is accepted at that school you are morally obliged to enroll the child there. You have asked for a favor and it would be rude to act otherwise.

After your interview, admissions directors agree that a thank you note is nice. "I keep it in the file; it never makes or breaks a decision; when we look back, after the child is in, it shows that this is a nice parent and we were right," says a former director of admissions. But another admissions director said she was already inundated with mail and didn't want any more! If you receive a nice note from a school after the interview don't necessarily think the school is recruiting your child. Some schools send handwritten thank you postcards to everyone who looks at the school, even if they don't apply.

If parents have a clear first choice they can convey this information to the school in several ways: 1) Write a brief note to the admissions director. 2) Tell your nursery school director, who will tell the school for you. 3) Have a friend, already in the school, write a first choice note for you. There is no consensus about the effectiveness of first choice letters. Some schools say it helps them calculate their yield, others say they don't pay any attention to them because some families have been known to write first choice notes to many schools! That is unethical, as well as unwise, since schools do talk and you might need to apply to those schools again in the future.

DO'S AND DON'TS

Do

1) During the spring/summer before you're going to apply, start to make a list of schools in which you are interested. Right after Labor Day, call these schools for a brochure and application, or download them from the school's website.

2) Give your current school director the school report form from the admissions packet. Note: Some schools send this form directly to the nursery school once they have received your completed application.

3) At the same time, make sure that you have requested the

required admissions testing from the Educational Records Bureau; promptly fill out the form and return it to the ERB with your check.

4) Read the brochure and the information on the school's website before your tour and interview.

5) Call ASAP if you are going to miss an appointment, whether for a group tour or your child's interview.

6) Pose thoughtful, not provocative, necessary or important questions, that show you've really read the material and know the school. Know at what grade the school ends.

7) Say something nice about the school during the parent interview, and turn off your cell phone or beeper, and don't look at your watch.

8) Ask whom you might contact if you have any additional questions during the admissions process. Being able to call a parent in the school is very helpful.

9) Call the ERB to make sure your child's test scores have been sent to all of the schools to which you have applied, and call each school in early January to make sure your file is complete. The file should contain: 1) your completed application, 2) letters of reference if requested, 3) school report from your nursery school, 4) results of ERB testing.

10) Use discretion when discussing ERB testing results and acceptances. Feelings get hurt and friendships ruined by boasting.

11) If you genuinely have a first-choice school, let your nursery school director know and let the school know (in writing from you or a parent in the school who knows you). But realize that if you are accepted, your child is morally obliged to attend.

12) Do use pull if you have it before completing the application process. Don't wait until after your child is rejected; negative decisions are rarely changed. But use discretion; the thicker the file, the thinner the candidate.

13) If you are totally bewildered use an advisory service, but be discreet about it—some schools frown on consultants.

14) After admissions decisions have been made, call or write every school at which you have been wait-listed to let them know: 1) that you are still very interested or 2) that you have accepted a place elsewhere.

15) Revisit the school after your child has been accepted, and have your child sit in on classes if you need more information before making a decision.

16) Ask for a copy of the school's annual report only after your child has been accepted.
17) Recognize that you have the right to call a school and (politely) find out why your child was not accepted.
18) Realize that kindergarten is a transition year, and reevaluate your choice of schools every three to five years.
19) Be a supportive parent, try to see your child realistically, know his strengths and weaknesses, be his advocate.
20) Remember that there is no such thing as a perfect parent, a perfect child or a perfect school.
21) Realize that you don't know how good a school really is until you have a problem.

Don't

1) Pick a school because your husband's law partner and/or your best friend send their children there.
2) Excessively prepare your child for the ERB (WPPSI). (You can prepare your child for upper-level testing (ISEE or SSAT.)
3) Be late or miss an appointment without calling.
4) Send a personal essay, photos or any more recommendations than the school requests.
5) Ask for special treatment during the admissions process. Even celebrities have to take the group tour.
6) Ask them to convince you as to why you should send your child to their school.
7) Stand out on the tour by asking too many questions or taking notes as if you were writing an article or a book.
8) Brag about your achievements.
9) Offer money to or otherwise try to bribe the admissions director.
10) Think that you can change the basic style of the school.
11) Tell a school that it's your first choice unless you intend to enroll your child there.
12) Make the elitist assumption that all students of color are on scholarship.
13) Select a school solely on the basis of how many children get into Ivy League colleges. Do look at the range of schools to which students are accepted.
14) Forget that you're an applicant, not a supplicant.

THE ERB

The Educational Records Bureau
220 East 42nd Street (The Daily News Building)
Suite 100
(near Second Avenue)
New York, NY 10017
(212) 672-9800, fax (212) 370-4096
website: www.erb.org

If your child is applying for admission to an independent school, he or she will be asked to take the "ERB's". In fact, ERB is not the title of the admissions exam. It stands for the Educational Records Bureau, founded in 1927, ERB is a national, nonprofit agency that serves approximately 1,800 independent and public schools nationally and internationally, which administers and interprets different types of tests for children from preschool all the way through high school. Expect extensive voicemail instructions and a chilly reception. The ERB employs approximately fifty psychologists (examiners) during the admissions season. According to the ERB: "All of the examiners are at least Masters' level school or clinical psychologists, many of them are doctoral level candidates, and some are Ph.D's." They are all experienced examiners. The ERB has been under contract with ISAAGNY (Independent Schools Admissions Association of Greater New York) for over thirty years. For New York City independent schools, the ERB administers a collection of tests that sound like kitchen appliance attachments: the WPPSI for preschool through first grade; the WISC for grades two, three, four, and five; and the ISEE for applicants to grades six through twelve. The ISEE is administered in three levels and ERB's trained proctors oversee the group administration of this test in a variety of locations. The cost for group testing for applicants to grades 6 through 12 is $89. Parents may purchase "What to expect on the ISEE", from ERB for $15, and in 2009, ERB has three new specific preparation guidelines available online at no additional cost. The new guidelines are written for students but also have a section for parents. It includes sample questions, test directions, an answer sheet, and a full-length practice test complete with immediate scores.

"The lower level: entrance to sixth grade, the middle level: entrance to grades seven and eight, and the upper level: entrance to grades nine through twelve. Practice questions are included in the back of the student guide. The ISEE takes approximately three hours. The ERB's early childhood division, ECAA (Early Childhood Admissions

Assessment), serves children from pre-kindergarten through 2nd grade and tests on the premises of approximately sixty nursery schools. Tests are also administered at the ERB's offices, as well as at other locations throughout Manhattan. The cost of the WPPSI is $495; $545 for grades 3 through 5. The number of children who take the ERB, or WPPSI has steadily increased by approximately 100 children each year over the past decade, roughly totaling 3,300 children in 2009; and despite the sagging economy, continues to climb even though the number of seats at private school for kindergarten remains relatively static. For students requiring financial aid, there is an ISAAGNY Fee Waiver Program.)

If you are considering applying to Hunter Elementary or a New York City public school program for gifted and talented you'll have to go to an approved testing service for Stanford-Binet testing (approximately $125). (See Programs for Gifted and Talented Students, p. 498, *infra.*)

Having a central testing agency administer one test to all children is intended to "eliminate repetitive testing and thus minimize the strain on children and parents." Prior to the selection of the ERB, parents used to take their children for formal testing at each school to which they applied. However, many schools still require up to an hour of their own "informal testing," so you can still expect your child to be thoroughly scrutinized everywhere he or she goes. It seems to parents that it is the strain on the schools that has mostly been alleviated since they can now see many more than one child at a time.

At some nursery schools, says one parent, "the fall semester of the four-year-old group is like 'Kaplan' for the ERB." The students get worksheets for practicing matching skills, copying geometric shapes and tracking mazes. They are drilled in their colors, taught to write their names and play with parquetry blocks (for spatial relations). Some children even bring Weekly Readers home to work on.

The WPPSI determines strengths and weaknesses and where along the developmental scale a child falls. The head of an elementary school described the ERB to touring parents as "a measuring stick against which all the children stand." The WPPSI was not devised as an admissions test, and a national sampling, not an independent school norm, is the measuring standard. It is an evaluation of the child's development in language and visual/motor skills. Like all standardized tests, it is a snapshot of the child's development taken on one day.

Children are compared with others their age; there is no advantage in holding off testing with the idea that "they will know more." In fact, they are expected to do more as they become older; in some cases the younger child may have a slight edge. Also, the later in the year it is, the more likely it is your child may have a cold or other illness. In fact, ERB introduced the option of spring testing in 1992. If your nursery school director thinks your child is ready "and will separate readily" the spring might be better. Each report is individually written, carefully reviewed and mailed in the order of the test date. Remember to schedule well in advance of school deadlines. It usually takes three to four weeks to receive the ERB report.

Parents are sent a copy of the confidential ERB report. You can discuss the results with your nursery school director or you may schedule a private consultation with the ERB.

The WPPSI is composed of four verbal and four nonverbal (or performance) sections. Children do not have to read or write to take this test.

Verbal

Comprehension: Commonsense; social awareness.
Vocabulary: Word knowledge; expressive skills.
Similarities: Ability to perceive relationships between things and ideas.
Word Reasoning: Deductive reasoning, social awareness.

Performance

Matrix Reasoning: Sequencing skills; non-verbal reasoning.
Coding: Visual motor speed and accuracy; short term memory.
Block Design: Ability to perceive and analyze patterns.
Picture Concepts: Non-verbal ability to perceive relationships between pictures.

It is common belief that some of the very selective schools have a fixed cutoff score below which they will not admit a candidate. This is simply not true. Admissions directors have said, "You wouldn't believe some of the scores I have here," and I know some children with astronomical scores who were not admitted. But some schools are more likely to take an "at-risk child" (with very scattered scores) than others.

Every parent fears that on the day of the test the child will be ill or otherwise not his normal self. Schools, either nursery or ongoing, will know if a given test isn't reflective of their observations of the child, and if they determine it is necessary they can request a retest. Retesting is usually done at the request of the ongoing school. (But, of course, results of both tests will be under consideration by the school(s) to which application is being made.) It is rarely requested.

Some directors of admission place more weight on the narrative portion of the test (the second page of the ERB report), which describes the child's test-taking behavior. One admissions director told us, "It's a personality thing."

The parent must fill out a form requesting that the test results be sent to the ongoing schools to which a parent has applied. Results are routinely sent to parents, the child's current school when indicated and five participating ongoing schools. There is a $15 additional charge for each group of up to three schools and all requests must be in writing to the ERB. Be sure to follow up with the schools to make sure they received the results.

In sum, have faith in your child. You know him or her better than anybody else does. In the vast majority of cases your child will look on paper exactly as he or she actually is.

And remember, ERB reports are just one piece of your child's admissions application. Your child's interview, the evaluation form from your present school and the application are all given serious consideration.

SETTING THE STAGE

In preparing your child to take the ERB, don't say he or she is going to play games or be in a room with other children. Do tell your child, "You are going to work with someone like a teacher who wants to see the kinds of things you know. There'll be some new things and you'll get a chance to learn."

If your child attends one of the participating schools, the test is administered in the relaxed atmosphere of that school. Whenever possible, children should be tested in the familiar setting of their own school. The test is usually presented as enjoyable "special work." You might reinforce this gently beforehand if your child raises questions— but be light and casual.

You may use the same explanation if you are bringing your child to the ERB. Explain that he or she will do "special work" with someone like a teacher who is eager to see what 4, 5, or 6 year olds are able to do. Let your child know that you will be in the waiting room with other parents.

If the child is reluctant to separate from you, have your spouse or a caregiver bring him or her.

ERB will not test a child who is unhappy or reluctant. The anticipation of a pleasant experience is the best preparation for being tested.

The all-important question facing anxious parents is whether and how much to prepare (or coach) their child for intelligence testing. Administrators at the ERB, say emphatically, "Don't do it!" If your child has been coached, it is immediately apparent. One four-year-old walked into the tester's office and blurted, "I forgot it all!" The tester is looking for how spontaneous the child is in responding to a question never heard before, and for his problem-solving strategy as well as level of information.

Admissions directors at the on-going schools have their antennae out for any signs of familiarity with the test and if they suspect that your child has been coached; if, for instance, all of the scores are very high and this performance does not match the nursery school report or the informal testing done at the school, then the application will be compromised. There are plenty of other families about whom they do not have ethical qualms.

I am sympathetic to parents who feel they have to do something, to prepare their child, if only to ease their own anxiety, so I have listed below some age-appropriate activities that you and your child can enjoy doing together. Remember to keep it fun and it will be a treat for your child to have Mom or Dad's individual attention. When your child gets tired or fidgety, stop.

Playing with wooden blocks, lego blocks, connect-the-dot books and puzzles strengthen children's visual spatial abilities. Tessellation puzzles are fun and challenging. You can make your own unusual cutout images, and then ask your child to reassemble them.

Tic-Tac-Toe, "Quick Chess" (simple three-minute chess games for the super intelligent 4-year-old) and strategic board games also enhance visual spatial coordination (Keep in mind that some pre-schoolers get very upset if they lose—this is normal—and it's okay to let them win now; they'll learn about sportsmanship later.)

Reading aloud to your child increases his vocabulary and develops his pictorial imagination. There are poetry and non-fiction books that are appropriate for preschoolers, in addition to picture books. While you are reading ask your child questions based on the content, such as, "What do you think he's feeling?" "Where are they going?" "What do you think is going to happen next?" After you finish a simple story, ask your child to "tell" it back to you. Help him to put the events in order. Draw a simple picture story, or have him dictate his own stories to you. Another way to increase a child's vocabulary is to ask, "What do you call . . . (name things/identify objects)," also ask, "What do you do if . . . ?"

Incentive Publications, booklets that are available at Barnes & Noble, tap into preschoolers' verbal and math skills. Scholastic also publishes games for preschool children in reading, writing, learning and math. Phenome-based books like Dr. Seuss's *Hop on Pop*, and most of his other books, correlate sounds with the shape of a word in a simple way. There are CD-roms like "Reader Rabbit" and "Grammar Rock" that help develop early pre-reading skills. But whatever you do, don't push the reading! Learning to decode occurs when the child's brain is ready, not before; it's a little like losing teeth.

Always have lots of art materials on hand—crayons, paint, pipe cleaners, beads, markers, clay, stickers, etc.—for open-ended play. Children should learn how to hold a pencil correctly (there are special soft grips you can buy at any stationery store) and use it to try to write their names, run mazes and connect the dots. McGraw Hill Spectrum, (as well as other companies) publishes workbooks that focus specifically on fine motor control. Also, sewing with yarn, threading a big needle and beading (threading large beads on a pipe cleaner, for instance) help preschoolers' fine motor control. A former private school consultant has published a guide to kindergarten testing (www.testingforkindergarten.com) that has tips too.

A field of mass media called "edutainment" began with the Learning Company's CD-roms, including "Math Blaster," "Millie's Math House," "Slash Master," "Zoom Beanies," and "Math Rabbit," which bolster young children's math skills. Parents should ask their child to count, use flash cards and play board games (Sorry, Trouble, Candyland, Chutes and Ladders) and simple card games like preschool Uno. You can make up games too. Bake and cook with your child to increase his awareness of simple addition, subtraction, fractions and percentages.

There's no substitute for experience and a trip to a museum, lollipop concert, a farm, the children's zoo, the bakery and the grocery store, can all be opportunities for learning and will increase a child's general knowledge (ability to share and get along with others, form an appropriate relationship with the teacher, work independently, follow directions, and show "maturity"). In the past, kindergarten might be a child's first school experience, but today most children have been in a preschool program for two to three years and prior to that, countless parenting classes. "Kindergarten has become an experience for which children need to be ready when they arrive."[*] However, this does not mean that parents should or have to teach their preschoolers to read. There are some children who will learn to read before kindergarten (you know who they are because parents of such children will invariably boast about their "little geniuses"). However, educators stress that the majority of children are ready for formal reading instruction in first grade or when they are approximately six and a half years old. Admissions directors do not expect candidates for kindergarten to read, nor should you.

A good evaluation of a child, in the words of one nursery school director, is "Verbal, curious, good self-esteem, ability to concentrate, not fidgety, has enough to give to others." Then there is an intangible measurement dubbed "the likability factor" by an early-childhood consultant we know. We'd all like to think our children have it.

ADVISORS, TESTERS AND TEST PREPARATION

Aside from this book and the director of your school, there are other useful resources in Manhattan to help you select the right independent school for your family. Keep in mind that the best source of information is the school itself. Ask if the school you are interested in has spring tours. Perhaps you can rule out a school or take a second look in the fall when you apply. Once the fall admissions process gets rolling you will usually not be able to take a second look until your child is accepted to the school. Advisory services (or educational consultants) help parents approach the independent school admissions process in an organized manner and provide reassurance and advice to apprehensive parents.

Parents, whether you choose to use a consultant or not, please be advised that some independent schools admissions officers have admitted that they do not look kindly on applicants who use the services

[*]*Kindergarten, It Isn't What It Used to Be,* by Susan Golant and Mitch Golant, Ph.D. (Lowell House, Los Angeles, 1990)

of consultants. So if you choose to use one, don't broadcast it during your interview.

All except two of the services listed below require a fee; fees vary widely.

ADVISORS

1. EDUCATION FIRST, email: maura@nyedu1st.com; victoria @nycedu1st.com, website: www.nycedu1st.com

    Victoria Goldman, author of this book, and Maura Wollner, an expert in education and child development, advise parents on how to optimize their admissions strategies, select schools and explore New York City's extensive educational opportunities.

2. THE PARENTS LEAGUE OF NEW YORK, INC., 115 East 82nd Street, New York, NY 10028 (212) 737-7385, website: www.parentsleague.org

    The Parents League was founded in 1913 and is a nonprofit organization of parents and independent schools. Annual membership fee: $125 for one year or $300 for three years; hours of operation are Monday through Thursday 9AM-4PM, 9AM until noon on Fridays.

    The Parents League offers a School Advisory Service for member parents who need advice about the process of applying to schools and information about the schools. Please call for an appointment. The advisors are volunteers who have all served in the independent school community and are also trained in-house.

    The Parents League distributes the New York Independent Schools Directory, published by the Independent Schools Admissions Association of Greater New York (ISAAGNY). Anybody can purchase the book for an additional $20.00 at the office, $23.00 by mail or online. Please be aware that the entries in this book are written by the schools themselves.

    The Parents League sponsors Independent School Day, held in the fall, at which parents can pick up printed material, including brochures and applications, from various city independent schools; representatives from the independent schools are available to answer brief questions. Be prepared for a mob scene, but it will save you countless phone calls.

The Parents League sponsors a Forum on Admissions, at which admissions directors from five or six independent schools speak and then answer questions from the audience about the admissions process. It offers a summer advisory service and a special education advisory service. You must be a member of the Parents League to participate; there are no additional fees.

3. GREENBERG EDUCATIONAL GROUP INC., 334 West 86th Street, Suite 1A, New York, N.Y. 10024, Tel (212) 787-6800 FAX (212) 579-8200, email: eric@greenbergeducational group.com, website: www.greenbergeducationalgroup.com

Greenberg Educational Group, founded in 1991, is run by a Fieldston School and Wharton Business School graduate, Eric Greenberg, who provides test preparation, tutoring and educational advising. Greenberg Educational Group works primarily with families applying to grades sixth through college and graduate school. Sliding scale financial aid is available.

4. MADDEN & WARWICK, LLC, Mary Madden and Jane Warwick, 1112 Park Avenue, New York, NY 10128, (212) 831-3272, email: mam1750@aol.com; jwarwick25@aol.com, Mary Madden and Jane Warrick advise families about the private school admissions process from nursery through middle school. Rates vary according to need.

5. SMART CITY KIDS, Roxana Reid, 1619 Third Avenue, (located on East 91st Street between Second and Third Avenues), Suite #1, New York, NY, 10028 website: www.smart citykids.com, (212) 979-1829

Ms. Reid, a former kindergarten teacher with a Masters in social work, specializes in kindergarten and nursery school admissions. She holds workshops and private sessions that prepare parents and children for every aspect of the admissions process—how to handle interviews testing, skill requirements, applications and essays. Fees are approximately $225 an hour, workshops are two hours, call for exact rates.

6. VIRGINIA J. BUSH & ASSOCIATES, 444 East 86th Street, New York, NY 10028 (212) 772-3244, email: vjb@ virginiabush.com

Since 1975, Mrs. Bush has been advising families on secondary school and college options.

7. SCHOOLS & YOU, Sarah D. Meredith, Tel (718) 230-8971, website: www.schoolsandyou.com

Ms. Meredith provides information and consultations on school choices from nursery through eighth grade for both public and private schools in both Manhattan and Brooklyn. She will consult at your home or workplace. Resource materials accompany every consultation, workshops and seminars are also available.

8. HOWARD GREENE & ASSOCIATES, The Educational Consulting Centers, 39A East 72nd Street, New York, NY 10021, (212) 737-8866, website: www.howardgreeneassociates.com

The Educational Consulting Center was founded in 1969 by Howard Greene, former admissions counselor at Princeton University. Originally known for college admissions counseling, Howard Greene & Associates will also advise parents about secondary independent schools. There is a range of fees.

9. SCHOOL CONSULTANTS ON PRIVATE EDUCATION (SCOPE), 309 East 87th Street, New York, NY 10128, (212) 534-6531, or (888) 214-6590 (toll free), e-mail: camps4u@aol.com, website: www.summerscope.com.

Director Elaine Vipler, M.S.Ed., is the director of SCOPE, an advisory service that helps families select appropriate school and summer programs for their children. Ms. Vipler assists parents with every aspect of the admissions process. There is no fee for summer programs.

10. THE INDEPENDENT EDUCATIONAL CONSULTANTS ASSOCIATION, 3251 Old Lee Highway, Suite 510, Fairfax, VA 22030 (703) 591-4850 or (800) 808-IECA (4322), website: www.iecaonline.com

The Independent Educational Consultants Association will send a directory of listings in the New York City area, free of charge.

11. MANHATTAN PRIVATE SCHOOL ADVISORS, email: mpsa@nyc.rr.com, website: www.privateschooladvisors.com, (212) 280-7777 Amanda Uhry, founder of MPSA, is an alumna of Fieldston, The University of Pennsylvania, and the Graduate School of Journalism at Columbia University. Ms. Uhry offers comprehensive admissions counseling to families applying to private schools for all grade levels.

12. ABACUSGUIDE.COM provides listings and links for private, public, and parochial schools in the NYC area. You can e-mail questions about particular schools to *info@abacusguide.com*.

Emily Glickman, founder and director of the Abacus Guide, helps families navigate the school selection and admissions process.

13. SCHOOL SEARCH NYC, 155 Riverside Drive, Suite 12C, New York, N.Y. 10024, Tel (212) 316-0186, email: robin@schoolsearchnyc.com. Robin Arnow, PhD, holds a degree in Clinical Social Work. She consults families on school placement and holds workshops. www.schoolsearchnyc.com

14. ROBIN ARONOW, Ph.D., 155 River side Drive, Suite 12C, New York, N.Y., 10024, Tel (212) 316-0186 or (212) 866-9798, email: dragnet@tuna.net, Dr. Aronow's goal is to make the ongoing schools admissions process for kindergarten—both public and private—less daunting, provide emotional support and plenty of information. She is a trained social worker, not a psychologist, and does not believe in professional coaching.

15. HILTON & HAVES ASSOCIATES, LLC, 300 East 59th Street, Suite 401, New York, N.Y., 10022, Tel (917) 796-8238, June Hilton, jhilton5@nyc.rr.com; (917) 414-8029, Rita Haves, ritahaves@aol.com June Hilton and Rita Haves specialize in nursery and kindergarten admissions. June Hilton, formerly Director of Admissions at Trinity School, and Rita Haves who currently serves on the board of both a nursery and on-going school have over 65 years of experience in private school admissions combined. Fees vary according to parents' needs.

16. BRUCE BREIMER, bossbreimer@aol.com, Tel (212) 787-6955. Mr. Breimer was Director of College Guidance at Collegiate School for close to 40 years. Now, retired, he remains active on select school committees and offers private educational counseling with an emphasis on college admissions.

TESTERS

There are many testers; here are just a few names to consider:

1. SHARON H. SPOTNITZ, Ph.D,444 East 86th Street, New York, NY 10028, (212) 734-0095, email: shsphd@mac.com, Dr. Spotnitz, former executive director of ERB, is a licensed psychologist and child and school psychologist with a specialty in testing children who have learning disabilities. She

administers psychological and psycheducational evaluations in addition provides educational consultations and comprehensive assessments. Dr. Spotnitz tests students of all ages and grade levels ranging from preschool through graduate school.

2. LOIS BERMAN, Ph.D., 177 East 87th Street, Suite 502, New York, NY 10128, (212) 722-0250, email: loisberman@ earthlink.net

    Dr. Berman was the psychologist at Trinity School for seventeen years and has worked with many independent school families. As a licensed psychologist, Dr. Berman administers psychoeducational evaluations to children with suspected learning disabilities.

3. LANA F. MORROW, Ph.D., 350 Central Park West, Suite 1Q, New York, NY 10025, (646) 338-7676, email: lfm212@ earthlink.net

    Dr. Morrow administers neuropsychological evaluations and remediates children who have learning disabilities. She advises families as to which independent school will be best suited for their child.

4. SUSAN SCHWARTZ, Ph.D., 1160 Fifth Avenue, Suite 109, New York, NY 10029, (212) 426-0232, fax (212) 427-0612

    Dr. Schwartz administers comprehensive neuropsychological and psychological assessments that measure intelligence, academic achievement, attention, language, memory, and more. She also meets with school specialists and family members to discuss and plan remedial strategies.

5. TOPHER COLLIER, Psy,D. ABSNP, Clinical Psychologist, The Park West Practice, 115 Central Park West (entrance 1 W. 71st Street) New York, NY, 10023, (212) 675-2254, fax (212) 579-3430, email: DrTopherCollier@aol.com, website: DrTopherCollier.com, Dr. Collier is a licensed psychologist with advanced training in learning disabilities and neuropsychological, psychological and educational assessments. He has a full time practice where he provides therapy for children with a variety of learning and psychological issues.

6. ELYSE R. DUB, Ph.D., NCSP, Tel (917) 541-7340, email: elysedub@yahoo.com, Dr. Dub is a licensed psychologist who administers psycholoeducational evaluations.

7. DEBORAH L. LAZARUS, Psy.D., 1225 Park Avenue, Suite 1SC, New York, N.Y., Tel (722-7121, email: DeborahLaz@ aol.com, Dr. Lazraus specializes in child treatment and

psychotherapy and administers psychoeducational evaluations. Formerly, a school psychologist and elementary school teacher, she also consults parents about schools and placements.

8. PENNY MISHKIN, MS, OTR, 167 East 82nd Street, Suite 1B, New York, N.Y. 10028, Tel (212) 396-1062, email: HPenny1149@aol.com, Ms. Mishkin has a Master's Degree in occupational therapy and has been in private practice for over 15 years. She evaluates preschool age children for kindergarten readiness and prepares those in need of assistance. Her specialty is fine and graphomotor skills and visual-spacial perception.

9. ANTOINETTE J. LYNN, Ph.D., 350 Central Park West, Suite 1Q, New York, N.Y. 10025, Tel (212) 666-3180, email: ailynn@aol.com, Dr. Lynn is a clinical psychologist with a subspecialty in neuropsychology of children with learning disabilities. She has twenty-plus years experience and works with families in choosing schools, and also works with families to treat children with learning disabilities who can be mainstreamed into a variety of private schools.

10. NYU CHILD STUDY CENTER, 577 First Avenue, New York, NY, 10016 (212) 263-6622, website: www.aboutourkids.org.

TEST PREPARATION AND TUTORS

Many New York City parents have their children tutored, either privately or in a group for older children, for the ISEE (Independent School Entrance Exam for grades 6–12), the Hunter High School Entrance Exam (sixth grade), the SSAT, the Specialized High Schools Exam (Stuyvesant, Bronx Science, Brooklyn Tech) and the SAT I (the reasoning test) and II (the subject tests). *What to Expect on the ISEE* is a review book published by the ERB that includes practice exams and exact directions for the test.

Candidates for grades six and above should begin to review and refresh their knowledge several months preceding the exam using either a review book and/or a suitable tutor or review class. At the very least, students should look at the sample questions included in the registration materials.

Ideally, tutoring should boost a child's confidence in his/her abilities, familiarize the student with the kind of questions he will find on the test (multiple choice or essay type), teach test taking strategies and hone essay writing skills. It should be preparation that enables students to go into the testing situation thinking, "Hey, I know this stuff, I can do my best." Cramming for any exam the week or two before only results in a sleep-deprived and anxious candidate. Make sure your child has a good night's sleep and something to eat/drink before the test, and because most of these tests are over three hours long, bring a drink and a snack that doesn't make too many crumbs.

The best way to find a tutor is through inquiries at the child's present school or through word-of-mouth. In some cases the city offers review courses such as The Specialized High School Institute (see p. 498). National test preparation companies such as Princeton Review and Kaplan have offices in Manhattan. Parents have recommended the following resources to me; rates vary widely so be sure to ask how much it will cost before you sign up.

- **Advantage Testing,** Tel (212) 744-8800, 210 East 86th Street, Suite 601, New York, N.Y. 10028 website: www.advantage testing.com, Individual tutoring for standardized tests including, SSAT, ISEE and SAT specialists and graduate test prep for GMAT, MCAT and LSAT. Subject tutors are also available for a wide variety of courses, including APs.
- **Bespoke Education,** Tim Levin, (212) 286-2227 x 100, www.bespokeeducation.com. Tim Levin, a former biology teacher at Fieldston and test prep writer for Kaplan, offers test prep in Manhattan and Westchester for most standardized tests including the ISEE/SHSAT, the SAT/ACT and more. Bespoke Education also offers tutoring in most subject areas for middle and high school students.
- **GRF Test Preparation,** Richard Geller, (212) 864-1100, 50 West 97th Street, apt. 11T, New York, NY 10025. Test prep for the specialized science high school entrance exam (Stuyvesant, Bronx Science, Brooklyn Tech), ten three-hour sessions, offered at two locations in Manhattan, also in Riverdale and Queens. Cost: approximately $845 for ten 3-hour classes.
- **School Skills, Inc.,** (212) 861-5083, email: schoolskillsny@yahoo.com, Dianne Karlstein DeVizcaino, "Mrs. D." 210 East 73rd Street, New York, N.Y. 10021. Maybe it's the candy and pretzels she keeps on her desk, or her forty-plus years experience in teaching, but many children we know enjoy

going to "Mrs. D." In demand for ERB, ISEE and Hunter among others for test preparation, Mrs. D. also provides basic skills review, city-wide test preparation and college application essay writing.

- **Inspirica,** (formerly Stanford Coaching, Inc.) Tel (212) 245-3888 or (888) 245-9969, FAX: (212) 245-3893, website: www.inspirica.com, 850 Seventh Avenue. Inspirica provides one-on-one tutoring in most academic subjects, specialized programs for SSAT/ISEE, PSAT, SATs and other highly individualized programs, and also admissions consulting.

- **Empire Edge Education LLC,** Tel (212) 289-0068, FAX (212) 289-0033, 205 East 88th Street, Suite 4C, New York, N.Y. 10128. Jody Steinglass, founder, is a Yale University and NYU alumni, who offers expert tutoring in most subjects and test prep to elementary, middle, and high school students in student's homes.

- **John W. Harper,** 341 West 11th Street, apt 1F, New York N.Y. 10014 Tel (212) 727-3603, FAX (877) 242-8511, email: johnwharper@hotmail.com. John Harper is a former Harvard College tutor and instructor who specializes in individual test prep from grades 5 through 12, including, the ISEE, SSAT, SHSAT, CTP, PSAT, SAT and AP exams.

- **Yale Tutors,** Tel (212) 696-7896, website: yaletutors.com, Test prep for the SAT, SSAT, ISEE, ERB, Regent's, and APs among others plus for most academic subjects. In-home tutoring and flexible scheduling.

- **Overqualified LLC,** 358 West 45th Street, apt 4C, New York, N.Y. 10036 Tel (646) 387-5846 or (603) 548-7042, email: nycontact@overqualifiedtutoring.com, katherine_obrian@yahoo.com, website: www.overqualifiedtutoring.com. Founded by Katherine F. O'Brian, a Havard graduate, Overqualified is a comprehensive tutoring service that only employs Harvard graduates for tutoring middle and high school students in subjects, improving study skills, and essay writing and for standardized tests, including SATs.

- **InteractiveMathTutor.com,** Tel (212) 874-4105 or 1-866-MATH911, email: hmheller@interactivemathtutor.com, website: www.interactivemathtutor.com. InteractiveMathTutor.com is a Manhattan based math tutoring company formed in 1999.

The company provides both in-person and online tutoring in New York and throughout the country in all levels of math.

- **Schoolhouse Tutors,** Tel (917) 974-4997, email: jlane@ schoolhousetutors.com, website: www.schoolhousetutors.com. Founded in 2003, by Jeff Lane, Schoolhouse Tutors offers several series of workshops in Chelsea based on their unique technique, Power Academics that prepares middle and high school students in study and organizational skills, standardized test prep, reading comprehension, internet use and writing. Individual tutoring is also available.

- **Tutor Doctor, Inc.** Tel (212) 452-1204, Toll free FAX (866) 889-7963, website: www.tutordoctor.com. Michael Weiner, founder of Tutor Doctor, Inc., publishes periodic e-newsletters on a variety of topics and provides links to a other educational organizations, and experts.

- **Lorna Sheldon, MEd.,** 33 Central Park West, New York, N.Y., 10025, Cell (646) 326-7801, Home (212) 961-0750, email: LSheldon@ECFS.org. Ms. Sheldon is an early childhood learning specialist and a teacher at the Ethical Culture/ Fieldston School who preps children for ERBs, PSATs, SATs and ELA testing in reading, math, essay writing and organizational skills.

- **Ethan Todras-Whitehill,** Tel (718) 554-6202, email: mail@ ethantw.com. Mr. Todras-Whitehill tutors students individually for SATs.

- **Patricia Lynden,** 320 West 90th Street, apt 3B, New York, N.Y. 10024, Tel (212) 873-0239, email: plynden@nyc.rr.com. Ms. Lynden is a writer, editor and teacher who specializes in all types of writing including essays, research papers and articles.

- **Emma Kronman,** email: emma.kronman@aya.yale.edu. Ms. Kronman, a Yale alumna, tutors middle and high school students for SATs I and II, ACTs, ISEEs, SSATs, AP exams and academic subjects including, English, History, (U.S. History and World History), French, Italian, Biology, Chemistry and Math.

- **Adam Bresnick, Ph.D.,** email: abresnick@gmail.com. Dr. Bresnick teaches English to Upper School students at the Collegiate School, and tutors students in English, history, French and SAT prep. He also specializes in teaching students how to write essays for school-based assignments as well as for applications and standardized tests.

THICK OR THIN

Admissions decisions are usually made by committee (although the Director of Admissions acts alone at some schools.) The members of these committees vary from school to school. At some schools someone from the development office sits in, and sometimes parents of students are on these committees. There is usually a core group of children comprising siblings and legacies who are definite admissions and the committee tries to put together a balanced class around this core. Schools want a balance of personalities as well; they don't want all leaders or followers. If it is a coed school they need an equal number of boys and girls. So your chances vary from year to year depending on what kind of sibling year it is, or for unpredictable reasons. For example, in a recent year at Riverdale Country School, more applications were received than in any previous year, "over five hundred for approximately seventy spots," according to the Director of Lower School Admissions. So a rejection one year might well have been an acceptance the following year. Try not to take it as a judgment of your child.

Do admissions directors talk? The independent school world is small; admissions directors go to lunch and phone calls go back and forth during the admissions process. Usually, they will not talk about specific families. They will discuss whether the "pool" is up or down for girls or boys this year and so forth. But somehow, if you tell each school that it is your first choice, it will get around. So don't say it unless you mean it.

The yield figure is a mathematical formula, different at each school, which attempts to predict the number of children who, having been accepted to the school, will actually enroll. Anyone whose child is in an over-enrolled kindergarten class knows that this is an inexact method.

There are three elements that make up your child's file:
1) **ERB Testing Results**
   The examiner prepares an individual report for each child. Each report is carefully reviewed by a child psychologist for accuracy and clarity. Parents and schools receive the identical report.
2) **The School Report**
   A confidential report (parents never see it) that discusses your child in depth: his growth, maturity, strengths and weaknesses

usually over the past (three) years as well as information about the family such as how supportive the parents are, how promptly they pay tuition, if they have donor potential and so on. Nursery school directors have to be honest in this report; as a former Parents League president put it: "Report plus rapport equals respect." An honest report plus a relationship between the nursery school director and the director of admissions at the ongoing school equals respect for the nursery school director's recommendation. Admissions directors know how to read between the lines of these reports and the notation "Call me for additional information" implies there is more to the story than what's written on the page. An early-childhood consultant told us that "for an unconnected family without significant means, it's essential that your nursery school director have an established relationship with the admissions director at the ongoing school and be able to really go to bat for you." It certainly can't hurt to be active and involved in your nursery school, and if you're unsure whether to give time or money, give both.

3) **Parent and Child Interviews**

An admissions director who's been in the business for twenty-seven years says, "I never read a file until I meet the child." The child's profile should fit together like a jigsaw puzzle, says a representative from Ethical Culture admissions. "The nursery school report should correspond to behavior in the interview, the ERB reaffirms both. If a piece doesn't make sense, then we have to look further."

If you've got three out of three you're accepted (provided there's room), and a contract will usually be included with the acceptance letter (thick envelope). Two out of three and you might be accepted or wait-listed. One out of three is usually a nonacceptance (thin envelope containing only a nonacceptance letter). This is not gospel; there are mitigating factors and if the child is outstanding in some way that might outweigh one of the other factors.

MULTICULTURAL/SCHOLARSHIP PROGRAMS

A Better Chance
National Office
240 West 35th Street
9th floor
New York, NY 10001
(646) 346-1310 or (800) 562-7865
website: www.abetterchance.org

Founded in 1963 by twenty-three independent schools in the Northeast, A Better Chance, Inc. is the oldest national, nonprofit academic talent-search organization for minority secondary school students. The membership comprises over 300 independent day and boarding schools. Students are recruited and admitted to these schools on the basis of high academic achievement and personal initiative. Many of students apply in the eighth or ninth grade. Applicants must take the SSAT or the ISEE. Financial aid is provided by the member schools. A Better Chance provides ongoing counseling and support. A Better Chance has an Affiliated Colleges Program with a variety of colleges and universities that have demonstrated a commitment to increase their minority enrollment.

The Albert G. Oliver Program/ The Oliver Program
The School at Columbia University
556 West 110th Street
3rd floor
New York, NY 10025
(212) 430-5980 fax (212) 430-5981
website: www.theoliverprogram.org

The Albert G. Oliver Program, named after an outstanding New York City educator, is a nonprofit organization founded in the 1980s to help talented black and Hispanic youngsters gain access to day and boarding schools at the high school level. The brochure says "A primary

46

goal of the Oliver Program is to nurture the hearts of these gifted young people so they develop a sense of caring, love and responsibility that will make a positive impact on the lives of others." The Albert G. Oliver Program is unique in offering a mandatory community service program (150 hours total) and a summer internship program. Each year up to fifty black and Hispanic students are placed in independent day and boarding schools that offer strong support services including financial assistance. Oliver graduates attend many Ivy League colleges, other top universities,and have an alumni base of over 800 people.

Member Day Schools:

The Berkeley Carroll School
Blair Academy
The Brearley School
Brooklyn Friends School
The Browning School
The Calhoun School
The Chapin School
Collegiate School
Columbia Grammar and
    Preparatory School
Concord Academy
Convent of the Sacred Heart
The Dalton School
Deerfield Academy
Elisabeth Irwin High School
Emma Willard School
The Ethel Walker School
Ethical Culture Fieldston School
Friends Seminary
George School
The Governor's Academy
Groton School
Horace Mann School
Hotchkiss School
Kimball Union Academy
The Lawrenceville School

The Loomis Chaffee School
Marymount School
The Master's School
Millbrook School
Milton Academy
Miss Porter's School
The Nightingale-Bamford School
Northfield Mount Herman School
The Packer Collegiate Institute
The Peddie School
Phillips Academy Andover
Phillips Exeter Academy
Poly Prep Country Day School
Regis High School
Riverdale Country School
Rye Country Day School
The Spence School
St. George's School
St. Mark's School
St. Paul's School
Suffield Academy
Trevor Day School
Trinity School
Westminster Academy
Westtown School

Early Steps

540 East 76th Street
New York, NY 10021
(212) 288-9684 fax (212) 288-0461
website: www.earlysteps.org

Ms. Jacqueline Y. Pelzer, Executive Director

Early Steps is a membership organization, created in August 1986, to increase the number of students of color in city independent day schools at the kindergarten and first grade levels. Early Steps was an outgrowth of an Independent Schools Admissions Association of Greater New York (ISAAGNY) Minority Affairs Committee study that identified the need for schools to pool resources for the recruitment of younger students of color, and has enrolled over 2,000 children of color in many of New York City's private schools to date.

Early Steps provides counseling, guidance and referral services to families of children of color looking for and enrolled in city independent schools. Early Steps serves all families of color whether they need financial aid or not, it is not a scholarship program or a program for low income families. Financial aid is available but families should be prepared to pay a portion of the tuition. Some families pay full tuition.

Prep for Prep

163 West 91st Street
New York, NY 10024
(212) 579-1470 fax (212) 579-1459
website: www.prepforprep.org

The Prep for Prep program is a nonprofit educational organization founded in 1978. Some of the original group of Prep for Prep students attended Trinity School. Today, Prep for Prep identifies academically talented students from minority group backgrounds, provides fourteen months of intensive academic preparation and places these students in leading city independent schools and boarding schools with scholarships that are based on financial need and academic performance. The program is highly selective and rigorous. Once enrolled, students are provided with ongoing counseling and leadership development opportunities until high school graduation. The Prep for Prep community includes thousands of students and alumni.

The TEAK Fellowship

16 West 22nd Street
3rd Floor
New York, NY 10010
(212) 288-6678
website: www.teakfellowship.org

The Teak Fellowship prepares talented students from low-income families for admission to top public, private, and parochial high schools. Teak has a colorblind admissions process and accepts 30 low income, high achieving students per year. The program begins in seventh grade and follows students through their high school graduation, providing personal as well as academic support through tutoring and mentoring, test preparation, internship opportunities, leadership training and community service.

APPLYING FOR FINANCIAL AID

The rigorous process of qualifying for private school tuition assistance makes kindergarten admissions look easy. After your child has been accepted to an independent school, or if your child is already enrolled in an independent school and you are requesting tuition assistance (such needs may arise because of a divorce or the loss of a spouse's job) your first step is to contact the financial aid administrator in your child's school. The financial aid officer will give you a Parent Financial Statement or PFS which you must complete. Be forewarned that the PFS asks applicants to list all of their assets and expenses, including their country house, boats, family car(s) club memberships, lessons, summer camp, and vacations. The completed form must be returned to the SSS—The School and Student Service for Financial Aid. The SSS, an affiliate of the National Association of Independent Schools, is a nationwide service that assists independent schools in processing scholarship applications. The SSS is administered by the Educational Testing Service (ETS). Parents are usually asked to submit a copy of both parents' W-2 forms and the previous year's joint or separate Federal Income Tax returns in support of their application. If there are no young children at home, the SSS will impute an income for a nonworking parent.

In processing the PFS the SSS uses national guidelines set for independent schools; families who live in one state might be applying for financial aid from a prep school which is located in another state. A copy of the PFS is then sent back to the school with a recommendation from the SSS of how much tuition that particular family can afford to pay. The school then recalculates; some use specific software for this purpose, taking into account the cost of living in Manhattan. The final decision rests with the school. Most schools have a scholarship committee which reviews each application and then makes "recommendations to the family" as one administrator put it. It is up to each family to decide the financial sacrifices or lifestyle changes it is willing to make. Some families start out on financial aid and eventually become full-tuition paying families and vice versa. Some families choose to "live on peanut butter" and make other sacrifices, others will consider a move to the suburbs, or begin to look at public school options.

TRANSPORTATION

Once your child has been accepted into school, whether public or private, your next consideration is how to get him or her to school and back each day, safely and conveniently. If they live nearby, many parents walk their children to and from school. Those who live further away may rely on a bus service. There are different types of bus service, free and public, or private requiring payment. Depending on the size of your child's school, you might have a limited choice of transportation services. Some parents combine services, depending on their needs.

1. ATLANTIC EXPRESS SERVICE: (A/E or yellow school bus service):

Administered through the office of pupil transportation within the Department of Education, (718) 585-8592.

Atlantic Express has an excellent safety record and is free to public school students and private school students attending participating schools. Students must apply through their own school. To qualify, students in kindergarten through second grade must live ½ mile or more from school. Students in third through sixth grades must live 1 mile or more from school. In early September, the school provides students with a list of designated bus stops (usually along the avenues) and times for pick-up and drop-off. Middle and high school students are provided with subway and bus passes.

2. PRIVATE BUS SERVICE: The private schools contract with a bus company (such as SuperTrans NY INC. (914) 968-3300, fax (914) 968-5455, 60 Alexander Street, Yonkers, NY 10701, website: www.supertrans-ny.com) which provides pickup and drop off at specific times and many locations. This service is the most convenient and also costly. Roundtrip starts at approximately $2,500 per child per year.

3. SCHOOL VAN: Various private schools run their own van service which usually picks up and drops off at designated bus stops. The cost is less than for private van service.

Students attending a regularly scheduled after-school program one or more times a week often arrange with their school for private van service for dropoff to these activities.

EXTRA-EXTRACURRICULAR ACTIVITIES

There are a number of organized after-school athletic programs which feature quality coaching and team play and provide transportation from school to the program and home. Some schools have established relationships with one of these programs, or a number of other families in the school participate. Some are co-ed, others single-sex, fees vary, but the programs that include transportation are usually costly. Advertisements and listings for many of these programs are often found in community newspapers and other local parent publications.

Boys and girls who attend the traditional single sex schools have limited social contact with the opposite sex. This is somewhat ameliorated by coed theater and musical productions, interschool classes and activities. But what could be more fitting for the offspring of the socially prominent than charity dances for the pubescent set to introduce them not only to each other but to philanthropy as well? Miniature charity balls, sponsored by organizations such as Yorkville

Common Pantry, are usually held at one of the private schools and the money raised benefits a variety of local causes. These dances for teenagers attending Manhattan's exclusive schools are a quaint but benign form of organized dating for many 11 and 12-year olds as well as a time for parents to enjoy their last vestige of social control because before they know it their teenager will be out and about.

The "White Glove" social organizations listed below are traditionally "by invitation only." However, you no longer need the proper pedigree to participate; after all, good manners are for everyone.

The Barclay Classes are headquartered in Westfield, New Jersey, (908) 232–8370, website: www.the barclayclasses.com. For over 75 years, the Barclay Series has offered classes to children in the social graces, proper party attire and ballroom dancing. The classes meet ten times from September through April. Spit and polish is the order of the day and young ladies wear white gloves until sixth grade. There are real parties twice a year, usually with a theme. Children enjoy the classes because refreshments are served and prizes are awarded. You must contact the Barclay Series to request an invitation if one has not already been sent.

Dancing lessons offered by **The Knickerbocker Cotillion** begin in fourth grade and children must be invited to attend; unlike the Barclay Series, The Knickerbocker Cotillion is a not-for-profit organization, an older and some say, more exclusive group. The group's coordinator usually forwards applications to those who call; however, it is the organization's policy to refrain from publicity.

The Knickerbocker Greys: An after-school cadet program for boys and girls. Telephone: (212) 585-1881, website: www.knicker bockergreys.org. Once upon a time children from Manhattan's best families bought their school uniforms at Alex Taylor and their other clothes at Best & Company; the girls took dancing classes at Mrs. DeRhams' Dancing School at the Colony Club or if you were Jewish, at Viola Wolfe's, while their brothers drilled with the Knickerbocker Greys at the Park Avenue Armory. Originally linked with Patriotic and Historical Societies such as the National Society of Colonial Dames and the Society of Mayflower Descendants this organization appeals to any child who simply likes history and tin soldiers. Since 1881 the Knickerbocker Greys has offered boys (and now girls) ages 6–16 the opportunity to participate in parades, reviews and civic ceremonies in New York City. (Remember when you had to join the Girl Scouts just to march in the Memorial Day parade?) The Greys is not a military organization but they use precision drill and the "pomp and circumstance of beautiful old uniforms." Meetings are held once a week on Tuesdays only from September through May.

GLOSSARY

Alternative Forms of Testing: Testing that is not standardized, but rather a measure of an individual child's capabilities and progress relative to himself, not to other children. The most popular trend in alternative testing is portfolio assessment: A child will select his best work from the whole semester or year, and submit this work instead of taking a standardized test. This gives the child's judges the ability to gauge the child's progress over the course of the term, and gives them a fuller picture of the child's abilities, rather than a brief snapshot from a test taken on one particular day.

Child-Centered Program: A program in which learning in the classroom is facilitated by the teacher and directed by the students. Activities require active learning and motivation on the part of the student; the teacher does not lecture to a passive class. The phrase "child-centered program" is also used to describe a program in which a child is presented with age-appropriate, meaningful curricula.

Chicago Math: Chicago Math is a program developed at the University of Chicago that teaches children to reason logically, see mathematical patterns and relationships, and understand the usefulness of math in everyday life. Manipulatives, math games and literature are woven into the curriculum to develop abstract mathematical thinking while reinforcing computational concepts.

Classic Curriculum: Featured in traditional schools. A classic curriculum always includes Shakespeare, Virgil and the Greeks. The goal is "a cultured mind nourished by the humanist tradition."

Collaborative Learning: In a classroom that subscribes to collaborative learning, the students work in groups. It is assumed an individual student will be motivated to work because he or she will feel responsible to the group, that a student will learn to clarify his thinking through the need to articulate and debate his ideas within the group, and further, that he will learn new ways of thinking when he analyzes the ideas of other group members.

Cum Laude Society: The Cum Laude Society is an honor society modeled on Phi Beta Kappa, which has member chapters in several New York City independent high schools. The purpose of the Cum Laude Society is the encouragement and recognition of academic excellence. Many chapters (particularly at schools that no longer rank students or do not give grades) make selections by such criteria as character, honor and integrity. New York City independent schools with member chapters and year of induction are: Berkeley Carroll School, Brooklyn, 1989; Collegiate School, 1922; Horace Mann School, 1951; Packer Collegiate Institute, Brooklyn, 1976; Poly Prep Country Day School, Brooklyn, 1908; The Riverdale Country School, 1922; Trinity School, 1934.

D'Nealian Handwriting Method: Using the D'Nealian method young children are taught to form print letters with loops and rounded angles so that the transition to cursive writing later on is easier and more natural.

Departmentalization: When students leave their homeroom classroom to go to specialists for core subjects.

Different Learning Styles: This phrase refers to the idea that students learn in different ways, and under different conditions. Some students learn best from reading in a quiet room; other students learn best when engaged in debate. Teachers who subscribe to this theory will try to provide experiences that will accommodate different kinds of learners.

Experiential Learning: Learning through hands-on activities and first-hand experiences.

Integrated Curriculum: A curriculum organized around a central theme. All areas of study (reading, writing, math, science, social studies, art and music) are used to investigate this theme. In this way, the children learn process and content within a unified context. "Core curriculum" is a term that is often used synonymously.

Interage, Mixed-Age or Flexible Class Grouping: Classes that are not grouped according to calendar age. There might be a two-year age span within the class composed of children with "a diversity of achievement, capacity, talent and style, but who have enough intellectual and social congruence to work well together" (Bank Street School for Children brochure).

International Baccalaureate: The I.B. is an internationally recognized curriculum and examination. The I.B. diploma is required for admission to many foreign universities. The I.B. program is administered from Geneva, Switzerland, and taught in over four hundred secondary schools in about thirty-eight countries. It is a rigorous and demanding program; students must master a minimum of six subjects and demonstrate the ability to think clearly and communicate effectively. Many colleges and universities in the United States offer advanced placement and/or a year of college credit for superior performance on the I.B. Lycée Français and a very few other schools, all in Manhattan, offer an I.B. program.

Interschool: A consortium of eight New York City independent schools—Brearley, Chapin, Nightingale-Bamford, Spence (girls' schools); Browning and Collegiate (boys' schools); Dalton and Trinity (coed schools)—which share academic, extracurricular and administrative components.

Invented Spelling: What we all do when we try to spell a word: We make an educated guess. The use of this method allows children the freedom to write the words they may not know how to spell, instead of "dumbing down" their writing to avoid making mistakes. Invented spelling is used in a classroom for rough drafts; students must use the correct spellings of words for final copies.

ISAAGNY: Acronym for the Independent Schools Admissions Association of Greater New York. Composed of admissions directors and heads of early childhood programs, ISAAGNY was founded in 1965 in order to simplify and coordinate admissions procedures among independent schools in the New York Metropolitan area. It is now composed of approximately 150 member schools. ISAAGNY contracted with the Educational Records Bureau to administer uniform admissions testing. ISAAGNY also developed a uniform school report form and sets common notification and reply dates.

Kwanzaa: A seven-day African-American cultural holiday similar to traditional African harvest festivals. Kwanzaa means "first fruits" in Swahili. Kwanzaa coincides with the celebration of Chanukah and Christmas.

Learning Disability, Learning Disorder (LD or Learning Difference): The term currently used to describe a handicap that is neurological in origin, which interferes with a person's ability to store, process or produce information. The impairment can be quite subtle and may go undetected throughout life. The primary characteristic of a learning disability is a significant difference between overall intelligence and achievement in some areas according to the National Center for Learning Disabilities. If you or a school suspects that your child has a learning problem, your child will probably be asked to get an extensive psychoeducational evaluation.

Montessori Method of Education: Based on Dr. Maria Montessori's scientific observations of the behavior of young children who were orphaned, disadvantaged or, for other reasons, institutionalized. The Montessori approach encourages active, self-directed learning in a non-competitive environment. The Montessori classroom features multi-aged, multi-graded heterogenous groups and is based on the principle of freedom within limits. Children are free to work at their own pace with materials they have chosen, either alone or with others. Individual mastery is balanced with small group collaboration within the whole group community. The teacher relies on his or her observations of the children to determine which new activities and materials he may introduce to an individual child or to a small or large group. Several NYC Montessori schools that are members of the American Montessori Assocation, use an "eclectic" or "modified" approach, a comfort to those who think "pure" Montessori is too doctrinaire or rigid.

Multiculturalism: In the classroom, multiculturalism introduces subjects and authors that are not typically considered a part of the Western cultural canon. It is a theory of inclusion that allows many cultures a place in the curriculum, with the aim of increasing respect and understanding for the diverse populations of the world.

Multiple Intelligences: Intelligence is not restricted to a score on an I.Q. test but can encompass many areas of life. Some people may excel in music, some in leadership. These are not necessarily testable qualities, but they are forms of intelligence nonetheless.

People of Color (Children of Color) and Cultural Diversity: Inclusive terms of respect agreed upon by the National Association of Independent Schools' Committee on Diversity for people usually described as non-white ethnic minorities, including: African-Americans, Latinos, Asian-Americans, Native Americans, Pacific Islanders and natives of Alaska.

Progressive vs. Traditional School: These terms are in disrepute these days. Many of the traditional schools have incorporated elements of progressive education into their elementary school classrooms. Progressive schools remain in the vanguard in their use of innovative educational practices. A traditional classroom may have a teacher at the front of the room lecturing to students sitting in rows; children are grouped homogeneously by ability level and generally work on the same material at the same time. A progressive school is more likely to have an informal or seminar-style classroom with more discussion and is one in which children work in small groups independently. I find that traditional schools tend to be the older, established single-sex schools, which have a Latin motto, concentrate on the Western or classical canon, have a dress code or uniform, a handbell choir and "quaint" traditions.

Revolving Loan: At a school without a significant endowment parents are asked to give an interest-free loan to the school, refundable when the student graduates or leaves for any reason.

Waldorf Education: The Waldorf method is based on the scientific observations and pedagogical insights derived by Rudolf Steiner (1861–1925), an Austrian scientist, philosopher, artist, and educator. At the heart of the Waldorf philosophy is the belief that education is an artistic process. Innovative teaching methods address the whole child, working to develop clarity in thought, balance in feeling, and conscience and initiative in action. In a pure Waldorf school, students stay with the same teacher from grades one through eight and create their own Main Lesson Books for their core subjects. Students create their own textbooks based on classroom instruction. There is an emphasis on using natural materials and the arts. The program includes knitting, folklore, crocheting and woodcarving usually reserved for the afternoons. A typical Waldorf curriculum offers phonics, grammar, English, two foreign languages (in many schools German is one of the languages), music, eurythmy (a form of music and movement), mythology, drama, art, crafts, science, math and world history. The school aims to encourage close human relationships that help students develop a strong sense of themselves and an awareness of others.

Whole Language: A practical body of ideas about education that originated in New Zealand with the seminal work of Sylvia Ashton-Warner. The connections between reading, writing and speaking are made complete in the Whole Language classroom. Students in a Whole Language classroom read literature (not basal readers) and write stories, plays and poems (instead of filling out workbooks). A Whole Language classroom uses an integrated curriculum, so learning centers around one subject. In this way, students learn both process (the mechanics of learning, like long division) and content (long division is used to answer a question about the subject under study) simultaneously. Learning becomes relevant to the student, and ceases to be an abstraction. There is some controversy surrounding Whole Language. Some educators would like to see more of the "old-fashioned methods," particularly an emphasis on phonics, included in any Whole Language program, and on drills for matters that must be remembered and reproduced quickly and accurately (such as multiplication tables, spelling, grammar).

Writing Across the Curriculum: Teachers who believe in writing across the curriculum will not confine writing to language arts; instead they will provide writing experiences throughout the curriculum. This will help students refine their writing and will demonstrate that writing can serve a variety of purposes and is used in many disciplines.

Writing Process or Writers' Workshop: The teaching of writing in which students are taught to discover what they think about the topic in question and to clarify those thoughts through the process of writing, editing, rewriting and publishing: 1) drafting (brain drain), 2) revising (sloppy copy), 3) editing (neat sheet), 4) finalizing (final fame). Grammar, usage and spelling are taught within the context of the individual student's writing needs rather than in isolation.

THE PRIVATE
SCHOOLS

The Abraham Joshua Heschel School

(Nursery–5th grade)
270 West 89th Street
New York, NY 10024
(212) 595-7087
website: www.heschel.org

(6th–8th grade)
314 West 91st Street
New York, NY 10024
(212) 595-7817

(9th–12th grade)
20 West End Avenue (at 60th Street)
New York, NY 10023
(212) 246-7717

Coed
Nursery—12th grade
Accessible

Ms. Roanna Shorofsky, Head of School
Ms. Marsha Feris, Director of Admissions

Birthday Cutoff   Children entering nursery school must be 3 by August 31
Children entering kindergarten must be 5 by August 31

Enrollment   Total enrollment: 800
Nursery 3's places: 26
Pre Kindergarten places: 14-16
Kindergarten places: 10
9th grade places: 35-40
Graduating class size: approximately 75

Tuition Range 2009–2010 $21,700 to $33,900,
Nursery 3's (½ day)–12th grade

Financial Aid/Scholarship   Available for students in all grades

Endowment   A $42 million capital expansion and renovation is planned for Kindergarten through Eighth Grades; Heschel's $100 million capital campaign is almost half way completed

61

After-School Program   Heschel After-School Program: until 5:30 P.M.; creative and recreational activities; an additional payment is required

---

The Heschel School was founded in 1983 to honor the memory of Rabbi Heschel by a group of educators and lay people from a broad spectrum of the Jewish community. The student body is composed of Jewish families from reform to modern orthodox. "Heschel is a Jewish school as opposed to a religious school," that uses a "holistic, child-centered approach." Girls participate fully in all aspects of the school. Heschel offers an excellent Jewish education to a community of families who are dedicated to making Jewish values a vibrant part of their children's lives. The school day is long, 8 A.M. to 5 P.M. Every day starts with prayers, and although there are seven different prayer groups, some meditative and simply spiritual, most are Jewish. The school honors the dietary laws of kashrut.

Interest in Heschel is increasing because, one parent surmised, "Heschel is the answer to the current quest for spiritual renewal without being doctrinaire or rigid."

Heschel is committed to Jewish life, ethics and values, appreciation of the needs of the whole child, and responsibility to Jewish and world communities. There are social action projects on every level throughout the year. Students in the early childhood division bake cookies for weekly soup kitchens; lower school students conduct coat drives, toy drives; middle school students visit nursing homes and high school students get involved in a variety of interesting ways.

Getting in: Parents of applicants for grades nursery through eighth are required to attend a tour in the fall before submitting an application. "You walk around and get a sense of what we're about," explains the Director of Admissions, who encourages a tour before applying. The school looks for the child who is "bright, has stamina, is inquiring and verbal, and a family who can see themselves as part of the Heschel community." Applicants for grades nursery through first attend a play group visit. Parents meet with an administrator. All applicants for kindergarten and above must submit the results of ERB testing. Applicants for grades second through eighth are invited to spend some time visiting a classroom. High school applicants should call for an application and plan to attend an Open House. Once an application is received, prospective students and their parents are invited for an individual family tour, a meeting with the Head of the high school and submit the results of their ISEEs.

Parents: A parent told us: "Heschel has a very West Side feeling even to a West Sider." According to her, "There are many professionals and lots of academics with Ph.D's—the type who subscribe to *Tikkun* magazine." There is no dress code except for the yarmulke which must be worn during meals and Judaic studies.

Program: The lower school is composed of grades one through five. The Heschel School offers a rich, rigorous and structured program. Each class has two teachers all the way through fifth grade, and classes often break into many small groups; every part of the school day is planned; teachers discuss readings, projects and go on field trips to engage students.

Formal Hebrew and Judaic studies begin in first grade. Heschel's dual curriculum is composed of Jewish history, culture, and Hebrew language integrated with language arts, math, science, social studies and the arts. "The Jewish and secular curricula are intertwined in an organic and relevant way," parents say. Experiential learning is stressed and there is an emphasis on creativity and critical thinking. Computer projects are integrated into many curriculum areas.

The middle school is for students in grades six through eight, subjects are departmentalized. The program is geared to early adolescents. Students explore sophisticated concepts and abstract reasoning skills, exploring challenging text, writing creative and persuasive essays, and participate in scientific and mathematical inquiry. There's a 6th grade trip to Philadelphia, a 7th grade trip to Washington, D.C., and an 8th grade Israel Experience. The middle school also stresses art and music, many students play an instrument or sing, draw and paint with specialists.

The high school, opened in 2002, is housed in a beautifully designed, bright, state of the art facility that includes a chapel, full-sized gym, a large, shiny, bright, kosher cafeteria on the main floor, three science labs, library, and art, music and dance studios. Now operating at full capacity with approximately 75 students in each grade, for a total of 300 students, Heschel's high school is in full-swing. Every student has a laptop; the classrooms are wireless, as is the entire building. Students hail from all over the greater New York area, including, Manhattan, Brooklyn, Queens, New Jersey, Connecticut, Long Island and Westchester. The sha'ar is a two-year program for students who have not previously attended a Jewish school.

The high school offers a rigorous program with a general studies core enhanced by the arts. There are no APs, by design. There are intensive courses in Hebrew language, Bible Talmud text analysis, and Jewish history. The dual (Jewish and general studies) curriculum is integrated with college prep. The school is pluralistic in every sense; all signage throughout the school is in English and Hebrew, some classrooms have arks with torah scrolls alongside Smartboards. The center of the third floor of the high school embodies the Faculty Room, an open room with no walls; every faculty member has a desk, computer and laptop.

Technology is fully-integrated into all aspects of student life.

The high school faculty hosts many with doctorate degrees and expertise in adolescent behavior.

The art and music programs are spectacular. The large art studio oozes with creativity. I saw at least 20 students one afternoon drawing their hearts out. The lobby, halls and common areas are covered with student's works, etched glass (inscribed from a Holocaust prisoner), and other works of art. The several music studios I visited were all fully-equipped with the latest in sound systems. Students were playing a wide variety of instruments—guitars, violins, horns, woodwinds, drums, and keyboards. Other offerings include, a capella, choir, jazz, sculpting, photography, creative writing, public speaking, an award-winning debate team, 30 clubs, and more.

The science and math are part of the core curriculum; additionally, there is a science and math research initiative available for students who choose to focus on an area of individual research. A member of the science department coaches students in science/math journal reading and research methodology. Summer programs are coordinated and many compete in the New York State Science and Engineering Fair and in the Intel Competition.

Athletics in the high school is organized into league sports played over three seasons in two leagues for a total of 11 teams of junior varsity and varsity athletes. The "Heschel Heat," with their blue and orange, compete in basketball, (the JV teams recently won a championship), volleyball, floor-hockey, soccer, cross-country, tennis, softball, baseball, and ultimate Frisbee in the spring.

Popular College Choices   Typically about one-third of the class spends a "gap" year in Israel; Bard, Barnard, Boston University, Brandeis, Brown, Colby, Columbia, Cornell, Harvard, Johns Hopkins, McGill, Middlebury, NYU, Oberlin, Rochester Institute of Technology, Rutgers, Sarah Lawrence, SUNY Binghamton, Tufts, Tulane, University of Chicago, University of Maryland, University of Pennsylvania, Vanderbilt, Vassar, Yale

Traditions   Celebrations of Jewish as well as a few various other seasonal holidays and festivals

Publications   Schools Newspaper *Helios*
Literary Magazine *e.pit'.o.me*

Community Service Requirement   There is no specific community service requirement as service is an integral part of the school's culture.

Hangout   Only seniors can leave the building; the fountain at Time Warner, Trump Parc, Starbucks at Columbus and 59th Street

The Alexander Robertson School

3 West 95th Street
New York, NY 10025
(between Central Park West and Columbus Avenue)
(212) 663-6441
e-mail: info@alexanderrobertson.com
website: www.alexanderrobertson.org

Coed
(Kindergarten–5th grade)
Not accessible

Rev. Leslie Merlin, Headmistress
Ms. Fran Pitts Smith, Principal
Miss Carrie Schantz, Director of Admissions and Exmissions

Birthday Cutoff   Flexible

Enrollment   Total enrollment: 40
Kindergarten–1st grade places: 15
1st grade places: 5
Graduating class size: Approximately 9

Grades   Four terms

Tuition Range 2009–2010 $19,200 for all grades

Financial Aid/Scholarship   Aid is available

Endowment   N/A

After-School Program   A variety of creative and recreational activities from 3:00 P.M. until 6:00 P.M. Monday through Friday, operated by Oasis Day Camp. A separate fee is required.

Summer Program   The school acts as a host for the Oasis Day Camp.

Founded in 1789, The Alexander Robertson School is one of the oldest coeducational schools in New York City. The school is named for its founder, a prosperous Scottish businessman and member of the

Second Presbyterian Church. Among the original students were immigrants and freed slaves. Although The Alexander Robertson School is still owned and operated by the Second Presbyterian Church, it is nonsectarian "while strongly espousing Judeo-Christian values and traditions." In 1998, the Reverend Leslie Merlin became Head of School. The Reverend Merlin was Associate Pastor of The Brick Presbyterian Church for eighteen years, and as such was closely associated with the Brick Church School. She taught in the U.S. and abroad before entering Princeton Seminary, where she received her Master of Divinity degree in 1976.

The student body represents the diversity of the surrounding neighborhood. The ERB is required for entering students. The style of the school is traditional and structured. The program follows a logical sequence through all grades with emphasis on basic skills and study habits. Teachers are sensitive to individual learning styles and differences.

ARS's EveryDay Ethics program teaches children social and emotional skills such as empathy, emotion management and problem solving. Etiquette and protocol are also taught using mealtime as a model—the school eats as a whole with tablecloths, in the newly renovated gym. Students bring their own lunch as well as their own cloth napkins from home to practice table manners.

Classrooms have been recently renovated, and are bright and clean.

The pre-first class focuses on socialization, exploration of the neighborhood and world, and beginning academic foundations. Reading through phonics is emphasized in first grade, with greater proficiency encouraged in second grade. Basic math skills are taught using traditional methods and manipulatives. Creative and critical thinking and writing skills are introduced and cultivated in the middle grades leading to clear, concise, expository writing, including reports in social studies and science in the upper grades. ARS's art program has earned awards for its students both locally and nationally. The music program includes movement, Orff instruments, recorder instruction, theory, introduction to the classics and vocal training. French is taught in all grades and each week a class eats together in the French room which transforms into "Café ARS," and all speak French and occasionally watch French movies. Students also make use of Central Park for recreation and science.

Popular Secondary School Choices   Graduates attend over thrity private schools, including Bank Street, Calhoun, Chapin, Claremont Prep, City and Country, Columbia Grammar and Prep,

Dalton, De La Salle Academy, Dwight, Fieldston, Friends, Horace Mann, Manhattan Country, Marymount, Master's, Nightingale-Bamford, Packer Collegiate, Professional Children's, Riverdale Country, Rudolf Steiner, Loyola, St Hilda's and St. Hugh's, Studio, Trevor Day, Trinity, UNIS, and York Prep.

The Allen-Stevenson School

132 East 78th Street
New York, NY 10021
(212) 288-6710, fax (212) 288-6802
website: www.allen-stevenson.org

All boys
Kindergarten–8th/9th grade
Not accessible

Mr. David R. Trower, Headmaster
Ms. Ronnie R. Jankoff, Director of Admissions

Uniform   Lower School: Allen-Stevenson polo shirt with emblem, pants (no jeans), sneakers allowed kindergarten–3, no sneakers grades 4–9
Middle and Upper Schools: blazer, dress shirts, tie and pants (no jeans)

Birthday Cutoff   Children entering kindergarten must be 5 by September 1
Children entering 1st grade must be 6 by September 1

Enrollment   Total enrollment: 400
Kindergarten places: approximately 45–48
Graduating class size: approximately 22–25

Grades   Semester system in the Lower School
Trimester system in the Middle and Upper Schools
Lower School students receive anecdotal reports and checklists
Letter grades begin in 5th grade
Departmentalization begins in 6th grade
Practice exam given in 6th grade
First final exam given in 7th grade

Tuition Range 2009–2010 $35,500 kindergarten– 9th grade
All fees are included in the tuition
An alternative payment plan is offered through the Wachovia Bank

Financial Aid/Scholarship   Approximately 12%–14% of the student body receive some form of aid
$1.5 million available

Endowment   Approximately $20 million

Diversity   Prep for Prep, Early Steps and Boys Club students are enrolled
Multicultural Committee for parents
Multicultural elements are incorporated into the curriculum at all levels

Homework   Kindergarten: none
1st–3rd: 15–30 minutes
4th–6th: 1 to 1½ hours
7th–9th: 2½ to 3 hours

After-School Program   Alligator Soup: open to A-S students only, kindergarten through 6th graders, 3:30–5:00 P.M., fall, winter and spring; a variety of creative and recreational activities; an additional payment is required
Middle School and Upper School intramural program
Junior varsity and varsity sports

Summer Program   Sports and Discovery Camps: Open to all boys from all schools; from mid-June through late July; for kindergarten through 6th grade, a variety of athletic and recreational programs; for incoming kindergarten students a Rookies Camp program helps new students to meet teachers and other members of the A/S community, make new friends, and experience a variety of creative and recreational activities; from mid-June through late July, boys must bring their own lunches and beverages, snacks are provided; an additional payment is required for all summer programs.

The Allen-Stevenson School was founded in 1883 by Mr. Francis Bellows Allen, who was later joined by Mr. Robert Alston Stevenson

69

as administrative head of the school. Allen-Stevenson was originally located in a brownstone next door to The Chapin School on East 57th Street. During this time, a group of A-S boys once climbed across the roof of the building and into the proper girls' school next door and were severely punished. Perhaps to avoid unnecessary temptation, in 1924 the A-S school moved uptown to its present location on East 78th Street. In the 1920s, A-S boys would roller skate and roll hoops to school whereas now they scooter. A-S is a traditional school with an emphasis on hands-on learning within a structured setting. A-S has always had an emphasis on physical hardiness, music and language arts. Parents say that A-S graduates are very well-rounded and well-mannered.

Allen-Stevenson is located on the Upper East Side. It has a neighborhood school character; parents say the school provides a small and warm community. Allen-Stevenson has completed a major renovation that increased its physical space by fifty percent. Each division of the school now has its own level with flexible "town centers" for divisional meetings. There's also a new multi-purpose auditorium that holds up to four hundred people, a large library/media center, a separate Lower School library, a "Smart" classroom, an additional science lab, a science suite, a new music area, and art and woodworking space.

Getting in: The number of applications to A-S has increased over the past few years resulting in a much more competitive admissions process. After an application has been filed, parents tour the school with a parent tour guide. Parents meet individually with the director of admissions, then parents are invited back with their sons for a small group visit (six to eight boys). While the boys are busy in a classroom with members of the admissions staff, parents are invited to the library to watch a video about the school and to talk with the headmaster and the head of the Lower School. The visit lasts about one hour. The school maintains an active wait list and there is a sibling and legacy policy, but admission is not automatic. The most important criteria for admission is a good fit between the school, the boy and the family.

Parents: Parents are very comfortable at A-S. One parent described it as "an open, warm environment, a wonderful place." She described the parent body as "low key, with a lot of professional people." Another parent said, "It's a normal cross-section of independent school families." Annual class cocktail parties are held in the fall at the school as well as at parents' apartments. Fund-raising events include a Holiday Raffle, Book Fair and spring fund-raiser. There are annual holiday and spring concerts. New parents are invited to an evening reception at the school to meet the Lower School teachers and administrators. The school has no religious affiliation.

Program: Headmaster David Trower, who came from the Collegiate School, is credited with revising and updating the curriculum and attracting good faculty. Parents say, "Mr. Trower's door is always open and he goes out of his way to know you and your son," "He shakes every parent's and boy's hand." In a recent issue of *The Lamplighter*, Mr. Trower is quoted on the tone of Allen-Stevenson: "Our strong academic expectations of the boys are set within a nurturing context. This combination makes Allen-Stevenson unique."

Allen-Stevenson has a very strong music program and boasts one of the finest elementary school orchestra programs in New York City. All students learn to sing and read music. The Middle School Chorus has sung on the White House Ellipse.

The Artist-in-Residence Program during Book Fair Week at A-S features an artist or writer with a specialty. Artwork frequently coordinates with other subjects. For instance, fifth grade boys study ancient civilizations in history and in art class, reinterpreting the art of ancient civilizations: they make ceramic vessels based on ancient Greek vases decorated with narrative scenes or patterns. Trips to the museums support the study of "Ancients" in both art and history. The shop program is extensive and combines art and math skills. Beginning in seventh grade students select an elective arts course during the three weekly "creative" periods.

Public speaking and the dramatic arts are also important at A-S. Upper School boys participate in the annual public speaking contest. Every year there is a Middle School play with a student cast and crew. The popular fifth through ninth grade annual Gilbert and Sullivan production often includes faculty in cameo roles or chorus. A classic American play is produced by seventh graders. Girls from the Nightingale-Bamford School play the female roles in the annual Upper School Shakespeare production as well as the sixth grade and seventh grade plays.

At A-S technology is used to enhance teaching and learning. Boys are taught how, when and why to use computer systems beginning in kindergarten and technological tools are appropriately used by teachers and students in every grade as aids for thinking, producing and presenting work in all areas of the curriculum.

The Lower School at A-S is composed of grades kindergarten through third. Parents say that the Lower School has a non-pressured approach to learning. The teachers employ an eclectic array of materials to teach basic concepts and skills. Reading, writing and math skills are taught in small, fluid groups. There are computers in all of the classrooms. In addition to their classroom teachers, boys interact regularly with a science specialist, art and music teachers, computer teachers and the Physical Education staff. Artwork displayed throughout the school reflects A-S's commitment to the integration of the art into the overall curriculum. At the first of many science fairs, Lower School boys participate in "The Invention Convention," an exercise in problem solving. One boy solved the problem of soap sinking in the bathtub (he inserted a cork), another solved the problem of the spoon sinking into the sauce pot with a magnetic spoon holder. Seventh through ninth graders participate in the annual Science Fair while fourth through sixth graders have their own Science Festival each winter.

Middle School at A-S is composed of grades fourth through sixth. The boys now wear navy blue blazers with the school emblem on the pocket, a dress shirt and tie. Toward the end of third grade, the boys are invited by the fourth grade to a special "tie ceremony" where they are taught how to knot a tie.

The goal of the Middle School program is to develop a student's abilities and self-confidence so that he can begin to take more responsibility for his own learning. Critical thinking is emphasized in English. Science instruction encourages investigation, observation and interpretation of information. In mathematics boys now explore conceptualization, problem solving and logical interpretation of math facts. Fourth graders study map skills and geography as it applies to explorers and exploration as well as current events. The fifth grade history program covers The "Ancients": Near East, Egypt, Greece and Rome, integrating art, music and literature. Sixth graders begin the study of American history which continues into seventh grade. The school library is completely computerized with CD-rom, on-line access, and a variety of on-line data base subscriptions. Middle and Upper School boys use the computer for writing and research. The Learning Resource Center offers support to students needing extra help in acquiring study skills and strategies as well as enrichment at all levels.

The level of work becomes more demanding in the Upper School (grades seven through nine) as the boys prepare for secondary school admissions. Critical reading of both classical and contemporary literature is emphasized. The boys also complete large "theme projects" such as "Facing History," an inter-disciplinary program dealing with the social implications of the Holocaust. The history curriculum incorporates geography and covers the study of the U.S. and the world.

Upper School mathematics covers the study of algebra, geometry and introductory trigonometry. The science curriculum is designed to develop scientifically literate, independent researchers who are ecologically aware and informed about global issues. Weekly labs provide hands-on experience in life science, physical science and biology.

Study of Spanish is offered in grades 2 through 9. French is offered in grades 6 through 9. Language fundamentals are made clear through the study of Latin, introduced in third grade. The arts are taught by professional artists and musicians. Art and music courses are required through seventh grade; afterward they are offered as electives.

In keeping with the longstanding emphasis on physical hardiness at A-S, there is ample opportunity for exercise. Boys in the Lower School go to Central Park for "field" three times a week. There is gym on the other days. "A certain level of fitness is expected," said one parent. Another parent said, "The A-S boys are sports-minded but it's not a jock school." A-S offers ice hockey at Chelsea Piers and swimming at the Asphalt Green Aquatic Center. Team sports begin in Middle School. Upper School boys go to Randalls Island four times a week in the spring and fall. School colors are blue and gold. One of Allen-Stevenson's big rivals is The Buckley School, just down the avenue.

Allen-Stevenson has traditional Lower School weekly assemblies that feature a variety of guest speakers, class performances, poetry readings and so forth. At Middle and Upper School weekly "morning meetings" a member of the faculty will discuss subjects of concern to the A-S community. Topics have included the AIDS epidemic, community service projects and alternatives to watching television.

Project Charlie, the anti-drug program, begins in first grade. Education about health issues is part of the curriculum in grades seventh through ninth, including AIDS prevention. Seventh through ninth graders attend an advisory period once a week to discuss a variety of issues.

Boys participate in special projects in community service throughout their years at A-S. Ninth graders hold Community Service Week and are required to perform twenty hours of community service.

Extracurricular activities in the Upper School include: orchestra, theatre, yearbook, chorus, photography, painting, woodworking, printmaking, newspaper and student council. (Music rehearsals are scheduled so that they don't interfere with other extracurricular activities.)

Special privileges for ninth graders include overnight trips, the use of the seminar room and permission to leave school for lunch once a week.

There are numerous awards in recognition of excellence at A-S. The Anthony G. Couloucoundis Memorial Award is presented to a sixth grader for "scholastic excellence; all-around participation in athletics, the arts, and community service and above all, the gift of friendship." Other awards distributed on Prize Day include the Alumni Medal, DAR Medal, an athletic award, the Charles E. Horman Award for Independence of Spirit and for Citizenship as well as awards in many of the academic disciplines, creative writing, public speaking, Latin, music, shop, art and drama. Closing ceremonies are held in the upper gym.

Popular Secondary School Choices   Graduates attend a variety of New York City independent secondary schools, including Columbia Prep, Fieldston, Riverdale Country, Horace Mann, Trinity, Dalton, and boarding schools including Hotkiss, St. George's, Choate, Lawrenceville, and Peddie

Traditions   Founders' Day, Grandparents' Day, Mother's Day Lunch, Father/Son Breakfast, Father/Son Dinner, Holiday Concert, Spring Concert, Headmaster for a Day, Dinosaur Parade, Field Day, Science Fair, Book Fair, Arts Festival, Middle and Upper School picnic, annual Gilbert and Sullivan production, annual Shakespeare play, Young Alumni Day

Publications   Alumni publication: *The Lamplighter*
Lower School literary magazine: *Rabbit Pie*
Middle School literary magazine: *What We Write*
Upper School literary magazine: *Pages*
Newspaper: *The Allen-Stevenson Weekly*
Yearbook: *The Unicorn*

Community Service Requirement   Special projects in Middle and Upper School; 20 hours in 9th grade; 9th grade Community Service Week

Hangout   The steps outside school

Bank Street School For Children

610 West 112th Street
New York, NY 10025
(212) 875-4420 (main number)
(212) 875-4433 (admissions), fax (212) 875-4733
website: www.bankstreet.edu

Coed
3's–13's (interage groupings)
Accessible

Mr. Alexis Wright, Dean of Children's Programs
Ms. Marcia Roesch, Director of Admissions

Birthday Cutoff   September 1st of the year of entry

Enrollment   Total enrollment: Approximately 425

Nursery   3's places: 16
4's places: 25
5's places: 5–10
Graduating class size: approximately 40–44

Grades   Semester system
No letter or numerical grades
Bi-yearly parent conferences and reports
Departmentalization begins in the 10's (beginning of Upper School)
No formal exams or testing but there are "curriculum tests" and
standardized tests in the Upper School

Tuition Range 2009–2010 $30,325 to $32,530, Nursery 3s–13s
Tuition payment plan available

Financial Aid/Scholarship   Approximately 33% of the student
body receives some form of aid

Endowment   Bank Street College: approximately $25 million; Bank
Street School for Children : approximately $2.5 million

Diversity   Approximately 34% of the student body is diverse; Parents of Children of Color group; Teachers by Adoption; Gay and

75

Lesbian Parenting Group; Learning Styles and Study and Support Group; Teacher of Color Group; Kids of Color Group; The Buddy Program
Prep for Prep students and Early Steps students enrolled

Homework   Nightly reading for all children (either being read to or reading by oneself) 6/7's: When appropriate
7/8's: 30 minutes, builds to 3 nights a week
8/9's: 45 minutes, 4 nights a week
9/10's: 1 hour, 5 nights a week
10/11's, 11/12's: 1½–2 hours, 5 nights a week
12/13's, 13/14's: 2–2½ hours, 5 nights a week
There are group and individual assignments

After-School Program   Bank Street After-School Program: for children ages 4 and up; 3:15–6:00 P.M., five days a week
Children 5 years and older have a variety of activities to choose from including: sports, art, violin, woodworking, puppet making, theater, judo, flute and quilt making
An extended day program of supervised play is available from 4:30 P.M. until 6:00 P.M.
School vacation program: Bank Street will operate a full day program of activities for children age 4 and older when registration warrants. These programs require an additional payment

Summer Program   Bank Street Summer Camp: during the last weeks of June and the month of July

---

The Bank Street School, a demonstration school for children, is part of the prestigious Bank Street College of Education which also includes an independent Graduate School of Education, a Division of Continuing Education and the Bank Street Bookstore. The Bank Street School uses the "developmental interaction" approach to education, which is based on the views of visionary educator Lucy Sprague Mitchell.

Lucy Sprague Mitchell, the founder of the Bureau of Educational Experiments (which later became Bank Street) was part of a group of educators in the 1920s who believed that children learn best "when they are involved in the process of learning, in a developmentally appropriate environment." Concurrent with this philosophy is the belief that children construct meaning out of interaction with the world—they learn best from direct experience. Mitchell's vision of the "classroom as a community" was very different from the nineteenth-century "factory worker model" for schools. Today at Bank Street these elements of "progressive" education are put into practice with a diverse group of children, implemented by a dedicated and highly skilled staff.

Lucy Sprague Mitchell also believed that when children learn to be members of classroom groups that work together and care about each other's welfare, this lesson will extend to caring about the welfare of the society in which we live. The Bank Street College of Education was involved in designing the Civil Rights Act of 1965 and the Head Start and Follow Through Programs.

Getting in: Applications, Open House registration, and all admissions-related information are available on the school's website (http://www.bankstreet.edu/sfc/admissions.html) in September right after Labor Day. Once an application is received, the admissions office will schedule the child's visit and parent tour, which occur at the same time with the exception of the 3s program. At the Open House I attended, the school's spacious auditorium was packed. Parents are shown a video that illustrates the philosophy of the school. This video was unique—not a public relations tool but a real snapshot of class-room life. Student guides from fifth through eighth grades are present during the refreshment time to answer questions and share their experiences. After the Open House presentation, a tour team of a parent guide and typically two student guides take parents through the facilities. The WPPSI is not required for admission to the Lower School (but ERB testing is required for admission to the Upper School starting at age ten.) Parents bring their child to Bank Street for a small group interview (approximately four to five children); separation is handled gently. Parents observe two classrooms for about ten to fifteen minutes while their child is being interviewed. The final step in the process is the parent interview in which there is an exchange of information. The interviewer will share what she observed about your child. Parents might be asked, "What are you looking for in the next twelve years?" In addition to a diverse student body, the brochure says the school "seeks children who give evidence of becoming adventurous learners and who will use the school experience well." An admissions committee of eight staff members makes the final decision.

Parents: Parents describe the atmosphere at Bank Street as informal: "Everyone is on a first-name basis." Professors from nearby

Barnard College and Columbia University send their children to Bank Street, although one parent said, "There's more money at Bank Street now than there was before," Bank Street is committed to a diverse student body and 33 percent of the student body receive some form of financial aid. Parents are welcome everywhere in the school. "In Lower School you might see ten parents listening in at morning meeting," a mother told us. The cafeteria is the gathering place for parents in the morning. Potluck breakfasts and dinners are held. Parents often serve on committees or task forces; for example, recently both the music curriculum and the Spanish program were reviewed. Parent education is an important component of Bank Street. The school conducts a series of evening classes for parents about how math is taught to their children. Parents say that the administration is always "looking, questioning, improving" the school.

The Parents Association consists of four elected officers and a president and vice-president for each division (Lower, Middle and Upper). In addition, the class parents meet with the dean of children's programs. There are a number of fund-raising activities undertaken in an effort to boost teacher's salaries.

Since holidays are not celebrated at Bank Street, the Bank Street Winter Fest is an eagerly anticipated community celebration. Each year a central theme is chosen for the event (a celebration of the winter solstice). The whole school gets involved by writing skits, creating scenery and costumes, and performing. Tickets are free for this three-night event. There is also a Fall Fair and Auction.

Program: The program at Bank Street requires a lot of student initiative but the teachers are "engaged facilitators," explains the school's Director of Admissions, Marcia Roesch. "They have an amazing amount of energy for the children," a parent said. Graduate students from the Bank Street College of Education do their student practicum within the classrooms. There are two teachers in every classroom until fourth grade, then two core teachers for math and humanities. One-quarter of the teachers at Bank Street are men. A typical 4/5's classroom of twenty-one children has a head teacher (who holds a master's degree), a full-time assistant, one or two graduate assistants, lots of blocks, puzzles, books, art materials, snails, and plants.

The teachers at Bank Street "lead from behind" rather than lecturing in front of the classroom. They are actively involved with the students, guiding them in their choices. "The teaching is always adapted to the child's style, that's what they pride themselves on," a parent told me. In addition to the established social studies core curriculum, teachers are encouraged to derive much of the curriculum from student interests and from the students' cultures or environments.

The Lower School is composed of ages three through six. Flexible or mixed-age groupings are used throughout Bank Street. In addition to the 3's, there are two 4/5's classrooms and two 5/6's classrooms. There is typically a 14-month age span within the classroom groupings. Smaller groups are formed for reading and math. Activities are geared to the appropriate developmental level of the child. For instance, "pre-operational" thinkers are not pushed to master a task that will come naturally at age seven. The brochure says "the creation of meaning is the central task of childhood." In practice, children make sense out of concrete experience using concrete materials. (Bank Street students were among the first to use the Cuisenaire rods, unifix cubes and pattern blocks that have become standard materials used to teach math in many elementary school classrooms.) These are noisy, productive classrooms—there is the time and space for exploration, and work with materials. There is, however, an underlying structure. Each day begins with a meeting at which students exchange ideas and learn to listen to each other. All of the students have classroom "jobs" that they take very seriously. Parents say students learn organizational skills right from the beginning.

The daily schedule posted in the meeting area usually includes reading, writing, math, music, movement, gym time and recess and Spanish exposure. (By sixth grade students choose Spanish or French to study more formally) The youngest children play on the deck for one hour each day. Older students use Riverside Park. In the Lower School, movement, gymnastics and imaginative improvisation are all part of the physical education program. Students ten and older participate in interschool teams in soccer, basketball and softball.

The writing program includes teaching of reading from a literature-based program and involves all areas associated with language: listening, speaking and writing. (The Bank Street Readers were the first multiracial readers geared to young children growing up in an urban environment.) Recently, a 4/5s class visited the Bank Street Bookstore and then made their own bookstore in the classroom that they ran for one week as a real store. They sold library books and homemade books and ordered books by telephone. Other classes and parents came in. The money they made was donated to a charity.

The Middle School at Bank Street comprises ages six through ten. Students leave the classroom for woodworking, art, drama, music and gym. The class often breaks into half groups; one-half of the class will go to computer lab while the other half does writing in the classroom.

In these years, students make the connection between the use of the concrete materials (Cuisenaire rods, unifix cubes and blocks) and the use of symbols.

In science students conduct experiments with natural and synthetic matter; they learn about simple machines. They examine hermit crabs and salamanders, and they experiment with the Nile Delta Stream table.

Beginning in first grade, the students break into reading response groups in which four to five students read the same book and discuss it. Parents say, "At Bank Street the children's opinions are really valued." By the 7/8s "they're picking magnificent books to read by themselves." Students write and revise their own work with their peers acting as gentle "critics." Using the computer the students then "publish" their work, which becomes part of the classroom library. There are two computer labs with Macintosh and PC computers and students begin writing on the computer in the 7/8s. Parents say there is a lot of independent reading and writing under the watchful eye of the teacher(s). Because of the low student-teacher ratio, learning difficulties are recognized quickly and a reading specialist works with children in the classroom. Field trips are often integrated into the writing program. All students write in notebooks every day.

Beginning with the 6's, students visit the art studio and woodworking shop. Students are introduced to many media including: sculpture, weaving, batiking and printmaking. Art is frequently integrated into the curriculum. Murals are done in groups—I saw an impressive "Egyptian" collaborative mural, in the 9/10s (Fourth Grade).

In the 6/7s (First Grade), the social studies curriculum expands from the study of neighborhood and community to the study of what people need in a neighborhood in New York City. A class of 6/7s studied buildings around the city and the students created their own neighborhood complete with video store, pizza shop, and grocery store, all made from wooden crates which they painted and furnished. This "crate city" was then peopled with handmade puppets.

The 7/8s study the evolution of The Hudson River. The unit culminated in the creation of a huge papier-mâché model of The Hudson River displayed in the classroom. The focus of the 8/9s curriculum will be the Explorers and New Amsterdam.

The music program is multicultural and the Orff method is used. The 7/8s learn to play the recorder. There are instrumental ensembles and chorus in the Middle and Upper School, and a new string program.

The Upper School comprises students ages ten through thirteen. For Upper School students, the Humanities Core (social studies and language arts), and math and science teachers provide the home base for each class. In addition to teaching content, these teachers serve as advisors and are first in line to speak with family members or other support people. Students leave their classrooms for art, wood-working, music, drama and Spanish in the 8/9s and 9/10s. Science is taught to the 9/10s three times a week. All older children elect Spanish or French and go to those rooms for instruction. They have physical education four times a week and in addition to the arts that are integrated into the academic subjects, students also study art, shop and music. As in the rest of the school, students learn using both tradi-tional and experiential methods. Each age group takes day trips and an overnight trip. Each learns how to do research and participates in role-playing and simulations based on this research. For example, the 13s/14s participate in a Mock Congress, and go on a four-day trip to Washington, D.C. during which they speak directly with members of Congress. Classes publish and share their research projects via hand-made books, displays, "coffee houses," newspapers and magazines. Each year, in Science Expo, teams of students conduct real scientific investigations and share their results with the community. One stu-dent wrote about "our debt to the Greeks" after her Washington trip.

Only the 13/14s may leave the school building for lunch only.

Popular Secondary School Choices: Bank Street graduates attend a variety of independent day schools (Fieldston, Dalton, St. Ann's and Friends Seminary are popular) and New York City public schools

Traditions   Fall Fair, potluck dinners and breakfasts, parents' fund-raiser dance, Thursday morning meetings, overnight class trips (beginning with the 9/10s), Washington, D.C., trip for 13s, Winter Fest (celebration of the winter solstice), 13's play/musical, Spring Concert, alumni reunions, Arts Day, New Parent Welcome Dinner, New Student Pizza Party, Spring Auction

Publications   Newsletter: School for Children Network
Yearbook
Various publications of Bank Street College Parents Association:
PA Newsletter: Connections

Community Service Requirement   Community service projects vary from classroom service to working for organizations with worldwide missions.

The Berkeley Carroll School

Lower Division (Pre-Kindergarten–Grade 4)
701 Carroll Street
Brooklyn, NY 11215
(718) 789-6060

Middle and Upper Divisions (Grades 5–12)
181 Lincoln Place
Brooklyn, NY 11217
(718) 789-6060
website: www.berkeleycarroll.org
e-mail: bcs@berkeleycarroll.org
twitter: BerkeleyCarroll

Coed
Pre-Kindergarten–12th grade
Not accessible, Lower Division
Accessible for 5th–12th grade

Robert D. Vitalo, Head of School

Birthday Cutoff Children entering kindergarten should be 5 by September 30 but readiness is key

Enrollment Total enrollment: 815
Pre-K places: Approximately 40
Kindergarten places: Approximately 15
Graduating class size: Approximately 55

Grades Trimester system, Pre-K through 12.
In all grades, extensive narrative written reports twice a year, as well as family conferences. Beginning in 7th grade, students accompany parents at conferences.
Letter grades and Honor Roll begin in 6th grade
Departmentalization in English, History and Math begins in 5th grade
Required foreign language study begins in 5th grade
First final exam begins in 8th grade

Tuition Range 2009–2010 $14,500 to $29,900, Pre-K (½ day) through 12th grade

Financial Aid/Scholarship Approximately 30% of the student body receives some form of aid

Endowment $3.5 million

Diversity Berkeley Carroll enrolls Prep for Prep students, and is an Early Steps participant; the school offers a variety of diversity programs

Homework Kindergarten: Begins in the spring with "think about" assignments one night per week
1st: Twice a week, 15–30 minutes
2nd–4th: nightly, Monday–Thursday, 30–60 minutes, lengthening as age increases.
4th: all assignments are given at the beginning of the week to facilitate longer-range planning. Longer term projects are added
5th/6th: 1½ hours per night with an occasional long-term project
7th/8th: 2–2½ hours per night
9th/12th: 3 hours per night

After-School Program After-school programs in music includes instruction in virtually all instruments and voice. Older children can select from a large variety of mini-courses including: cooking, quilting, chess, puppet-making, fencing, and gardening. The Lower School division participates year-round in the nationally recognized Hands-on-Science program. Extended day program and early morning (7:30 A.M.) for Berkeley Carroll students only: for Lower Division, from 3:00 P.M. until 6:00 P.M. A variety of academic, creative and recreational activities; an additional payment is required
Interscholastic and intramural athletic competition for Grades 5–12
Music and voice instruction available

Summer Program The Berkeley Carroll Summer Programs run from mid-June through mid-August and are open to students from other schools; an additional payment is required for all summer programs
Summer Day Camp: for Pre-K–4th graders; a variety of creative and recreational activities including swimming trips and weekly BBQ

Creative Arts Camp: for 8–14 year olds; a variety of creative and recreational activities with an emphasis on the performing and visual arts; spring break camp programs are offered and popular

---

The Berkeley Institute, named in honor of Bishop George Berkeley, was founded in 1886. Bishop Berkeley envisioned a white glove school in which the classics were taught along with the arts. One hundred and ten years later the Bishop's vision is only a tintype memory. In 1982 the institute merged with the Carroll Street School, a growing Montessori-based elementary school. In 1996, The Berkeley Carroll School was one of four independent schools in the NYC area to be designated a Blue Ribbon School by the U.S. Department of Education.

Tucked away in the heart of Brownstone Brooklyn, within walking distance of the Brooklyn Botanic Garden, the Brooklyn Museum and Prospect Park, the Berkeley Carroll School's four coed divisions are housed on two campuses only four blocks apart. "Class Links" programs provide opportunities for the youngest toddlers to mingle with senior students, for activities such as crafting pottery or a walk in the park.

A capital campaign completed in 1992 nearly doubled the space of the Lincoln Place (Middle and Upper School) campus and the award-winning classroom complex also houses administrative offices, a student commons, and floor-through Visual Arts Center. In 1994 a new Media Center was added; an athletic center, including a swimming pool, opened in 2001, as well as a child care center for 1 to 3 year olds.

Getting in: Parents can check the school's website and attend one of the many open houses that are offered. All Lower School applicants are interviewed either individually or in small groups, depending on the grade to which they are applying. Applicants for grades two through four visit a classroom. Candidates for grades kindergarten through four must be tested by the ERB. Parents meet with the Director of Lower School Admissions or the Division Director during their child's visit. Berkeley Carroll looks for students who are a good match for the program, "A child who is bright and motivated and demonstrates an interest in learning and doing." I was told by a member of the admissions staff,: "Every student we enroll brings distinctive strengths so that students may excel in all areas—academics, the arts and athletics."

Parents: Parents automatically become members of the Parent's

Association. The PA sponsors parenting workshops and parents are also welcome to serve on committees, volunteer at the library, and accompany children on trips. At BC parents have a real voice in how their school is run because they serve on the school's 25 member board of trustees where they constitute the majority of members, but the school is not a parent co-op; the administration remains firmly in charge of academic direction, class placement and faculty appointments.

Parents who are also authors (and there are quite a few) sign their latest books at the two PA book fairs. Parents created the elementary division's Law Day, helping students stage mock trials at one of which the appropriate sentence for the Wolf in Little Red Riding Hood was adjudicated. Parents also organize and participate in Career Day at which students have the opportunity to create architectural models, write legal briefs and so on. Parents are involved in the social life of the school from planning a year-end trip for graduating seniors to organizing the fifth grade bowling party.

Program: Active hands-on learning is the credo of the Berkeley Carroll School and there is an emphasis on writing, both expository and creative. In a pre-school classroom you might see several children stroking the ears of the class rabbit while charting its growth with pencil and paper. Others will be working independently on a classic Montessori activity such as fitting cylindrical shapes into self-correcting slots or might be gathered around the head teacher, mastering the "M" sound by carefully tracing the shape of a sand-paper letter.

Reading activities begin in kindergarten in a self-paced instructional setting. Many learning styles are accommodated; worksheets are available for those children who gravitate to them. Phonics and whole-language approaches are used to teach reading and all children work one-on-one with the Head Teacher. Children are taught to read with a blend of phonics and whole language, starting with literature in pre-kindergarten and kindergarten. To complete a book is more than an exercise in pronouncing the words: children master vocabulary, spelling and answer reading comprehension questions after which they are "given" the book as part of their personal "library." By the end of the year, some six-year-olds have acquired a library of 12 books or more, testament to their diligent efforts. Grades 1 and 2 have reading roundup, where the entire grade is split into groups to work on individual skills. The math program uses hands-on materials and Mad Minutes to reinforce number facts.

There is a weekly assembly program. Students receive a solid grounding in the basics through an integrated approach to learning. A first-grade unit on "community" might include activities related to the history of the school, and include field trips to several social service organizations.

The teaching of writing begins with journals and progresses to include the use of dialogue, appropriate punctuation and grammar skills. Lower School students study science, art, music, computer, dance and physical education and swimming. Music study uses some Kodaly methods and Orff instruments to begin with, then introduces the recorder and reading music to third and fourth graders. Good sportsmanship and fundamental skills are taught to prepare students for competition in the later grades.

Technology is integrated from kindergarten through fourth grade. There are laptops and projectors available, Smartboards and a computer lab. First and second graders have dedicated computer time in the lab, third and fourth graders use computers in their classrooms.

Field trips are an integral part of the curriculum beginning in preschool with visits to pumpkin farms and to dramatic performances.

The Middle School program at BC "recognizes that children are going through major developmental hurdles. We watch and guide children in every aspect of this development." The student/teacher ratio is roughly about 16/17 students to 1 teacher. Every student is part of an advising group and every teacher, including the Middle School director, has a role as an advisor. Groups of sixth, seventh, and eighth graders spend three years with the same advisor; an average of eight students; cross-grade relationships are organic.

Middle School students gradually master expository and creative writing. At all grade levels, revision is a major component of the writing process and there is extensive peer and teacher review. In sixth grade, students begin a photo-journalism essay with the theme "My Brooklyn" that highlights some aspect of their lives within a family or a community unique to where they live. Seventh graders spend a month researching an actual Supreme Court case that relates to national security.

The foundation of the Middle School math curriculum is mastery of the basics with an emphasis on creative problem solving, such as finding the most efficient routes from one place to another. Advanced students finish algebra by the end of eighth-grade—some more quickly than others. The Middle School Science program is spiral-based, and explores the scientific method. Biology, geology, chemistry and physics reappear each year. There are several computer labs at BC. All campuses are hooked up to the Internet and the school's e-mail system allows for virtual links among teachers and between teachers and parents. The libraries are fully automated and up to date.

Arts offerings include drawing, ceramics, theater tech, acting, dance and music. Fifth and sixth graders study musical instruments and the elective program gives students a chance to choose between jazz or chamber music or chorus. There's a debate team, intramural teams for fifth and sixth graders and interscholastic sports teams for students in seventh and eighth grades.

In the Upper Division students model calculus derivatives on state-of-the-art calculators and computers. In 1996 the Upper Division science curricula were redesigned to put greater emphasis on biochemistry in the mandatory biology course. As a result, physics is taught in ninth grade, chemistry in tenth, and biology in the junior year. More than three quarters of the students take AP courses.

Choice within structure best summarizes the Upper Division at BC and students have several options in arts and athletics. A highly motivated student might play varsity baseball in the afternoon and sing in the choir at night. From ninth through twelfth grades, students take five core academic courses: history, science, English, math and foreign language. They also enroll in two rotating semester electives. (Fifteen electives are offered in everything from chamber orchestra and jazz band to photography and ceramics.) There are often multiple ways of meeting the course requirements—some more rigorous, others explore an interesting aspect of a familiar subject. For instance, juniors may opt for AP American History or select a course on Democracy in America or American Social and Cultural History.

A hallmark of BC's commitment to making the city their campus, all freshmen are offered a program call New York at Night, where the entire grade attends a quintessential New York event on five Friday nights over the course of the year. Upper School students also participate in the United Nations Students Conference on Human Rights and Climate Change every December.

Students participate in semester programs including The Mountain School, The Island School, and High Mountain Institute as well as exchange trips to Belgium and Spain and community service trips to New Orleans, Argentina and Costa Rica. Student's have won awards from Scholastic Gold Keys on both regional and national levels and yearly acceptances to the Breadloaf Young Writers' Conference at

Middlebury College. Additionally, there's a visiting writer's program and a visiting artist's program. Upper School seminars inspire students to question and look for creative solutions to problems.

The school helps students with placement and contacts; internships range from finance and medicine to photography, music, fashion and advertising.

Athletics are an important part of the program at BC but this is not your typical "jock" school. Berkeley Carroll has won first place in judo championships.

Popular College Choices   Oberlin, Brown, University of Pennsylvania, Washington University, Wesleyan, Bates

Traditions   All-School Theme Write-In (recent topics include gender differences, justice and fairness, and leadership), Arch Day, Lower Division Spring Festival, Thanksgiving Sharing Assembly, Holiday Candle Lighting Ceremony, Middle and Upper Division Prize Day, Parent Association Speakers Bureau, Halloween Party, Sesame Place Trip and Annual Auction

Publications   Lower School quarterly creative-writing compendium: *Explorations*
Newspaper: Blotter
Literary magazine: *Reflections*
Yearbook: *The Lion*

Community Service Requirement   80 hours minimum for Upper Division students—all participate; community service starts in the preschool years with food drives for Thanksgiving. Older children devise their own community service projects. By the time students reach the age of 18 they are volunteering in soup kitchens, geriatric centers or on park clean-up crews. Upper Schoolers are required to perform 50 hours of community service but many graduate with more than 200 hours.

Hangout   Ozzie's Coffee Bar, Roma's Pizza, Prospect Park playing fields

The Birch Wathen Lenox School

210 East 77th Street
New York, NY 10075
(212) 861-0404
website: www.bwl.org

Coed
Kindergarten–12th grade
Accessible-elevator

Mr. Frank J. Carnabuci, Headmaster
Ms. Julianne Kaplan, Director of Admissions

Uniform   Lower School: Boys (grades K–5): Tan or gray trousers, white shirt with BWL logo; Wednesdays (dress-up day): dress tie and navy blazer with BWL logo; dress shoes. Girls (grades K–3): Early fall and spring, pink uniform jumper, white shirt with BWL logo, dress blouse or collared polo. Late fall and winter, dark blue and green plaid uniform jumper. Girls (grades 4 and 5): early fall and spring, pink uniform skirt, white top with BWL logo; late fall and winter, dark green and blue plaid skirt, white top with BWL logo, shoes.
Middle School (grades 6–8): Boys: khaki pants, shoes, collared shirt; tie, blue blazer
Girls: fall/spring, khaki skirt or pants with BWL logo; winter, blue skirt or pants, short sleeve polo top (white, yellow, green or blue), socks/tights/leggings, shoes
Upper School (grades 9–12): Boys (all year): khaki pants, collared shirt, tie, shoes; Girls: fall/spring, khaki skirt or pants with BWL logo; winter, blue skirt or pants, any color short sleeve polo top, socks/tights/leggings, shoes

Birthday Cutoff   Children entering kindergarten must have turned 5 by the beginning of school

Enrollment   Total enrollment: 550
Kindergarten places: 40

Graduating class: approximately 45

Grades   Semester system in the Lower School and Upper Schools Trimester system in the Middle School

Letter grades begin in 6th grade
Departmentalization begins in 6th grade

Tuition Range 2009–2010 $30,410 to $32,912, K–12th grade
Additional fees: for trips, books, lunch, PA dues, and activity fees,
approximately $1,600. Lunch program ($1,200) is optional for
10th through 12th graders; there is a 12th-grade graduation fee of
$585

Financial Aid/Scholarship 15% of the student body receive some
form of aid

Endowment $5.2 million

Diversity 17% children of color

Homework 1st: 15–30 minutes, increasing during the year
2nd: approximately 30–45 minutes per night
3rd and 4th: approximately 1 hour per night
5th: 1 1⁄2 hrs per night
6th–8th: 20 to 40 minutes per subject per night
9th–12th: 3–4 hrs per night

After-School Program Open to Birch Wathen Lenox students
only; a variety of creative and recreational activities; extended day
until 6:00 P.M. daily for Lower School; an additional payment is
required
Junior varsity and varsity teams

Summer Program A two-week camp for children in grades 1
through 5

In 1991, the Birch Wathen Lenox School was created by the
merger of two established schools: The Lenox School (founded 1916)
and The Birch Wathen School (founded 1921). The sale of the former
Birch Wathen and Lenox School buildings created a substantial
endowment enabling the school to weather the transition. Headmaster Frank Carnabuci, who had been the assistant head at The
Dalton School for eleven years, and almost 20 at BWL, brings sea-
soned administrative skills and endless enthusiasm to the job. Parents

say he knows every student by name and has implemented interesting new programs such as the overseas study program, and yearly school-wide themes such as The Year of Mythology, The Year of the Headline, and The Year of New York City as a Classroom.

Getting in: The ERB is required for admission to the school. Parents tour and student interview/assessments are also part of the process.

Parents: Parents are around school a lot. "Usually you will see either a parent drop off or pick up until about sixth grade when the kids are allowed to walk home," says a parent of a middle school student. "Although there are a few students from the West Side, there's a healthy sprinkling of everything." Fundraising includes the School Gala, Phone-a-thons, Winter Fest, a shopping bazaar offering goods and services staffed and supplied by parents. For the Spring Street Fair, each grade has its own booth, and 77th Street is closed. The Fair is completely supported by parents, "It's so sweet," says one tireless parent volunteer. "Everyone lets their hair down and they make a little cash."

Program: The Birch Wathen Lenox school is a traditional school with a nurturing atmosphere.

Birch Wathen Lenox's strength is the ability to individualize the curriculum to fit the child. The student to teacher ratio is very small. Parents say, "Nobody falls through the cracks." Specialists work with tutors and parents to resolve learning difficulties. One parent, a private school alumna, who has four children at the school describes BWL: "Having been through every grade in this school, and although it is a small school, it has pretty much everything that a big school offers, but in a small school setting, everyone is very responsive. If anything is wrong, they are listening and issues are handled in a very timely manner, it's not 'Oh you again.'"

The BWL School offers a traditional, comprehensive academic program that features small classes (average of 12 to 15 students per class) and serves a range of students. The school is able to meet the needs of a wide range of abilities through the use of an academic tracking system that separates students into groups based on their ability levels in specific subject areas. Tracking is a method familiar to most baby boomers but has long been out of favor with educators and is considered by many to be "politically incorrect." BWL, bucking the trend, says, "An academic tracking system allows students to progress at a pace that appropriately challenges them, while ensuring the greatest degree of success." Most learning specialists stop working with students intensely by the end of fifth grade, according to a parent, "By sixth grade everyone is expected to be at a certain level."

Even though BWL is small socially, parents say there is something very comforting about it. "Everyone watches out for each other," explains one parent, "It's a school for everyone."

Teacher's credentials and dedication at BWL are impressive, "There are two teachers with PhD's," says a parent of an eleventh grader. "And," she adds, "The school is warm and fuzzy, but has rigorous academics. All of my child's teachers really know him, and if something goes wrong, I hear about it that minute."

The school has expanded by adding a new theater and renovating the gymnasium and classrooms. An extra elevator has been installed and at least eight extra classrooms were added to the school. The cafeteria, also recently updated, has panini presses, a salad bar, organic fruits and yogurt and whole grain bread among other options.

The school is fully networked, with a T1 connection to the Internet. Computers are introduced in kindergarten. Students begin the study of French language and culture in fourth grade. Departmentalization begins in sixth grades in Middle School, where a traditional core of studies, including English, mathematics, history and science, and foreign language, are rounded out with computer science, music and art. In the Upper School, a traditional college preparatory program allows students more choices and independent study opportunities. Recently, three AP courses were added along with a nationally recognized Peer Leadership program.

BWL offers an overseas study program during spring break that enables students to go to France, Italy, Spain, Britain, Russia and various other locations. The program is linked to the school curriculum; daily assignments and a travel journal are required.

The school is completely sensitive to children with food allergies. "So sensitive," recounts a parent of a lower school student, "that every single person in our classroom must use sani-wipes on their mouth and hands before they enter, hence, we all have been getting sick less!"

The extra-curricular athletic program is broad and includes championship teams in girls' volleyball and tennis, and championship boys' basketball, softball and soccer teams. The Middle School athletic program offers soccer, softball, basketball, track and field, tennis, ice hockey, golf, and swimming. There is a professional hockey coach and other expert coaches. Recently the boy's varsity basketball team went undefeated. BWL teams make use of a variety of the city's gyms, pools and fields. Most parents would like to see an improvement in the athletic facilities, perhaps the addition of another building, "That's the direction we're heading," concludes the parent of four.

Popular College Choices   Princeton, Dartmouth, Cornell, University of Pennsylvania, Stanford, Columbia, Connecticut College, University of Virginia, Vanderbilt, Northwestern, Emory, Harvard, Yale, Washington University, RISD, Syracuse

Traditions   Winter Fest, Holiday Pageant at All Souls Church, Arch Day, Field Day, Spring Fair, "Year of" theme, Senior Art Calendar, Fall Convocation, 100 Nights Dinner, Harrison Moore Award, International Night, Spirit Week

Publications   Lower School newspaper: *The Upbeat*
Middle School Newspaper: *The Black and White Ledger*
Upper School newspaper: *The Clarion*
Alumni Magazine: *The Banner*

Community Service Requirement
Middle School: Grades 6,7,8   30 hours
Upper School: Grades 9,10   30 hours
Grades 11,12   30 hours

The Brearley School

610 East 83rd Street
New York, NY 10028
(212) 744-8582 (main number) (212) 570-8600 (admissions)
website: www.brearley.org

All girls
Kindergarten–12th grade
Accessible–elevator

Dr. Stephanie J. Hull, Head of School
Ms. Winifred Mabley, Director of Lower School Admission
Ms. Joan Kaplan, Director of Middle and Upper School Admission
and Financial Assistance
e-mail: admission@brearley.org

Uniform   Lower School: navy blue jumper, white socks and shirt, navy leggings on cold days, sneakers permitted but no clogs or boots
Middle School: navy-blue skirt, shirt or blouse (with sleeves), shoes or sneakers, sweat pants on cold days
Upper School: none

Birthday Cutoff   Girls entering kindergarten must have reached their 4th birthday on or before September 1 of the year in which they apply

Enrollment   Total enrollment: 675
Kindergarten places: 50–52
Graduating class size: approximately 45–50

Grades   Semester system
Kindergarten: parent conferences twice a year
Classes I–III: fall parent conference; spring narrative report
Class IV: fall parent conference; midyear and spring anecdotal reports with grades
Classes V: fall parent conference with the homeroom teacher
Class VI: February parent conference with core subject teachers and advisor
Class VII: fall parent conference with the Head of Middle School
Class VIII: fall parent conference with the Head of Class VIII

Classes V–XII: marks are given in every subject with comments and suggestions

Classes V and VI: receive marks and comments four times a year

Classes VII and VIII: receive marks and comments three times a year

Departmentalization in science, music, physical education, library and art begins in Lower School; math departmentalization begins in class IV; computer departmentalization in class II

Exams: before class VII, classroom tests are informal and marks are averaged with the term's work; once-a-year examinations begin in class VII and are held in March

Tuition Range 2009–2010 $34,000 to $34,350, Kindergarten through 12th grade, which includes fees for books, supplies, trips, food, and/or snacks

Financial Aid   20% of the student body receives some form of aid; recently, approximately $3.5 million was awarded

Endowment   Market value as of June 30, 2009 $101 million

Diversity   37% of the student body; Brearley enrolls students from Prep for Prep, TEAK, The Albert G. Oliver Program, A Better Chance, and Early Steps; The Parent Diversity Forum which meets monthly and holds a Festival of Cultures every other year; Middle and Upper School diversity groups meet weekly, and in the Upper School elected student representatives lead discussions for all classes in the division four times a year. A faculty/staff Diversity Council meets regularly to facilitate discussions among the entire staff. Upper School groups include affinity groups such as, Umoja (a support group for black students), Ella (a support group for Latina students), Asian Awareness and GASP (Gay and Straight Partnership)

Homework   Lower School families are expected to read aloud with their children from kindergarten on; when girls have learned how to read they are expected to spend ½ hour per night reading, as well as being read to

Classes II and III: weekly spelling assignments, math facts and puzzles, 20–30 minutes, plus nightly reading

Class IV: 30 minutes on weekdays, 60 minutes over the weekend, plus nightly reading
Class V–VI: 2 hours
Classes VII and VIII: 2–2½ hours daily
Classes IX–XII: 2½–4 hours daily

After-School Programs   Afternoon program: The Clubhouse, a joint after-school program with Chapin for girls in kindergarten through Class VI; a variety of activities including sports, crafts, homework help from 2:30 P.M.–5:45 P.M., an additional payment is required, financial aid is available; In Middle School, there is traditional Class VII Gilbert and Sullivan performance (December-May), and Class VIII drama (September-March), additional activities, Upper School students can audition for Fall Drama, Winter Musical, Spring Drama, all including boys from city schools; students also choose from a wide variety of activities including, the school newspaper, literary magazine, yearbook, math team, Classics, Model U.N., Habitat for Humanity, Summer Heart, Bridges to Learning, Brearley Enviornmental Action Committee (BEAC), and a host of arts options; there are 11 school-run activities and 20 student clubs and common interest organizations

Summer Program   SummerStart, for children grades K–VI; 2 weeks in June; creative and recreational activities for an additional fee; open to children in the community
Basketball Camp for grades V–XII held at the Field House at East 87th Street
SummerInterlude, a two-week June program, open to students from other schools in grades 4-8; musical activities are taught by members of Brearley's music department along with music faculty from The Rudolph Steiner School); an additional fee is required
Upper School students are eligible for summer study scholarships and exchange programs and can choose from a range of study/travel programs in the U.S., Europe (including Turkey and Greece) and Asia; the school also offers two 3-week travel/study programs to India or China in June

Brearley was founded by Harvard and Oxford-educated Samuel A. Brearley, Jr. so that girls could receive a college preparatory education comparable to that offered at the independent boys' schools. Brearley opened its doors in 1884, originally serving many of New York's socially prominent families, including those of German Jewish background. Today's diverse enrollment is a vibrant cross section of New York City. Since 1930 the school has had only five heads: Millicent Carey McIntosh (who later became Barnard's first president); Jean Fair Mitchell, Head of School for twenty-eight years; Evelyn J. Halpert, a Brearley alumna, who succeeded Miss Mitchell in 1975 and served until her retirement in 1997; and Dr. Priscilla Winn Barlow who led the school until 2003. Brearley's current head, Dr. Stephanie J. Hull comes to Brearley from Mount Holyoke College where she served as Assistant to the President and Secretary of the College. Dr. Hull has taught both French and Women's Studies at Dartmouth College and served as Assistant Dean while at Dartmouth. In her remarks at one recent "Last Day," Dr. Hull advised graduates "To maintain both an open mind and a healthy skepticism, a sense of humor."

Located steps from tranquil Carl Schurz Park, Brearley's twelve-story red brick building on East 83rd Street overlooks the East River. Brearley also has a 12,000 square foot Field House on East 87th Street, a short walk from the school. From the windows of the library in the school building on East 83rd Street, you can watch the sailboats and barges going by. Although at first sight Brearley might appear staid, when the girls are bustling through the halls or speaking forthrightly in class, informality reigns. There are no bells to signal the changing of classes. The atmosphere is relaxed; and you can also feel the exuberance spilling out of the classrooms as you walk down the halls or peek into the common spaces. Here girls receive a superb education in an environment characterized by shared intellectual exploration, tolerance and social activism. A parent characterized the school as being "like my kindergartner's indestructible Brearley tunic: sturdy, practical, and essential. It might come home encrusted with flour, paint, or papier-mâché but it washes clean and ready to go the next day." Brearley encourages students to take time to think, to make good choices, and to achieve a balance among their academica co- and extra-curricular activities. The focus is academic, but there is always time for the impromptu, lighthearted moments that are part of everyday school life. A sense of frivolity prevails at the annual Lower School ice skating parties; Middle School social events such as the Class VIII Carnival and Class VIII Dance and many Upper School events that are sponsored by the Self-Government Association and student clubs and committees.

Brearley girls are just as well mannered as "the green and yellow 'ladies' down the street at Chapin," and also strong, brainy, confident, poised and prepared. "These aren't shrinking violets; everyone has a distinct personality," says a parent.

Getting in: Brearley's admissions packet is welcoming and has all the information needed for a good look at what Brearley has to offer along with the school's wonderful and easy to navigate website: www.brearley.org. Additionally, Brearley's Viewbook and General Catalogue provide prospective families with both a broad and detailed perspectives of the Brearley experience from grade Kindergarten through Class XII. Applications must be filed by December 1 for Lower School, Middle and Upper School. Parents must apply before touring the school. Both parents should come. Tours for Middle and Upper School applicants are given by Upper School students. Parents of Lower School applicants are given tours by admissions office personnel. One prospective parent said, "It looks like a school: wide hallways, bright classrooms and everything is up to date and spotless." After your tour you meet with with an admissions officer. There is plenty of time for parents to describe their daughters and ask questions. Brearley attracts and enrolls candidates from a broad base; in a recent year the kindergarten class came from 32 different nursery programs. What are they looking for? "Eagerness to learn, a sense of curiosity and the willingness to take learning risks," says an admissions officer. "We don't expect the girls to come to us as finished products. We nurture each girl in her individual development, while instilling values of simplicity, generosity of spirit and respect for others." During the child's visit, the school looks for the beginnings of critical thinking skills and at how the child approaches a challenge. "Above all, we want to be sure that students can take full and joyous advantage of all that Brearley has to offer."

Interview appointments for applicants are made from mid-September to mid-January, and a very helpful letter is sent prior to the interview to describe the process in detail. When you arrive with your daughter there are children's books in the waiting room (no squirm test here) and the children go into a classroom with age-appropriate materials. Children might be asked to play a game, tell a story, complete a puzzle or draw a picture while chatting with a teacher. The parents meet with the head of the Lower School and the Head of School, giving them an opportunity to learn more about the school. One parent inferred, "They are also looking at the parents."

Preference is given to siblings and legacies, but they are not automatically accepted.

Financial aid is available beginning in kindergarten; it is need-based, and individual family circumstances are taken into account.

For applicants to Classes I–V, tours are for parents only and are given in the morning and last about an hour. After the parents have visited the school, an appointment will be made for a small group interview for applicants, which includes an assessment of the student's academic abilities. For students applying to Class VI and above, tours are given to applicants and their parents by Upper School students and last about forty minutes. An admissions officer or division supervisor interviews applicants and parents directly after the tour. A standardized exam (ISEE) and teacher references are required. Candidates also sit for Brearley entrance exams whose dates of administration can be found at the back of the school catalogue. What are they looking for? "We are looking for intellectual agility and stamina, eagerness, resourcefulness, kindness, humor and the wit to differentiate the essential from the extraneous," says one representative from the admissions staff.

Parents: The parent body at Brearley, according to one alumna, is eclectic, and hard to stereotype. "Investment bankers, Wall Streeters, doctors, health care workers, police officers, civil servants, recent immigrants, lawyers, architects, academics, actors, artists, writers and musicians are all included. The Brearley community includes families from every part of the city, and all feel welcomed and comfortable," says a parent. There is an active Parents Association, a monthly parents' newsletter and a comprehensive Brearley family web page.

The Parents Association benefits at Brearley are the best in the city; they rotate between events for families and those for adults. "One-of-a-kind" is a recurring theme. In 1999, the benefit "Brearley on Broadway" brought talent together for a nostalgic look at the school through the music of former notable Brearley fathers; Irving Berlin, Leonard Bernstein, Frank Loesser and Richard Rodgers. More recently, benefits have featured screenings at the Tribeca Film Festival and "Brearley Jane," an evening of music by alumnae, parents, students, and faculty, including the Brearley Rock Band, at Chelsea Piers, Pier 40. The entire community is invited to celebrate and support the school on Founder's Day, a special spring evening with a morning symposium and an evening gathering.

Over the years, Brearley has made connections to the families of the girls. "They know a tremendous amount about each girl, but they don't intrude, they feel that the school isn't a parent," said a former teacher. Beginning in Lower School, the girls learn to be their own advocates in social and academic matters, parents report. A parent said she was surprised "at how tremendously observant and psychologically astute the teachers and administration are about each girl."

Program: The Brearley kindergarten has sixteen to nineteen girls in each classroom. Separation is handled gradually. Monday through Thursday dismissal is 2:00, 12:30 on Fridays. Kindergarten girls have specialist teachers for library, music, science, dance and physical education. In music they sing, move and use percussion instruments. In Class III, girls are introduced to a stringed instrument or recorder and hand bells. Lower School girls sing together at Assembly each week and recorder and hand bells are played by Class IV girls at various assemblies as well as at the Winter Assembly and Last Day. Although not "academic" in the traditional sense, the kindergarten year at Brearley is rich with creative learning experiences that are carefully designed to enrich language and math and thinking skills. One of the three kindergarten classes studied breads from around the world, made flour from wheat stalks, baked bread and sold bread from their classroom "bakery." In another kindergarten class each girl had a chance to bring Paddington Bear (and his knapsack with pj's and toothbrush) home overnight along with a journal in which they recorded his every experience. During the year the girls get to know each other as they meet in half groups for gymnastics, PE, music, or play with balls, bikes and wagons on "the pier" or play roof and in Carl Schurz Park.

Formal academics begin in Class I and II. In Class I reading is taught in small groups. One parent said the atmosphere is more relaxed than at some of the other very selective schools and "There is free time in the morning during snack to visit other grades and classrooms." The aim of these early years, according to the brochure, is to help each girl to "form good work habits and to encourage her to be adventurous, responsible and kind." Emphasis is on cooperation, not competition. In Lower School, there is also an emphasis on public speaking with opportunities to recite poems and act in plays. One parent said girls get the sense that "everyone is good at something and the school fosters a sense of security and independence."

In Classes II and III homework includes a "math puzzle of the week" and some spelling words as homework. Starting in Class IV homogeneous math groups are formed but there is movement between groups and the girls all learn the same material, albeit at different paces.

Lower School girls have their own science lab where members of the science department oversee a hands-on approach: To study aerodynamics girls make parachutes and paper helicopters. One of the strengths of Brearley is that all of the faculty teaches across the grades so they get to know the girls as they grow.

"Mandarin has been introduced to girls in Class I and II in 20-minute sessions," explains the Head of the Lower School. "The emphasis is on playing with new words and sounds, so the girls develop their skills without any stress."

In Class II, the girls are introduced to formal computer classes once a week which increases to twice a week in Class III. The Lower School computer room is fully equipped and staffed by computer teachers. The girls learn how to keyboard, create graphics, do word processing and work in multimedia. Computer teachers work closely with homeroom teachers to integrate computer activities with other subjects. Students in Class IV visit the computer room twice a week for a Creative Writing Workshop that focuses on word processing, concept mapping, timelines, and creating a multimedia slide show.

Taking into account the fact that students learn at different rates, students may take a modern language or a reading and writing skills class in Middle School. New students or continuing students can have a skills class in Class VI, or can take beginning French in Class VII. French, Spanish, and Mandarin Chinese may begin in Class V and can be continued through the Upper School. A structured advisory program in the middle and upper schools helps to create dialogues among teachers and students to better monitor students' progress and their workloads. Advisory groups are small with approximately eight to ten girls per advisor and meet weekly. Latin is required in Classes VII and VIII and there are also introductory classes in modern languages (French in Class VII, Spanish or Mandarin in Class IX).

The curriculum in the Lower School is integrated with close coordination among the subjects. Frequently, English readings are related to topics in history and geography. One parent gave an example: "For a unit on China they studied the music, language, history, culture, customs, arts and foods of that country. The walls of the Lower School were lined with all things Chinese."

The Music Department offers private instrumental study to students in Classes II through XII on a variety of instruments. A girl may choose from almost any instrument, from the recorder to the double bass or harp. There is an additional fee, but financial aid is available for those who qualify.

Middle School at Brearley consists of Class V through Class VIII. A quaint tradition at Brearley is the stuffed animal mascot for each class handed down from Class XII to the upcoming Class V. (This is not to be confused with the official Brearley mascot, the beaver.) By Class VI all subjects are fully departmentalized. Attention is still paid to individual learning styles, placement and pace. Some coordination of subject matter continues. In sixth grade English the girls read "The Odyssey" while they are studying Greek and Roman history as part of a broader course in the History of the Ancient World. In sixth and seventh grades, the work load increases. A parent said, "By seventh grade expectations are high and the girls are well aware of their strengths and weaknesses." The parent of a seventh grader said that "reading selections are two years ahead of other schools, and high-level, sophisticated written work is required. Papers are returned with many red lines, sometimes with comments as long as the paper, but their work is the better for it."

In Class VII the girls are reading Dickens and Shakespeare and studying global medieval history, including an introduction to European, Islamic, East Asian, South Asian, and African civilizations. In the spring term they perform a Gilbert and Sullivan operetta. Drama, music and studio art classes are held once or twice a week.

Girls in Class VI take human biology, in which they study all the systems of the body including reproductive, as well as nutrition, drugs, alcohol and cigarette use. Health issues are addressed again in Class VIII to fulfill the New York state requirement. Students also take a one-semester community service course in Class IX, and volunteer in school or in the community throughout their Upper School years. Teams in gymnastics, volleyball, soccer, softball, basketball, swimming, track and lacrosse are formed at this point.

The Upper School: The catalog says that Brearley students need nineteen credits to graduate but most leave with twenty or more. For students who qualify, two classes may be taken in the same discipline. Students have about four to five frees (free periods) a week. Homework now averages four lessons a day of fifty minutes to one hour each. Formal testing begins in Class VII.

Advanced Placement (AP) exams are usually offered in at least seventeen subjects. No "AP" or "honors" courses are offered but most girls take a number of AP exams based on the preparation they get in regular Brearley courses. Math is required through Class XI, though most girls go on to Calculus and Finite Math, offered to XI's which gives students tools that apply to the business world. Linear Algebra, a standard tool for science and engineers, is offered to XIIs. Most Upper School students take more than three Upper School lab science courses. Science and environmental awareness and sustainability courses abound; honors and/or advanced classes are offered in almost every area of science throughout the Upper School. Those with proficiency in science can participate in the Columbia Science Honors Program. Any student can choose from five science courses in Classes XI and XII.

Brearley girls are hot for science, technology and math competitions; recent honors include finalists and semifinalists for The Intel Science Talent Search and the Siemens Competition in Math. Middle and Upper school students participate in Robotics as an activity, and along with a joint team from Chapin, have received awards from FIRST, For Inspiration and Recognition of Science and Technology, an organization that organizes a national science competition.

Seventh graders learn logo-programming in math class; students in Classes V-XII are required to have access to a computer at home with Microsoft Office, Geometer's Sketchpad (provided by the school), and an Internet connection. Financial aid is available for this program. There is no computer science requirement as such, but keyboard proficiency is expected by eighth grade and computer use is an on-going component of Lower, Middle and Upper School math, science, history and language classes. The Upper School offers two computer electives for eleventh and twelfth grade students: Web Design and Multimedia are offered in alternating years. Greek courses are also offered.

Class IX English is devoted to close readings of complex texts. In addition to such classics as Jane Austen and Shakespeare, the girls explore their own voices as writers. All students take a course in Twentieth Century World History. In Class X students take "American Literature From the Puritans to the Moderns" and "United States History Survey." Their studies culminate in a trip to Washington, D.C.

In Classes XI and XII there is a winter requirement of Sophocles' Theban tragedies and Shakespeare's *King Lear*. Spring electives in English are determined by student interest, but even when given a choice, Brearley girls don't seem to stray too far from the classics. Past choices include: Dostoyevsky, modern British fiction and Milton's *Paradise Lost*. More recent electives have been African-American fiction and Virginia Woolf. History electives in Class XI and XII include: "History of China and Japan," "Political and Social Philosophy," and "Modern European History."

Students take art, music or drama throughout the Middle School and continue in one or more of these disciplines in the Upper School. Class VII performs an annual Gilbert & Sullivan operetta and Upper School students perform in three main stage plays including one coeducational musical comedy production (*Bye Bye Birdie, Antigone, Metamorphoses,* and *The House of Bernardo Atha* are recent examples), as well as numerous class drama productions.

For students who are still developing their reading and writing skills, the Brearley Learning Skills Department provides support. In addition to the Lower School's reading program, there are small classes in the Middle School for girls who need significant help in some aspect of language. In the Upper School, a few girls continue to benefit from the individual attention that is offered by this department.

All students have a homeroom teacher and Brearley now has a full-time school counselor who, with the school nurse and a part-time psychologist, form the Brearley health team. There is also a peer leadership program to keep a finger on the pulse of the student body. Seniors who have completed one trimester of training during their junior year serve as a resource for younger students under the supervision of the school counselor and school psychologist.

In the spring term seniors have several options. They can choose independent study—for example, an extracurricular project, job or internship. A recent project was a student written, directed and performed ensemble production. Girls are also encouraged throughout the Upper School to do volunteer work. Girls in Class IX have a year-long community service requirement and select a project or agency they will work with for an entire year. One opportunity is "Bridges to Learning," a highly successful student-run effort that organizes five or six Saturday programs in the spring for students from Harlem Charter Day School, who come to Brearley for a day of arts, crafts, carpentry, computer and other activities. In addition, there are numerous community service drives throughout the year at Brearley, including the fall coat drive, books for Project Cicero, cans for Yorkville Pantry, and Class IV Penny Drive and Class VIII Carnival which benefits causes selected by students and an annual Mitten Drive in which mittens are bought and donated to a food pantry. Brearley supported and raised funds for the Asphalt Green AquaCenter.

There are opportunities to nurture the adventurous spirit of the Brearley girl. In addition to Mountain Day, a day of outdoor activities for Classes V through XII at Bear Mountain, Class XI girls may spend a semester at the Mountain School program of Milton Academy in Vermont, or attend the Maine Coast Semester program of the Chewonki Foundation. In addition to the school's summer travel/study programs in India and China, students may also apply to study in China, France, Spain, Italy or Vietnam under the School Year Abroad Program. Other exchanges include London for Class IX; numerous scholarships for summer study and travel abroad are awarded to girls in the Upper School.

While academic pressure is a fact of life at Brearley, (the school motto, is "By Truth and Toil,") steps have been taken to ease some of the pressure and provide more support for students. Classes in the Middle School continue to run for 40 minutes, but in the Upper School, the schedule allows for flexibility in the way that class time is structured. Language classes in Classes IX and X continue to meet for 40 minute periods, but a Class IX science course, for example, will configure its classes to meet fewer times per week and for a longer period. In addition, the school has taken steps to help students manage their assignments. In the Upper School, there are only three "major assignments" (papers, tests, and lab reports) a week and only one on any given day. In Classes XI and XII, students may make individual arrangements with faculty members when there is a schedule conflict.

Dr. Hull, the division heads, and the department heads coordinate the curriculum and homework and test schedules. Dr. Hull says that "a Brearley education encourages girls to take intellectual risks in an atmosphere that is both challenging and supportive." "The school has taken a lot of steps to help students manage pressure and address social and emotional needs," says a parent.

Course titles don't tell you everything. One alumna said that "there is an international excitement to classes, especially English and history. All subjects are thought through; students are taught to be skeptical of assumptions. Teachers are sensitive to classroom diversity concerns. The goal of Brearley's commitment to diversity is to create an inclusive community, and to develop on-going programs to continue the process.

Students at Brearley are aware of gender issues, and most girls are appreciative of the many benefits of single-sex education. All Brearley students and faculty read a common book each summer and then meet in small groups and discuss it in the fall. Recent books have included *Dreams from my Father*, *Persepolis* and *Where the Girls Are*. One alumna notes, "Students at Brearley never doubt that they can accomplish what they set out to do." The school's emphasis on the written word is evidenced by the large number of alumnae authors.

Two topics which propel ongoing debate and self-evaluation are diversity and leadership. Differences of opinion are respected at Brearley. There is a leveling of socio-economic differences at Brearley because of the emphasis on intellectual achievement. "Brearley girls never want to appear too rich, too social or too fancy. There's an inverse snobbism," says an alumna.

There is recognition that Brearley girls need opportunities to socialize. As one parent said, "It's not a party school; your socializing is postponed for another time." The school does arrange a number of activities with the opposite sex. Friday night dances start in Class VIII and The Middle School Orchestra performs with two local boys' schools during each year. Coeducational activities for the Upper School students include drama department productions, joint chorus concerts with a boys' school near Philadelphia, and with Collegiate, and there are events planned by various student clubs. There is a Holiday Semi-Formal in December and seniors may invite boys or go solo to the "Six Schools" prom held each year at the Waldorf Astoria.

The Class X trip to Frost Valley with five other single-sex schools from Interschool, including boys' schools, is very popular. Also, Brearley is a member of Joint Schools, which plan co-ed activities including an art show, poetry readings and community service days.

Student government is called Self-Government. In the Upper School, two girls form a team and they run for the positions of co-presidents. There are at least thirty student organizations, some for Class V and up, some only for Classes VII through XII. The Service Committee organizes a variety of drives. The Tech Club builds sets for plays. Other popular clubs include the Harvard Model U.N., Asian Awareness and Harvard Model Congress. The Brearley Environmental Action Committee is an active organization that is spearheading student involvement in the N.Y.C. Department of Sanitation's WasteLe$$ program in which Brearley was one of three schools invited to participate. BEAC also maintains a small "techno-trash" bin in the lobby for small electronic items. The students have performed a vital role in data collection and focus the attention of the school community on environmental issues such as recycling and was a recent winner in the Golden Apple Awards Trashmasher Super-Recyclers Contest.

Brearley offers all students a wide-ranging health program. From the Lower School's Respect and Responsibility Class in K-Class II and Life Skills in Classes III and IV, to the Middle and Upper School advisory programs, and extending to the Class IX health course, diversity discussions, seminars for juniors and seniors, decision-making, and nutrition courses, guest speakers, and more, Brearley covers all the bases.

In the Senior Seminar, all Class XII members learn about life skills, business letter writing, interviewing, health care in college, money management, basic auto mechanics, and cooking. Dr. Hull's senior seminar focuses on ethical issues raised by current events.

Brearley offers 13 interscholastic sports teams and a dance troupe. Brearley teams have won more than thirty AAIS titles over the last ten years. Recently, teams captured AAIS championships in cross-country and a NYSAISSA championship in track. There's a no-cut policy for middle school teams.

A music faculty made up of approximately thirty outstanding performing musicians offer group and private lessons to Brearley students and performs regularly at the school throughout the year.

There is praise for an extraordinary faculty. A building was purchased in 1987 on East 77th Street for faculty housing. Appreciation for the gifted faculty is evident from the numerous (nineteen) chairs and faculty awards provided. The school's Professional Development Fund helps to defray a portion of graduate tuition for the faculty and the cost of short courses and workshops. There are also annual professional development days. One class bestowed the Faculty Award Fund (recipients nominated by the senior class) in recognition of "the extraordinary commitment of the Brearley faculty to their students and to the entire Brearley community." At the end of the year the students write thank-you notes to their teachers.

Parents praise the faculty as one of the best among the city's top private schools: "Brearley's greatest strength is its faculty members, who combine experience and skill with genuine warmth and attentiveness to the girls as individuals. Our teachers do an excellent job of conveying not only the concepts in their classes, but also their own love of learning and teaching," and Dr. Hull concurs.

The school has continued its emphasis on providing a rigorous classical education while continually reviewing its academic and extracurricular offerings to keep them relevant. "Brearley's academic program," says Dr. Hull, "with its emphasis on independent thinking, self-expression, and both individual and collaborative problem-solving, has a proven tradition of preparing students to succeed at whatever they choose to pursue."

Brearley makes use of many graceful euphemisms, such as, "Last Day" instead of graduation. "We don't have AP courses—our courses are just impossible. We don't wear underwear—we wear bloomers," remarks one alumna. "We don't get 91's—we get Very Good minus minus plus slash good plus plus minuses. And we don't graduate—we Last Day Exercise." White dresses are worn at Last Day. There is an Awards Assembly at which school prizes in all subjects and scholarships for study and travel are presented. Students are recognized for community service work, and artwork from each class is placed in the school's permanent Kunz Collection. There is also a "Head's Award" for contributions to the school community.

In the late nineteenth century when college choices for women were extremely limited, Brearley prepared girls almost exclusively for Bryn Mawr College. Since then, Brearley has been very successful over the years in matching its students with excellent colleges and universities. Ms. Melanie W. Choukrane, who has extensive experience in college admissions and as a high school college advisor, became Brearley's college advisor in 2004.

Does Brearley churn out a yearly crop of super women? Former Head of School Evelyn Halpert had said that the school's objective is to "turn out young women who will be good citizens in a democratic society . . . whether successful by the standards of our society or not. It would be wrong, I think, to suggest that we want everybody who leaves this school to be a leader or a powerful person. We want all our students to leave this school happier and stronger because of the experiences they've had here and what they've learned."

Legacies say, "I'm Brearley born and Brearley bred"; "Alumnae gatherings are so exciting, there's never a boring person"; "College was disappointing after Brearley." An alumna writes of her years at Brearley: "A superb education and a permanent love of learning. Friendships that last a lifetime." From a Last Day speech by the co-heads of Self-Government: "Brearley teaches us to respect one another. It becomes second nature to care about each other and to get along despite our differing backgrounds, experiences and politics.

Brearley brings people together, though everyone here is unique, we share a common bond. The ties formed here are wound tight with so many remarkable experiences that they will never unravel." The process of learning is lifelong and many Brearley girls become distinguished scholars, writers, journalists, scientists and professionals of all kinds. An alumna now heads The Ford Foundation, and another is head of the Philadelphia Museum of Art, and the list goes on and on.

Popular College Choices   Harvard, Yale, Columbia, Princeton, Georgetown, Johns Hopkins, Bates, Macalaster, NYU, Stanford, Swarthmore, Williams

Traditions   "The best food of all the independent schools," Field Day, Mountain Day, Chorus Performing at Winter Assemblies, Biannual Festival of Cultures, Prom, seventh-grade Gilbert and Sullivan production, eighth-grade Carnival with a surprise theme, Book Fair, Brearley General Store, ice skating parties, Last Day Exercises

Publications   Student Newspaper: *The Zephyr*
Middle School publication: *The Blue Skirt Literary Magazine*
Middle School: *Balderdash*
Upper School Literary Magazine: *The Beaver*
Yearbook
Parents Association: electronic monthly newsletter: e-news from Brearley; *The Brearley Bulletin* special web pages for families and alumnae

Community Service Requirement   Students in Class IX are required to try three different activities in addition to participation as a group in a weekend work camp; Class X and XI students must choose one organization and make a sustained commitment to a minimum of four visits over the course of a school year.

Hangouts   The Mansion (a diner at 86th and York), the library, the "Promenade"

Brooklyn Friends School

375 Pearl Street
Brooklyn, NY 11201
(718) 852-1029, fax: (718) 643-4868
e-mail: bfs@brooklynfriends.org
website: www.brooklynfriends.org

Coed
Toddler–12th grade
Accessible

Dr. Larry Weiss, Head of School
Ms. Sara Soll, Director of Admissions, Preschool
Ms. Jennifer Knies, Director of Admissions, Kindergarten through
12th grade

Birthday Cutoff   Children entering the Family Center must be 20 months old by September 1
Children entering preschool must be 4 by October 1
Children entering kindergarten must be 5 by October 1

Enrollment   Total enrollment: 590
Kindergarten places: approximately 15
Graduating class size: 40

Tuition Range 2009–2010 $15,200 to $29,500, Preschool (Family Center, 2's)–12th grade
For grades 4–12 lunch is included

After-School Program   A variety of creative and recreational activities are offered from 3:00 to 6:00 P.M.; an additional payment is required

Summer Program   Summer camp: From mid-June through mid-August. For children from preschool through 2nd grade, an additional payment is required

---

Brooklyn Friends School is a Quaker college preparatory school founded in 1867 by the Brooklyn Meeting of the Society of Friends. The school is housed in a seven-story art deco building. When you enter through the brass doors you are greeted by lobby displays of student work, from digital photos to paper mâché. In addition to classrooms, four science labs and two libraries, the school boasts a darkroom, music, art, sculpting, ceramics and dance studios, a woodshop, three computer labs, a video production and editing room, two gyms, a roof top playground and a 300 seat theater. The style of the school is informal and there is no dress code.

The school is guided by the ideals of tolerance, equality and the peaceful resolution of conflict. Although Quaker traditions permeate the school parents say that the school is not in the least sectarian. "It manages to provide an enriching academic experience while fostering the sense that there is not a dichotomy between the secular and spiritual aspects of our lives." Students meet in silence for weekly Quaker Meeting and courses in ethics and social justice are offered in the Upper School.

Getting in: Open house tours give prospective applicants a chance to meet parents and faculty. A personal interview is required for all applicants. ERB's are required for kindergarten through fifth grade applicants. The ISEE is required for application to sixth through eleventh grades. One-third of the student body receives some form of financial assistance.

Parents: The parents at Brooklyn Friends are an eclectic mix of artists, office workers, lawyers, educators, physicians and Wall Street professionals who share a common philosophical commitment. According to one parent: "We looked for a private school that reflected and fostered our moral values, where the students were aware of their advantages but were not elitist." The parents play an important role in the school as class parents, library volunteers, and as members of the PTA, they engage in fundraising and community building.

Program: Experiential learning is emphasized in the pre- and lower schools. All classes are actively engaged in creating, hypothesizing and building. The pre-school curriculum is based on the idea of play as "the work of young children" and fosters independence and the development of language and self-expression through the arts, dance and music. Students work to develop and increase basic skills as well as taking part in art, dance, music, library and physical education. Computer science, woodworking, community service, and Japanese language and culture are also part of the Lower School program.

The Middle School is made up of fifth through eighth grade. Fifth and sixth graders stay in the classroom for reading, language arts, and social studies. They see specialists for science, math and foreign language. Latin instruction begins in fifth grade; students can select from Spanish, French or Latin thereafter. Seventh and eighth grades are fully departmentalized. The humanities program includes ancient history, the Middle Ages, the Renaissance and the Age of Exploration and American History. Environmental studies and discussions of new technologies enrich the traditional science curriculum. The school has ability groupings to ensure students are challenged in math; there are several new computer labs.

Upper Schoolers (grades 9–12) take four years of English, math, and physical education; three years of social studies, a foreign language, science, and art; one each of computer literacy and application, Quakerism and ethics. AP classes are also offered in math, foreign language, science and history.

Computers are integrated into the classroom curriculum from the Lower School through Upper School. The school recently installed a T1 line for Internet access throughout the building. In addition to classroom computers, students have access to six computer labs with Dell Optiplex systems. Upper Schoolers edit, write and explore scientific and mathematical formulas through a number of software programs. Brooklyn Friends has a website that is up and running.

Four days of community service are integrated into the school's calendar for group projects. Students also perform one hundred hours—80 outside, 20 inside—of service.

Many high school students play on a sports team. For a relatively small school, the teams are quite successful. BFS recently won the volleyball league championships and a New York State Independent School Soccer Championship title. Athletics are seen as an opportunity to build skills and develop good sportsmanship; despite their recent successes, BFS is not a "jock" school; sports are seen as an opportunity to do one's best.

From second grade through the Upper School, students take overnight trips to develop peer leadership skills, for academic study and for personal growth.

All high school students have an advisor who remains with them until they graduate. Recently, high school students began an exchange program with the Ackworth School, a Quaker boarding school in England.

For six weeks, at the end of senior year, all students engage in internships in areas of academic or personal interest.

Popular College Choices   Amherst, Barnard, Brown, Drexel, FIT, George Washington, Wesleyan, NYU, Sarah Lawrence, Skidmore, Smith, Saint Lawrence, SUNY Purchase, Vassar

Traditions   Holiday Crafts Fair, Dance Concert, All-School Art Show, Middle School Sports Night, Drama Productions, Sports Dinner, Spring Gala and Auction

Publications   Pre/Lower School Poetry Magazine
Middle School Literary Magazine
Middle School Newsletter
Upper School Literary Magazine
Yearbook
School Journal
Parents Notes Newsletter
Traditions, Alumni Newsletter
E-News, a weekly on-line publication

Community Service Requirement   All students take part in community service from pre-school through Upper School. Upper School students are required to complete 20 hours of community service in school and 80 hours outside of school in order to fulfill graduation requirements

The Brooklyn Heights Montessori School

185 Court Street
Brooklyn, NY 11201
(718) 858-5100, fax (718) 858-0500
website: www.bhmsny.org

Coed
2-year-olds–8th Grade
Accessible

Mr. Dane L. Peters, Head of School
Elise Mattia, Director of Admissions

Birthday Cutoff For the 2's Program, the child must be 2 by July 31 in year of entry; for preschool through 8th grade, child must be of age by October 31

Enrollment Total enrollment: approximately 260
2s Program: approximately 20
Pre-K and kindergarten places: approximately 110-115
Grades 1–3: approximately 60
Grades 4–6: approximately 40
Grades 7 and 8: approximately 20-30
Little Room: approximately 30

Grades 1st through 8th Grade progress reports; advisor program starts in 1st grade
1st through 3rd grades are on a semester program
4th through 8th grades are on a trimester system
Parent-teacher conferences twice a year for 2s through 8th grades

Tuition Range 2009–2010 $7,450 to $128,500, 2s–8th Grade
Tuition is all-inclusive, without added charges for trips, books, sports teams, uniforms, or early morning drop-off.

Financial Aid/Scholarship 9% of the school budget is allocated for financial aid. The Little Room is entirely funded by the Department of Education

Endowment $2 million

Homework Starts in 1st grade, averages 30 minutes each night
Homework increases gradually to an average of 2 hours each night in 7th and 8th grades

Diversity 32% of the student body

After-school Program A variety of recreational and creative activities are offered for three-year olds through 3rd grade. The program is open to non-BHMS students. An additional payment is required.

Summer Program A Montessori Summer is a full-day program offering a wide variety of creative and recreational activities. The program runs from late June through July. The summer program is for children 3 years old through 6th grade; the program is open to non-BHMS children; an additional payment is required

---

The Brooklyn Heights Montessori School opened its doors on October 1, 1965 with twenty children attending the one-room school in the First Presbyterian Church on Henry Street in Brooklyn Heights by a group of parents who desired a Montessori preschool in their neighborhood. In 1970 The Little Room program was started. Funded by the Department of Education, it is for children with speech and language delays. In 1988, the school expanded and moved to the Cobble Hill section of Brooklyn. Since then, the school has added elementary and middle school grades. BHMS completed an award-winning 32,000 square foot expansion, which includes not only spacious light-filled classrooms, but also a library, gymnasium and a multi-purpose performance space.

Getting in: Parents are invited to tour the school before applying. After the school tour, a parent interview, and a student visit are required of all applicants. BHMS asks that parents visit the school's website: bhmsny.org for further admissions-related details.

Parents: Parents play an important role in the vibrancy of the school's community. In fact, the school's board of trustees is primarily composed of parents. Parents are widely encouraged to be involved in the school and the Parents Association is very active.

Program: There are currently six divisions of BHMS: the Twos, the Montessori Preschool, the Montessori Lower Elementary and Upper Elementary Programs, Middle School, and The Little Room.

All learning at BHMS is designed to happen within the Montessori model of mixed-age classrooms which are carefully prepared environments organized to offer children a wide range of experience and to facilitate the growth of their skills, confidence and concentration. Independent work, freedom of choice and movement, depth of study, critical thinking, respect for and understanding of others, are all emphasized by a supportive and developmentally oriented staff at all age levels. The teacher's role is one of facilitator in collaborative learning. At each stage of technology is used to enhance skills, share creative ideas and communicate thoughts. BHMS emphasizes developing a sense of responsibility for the ethical considerations inherent in the use of new technology.

The Twos Program offers a gentle introduction to group experience while responding to a two-year-olds need to explore and exercise independence. Montessori inspired classrooms are tailored to this age group's stage of development. The twos are not a mixed-age group.

In the preschool and kindergarten classrooms the environment is nurturing and supportive. The educational philosophy and the teaching materials developed by Maria Montessori provide the underlying structure for the program. The BHMS faculty is concerned with the overall growth of each child, so teachers regard social, physical and emotional development as going hand in hand with intellectual growth. The groups are all mixed-age.

In the Lower Elementary Program, grades 1 through 3, the curriculum integrates all subject areas in a three-year cycle. Studying other cultures and countries helps children to understand themselves and their community in relation to the larger world. A unit related to the United States is included each year. Older elementary students expand the level of study by viewing cultures from a historical perspective. Problem solving provides a primary focus for the math and science programs. Courses concentrate on global cultures, math, science, Spanish, and develop reading and writing skills.

The Upper Elementary Program, (grades seven and eight), focuses on conceptual modules like revolutions, building a democracy, ethical responsibility and conflict and their impact on this country. As students are encouraged to become more abstract thinkers, the curriculum challenges them through a variety of independent research projects that require in-depth study, research, and managing documents. Students deepen their exploration of math, science and technology, and apply what they have learned to real life projects, including a guided independent year-long research-intensive "expert project."

116

Middle School students also explore ways that they can contribute to the larger community. There is an annual Shakespeare play in May, and three overnight trips each year in addition to local field trips.

BMHS teams, the Mustangs, are coed and open to all 6th through 8th graders.

Great care, time and attention is a priority in preparing students for high school admissions process. Families are provided with guidance and counseling.

The Little Room is a special educational program (Preschool) which serves children with speech and learning difficulties. Housed in its own space at BHMS, The Little Room shares much of the Montessori educational philosophy and practices. Integral to The Little Room is a unique mainstreaming program (the oldest in the city for preschoolers) which has been extremely successful in helping students move on to "typical" class placements.

Students in the mainstream classrooms also gain an opportunity to become comfortable with differences in people by participating in mainstreaming activities with the children in The Little Room Program.

Popular Secondary School Choices: Berkeley Carroll, Brooklyn Friends, Bay Ridge Prep, Calhoun, Packer-Collegiate, Collegiate, Elisabeth Irwin, Marymount, Poly Prep, Brooklyn Latin, Beacon, Stuyvesant, La Guardia High School as well as boarding schools, including, Millbrook, Hun, Miss Porter's, Putney, Gunnery

Traditions   Annual Picnic, International Festival, Valentine Card-Making Party, Spring Auction, Middle School Shakespeare performance

Publications   Newsletter: *Handprints*
Weekly Bulletin

Community Service Requirement   Is introduced in the Preschool and extended through Middle School

The Browning School

52 East 62nd Street
New York, NY 10021
(212)838-6280, fax (212) 355-5602
website: www.browning.edu

All boys
Kindergarten–12th grade
Not accessible

Dr. Stephen M. Clement, III, Headmaster
Ms. Liane Pei, Director of Admissions
Ms. Christine Bramble, Director of Middle and Upper School
Admissions

Uniform   Dress code for all grades (coat and tie with an option of polo shirt or turtleneck shirt in the Lower School)

Birthday Cutoff   Boys entering Pre-Primary or Kindergarten must be 5 by September 1

Enrollment   Total enrollment: 375
Pre-Primary or Kindergarten places: 30
Graduating class size: Approximately 30
12 Prep for Prep students as of Fall 2003

Grades   Trimester system
Letter grades begin in 5th grade
Departmentalization begins in 7th grade
Two reports per trimester providing parents with three informal reports each year; parents also receive progress reports every six weeks. In addition to regular parent/teacher conferences, additional meetings can be scheduled

Tuition Range 2009–2010 $34,600 to $35,245, Kindergarten through 12th grade (includes books and lunch and PE uniforms Tuition payment plan available

Financial Aid/Scholarship   Approximately 14% of the student body receives some form of aid

Endowment $14.5 million

Diversity   Browning typically admits students from programs such as Early Steps, TEAK, The Albert G. Oliver Program, George Jackson Academy, and Prep for Prep. Approximately 10-12 students are enrolled each year

Homework   Pre-Primary or Kindergarten: approximately 15 minutes each night plus reading log
Lower School: increases to 1 hour each night plus reading log
Middle School: about 2 hours each night
Upper School: about 4 hours each night

After-School Program   The Browning After-School Encore Program for students from Pre-Primary through Grade 6 offers a wide variety of creative and recreational activities including, cooking, Mandarin Chinese, computer, music lessons, hands-on science, arts and crafts, and after-school study guided sessions, golf, lacrosse, and a parent-led ice hockey program
The Browning Sports Club (Intramurals)
Junior varsity and varsity athletic competition
The after-school chess program is popular and integrated throughout the school. Professional chess masters teach the fundamentals of chess and The Chess Club is open to all Lower and Middle School students. The school hosts tournaments sanctioned by the US Chess Federation

Summer Program   There is a two week recreational program available for the Lower School in June, including students entering Pre-Primary as well as various camp programs in basketball, soccer, and baseball; an additional payment is required

---

The Browning School was founded in 1888 with five boys as a college preparatory school by teacher and scholar John A. Browning and John D. Rockefeller. It is a traditional school, at one time very socially exclusive in its student body. Today, Browning boys are culled from a more diverse population; the school stresses "the importance of developing well-rounded gentlemen." Parents say Browning offers a small, nurturing, supportive environment. "They are extraordinarily understanding and caring about the development of boys," said a parent. "It's a gem that people haven't discovered." Browning has a library, Smartboards, Mac computers, Wilson Music and Drama Room, four science labs, The Henry Luce III Art Center with Juan Metzger ceramics studio, the Morrison play deck, two gyms, and a fitness center. The cafeteria, also known as "Ruby's Kitchen," serves lunch daily. Menu choices include a full salad bar, sandwiches, bagels, soup, hot meals, fruit and yogurt.

Getting in: Parents should visit the school's website. Beginning in the second half of August applications are mailed out in the order that requests are received. There is no cut-off date for applications, but the school stops accepting applications when there are no more appointments available. Once families apply, a member of the admissions staff will call to schedule appointments for tours and interviews for parents and applicants. Postcards confirming dates are sent to families. Parents of Lower School applicants take a tour of the school with a parent tour guide. After touring, the Director of Admissions meets with parents. Approximately two-weeks later, Kindergarten or Pre-Primary applicants are invited to visit for a one hour small group meeting. Parents are asked to pick up their sons after the group meeting. Applicants to Grades 1 through 4 will be invited to spend half a morning visiting classes and activities with their age group and Browning teachers. Middle and Upper School families take small group tours with the Director of Middle and Upper School Admissions and a current student, followed by a parent interview with the Director of Middle and Upper School Admissions and the boy's interview with the appropriate Division Head. Upper School applicants are encouraged to schedule an additional visit to observe morning classes and an interview with the Head of the Upper School. Siblings and legacies are given priority, but acceptance is not automatic.

Parents: "I thought it would be very Muffy and Buffy, which it is," said a parent. "But, in my son's class of fifteen children, there's a family from England, one from Thailand and one African-American. In the other class, there's a South American family and an Italian family." Parents can volunteer for the Parents Association which sponsors a variety of events that support the school. The Parents Association also offers summer study stipends to faculty members to support professional development.

Program: Browning is composed of three divisions: Lower School (Pre-Primary or Kindergarten through Grade 4), Middle School (Grade 5 through Form I-II)and Upper School (Form III [ninth grade] through Form VI [twelfth grade]).

The School is small and provides lots of individual attention. The student/teacher ration is 1:8. The Lower School is carefully structured and geared to develop basic skills in literacy, math, and interpersonal skills. Special attention is placed on critical and creative thinking and communicating effectively using language and numbers. The Language Arts program uses structured reading programs and classic children's literature. Students are taught to be critical, purposeful and careful readers, thinkers and writers. Written work stresses clear, neat handwriting, accurate spelling, grammar and punctuation. There are annual spelling bees, a school-wide public speaking program and the Betty Jean Johnson Poetry Contest. The Lower School at Browning "lets boys be boys, and is structured, but nurturing. My son needed the structure and the small classes. I am beyond thrilled with the school," one parent said.

The enrichment program enhances the language arts curriculum meeting specific needs. Interdisciplinary study units on fairy tales in Grade 2, biographies in Grade 3 and Ancient Egypt and Italy in Grade 4 improve study skills and organizational skills. By Grades 5 and 6, the boys have honed techniques that enable them to become successful independent learners with solid study habits who can explore problem-solving strategies.

Classroom teachers work closely with specialists in art, science, music, library, health, computer, chess and physical education along with Division Heads who help foster a team taught experience throughout the Lower School Program. In social studies students learn about the diversity of their school, community, city and country as well as geography and history. The math program uses manipulatives so that the boys can "learn by doing," says one teacher. By the end of Lower School students are expected to be proficient in addition, subtraction, multiplication, and division using whole numbers and also begin to tackle word problems, fractions, decimals and simple algebra and geometry. The science program explores science from many aspects. Boys begin learning about the five senses in Pre-Primary and Grade 1, and move onto the study of the human body, nutrition and then learn about light, color, floating, and sinking. Most boys really enjoy the opportunity to study living things and compare various aspects of animal behavior of different animals and plants. By Grades 2 and 3 the metric system is introduced and used for scientific investigations into taxonomy, ecosystems, biodiversity, preservation and magnetism, the solar system and earth science. Grade 4 covers a comprehensive study of plate tectonics, earthquakes and volcanoes including rocks and minerals as well as the study of living things and what exactly constitutes living matter, the Linnaean classification system and plant growth. Additionally, Lower School boys take a trip to Black Rock Forest, a four-thousand-acre forest ecology research preserve near Cornwall, N.Y. to record the beauty of nature.

The proper use of art techniques is also stressed at Browning through the Fine Arts Program. All boys express their creativity using a variety of mediums including, drawing, painting, working with clay, sculpture, printing crafts and general design. The works of various artists are studied and explored through the city's vast resources, through field trips to museums and galleries. There's a fully operational pottery studio and an Annual Art show, a school-wide celebration of the arts.

The music program focuses on rhythm, pitch, timbre and improvisation. Orff and Kodaly methods are used. The boys learn to read and write simple rhythmic and melodic patterns, learn musical styles, and study composers; in fact there's a Composer-of-the-Month series that spans Brahms to Bob Marley. Students in Grade 4 are introduced to the recorder and a basic understanding of music theory. The Lower School choirs sing at assemblies, concerts, recitals, and at the Holiday Program.

Each year, Lower School boys have an opportunity to perform in theatrical productions by grade level. By Middle and Upper School, Browning boys participate in plays with several of the girl's schools. Recent productions include *The Tempest* and *a Midsummer Night's Dream*. Older boys really stretch themselves in the arts at Browning through an expanding awareness and appreciation of the performing arts, music and art. There are Middle and Upper School choruse, a Music Club, and a Drumming Circle. Members of ensembles and choral groups can receive academic credit in Upper School. Concerts are held both in- and outside of school.

Browning's attention to technology is sharp and school-wide starting in the Lower School with Smartboards and computer classes in operations, typing, word processing, research and the appropriate use of the Internet. In Grade 2 there is a typing tournament to improve speed and accuracy and boys are exposed to subject-related software programs including Microsoft Word and PowerPoint. The Technology program extends through the Middle and Upper Schools where computers are an integral part of each student's life. Programs for older students include GoogleAppsMoodle, Lego Mindstorms NXT, AdobeFlash, Garageband and making iMovies in HD.

Navigating the library, using the Reference Room as well as using the library's own reference collection of materials and databases is learned by each student. Many students use the library during study halls or free periods to get their work done.

The Middle School program focuses on strengthening study and organizational skills as well as offering a developmentally appropriate curriculum that is supported by a well-managed advisory program. By fifth grade the program is fully departmentalized. In Health, students are taught to focus on healthy habits, self-esteem, good decision making and the environment. Special programs reinforce the transition from childhood to adulthood. Foreign language study begins in fifth grade with a choice of French or Spanish. Latin is required in Forms I and II. Core academic subjects, like writing, grammar and critical reading are focal points of the Middle School program along with math, world culture, Medieval, Ancient and American history, map skills and computer literacy. For example, Forms I and II present a two-year comprehensive research sequence in American history from 1607 to the present.

Middle School math moves from starting algebra to refine the understanding of algebra, geometry and other more advanced concepts such as elementary statistics, graphing techniques, polynomials, linear and quadratic equations, word problems, slopes, exponents, and square roots. In science, reading and report writing are taught with a major focus on direct experience and laboratory investigations. General discussions about sustainability and global issues are integrated with the concepts of motion, machines and different forms of energy and math formulas. Astronomy, galaxies, the universe and the solar system are explored along with what's going on in Central Park with respect to spring hatchings, bird and people watching. Grade 6 focuses on water and its properties, its distribution on earth, its chemistry and importance. Form II focuses on the formal aspects of physics and chemistry laying the groundwork for high school level courses. Middle School Math-Science Night, held in February, features displays from each student's six-week project.

Browning's Upper School students are expected to recognize their role as leaders and role models of the school. For example, The Peer Leadership Program, trains select seniors to work with younger Upper School students. Academically, the boys continue to hone their skills, study habits and strategies that will be required for college. Academic excellence is honored with prizes and awards. Boys who have a grade point average of 3.75 are placed on the Headmaster's List, those at or above 3.5 but below 3.75 make the Honor Roll. Prizes for good citizenship and community service are also awarded. Upper School students are required to complete a minimum of three years of one foreign language in addition to basic requirements in English, history, math and science. A variety of AP courses are offered in almost all disciplines. Readings in English include both the Classics and contemporary authors; the history offereings cover a wide range from religion and the ancient world, the French Revolution to the rise of single-party dictatorships, democracy and World War II. All kinds of math courses are offered and often integrated with science courses.

Art is equally important for Upper School boys. All Form IV students are required to take a trimester course in the Foundation of Art and may pursue their interest through AP Studio Art Portfolio.

From Lower School through Upper School, Browning stresses physical education and fields strong teams in soccer, basketball, baseball, touch football, lacrosse, floor hockey, cross-country, track, golf, crew, fencing, and team handball and tennis. There are Middle School teams, Junior Varsity and Varsity teams. Boys practice and play at Randall's Island, Chelsea Piers, Central Park, Van Cortlandt Golf Course, Mosholu Golf Course and at the National Tennis Center. Field Day is a popular annual event.

Browning is a member of Interschool among other organizations. Beginning in fifth grade, Browning boys participate in a variety of activities with a number of girls' schools including exchange days, field trips, concerts, joint assemblies, dramatic productions and community service projects. There are numerous clubs and Middle and Upper School student councils.

College advising begins in Form III, individual conferences for students and parents with the Director of College Guidance typically begin in Form V after College Night. Students in Forms V and VI have the opportunity to experience the annual College Trip, where they visit roughly eight different colleges.

Popular College Choices Brown, Columbia, Davidson, Duke, George Washington, Middlebury, NYU, Skidmore, Tulane, University of St. Andrews, University of Chicago, Wesleyan, Yale

Traditions Father/Son Dinner, Public Speaking Competition, Brother's Breakfast and Picture, New Parent Dinner, Book Fair, Field Day, Grandparents Visiting Day, Public Speaking Competition, Spelling Bee, Holiday Skating Party, Annual Benefit, School-wide Annual Art Show, Middle School Shakespeare Play, Middle and Upper School Overnight, Three Day College Trip for Forms V and VI

The Buckley School

113 East 73rd Street
New York, NY 10021
(212) 535-8787
website: www.buckleyschool.org

All boys
Kindergarten–8th/9th grade
Accessible

Mr. Gregory J. O'Melia, Headmaster
Mrs. Jo Ann E. Lynch, Director of Admissions

Uniform   Beginners (Kindergarten): prescribed knit blue or white
Buckley polo shirt, pants (no jeans), leather shoes, no sneakers
Grades I–IX: jacket, tie, slacks and leather shoes
All grades must have neat and clean hair, off the collar and above
the eye-brows

Birthday Cutoff   Children entering kindergarten must be 5 by September 1

Enrollment   Total enrollment: approximately 370
Kindergarten places: 40
8th grade graduating class size: approximately 35; more than half will
choose to attend New York City schools, some will on to boarding
schools, the rest will stay for grade IX
9th grade class size: approximately 15–17 Approximately 40%
of Buckley graduates attend NYC independent day schools and
60% attend boarding schools; boys graduate in either Class VIII
or IX

Grades   Trimester system
Kindergarten through 3rd grade students receive anecdotal reports
and checklists
Letter grades begin in 4th grade (6 times a year)
Departmentalization begins in 6th grade, there are practice finals
in 6th grade in most subjects
First final exam given in 7th grade

Tuition Range 2009–2010 $33,500, Kindergarten through 9th grade

Financial Aid/Scholarship   Approximately 8.1% of the student body received some form of aid; approximately $850,000 in financial aid was awarded

Endowment   Capital fund valued at $30 million

Diversity   Children of color represent 10% of the student body

Homework   Beginners: none
Class I: approximately 20 minutes, weekly spelling tests
Class II: approximately ½ hour, daily
Class III: 45 minutes–1 hour
Class IV: approximately 1½ hours
Class V: approximately 2 hours
Classes VI and VII: 2–2½ hours
Classes VIII and IX: 3–4 hours

After-School Program   Boomerang, Monday through Thursday, after-school activities for Classes Beginners through VI, activities include chess, computer, art and science; Classes I through IX are required to participate in a variety of after-school sports
Interscholastic athletic competition in the Manhattan Private School League, the Metropolitan Middle School Track and Field Association, and with some schools outside of these leagues.
Monday/Wednesday/Friday Afternoon Lower and Middle School Gymnastics, a Middle and Upper School Basketball program, Varsity Singers, French Club, Cooking Club, Spanish Club, Myth Club, Chemistry Club, Ancient Greek Club, and 4 rock bands; Saturday Sports Club (10 A.M.–12 P.M. in the Buckley gym)
Vacation Sports Club (10 A.M.–12 P.M. in the Buckley gym)

Summer Program   The Buckley June Program; 2 weeks in June: swimming, computers, arts and crafts, games and sports at Buckley and Ward's Island; an additional payment is required

---

Founded in 1913 by educator B. Lord Buckley, historically The Buckley School has groomed the sons of New York's captains of industry (including a few Vanderbilts, Rockefellers and their latter-day counterparts) for the elite boarding schools. Today, "leadership, citizenship and academic excellence" are still valued at The Buckley School, which is traditional in the best sense of the word, but the

126

student body now includes children drawn from a variety of socioeconomic backgrounds—more than a few from neighborhoods far beyond the tony Upper East Side. While most of the current graduates still go on to schools like Andover and Deerfield, Buckley also sends many to New York City's independent day schools, such as Horace Mann, Dalton and Collegiate, Trinity and Riverdale.

Some elements of the past remain: Buckley still has "travel days" on either side of the spring vacation, a formal tea complete with finger sandwiches is served at The Spring Art Exhibition Day, the male teachers and athletic instructors are addressed as "Sir" and female teachers are addressed as either Miss, Mrs., or Ms. The boys are served by the kitchen staff family-style with teachers present at each table.

The Buckley School is far removed from the turmoil rocking the public schools. Prospective parents who have toured Buckley are impressed by the sense of clarity and order. The Lower School Director says, "Clear goals make clear kids." The emphasis on a classic curriculum, the strict dress code and unabashed respect for God and country have tremendous appeal to this generation of parents dubbed "the new traditionalists." Applications to The Buckley School have been at record levels in recent years.

Is there a typical Buckley boy? Parents say: "A boy who is very interested in sports, very smart, follows directions." It is very important for the boy to be able to handle the workload, because by fourth and fifth grades the curriculum is demanding. Buckley boys are not only hard working academically: Touring parents might see boys with their ties tucked into their smocks painting in the airy art room with classical music playing in the background. First graders recite poetry, Lower School boys perform in the annual rhythm band assembly, all classes put on a class play. Unfortunately, parents do not tour Ward's Island, where the extensive outdoor afternoon sports program (fall and spring) harnesses the boys' more athletic and competitive instincts.

Mr. Gregory J. O'Melia, a Boston-born Harvard man, succeeded Brian Walsh as headmaster in July 2001. Mr. O'Melia has extensive experience teaching and coaching in a range of private schools and was previously headmaster of Charleston Day School in South Carolina.

It is acknowledged that Buckley boys are very competitive, but the belief is that this competitiveness can be positive (and a great motivator) if used appropriately. Middle School pins are given largely for academic excellence. Grades in core subjects are averaged over the year—top boys receive pins. It is noteworthy that the highest awards at graduation exercises are for character, not the highest G.P.A.

Of course, any school is only as good as its teachers, and at Buckley there is tremendous respect for teachers and teaching. Approximately 80 percent of tuition goes toward faculty and staff salaries and benefits. Teachers are evaluated by division directors with the assistance of the headmaster.

Getting in: An important criterion is "a match in values between school and home." Although many of the boys (including legacies and siblings) still hail from nursery schools like Park Avenue Christian, Madison Avenue Presbyterian and Episcopal, the kindergarten class is composed of boys from typically more than 50 different nursery programs.

Admissions at Buckley consists of four components. After the application is received the parents tour the school and have a group meeting with the headmaster, 2) the parents interview with the director of admissions, 3) the applicant attends a interview and 4) the ERB and nursery school report are submitted. Both parents are requested to attend the interviews and the tour; decisions are made on the basis of the group interview, observation at the child's preschool, ERB and school report. However, the school will accommodate scheduling difficulties and meet with the parents separately, if necessary. The group interview is about one hour long (during which the boys are observed playing a variety of "games"). One mother said her son enjoyed the experience so much he drew a picture of himself going to Buckley while at his Trinity interview.

What are they looking for? According to Jo Ann Lynch, Director of Admissions, a boy with "a love of learning, good self-esteem and curiosity, who is fun to be with." They are also looking at how the boy socializes in a group. According to the Lower School Director, "the ERB is a measuring stick against which all the boys stand." And of course, they also look at the family. There is a sibling and legacy policy (some boys' fathers attended Buckley); however, the school will not automatically admit a child who they feel would not do well there. Buckley does maintain a wait list.

Parents: The first Buckley Parents' Committee began in 1982 with the purpose of "service and communication." There is only one officer—the president. Class representatives are selected by the homeroom teachers and division directors. Once a month there is a Parents' Committee meeting, several of which are open to all parents, and twice yearly at an all-parent open meeting, where academic, art or sports programs are presented, and the minutes are distributed to all parents. Parents praise the Buckley mothers, who are "time givers to benefit the school, a cohesive group of women working towards a common goal." School benefits are well organized and well staffed.

The tone at Buckley is definitely formal and very Upper East Side. The parents are Wall Street bankers, lawyers and doctors, ministers, with a sprinkling of writers and business people. But as one parent said, "It's a cosmopolitan mix of French, Chinese, Japanese, African-American, Jewish and Muslim." Another parent had a different perspective: "Boring, old money, coupon clipping . . . they are more dressed in the morning than Brearley parents are in the evening." However, others find that most mothers drop-off their sons in sweats, and either head to the gym or for a run in the park. Most parents dress appropriately for all school events, some mothers wear jeans, although Buckley is formal. The class cocktail party is usually held in a parent's elegant Upper East Side apartment.

The school has no formal church affiliation though throughout the year both Christian and Jewish events are acknowledged and celebrated. Christmas and Chanukah songs are sung at the Beginners' Christmas party. The Nativity play for Classes I and II is an annual event, and after the pledge of allegiance, boys are invited to recite the Lord's Prayer at assemblies. However, families of many faiths are comfortable here; the commonality seems to be one of a basic conservatism.

Traditions are important at Buckley. The used clothing sale and preview party, where parents can purchase gently worn Brooks Brothers pants and blazers for their sons, is a popular event. The Father-Son Overnight (kindergarten through ninth grade) is an annual rite, where the Fathers' Committee selects the Saturday night entertainment. The boys have a marvelous time playing tennis, fishing, throwing a football with Dad (substitute dads are available). Older boys attend the annual Father-Son Dinner, which features speakers such as Roger Goodell, Jim Nantz and John Negroponte. In addition, the annual Father-Son Day at Citifield or Yankee Stadium and family skating party help to bond the Buckley community.

Programs: Buckley's main facility consists of two fully renovated connected buildings on East 73rd and East 74th Streets. The adjacent townhouse was purchased in 1996. It has been completely rebuilt to provide additional classroom space for small group instruction and technology. It will also house some of the facilities now in the 74th Street building which provides additional classroom space. In addition, a new Assembly Room with a balcony has been constructed providing more seating space and doubling the stage area of the old facility. The Hubball Building, two blocks away, named for James M. Hubball, headmaster for thirty-two years, houses three full-size gymnasiums plus the two Beginners' classrooms. Parents like the fact that the Beginners have their own little world, although they travel to "Big Buckley" for Friday assemblies each week. There is a Big Brother Program to help integrate the boys into Big Buckley. Lower School boys write "fan mail" to boys in other grades after watching them perform in school productions.

The Lower School at Buckley is composed of kindergarten through grade 3. Each grade level has two homeroom classes that are reshuffled through the grades so the boys relate to different friends. "Kindergarten at Buckley is a gentle transition into grade school," parents say. Mondays and Fridays are short days, so there is time for play dates and for just settling in. "Except for a few leftover nursery school cliques, friendships seem to shift weekly in the kindergarten year," said one parent. The Friday afternoon gymnastics and basketball clubs (for an additional charge) are "more social than athletic" and most of the boys attend. Boys who want to learn gymnastics routines can attend afternoon sessions at the school beginning in first grade. After school several boys attend art classes at the Metropolitan Museum of Art, others go to religious school, take Chinese, piano or karate, and if they have not had enough sports already, some Lower School boys attend the Cavaliers after-school sports program. Additionally, all boys in Beginners through Grade IV are eligible to attend "Boomerang," the after-school activities group.

The Beginners' classroom is traditional with block and lego corners, listening center, library corner and an adjoining outdoor play roof. On three extended days (until 2:45 P.M.), the boys alternate among gym, creative movement and outdoor play. They also have science and library every week. The kindergarten day is organized but not overly structured. Parents say, "They are really tuned into the rates at which little boys develop. Throughout Buckley the boys are challenged, but they are given the skills to meet those challenges." Kindergartners end the year with the Teddy Bear Picnic, to which boys bring their favorite stuffed bear (or other well-worn animal).

Beginning in first grade boys wear a jacket and tie to school, changing into their "Buckley blues" for after-school sports each day. The day is structured and the boys leave the classroom for art, crafts, music, science and library. First through third graders go to the science lab twice a week. There is a recess every morning and an hour of sports in the afternoon. Project Charlie is an anti-drug program and values class in the Lower School that fosters good self-esteem and responsible decision-making.

While each boy is challenged, fundamental skills are taught in small groups and there is never the expectation that all the boys should be at the same skill level at the same time. Homework is given to teach study skills and responsibility. Parents say that "by third grade the pace is quicker, there is serious traditional work, a certain amount of maturity is expected." Third grade boys know how to use the library, and also have access to the New York Society Library on East 79th Street.

The emphasis at Buckley has always been, and remains, on a "sound traditional curriculum and a common program which every boy partakes in." The Buckley School brochure is notable for its brevity regarding the yearly curriculum, but there is more here than meets the eye. Social studies in the Lower School incorporates multicultural viewpoints. Boys learn to work in collaborative groups as well as individually. There are workbooks that reinforce reading, math and handwriting skills. Journal writing begins in kindergarten and first graders write daily. Formal reading instruction begins in first grade—boys break into reading groups based on ability. There is a lot of movement between these groups. The Lower School Head explains that the reading program is literature based and includes the teaching of phonics. Buckley is quick to identify learning problems before a boy's self-esteem is affected. The Skills and Language Arts Program (SLA), provides support where needed. There is a computer in the kindergarten classrooms that is used for games. Boys in the Lower School "publish" their own books using the computer and there is a Lower School literary magazine, *World of Stories,* that is a desktop publication.

Computer classes and related technology at Buckley include learning to create websites and researching information on-line. Subject teachers collaborate with computer teachers to support the curriculum.

Throughout the Lower School art is frequently integrated into the curriculum. For a unit on the Middle Ages and Islam boys in Class V went to the Arms and Armor Exhibit at the Met and to the Cathedral of St. John the Divine to see and sketch Gothic architecture. Kindergartners make stick puppets and papier-mâché masks. First graders study the cultures of ancient Mexico and Japan. They study Mayan culture, make their own pottery, pictographs, patterns and write illustrated stories. After visiting the Brooklyn Botanic Garden, one class designed their own Japanese gardens. The Japan unit culminates in a visit to the Urasenke Center for a traditional tea ceremony. Second graders make papier-mâché skyscrapers, study immigration and make a map of Manhattan.

The range of the art program at Buckley is visible on Exhibition Day. Works range from terra-cotta dinosaurs to seascapes inspired by Monet, from jungles à la Rousseau to multimedia sculptures and computer projects. There are collaborative murals and freedom quilts. The older boys make actual-size self-portraits of what they would like to be when they grow up, paint from still lifes on canvas, and learn the art of basic printmaking, creating dry point and mono prints. In crafts, the projects range from letter openers, toys, small benches and finely crafted, wooden bowls. Boys spend their final year at Buckley creating a carved wooden plaque of a motif that they would like to be remembered by. The plaques, dating back to 1919, grace the walls of the school's lobby. Every graduating Buckley boy is connected through these series of wooden plaques that serve as snapshots of each particular boy, and are emblematic of the era that they attended the school. Playboy bunny impressions personify the 60's, and a variety of interests have been depicted since, including soccer, cartoons, health and sailing.

Middle School at Buckley is composed of fourth grade through sixth grade. Beginning in Grade IV, homework requires more sophisticated thinking and time; parents say it takes between forty-five minutes and two hours. There are more long-term assignments and letter grades begin in this year. Boys choose a book for their book report (one self-described nonconformist told us he chose Stephen King's *Nightshift*). The boys study the ancient world and write research reports. They have their own Olympic games. French and Spanish are offered for the first time; Latin is required beginning in seventh grade.

The fifth graders study the Middle Ages, culminating in a Medieval Feast. Parents dress in luxurious costumes, the boys make banners, shields and stained glass windows. Middle Schoolers study earth science, physical science, human systems and write carefully researched history papers.

Buckley takes athletics seriously and offers a highly organized, competitive sports program. Blue championship banners line the walls of the Hubball Building and the trophy case is full. The brochure says: "Physical fitness and skill development are emphasized." Per von Scheele, the director of athletics at Buckley for roughly the past forty years, rollerblades to school and leads ski trips to Italy during spring vacation. In fall and spring the boys travel to Ward's Island for field sports. There are weekly assessments to determine progress. Membership in the Strength Club, the Super Strength Club or Gladiators bestowed in "recognition of achievement of athletic strength at a level several years beyond a boy's grade level" is highly prized. Those who meet certain standards get a T-shirt.

By seventh grade, afternoon sports are seventy-five minutes long and one mother told us "the boys come home around 5:30 P.M., do a load of work and go to bed." Not every boy needs to be a jock, but the boy who is totally uninterested in athletics will not be happy here (boys do receive an effort grade in athletics on their report cards). Boys who love to compete and are talented will thrive. Buckley gym birthday parties are popular and parents must book them about a year in advance.

There are Middle School intramural leagues and beginning in seventh grade there are Varsity A and B teams. All boys must participate in one sport each trimester without exception. In fifth grade the boys begin playing football. The Buckley Blue Demons are a source of tremendous pride and school spirit. The wrestling team has won many consecutive championships in wrestling as have the track and field team. In addition to football, Buckley has championship teams in soccer, wrestling, gymnastics, baseball, lacrosse, and basketball. At the end of each season awards are given out recognizing outstanding individual and team achievement. At the end of the year, the most physically fit boy in Classes IV through IX is given special effort recognition through personal fitness index scores.

At the Middle School closing assembly eight different awards are bestowed. Pins are awarded for achievement in the areas of French, athletics, English composition and positive attitude. The Gold Founder's Pin is awarded for the student who made the greatest progress during Middle School, and the George Lane Nichols Award is given for "courage, loyalty, helpfulness and reliability."

The Upper School at Buckley consists of grades seven through nine. In classes VII and VIII boys read *The Iliad*, tackle algebra, hone their lab skills and study American and European history. They continue their study of French, Spanish and Latin. During the spring term, seventh grade boys write a 2,000-plus-word research paper on a topic of their choice in American history (subject to teacher's approval). Classroom discussions in the Upper School become increasingly animated. In eighth grade the boys read more classics: *The Great Gatsby, Julius Caesar, To Kill a Mockingbird;* they complete another spring research paper, and study modern European history up to the Franco-Prussian War.

According to the handbook, ninth grade "readings are chosen for their relevance to the student's developing sense of ethics and justice." They read *The Catcher in the Rye, Huckleberry Finn* and *Macbeth*. There is a weekly debating period and the Gates Bowl debate ends the year. Boys study Euclidean geometry, physics and modern European history through the present. Ninth graders take trips to Boston and Washington, D.C. (where the boys visit the Lincoln and Jefferson Memorials, Arlington National Cemetery, as well as the Holocaust Museum). The most popular ninth grade trips are weekly visits in spring and fall to many of New York City's museums and sights. Ninth graders must complete a major research papers during the year and present a multi-media project in history.

Ninth graders take a year-long class in debating and engage in a formal debate before the student body. Classes VII and VIII have Values Classes with the Headmaster; the Class IX leadership class is also taught by Mr. O'Melia. Ninth graders drop one language and take only five academic courses. They have the privilege of leaving school for lunch on Wednesdays during winter term so that they can use local libraries to work on their term papers. They also spend Wednesday afternoons on field trips all over Manhattan with the Assistant Headmaster.

There are many opportunities for boys to gain confidence speaking and performing in front of their peers and larger audiences.

The annual class play, a tradition at Buckley, starts in kindergarten. The boys soon become very comfortable onstage. Every boy participates in making scenery and has a speaking part. First graders perform in the Nativity play and a poetry recital. The annual class plays become more sophisticated in the Middle and Upper Schools; many of these productions offer a contemporary twist on the classics, for example: *Twelve Angry Men, Catch 22,* and *Hamlet II: Better than the Original.* For the Upper School spring operetta, students from one of the independent girls' schools play the female roles, but in Middle School, boys play all operetta roles. In the annual Jack Woodruff Public Memorial Speaking Contest for seventh and eighth graders, boys must go through four rounds of speaking for four to five minutes on controversial current issues. Recent topics have included the Patriot Act, continued funding of NASA's Mars program, and tax incentives for reducing carbon footprints. The boys are judged on delivery and content.

The student council for grades four through nine is elected by popular vote, with some representatives appointed by faculty. Other extracurricular activities include the popular Glee Club, which offers three concerts a year as well as the Upper School operetta and an annual Middle School operetta. Boys can elect to work on the literary magazine *The Dawn* (named by Mr. Buckley after *The Salutation of the Dawn*, from the Sanskrit), the Upper School newspaper *The Shield* and The yearbook, *Horizons,* or join the Environmental Club. Community service activities include Glee Club Concert visits to the Mary Manning Walsh Residence, and participation in Operation Santa Claus, where boys in Classes VIII and IX team with faculty to provide and wrap gifts for children in the Family Health Services Programs of The Little Sisters of the Assumption Convent in East Harlem, but there is no hourly requirement.

At Upper School closing exercises the Gold, Silver and Bronze Pins are awarded for academic achievement. There is a first and second honor roll, a student athlete award, as well as individual awards in most subject areas. The Harrison S. Kravis Award is given by the Lewis Eisenberg family in recognition of "progress, citizenship, participation in school activities, generosity of spirit." Four major athletic awards, most of them emphasizing character, effort and sportsmanship, are given.

Buckley boys have good manners, excel at sports and speak well in public and are always comfortable wearing a tie and jacket. Parents say that they are well prepared for the most rigorous secondary schools in the nation: "Buckley is prepping our son for life, with high standards in many ways," concludes one alumnus parent.

Popular Secondary School Choices   Whereas decades ago nearly every Buckley boy went to boarding school, now about 40 percent go to New York City-area day schools and 60 percent consistently go to boarding schools. Deerfield, Hotchkiss and Andover lead the recent boarding school choices; Trinity, Riverdale, Horace Mann, Dalton and Collegiate are popular day school choices.

Traditions   Friday assemblies, Father-Son Overnight at Camp Sloane in Lakeville, Connecticut, Father-Son Beginners' Breakfast, Father-Son Dinner, Father/Son Baseball Game, Grandparents' Day, Book Fair, Buckley Skating Party, Class V Medieval Feast, Rhythm Band Assembly, Spring Exhibition and Tea, Middle and Upper School Glee Club operettas, Field Day, Nativity play, Holiday Concert, Annual Jack Woodruff Memorial Public Speaking Contest, Class IX trips to Boston and Washington, D.C., Fathers' Committee softball game vs. Class IX graduates, used clothing and book sale and preview parties, theatre benefit, alumni party, Gates Bowl Debate, Oral English Assembly

Publications   Lower School literary magazine: *A World of Stories*
Literary magazine: *The Dawn* (since 1926)
Upper School newspaper: *The Shield*
Yearbook: *Horizons*
Annual report
School and alumni news: *The Buckley Letter*

Community Service Requirement   No hourly requirement; past activities include Yorkville Common Pantry, Clown Care Unit at New York Hospital, and the Association to Benefit Children.

Hangouts   The Buckley Gym, EJ's Luncheonette

The Caedmon School

416 East 80th Street
New York, NY 10075
(212) 879-2296, fax (212) 879-0627
website: www.caedmonschool.org

Coed
Nursery (2.9 year-olds)–5th grade
Not accessible

Dr. Greg Blackburn, Head of School
Erica L. Papir, Director of Admissions
Lynne A. Burke, Assistant Director of Admissions

Birthday Cutoff   Children entering the Beginners' class must be 2.9 years-old by September 1st
Children entering the Early Program must be 3-years-old by September 1st
Children entering kindergarten must be 5 by September 1st

Enrollment   Total enrollment: 240
Nursery 2s (Beginner's) places: 12-14, Nursery 3s (Early Program and largest point of entry) 18-20
Kindergarten places: 6-10
Graduating class size: 22-24

Grades   Semester system
Detailed written reports 2 times a year and two conferences, the second of which is a portfolio review where 3rd–5th grade students are present with their family; one written report and two conferences in the Early Program (2.9–4-year olds); In addition to formally scheduled conferences, teachers and administrators are always available to families to discuss questions or concerns about their child

Tuition Range 2009–2010 $13,040 (½ day Nursery) to $21,238 (full day K–5th grades); there are no additional fees, books and lunch are included

Financial Aid/Scholarship   14% of the student body receives some form of aid

136

Endowment $3 million

Diversity 38% of students are from diverse backgrounds: FACES of Diversity committee, a group that hosts pot luck dinners, documentary screenings, book discussions and speakers

Homework Elementary school: Four days each week, increases as children get older; beginning in 1st grade, children receive daily homework in language arts and math; by upper grades, children also receive homework in social studies and some specialist classes

After-School Program An additional fee is required for Caedmon after-school programs; available Monday through Friday from 3:30 P.M. through 6 P.M., over 30 classes including foreign language, sports, technology and art; most activities are held in the school building except swimming; in addition, there is a dance club and chorus for children in the Elementary Program, plus an extended day program; approximately 70% of students enroll in at least one after-school activity: The Caedmon Music School is a community program open to children from other schools that offers private and group lessons in flute, guitar, cello, violin, piano and voice; lessons are offered during the week after school and on weekends

Summer Program The Caedmon School Discovery Camp offers a six-week summer program to children ages three through ten years old; two and four week sessions are available; open to children from other schools, the camp program is an around the New York City area travel-based program that includes field trips, swimming lessons, sports and games, computers, arts and crafts, drama, dance and movement, cooking, yoga, music and science; an additional payment is required

---

The Caedmon School was founded in 1962 by a group of parents interested in the philosophy of Maria Montessori; Caedmon offers a "modified Montessori" program. The school is housed in a bright and airy five-story building, with a beautiful new multi-purpose lobby that boasts a beautiful black baby grand piano. In almost every classroom I noticed a framed picture of the school's mission statement.

Facilities include, a private outside courtyard, sheltered from the street, has a safety surface playground. There is a large lunchroom with a full kitchen, which serves hot lunch to everyone. Classrooms are spacious and bright, the art studio is filled with a plethora of materials portfolios, the state-of-the-art science lab houses various animals and specimens. The tight, but tidy, gym has a rock-climbing wall among other athletic items, and there are lap-top carts that travel to every elementary classroom. Smartboards are also in all elementary classrooms and there is a cozy well-stocked library.

Head of School Greg Blackburn says, "Caedmon is a wonderful place for children to learn, with families committed to our mission and to remaining normal and calm in one of the most amazing cities in the world." Mr. Blackburn wore a bow-tie on the day I toured and met him at the school, and he was calm, relaxed, friendly, warm, readily available and conveyed that he was thrilled to be at the helm of Caedmon; as does the board of twenty-one trustees, of whom up to eight are Caedmon parents.

An "attitude of compassion," community service, multicultural respect and acceptance is woven into Caedmon's curriculum. Twenty-five percent of the student body is international; many parents work at the U.N. missions. One parent said, "My husband is with the U.N.; we move constantly and coming to New York City was overwhelming. Caedmon became an oasis for our whole family." Parents say that Caedmon is "warm and accommodating; they are very responsive to children's differing rates of development." There is praise for an "experienced, superb teaching staff" and for the "creative, well thought out homework assignments."

Getting in: The school has a fall admissions procedure; the application deadline is November 30. Applications are processed in the order in which they are received. The application fee is $50.00. The admissions process requires three steps: tour of the school (group tours are available in the mornings and evenings in late-September), attendance at an individual parent interview with an Admissions Officer and a playgroup interview for children, usually on a separate day.

Parents: Caedmon parents range from artists to investment bankers, and quite a few are originally from different countries. The board of trustees has twenty-one elected members, seven of whom may be present parents. "The families who come to Caedmon are under the radar families—-they come to Caedmon for what the school is and stay through fifth grade," explains Dr. Blackburn. The

Caedmon Family Association (CFA) is a well-organized, welcoming, friendly group. The CFA hosts coffees, Curriculum Night, an all-school fall picnic in Central Park, two book fairs, Spring Fundraiser, a teacher appreciation lunch, school photo day, Dad's Night, and a Mother's Day raffle.

Program: The school is dedicated to four basic educational tenets: academic excellence, and natural gifts, diversity, community building and service. From the earliest years at Caedmon, children follow a modified Montessori program. Children are introduced to materials for fantasy play, combined with an emphasis on group work and relaxed socialization amongst the children. Each morning Dr. Blackburn greets children personally.

The school is deliberately small, affording for much individual attention; classes are small, the overall student/teacher ratio is 10/8 to 1. The atmosphere is academic but nurturing. Children are placed into small groups for academic instruction.

The Beginners Class, 2.9 to 3-year olds, has up to fourteen children with two teachers, and first-time students are welcomed to a very warm school environment. The Early Program, a mixed-age group of children, ages three to four-years old, has an average of twenty children and two teachers, both programs have the option of morning or afternoon sessions, are Montessori-based and offer a variety of pre-academic activities and open-ended play. Younger children on a full-day schedule are scheduled for lunch and a nap.

The Elementary Program consists of kindergarten through fifth grade. Specialists work closely with classroom teachers balancing the curriculum with science, Spanish, library/research skills, computer, music, art, gym, yoga, and community service projects.

Throughout the entire school a modified Montessori approach is prevalent along with close attention to developmentally appropriate tasks. The emphasis is on Montessori materials and activities but also encourages creativity.

In kindergarten, the focus is on a language-rich reading, language arts and writing curriculum with particular emphasis on basic skills. The math program stresses the use of numbers, words (solving word problems) and graphic measurements. Using manipulatives and hands-on, experience-based learning processes, students learn concepts and establish a strong foundation for learning more complex skills. Kindergarten prepares five-year-olds for the more teacher-directed and academic demands of Caedmon's Elementary Program. "The teacher really understands that my five-year-old is both a playful child and a budding student," observed one parent.

As students develop skills their academic abilities increase to include reading comprehension, analytical discussions, research skills, work on short- and long-term projects, book reports and essay writing. The TERK math curriculum is incorporated into the math program along with typical math functions, plus sorting, collecting, probability and statics, measurement, two- and three- dimensional geometry, estimation, tables, and graphs.

Technology begins in kindergarten and is fully integrated into the curriculum. Children have access to computers from lap top carts and are taught how to research, write, problem solve and produce creative presentations. All fifth graders have their own lap tops.

The arts at Caedmon are exceptionally strong. Students in music class perform using Orff instruments, read music and participate in ensemble singing and dancing groups and performances hail from a variety of cultures. In addition to music class, children in kindergarten through third grade have group violin lessons. Elementary school students perform in an original play at the end of each school year that often ties into the curriculum. As a "senior" privilege, The Head of School directs a musical with the graduating fifth graders.

Caedmon's on-going school placement staff takes very good care to attend to the needs of families who are going through the admissions process. There is a tremendous amount of communication afforded to each applicant family. The process begins in spring of fourth grade, with a workshop. Both the Director of Admissions and the Head of School meet with each family in spring and again in fall or as needed. Additional after-school workshops foster writing and interviewing skills.

Popular Secondary School Choices Allen-Stevenson, Bank Street, Browning, Birch Wathen Lenox, Claremont Prep, Collegiate, Columbia Grammar and Preparatory School, Convent of the Sacred Heart, Dalton, Dwight, Little Red Schoolhouse Elisabeth Irwin, Fieldston, Hewitt, Horace Mann, School, Manhattan Country, Marymount, Packer Collegiate, Poly Prep, Riverdale Country, Trevor Day School, York Prep

Traditions Monthly all school assembly, Book Buddies (children meet weekly with each other throughout the grades), student musicals, Curriculum Night, annual apple-picking, annual spring beach trip, annual spring park day and picnic, new family reception, all-school Thanksgiving feast, end-of-year-play, Early Program Music and Movement Performances, international family reception, spring benefit, Grandparent/Special Friend Day, fifth grade over-night trip, fifth grade musical

Community Service Community service is an integral parent of the curriculum in fifth grade. Children and their families participate in a range of projects throughout the school year. Issues related to community service projects are often integrated into the program, such as a recent study of sub-Saharan Africa which raised funds for a sister school in Kenya through C.A.R.E.; also popular is the Pajama Program, which collects and distributes new PJs and books to children in need twice each year; food drives and "green-awareness" projects

The Calhoun School

(3-years olds-1st Grade)
Robert L. Beir Lower School
160 West 74th Street
New York, NY 10023
(212) 497-6550 (main number)
(212) 497-6575 (admissions)
fax (212) 721-2025
website: www.calhoun.org

(2nd grade–12th Grade)
433 West End Avenue (at 81st Street)
New York, NY 10024
(212) 497-6500 (main number)
(212) 497-6510 (admissions)
fax (212) 497-6530
website: www.calhoun.org

Coed
Preschool–12th Grade
Not accessible at 160 West 74th Street;
Not fully accessible at 433 West End Avenue

Mr. Steven J. Nelson, Head of School
Ms. Nancy Sherman, Director of Admissions, 81st Street
Ms. Robin M. Otton, Director of Lower School Admissions, 74th Street
Ms. Jenny Eugenio, Associate Director of Admissions, 81st Street

Birthday Cutoff Children entering preschool must be 3 by September 1
Children entering kindergarten must be 5 by September 1

Enrollment Total enrollment: 740
Preschool 3s places: 48, largest point of entry
Kindergarten places: 12
Graduating class 2009: 43

Grades Semester system
Letter and number grades begin in 8th grade
Foreign language begins in preschool 3's with Spanish. Mandarin

142

is added in Middle School, French in Upper School
Departmentalization begins in 2nd grade (2nd through 4th graders move in homeroom or "cluster" groups to specialists in all subjects.) Full departmentalization begins in 5th grade
Timing of first midterm or final exam varies

Tuition Range 2009–2010   Approximately $20,350 to $34,530 Preschool (½ day 3's)–12th grade (includes lunch for 2nd through 12th grades and all materials and books)
Additional fees: for trips (5th–9th grades, ranges from $200–$500); Parents Association fees, $50
Tuition plan of 10 monthly payments can be arranged

Financial Aid/Scholarship   27% of the student body receives financial aid

Endowment   N/A

Diversity   Membership in Early Steps, The Albert G. Oliver Scholars Program, Prep for Prep, ABC, and Faculty Diversity Search.

Homework   Preschool–1st grade: none
2nd–4th: approximately 15–45 minutes
5th–8th: 1–3 hours
9th–12th: approximately 2–4 hours

After-School Program   Calhoun ASP: a variety of classes offered each school day in both buildings, Monday–Friday, 3–5 P.M. daily daycare (74th street), 3–6 P.M. (81st street), with a homework help program and a variety of activities including robotics, knitting, chess, sewing, yoga, dance, ceramics, swimming, animated movie-making, and theater; karate, sports, cooking; an additional payment is required

Summer Program   Summercare: a six-week day camp program for children ages 3–7, directed and staffed by members of the Calhoun School faculty; from the third week in June through July, 8:30 A.M.–2:30 P.M; Calhoun Summer Dance & Video (CSDV): a two-week summer arts program for students ages 10-14; Calhoun Summer Theater (CST), for students ages 8-10, students

create their own original theater pieces; Calhoun Summer Shakespeare (CSS): for students ages 11-16, students are taken through
the stages of a Shakespeare production

———

Founded in 1896 as the Jacobi School for Girls, renamed in 1924
for Head of School Mary Edwards Calhoun. It became completely
coeducational in 1971. Committed to a progressive approach to education, Calhoun has always been a forward-looking institution known
for its innovative curriculum, individualized attention and small class
size. Within each division of the school, there is one floor of classes
with few walls or doors and no rows of desks, but rather areas assigned
to each discipline. Although the tone is informal, there is a strong
underlying academic structure. Parents say, "Calhoun prepares students well for college because they have learned how to be independent thinkers and achievers."

Calhoun has two locations: Since 1989, preschool through first
grade have been housed in the Robert L. Beir Building on West 74th
street. Since 1975, grades two through twelve have been located in a
modern building at West 81st Street and West End Avenue. In 2004,
four additional floors were added to the 81st Street building. The new
floors house a full-size athletic center, a state-of-the-art performance
center, studio art workshops, science labs and language rooms with
their own bank of computers. The school is organized into three divisions, each with its own director.

Parents have a high regard for the teaching staff at Calhoun. Parents describe Calhoun as a community consisting of administrators,
teachers, children and parents. Teachers and administrators are called
by their first names. Under the inspired leadership of Dr. Neen Hunt,
a gifted educator and former head of school, Calhoun attracted a dedicated and caring staff, some of whom have developed its innovative,
award-winning progressive curriculum. Faculty incentives such as the
Professional Development Program, a grant from the Edward Ford
Foundation and the Faculty Enrichment Grant allow teachers at Calhoun to continue to grow and learn. Parents say, "At Calhoun children
see good values that are reinforced by example." Current Head of
School, Steven J. Nelson, came to Calhoun in 1998, with experience in
a variety of private school and college settings, and with a deep belief
in the value of a progressive education. In describing his philosophy,
Mr. Nelson says, "We need to think about education in America in a new
way . . . We should identify and nurture the rich mix of intelligences that

accompany each child through the schoolhouse door. We should value the abstract painting as much as we value the calculation of compound interest."

Getting in: Parents interested in learning more about Calhoun can attend an open house in the Fall before applying. The application fee is $50. There are some short essay questions on the application, such as "Briefly describe your child's personality . . . distinctive qualities, temperament . . . special interests." The school views the ERB as just one component used to evaluate the match between the child and the school. Calhoun selects students with a broad range of interests and talents who have the potential to be focused and self-motivated and the intelligence necessary to meet the demands of its program. A kindergarten applicant's school visit is low-keyed; its aim is to get a sense of the child's personality and interests and to assess facility with basic skills and concepts. Parents participate in a question and answer session with the director of the Lower School and tour the entire school. The preschool program is very popular and the largest point of entry. There are some spaces each year for new four-year olds, and space also opens up at the kindergarten level. Calhoun gives preference to siblings whenever possible.

Parents: Socially, Calhoun is low-key. The primary focus is always on the child, not the parent or social scene. Calhoun counts on parents to be active in their child's educational life, and the school in turn is very supportive of parents. There are frequent conferences, and parents are invited to call or visit when they need to. The Parents Association (PA) is very active, and is supportive of the school's goals; the PA facilitates communication between school and home and serves as a warm and inviting social environment. Annual PA events include, Spring Carnival, the Book Fair at Barnes & Noble, a Tea to honor faculty and staff, and sports evenings in the school gym. Some parents say they feel a connection to Calhoun even after their children graduate, and they continue to attend school events. Wednesday evening volleyball has been going strong since 1978.

Program: At the Robert L. Beir Lower School building (preschool through first grade), classrooms are bright and airy. A strong, cohesive team of teachers collaborate to create an impressive curriculum that integrates art, music, theater, science, computers, Spanish, and physical education. Separation is handled gently on an individual basis: All children have a homeroom "cluster" area and a primary or "cluster" teacher; they travel from this cluster area to other rooms and specialists for certain subjects, depending on their grade level. Children in kindergarten and first grade have language arts, math, science, social studies, Spanish, block building, cooking, art, music, library, computer, physical education, theater and creative movement. Children have recess on the terrace or go to the park each day. Parents say, "Creativity and socialization and the three R's are all stressed in the Lower School." Discipline is recognized as an inner process that is developed with the aid of adults. Calhoun teachers are sensitive to the differing rates of social and emotional development in children. A parent said, "Many are creative kids who march to their own tune."

A broad based approach to teaching reading is employed, making use of Whole Language, phonics, and skill-based instruction techniques. In addition, an innovative program integrates children's creative writing and music. First graders, whose classrooms are on the top two floors of the Beir building, begin to gain spelling skills while given the freedom to use invented spelling. Throughout the school year, first through fourth graders proudly publish their own original books and research papers. First graders continue to follow a curriculum stressing hands-on learning, problem-solving and teamwork. Students begin a year-long study of Central Park. Visits to the park provide experiences that are further developed back in the classroom, including observational drawings of its plants, animals, statues and structures, and classification of the various leaves and rocks that are collected.

Second through twelfth grades are located in the West End Avenue and 81st Street building, where each of the three divisions has its own floor and there are four additional floors of shared spaces. There is a mix of closed and open classrooms throughout the building, giving students experience in both settings. Second through fourth graders (the continuation of Lower School at 81st Street) are divided by grade level into groups or clusters of twelve to fifteen students, and assigned an advisor. They travel as a cluster to other classroom and activity areas within the school. (Calhoun's cluster advisory system changes somewhat in the Middle and Upper Schools, where clusters are formed across the grades and students follow increasingly individualized schedules.) In keeping with Calhoun's philosophy of learning as a shared, connected experience, table groupings replace the traditional desks in rows.

An eclectic approach is used to improve reading skills. Teachers work one on one with students in order to address each child's individual needs. Students engage in creative and journal writing and learn the writing process. Research writing skills are introduced in first grade and developed further in successive grades. By the end of the eighth grade, each student chooses a topic and formal thesis; students are expected to have strong skills in research writing when they leave Middle School.

Math skills in mechanics and abstract thinking are taught in creative hands-on classes in which students participate fully, sometimes even writing their own math problems to share with other math students. Homework assignments reinforce skills as well as challenge students. Critical thinking and problem solving encourage divergent approaches.

The school recognizes the different talents, abilities and learning styles of individual children. The curriculum is flexible enough to address itself to varying developmental needs.

Calhoun's interdisciplinary approach to learning is most obvious, beginning at the Lower School level, when, for example, literature is integrated with social studies, science and other subjects. The artful interweaving of different subjects into a cohesive whole is the hallmark of the program, evident at each grade level.

Second graders spend a year studying New York City, beginning with Calhoun and extending to various neighborhoods and cultural and historical aspects of the city. Third graders study U.S. history and world geography, fourth graders delve more deeply into New York City's history, focusing on immigration, emigration, moving and settling, culminating in a research paper.

The Middle School at Calhoun is composed of grades five through eight. The integrated English and social studies curriculum for fifth and sixth graders was originally developed by two Calhoun teachers and won recognition from the National Conference of Teachers of English. "Ancient Civilizations" and "The Journey of the Silk Road" represent the two-year cycle in which students examine the roots of Western civilization and read the literature of different ethnic groups, including Greek, Roman, Egyptian, Chinese and Islamic. The academic curriculum is enhanced by related activities: art, music, drama, creative writing, or computer study. For instance, the art program, complementing the English and social studies curricula, might organize projects in ceramics for an Egyptian tomb (fifth/sixth grade ancient civilization studies).

All fifth and sixth graders study music, drama, studio art and woodshop, in addition to their academic core courses. Seventh and eighth graders choose arts electives like oil painting, digital video, Shakespeare, directing, creative writing and graphic design.

147

Eighth graders write a formal term paper. Each part of the research process is graded, and after the finished product is presented, further revision may be done. An alumna who went on to Stanford University says that papers at college are easier than those at Calhoun. The Middle School math curriculum is viewed as a process that extends over the four years of the division. Longtime math teacher, Phil Bender, takes his students on a trip across the George Washington Bridge to collect and process mathematical data as one example of Calhoun's experiencial approach to learning. At the eighth grade level, students begin their study of algebra.

Students begin formal instruction in modern language, taking Spanish in the fifth grade. Mandarin is taught beginning in sixth grade. The language program continues, adding French in the Upper School through advanced literature and conversation courses.

Calhoun's computer program spans all grade levels. In the Lower School, students use graphics and word processing programs, in addition to educational games which reinforce math, language, and problem solving skills. Lower school students (grades 2–4) use the computer as a tool to enhance the curriculum in all subject areas. By the end of fourth grade all children complete a keyboarding program and use application software in group projects. In Middle School, fifth graders are introduced to the broad concept of "netizenship," which allows for discussion about the proper and constructive use of computers, digital technology and the internet. Fifth graders do class projects around themes and build their own websites using the basics of standard coding languages such as HTML and CSS. Sixth graders expand upon the topics of the fifth grade class with a greater emphasis on information and media literacy through more involved research using the internet. Students are urged to take a critical look at the way media affects our society. Seventh and eight graders choose from a variety of technology-themed electives, often shaped to address interests and strengths that they have already shown. Students have the option to take an interdisciplinary Spanish and technology course which develops skills in both areas.

Basic Upper School computer courses include HTML and other programming, internet safety and multimedia presentations. Upper School students can also choose from advanced electives, including Java and C++ programming,. Several Calhoun Upper School students have parlayed their computer expertise into well-paying summer jobs.

The Upper School at Calhoun consists of grades nine through twelve. Parents describe the Upper School student body at Calhoun as diverse; students have different strengths and interests as well as different backgrounds.

Early fall activities for all ninth graders include an orientation day prior to the official beginning of classes, and a two-day overnight with peer leaders and faculty during the first week. Peer leaders, specially chosen and trained seniors, also lead weekly discussions with small groups of ninth graders throughout the year, in a course called Life Skills.

The cluster advisory system continues in the Upper School. Parents find that it is an excellent and easy way to keep communication open and consistent. Beginning in the Middle School and continuing through the senior year, students are scheduled once a week to meet individually with their cluster advisors. For graduation, 25 credits are required, including three in science, one-half in computer science and three in modern language. There are, in addition, the following non-credit requirements: four years of physical education and sixty hours of community service.

Classes are mostly discussion-based seminars. Parents say it is impossible for students to be lost in the shuffle because classes are small (typically 12-15 per class), and students are encouraged to be active participants. Parents and graduates praise the exceptional preparation in interdisciplinary writing and research. The school offers advanced coursework in all academic departments and in the arts. AP courses are not offered. Instead, the school provides college seminar style electives and, additionally, students have the opportunity to augment various courses to further their depth of study.

For one week in February, regular courses are suspended. Instead, teachers and students engage in Winter Session courses. These focused, intense courses provide an array of offerings. Some recent courses have been: Free Speech in Post 9/11 America; Rent, the Musical; Science Fiction/Science Fact; Draw and Sculpt and Human Form; Homelessness and Hunger.

Each May, all seniors complete course work early and for three weeks, work independently outside of school on a project of their choice. At the end, seniors present their projects to faculty and peers. Some sample projects have been: ecologically sound building, an equestrian project, a photo travel journal of NYC, a music CD. Students also can design their own projects for half or one credit in the subject of their choice, culminating in an oral or written presentation or performance before a Masterworks Committee. Sample projects have included play directing, a personal family history of the Holocaust, a collection of short stories, a sculpture, a dance demonstration/performance and vocal recital.

Calhoun participates in the Network of Complementary Schools, which offers a two-week exchange program for students as well as faculty at other innovative schools throughout the United States and Canada. For example, students may attend a school on a Navajo reservation in Arizona, a drama program in Putney, Vermont, an outdoor survival program in the Sierra Nevada mountains, or a study of Puerto Rican culture at Caribbean Prep. In the past, Calhoun has been host to students from the Navajo reservation, from Seattle, Washington and from a small rural town in Kansas.

An active Student Government Executive Council is made up of class officers from each class along with an elected president, vice-president, secretary and treasurer. The student government has, among its many activities, sponsored students at the AIDS Dance-a-thon and raised money for UNICEF.

The MCC (Multicultural Committee) organizes assemblies and discussions on cross-cultural issues. Green Group, GLASS, Students for Choice raise consciousness about social concerns. Other clubs reflect student interest in French, astronomy and Scrabble. Calhoun has a popular Model UN team whose many members have participated and won awards in various yearly events.

There are Middle and Upper School theater productions each year held in one of the school's two new theaters. Café Calhoun, sponsored by student government, is a showcase for Upper School student talent. Students may work on the staffs of the school newspaper, literary magazine and yearbook.

Varsity sports include league-winning volleyball, basketball and soccer teams, in addition to track, cross-country, golf, softball, and baseball.

In their weekly College Seminar, second semester juniors begin discussing the process of choosing and applying to colleges. This seminar continues through the middle of the senior year, and individual consultation continues until acceptances are received and final choices must be made.

Calhoun graduates go on to a variety of colleges, reflecting the diversity within the graduating class.

Popular College Choices   Brown University, Wesleyan University, Kenyon, Skidmore, New York University, Oberlin College, Vassar

College, University of Michigan, George Washington University, Bard College, and Pitzer College

Traditions   Harvest Festival (annual school Thanksgiving celebration with thematic activities organized around a community service project), Fall and Spring MS/US dramatic productions. Café Calhoun (Upper School talent show), Book Fair, Spring Carnival, Cluster and Grade Trip Days (special activities for grades 2–12), Winter Session classes/activities, Wednesday evening volleyball for parents, annual trustees' fund-raising event, Curriculum Expo (which includes an art show), Class Day, Athletic Awards Assembly, Commencement exercises

Community Service Requirement   60 hours

Publications   Newspaper: *The Issue*
Literary magazine
Newsletter/alumnae/i publication: *Calhoun Chronicle*
Yearbook

Hangouts   Riverside Park, the plaza on 81st Street outside Calhoun, neighborhood coffee and pizza shops, Barnes & Noble Bookstore

The Cathedral School of St. John the Divine

1047 Amsterdam Avenue
New York, NY 10025–1702
(212) 316-7500, fax (212) 316-7558
website: www.cathedralnyc.org
e-mail: admission@cathedralnyc.org

Coed
Kindergarten–8th grade
Not accessible

Marsha Nelson, Head of School
Kassandra Hayes, Director of Admission

Uniform   White or navy blouses/shirts, navy or khaki pants, skirts, jumpers, or shorts (in warm weather)

Birthday Cutoff   Children entering kindergarten must be 5 by September 1st

Enrollment   Total enrollment: Approximately 270
Kindergarten places: 36
Graduating class size: Approximately 30

Grades   The school functions on a trimester system, with parent/ teacher confrences twice yearly. The Lower School sends written comments twice a year. The Upper School sends grades each trimester and comments twice a year.
Letter grades begin in 5th grade
Full departmentalization begins in 5th grade

Tuition Range 2009–2010 $32,200 K–8th grade
Fees and lunch are included in the tuition

Financial Aid/Scholarship   33% of the student body receives some level of aid based on financial need

Endowment $5 million

After-School Program   The school has an extended day enrichment program for Cathedral School students. In addition, the Cathedral of St. John the Divine's A.C.T. program offers after-school and holiday programs. A.C.T. is open to students from other schools; an additional payment is required

Summer Program A.C.T. uses the 13-acre Cathedral Close for the summer program; a variety of creative and athletic activities are offered for an additional payment

---

The Cathedral School was founded in 1901 to provide choristers for the Cathedral of St. John the Divine. Now an Episcopal school for boys and girls of all faiths, the tradition of providing the choristers for the Cathedral is still one of the school's unique features. When the strains of evensong float out of the gothic cathedral over the 13-acre close of flowering shrubs and herb gardens, shade trees and strolling peacocks, Cathedral School seems like a place out of time, yet this school is very much in sync with modern life and the latest educational practices. One of the best-kept secrets on the Upper West Side, The Cathedral School is a vibrant community. Its popularity is due to not only its extraordinary location but also a strong academic program, an enthusiastic head of school, and a diverse and talented pool of students.

Getting in: Parents can attend information-gathering Admissions Panels in the fall or spring. They have ample opportunity to observe classes, attend special events and ask questions of school administrators and parents. The school retains an affiliation with the Episcopal Church but admits students of all faiths. The ERB is required for admission. Parents come for a tour and interview after submitting an application; applicants to kindergarten and first grade are interviewed in groups of 5 at the school, while applicants to grades 2 through 7 visit for a school day. Cathedral has always valued diversity and a full third of students receive financial aid. The school roster reads like a mellifluous mix of nationalities. Entering kindergarten students visit the school in late May. All new students attend a one-day orientation at school before opening day.

Parents: The parent body at The Cathedral School represents a hip cross-section of city life and includes some prominent writer/editors, well-known actors, academics from Columbia University, professionals, musicians, and artists. Parents value the inclusiveness of the community and everyone is made to feel welcome. Though most parents work, the Parents Association is very active and sponsors fundraisers, book fairs, class dinners, workshops, and picnics.

Program: Classes throughout the school are small. The atmosphere is academic but nurturing and the curriculum celebrates the diversity of the school's community. The Lower School is composed of grades kindergarten through four, and the Upper School is composed of grades five through eight. Each division has its own Division Head, faculty, schedule and special facilities, including Upper and Lower School science labs. Lower School students, working in a self-contained classroom setting, master basic skills in the three R's. French, Spanish and Mandarin Chinese are introduced in kindergarten through grade 3, and fourth grade students choose French or Spanish for continuing academic study.

Students enjoy music and art classes twice a week, library once a week, and physical education four times a week. Whenever possible, teachers in different departments join together to write and teach an interdisciplinary curriculum so that students learn the connections between subject areas. For example, Lower School students learn to program small robots called "PicoCrickets" in science class, then create themed settings and characters for the robots in art class. Sixth grade students study Ancient Greece in history, read Greek myths in English, and study Greek art and architecture and create three-dimensional temples and sets for their Greek play in art class.

The use of technology at Cathedral is curriculum driven. All classrooms have at least one computer and printer with access to the school's network and the Internet. The computer lab has eighteen computers, the library has nine and the science lab and art room share a class set of laptops. Eight classrooms are equipped with Smart-Boards; teachers have had extensive training regarding utilizing the SmartBoard to enhance instruction.

The Director of Technology works with teachers to integrate a sequence of technologically appropriate skills including keyboarding, word-processing, graphing, on-line research, PowerPoint presentation, spreadsheet, and multimedia design. Recent projects include a first grade web-based connection with a school in San Francisco, a fourth grade social studies project using an iMovie, an African folktale project in fifth grade, an Ancient Roman multimedia project in sixth grade, and an eighth grade portrait project that uses Photoshop Elements. New technology units are developed through brainstorming sessions with the Director of Technology, and subject-area teachers.

Art is integrated into the curriculum wherever possible and student artwork is prominently displayed throughout the school. Students work in traditional media as well as nontraditional art forms like mosaic, architecture, and wood-working. For good reason, the Medieval Studies curriculum at Cathedral School is the best in the city. Students tour every inch of the Cathedral and seventh graders celebrate the period's art, music, English and Latin in a Medieval Evensong, held in the Great Choir of the Cathedral of St. John the Divine. They carry personal coats-of-arms, wear period costumes, recite original sonnets of courtly love, and sing and perform a regal dance that they choreograph themselves.

The interdisciplinary music curriculum is skills based and emphasizes fun and appreciation. Through the study of musical concepts of melody, harmony, and rhythm, students learn to read music and experience song and dance from different cultures. Violin instruction begins in first grade. The eighth grade performs a musical each spring as a culminating project.

The Cathedral School, by statute and long-standing tradition, provides the choristers for the Cathedral. These choristers, auditioned from the pool of fourth through eighth graders, rehearse several times each week and provide the treble line of the choir for most of the Sunday and other special services throughout the school year. Choir stipends are available. Recently, the choristers joined other choirs to perform the Third Symphony of Gustav Mahler in Carnegie Hall. The choristers have also recently traveled to Boston and Montreal and to England over the summer, where they sang at services and concerts at Manchester and Sheffield Cathedrals.

The physical education department uses Cathedral's two gymnasiums and two outdoor playgrounds, as well as the adjacent playing fields in Morningside Park. A new playground, nestled alongside the Cathedral itself, opened in the fall of 2008. Interscholastic junior varsity and varsity sports are optional for students in grades five through eight, both single-sex and coed teams include basketball, soccer, baseball, track, cross-country, softball and volleyball.

Hot lunch (a salad bar and sandwiches are also available) is served family style with mixed age groupings at tables; grace is led by student volunteers, including kindergartners, and sung by all. Older students take turns as waiters and servers, helping the younger students.

The Lower School assembly each Friday morning is a long-standing tradition of the school; recently, the Upper School added an assembly period each week, continuing the tradition of this important aspect of school life. Lower School assemblies typically include singing, class performances, poetry readings, individual student performances and announcements. Parents come in droves to catch a glimpse of their children in action. Upper School assemblies include discussions of character development, as well as events planned by the student council, such as talent shows, or presentations on topics such as Internet safety.

The Upper School at Cathedral (grades 5–8) is departmentalized.

Each student carries a full program in English, social studies, math, science, French or Spanish. Latin teacher Dr. John Vitale makes a compelling case for the relevance of studying classical Latin today (and not just as a vocabulary booster for the SAT's).

Students visit the cathedral twice each week for services led by the chaplain. Services concentrate on stories, holidays, beliefs, and values derived from the world's great religious traditions. For example, the Upper and Lower School each celebrated a Passover seder. Students at the school represent a variety of religious traditions, including Buddhist and Muslim. "The goal is to develop our student's religious literacy and affirm each child's spiritual development." Parents praise the sense of spirituality which infuses learning at Cathedral School. Each fifth grade student works with the chaplain in an academic course called "World Religions."

The Secondary School Placement Director works individually with each student and their parents beginning in seventh grade to develop an appropriate list of high school options. Placement Counseling emphasizes self-awareness and a search for a school that would be appropriate for each individual's talents and interests.

Popular Secondary School Choices   Friends Seminary, Trinity, Riverdale, Dalton, Brearley, Beacon, Columbia Grammar and Prep, Fieldston, Marymount, Notre Dame, Boarding: Choate, Kent, Lawrenceville, St. Andrew's

Community Service Requirement   Students develop projects to support Cathedral outreach and environmental programs, care for Cathedral Close, or raise funds for outside organizations; Lower School Evensong in Action is a new initiative. The Upper School "Mission and Outreach" committee and the Student Council take leadership roles in student fund-raising activities. The school has a commitment to support 50 children in Tanzania through "Carpenter's Kid's," a mission of the Episcopal Church that enables children orphaned by AIDS to go to school.

Traditions   New parent dinners, all-school picnic on the grounds, class dinners, an annual fundraising auction, Earth Day, Alumni Reunion, Grandparents Day, Class Reps, Book Fair, Diversity Advisory Council, Spring Fair, Field Day, Upper School Camp Trip, Chorister Tours, Peace Tree Ceremony, Passover Seder, Kwanza Assembly, Eighth Grade Musical, Chorister Divestiture and graduation

The Chapin School

100 East End Avenue
New York, NY 10028
(212) 744-2335
website: www.chapin.edu

All girls
Kindergarten–12th grade
Accessible

Dr. Patricia Hayot, Head of School
Tina Herman, Director of Upper School Admissions
Therese Cruite, Director of Lower School Admissions

Uniform   Lower School: light green or dark green jumper, white blouse or polo shirt
Middle School: dark green pleated skirt with white collared shirt, khaki pants
Upper School: dress Gordon or dark green kilt or skirt, collared shirt or blouse, khaki pants
Uniforms can be purchased from the Corey Uniform Company

Birthday Cutoff   Children entering kindergarten must be 5 by September 1

Enrollment   Total enrollment: 675
Kindergarten places: 54
Graduating class: 40-50

Grades   Semester system in the Lower and Middle School
Trimester system in the Upper School
Kindergarten–3rd grade: detailed progress reports
Classes 4–12: letter grades and comments
Departmentalization begins in 4th grade
First final exam in 7th grade

Tuition Range 2009–2010 $31,500, Kindergarten through 12th grade Additional fees: approximately $950 to $2,500
School bus available for K–6; cost depends on type of service

Financial Aid/Scholarship $3 million in tuition aid for 19% of the student body

Endowment $49 million

Diversity 29%; the school works closely with Early Steps, A Better Chance, Albert G. Oliver Program, TEAK and Prep for Prep; the school has a diversity coordinator who oversees programs and clubs including the Cultural Awareness Program, the Gay Straight Alliance, and P.O.C.C. (Parents of Children of Color)

Homework Kindergarten: reading
Class 1: reading, plus some assignments
Class 2: 20–30 minutes
Class 3: 30–40 minutes
Class 4: 20 minutes per subject (average 3 subjects)
Classes 5–8: approximately 2–3 hours spent on an average of 4 subjects, depending on grade level
Classes 9–12: 3 hours

After-School Program The Clubhouse is an after-school program at the Brearley and Chapin Schools that provides a variety of classes for students in kindergarten through fifth grade, Monday through Friday. There is a play period before class when the girls are given a snack or, on Friday, lunch.
The school oversees the organization of various activities in fine arts, computer science and physical education for Middle and Upper School students
Middle School intramural program
Green and Gold team competition (girls in classes 4–12 at Chapin are either Green or Gold)
AAIS League interscholastic competition
Elective offerings in both the Middle and Upper Schools
Night Owl Study Hall

Summer Program June Jamboree, 2 week summer camp

The Chapin School was founded by Maria Bowen Chapin in 1901 as an elementary school called "Miss Chapin's School for Girls." After the death of Miss Chapin, in 1934, it became The Chapin School, Ltd. Throughout the years Chapin has had strong leadership: Miss Ethel Grey Stringfellow, headmistress for twenty-four years, was succeeded in 1959 by Mildred J. Berendsen, who, after leading Chapin into the nineties, retired after thirty-four years in 1993. Dr. Patricia Hayot became the sixth head of Chapin in 2003.

In the 1920s and 30s, Miss Chapin's School groomed New York's young women to take their place in Society. At that time, there were no afternoon classes. Some girls had great academic potential, and some less; classes were designated "general" or "college," depending on the aspirations of the individual.

Chapin in the new millennium, as in the nineties, has an excellent academic reputation and sends its graduates on to the very top colleges throughout the country, but the tone of the school remains decidedly traditional, although it takes great pride in maintaining a balance between innovative and traditional approaches to learning. At Chapin today, there are still handbells, but also African drumming, and the white gloves are gone. A parent told me, "We wanted a place where our daughter would feel valued and loved. They care about keeping our girls sweet." And she added, "They highlight what she does well."

A major building program was recently completed. Improvements to the school included building two new floors and a multitude of renovations including a fourth gym, a gorgeous greenhouse, seven new science labs, more classroom space, a dance studio, four art studios, and computer facilities. Additional construction completed in 1998 includes: a two-floor library/multimedia center, a new gymnasium, a drama classroom/black box theatre and a foreign language lab. The outdoor play yard, art studios and dining room were also renovated and a third kindergarten space was added.

Pat Hayot, a former Klingenstein Fellow at Columbia University's Teachers College, arrived at Chapin after serving as Head of The International School in Paris and the Columbus School for Girls. She is, unlike some of her predecessors, is more like Miss Chapin, who was an original a suffragette.

Planning ahead is first on Dr. Hoyt's agenda, as Chapin undergoes a massive strategic planning process. Some key issues are building a more global curriculum that is reflective of today's world, more electives for ninth graders, more AP classes, and even more personalized scheduling.

Spring 1998 marked the official opening of the new library, The Annenberg Center for Learning and Research. An outdoor playroof was converted to create this "Titanic" space which features porthole windows and a grand staircase. The library has a multi-media center with capabilities for video-conferencing, private study rooms and in one section—plush purple armchairs. On previous tours The Chapin

School felt a bit dark; the effect of the current renovation is like taking down the heavy drapery and letting in the light.

Modernization is underway in other areas of the school as well: In 1998 the Upper School at Chapin voted to add khaki pants to the school uniform, in addition to the Gordon Plaid kilt. The traditional Friday Morning Assembly, has been updated to include celebrations of a range of faiths. The girls now have a part in designing the program on Fridays which reflects the diversity within the school community.

The Life Skills Committee which began several years ago, reshaped life at the school. Two outgrowths of this committee are 1) Appointment of a full time coordinator of counseling services and life skills education who oversees the social and emotional growth and health of the school. 2) The introduction of a Peer Leadership program which prepares a select group of twelfth graders to counsel ninth graders.

Getting in: Parents tour Chapin after applying. Prospective kindergarten parents meet in a group with the Lower School head in the Reception Room for a short talk. Two families are given a tour by a parent tour guide and interviewed by a member of the admissions office staff. Parents return with their child for a play group interview during which Dr. Hayot and an Upper School student answer questions. Every applicant receives a plant from Chapin's greenhouse. After admissions decisions have been made, a wait list is maintained. The wait-list letter informs parents how to notify the admissions office of their continued interest in The Chapin School.

Parents: The Chapin parent body is very involved and supportive of the school. The school, in turn, is supportive of parents: "There is total emphasis on the whole child; kindness and warmth pervade the Lower School. They are sensitive to individual needs and are concerned when there is a divorce or sickness in a family," parents say. "They are interested in making life easier for parents."

Chapin is also social in the traditional sense. "You would never dress informally for a school event," said one parent. And, although khakis and hair clips have replaced suits and headbands at drop-off and pick-up and some do deliberately dress down for school events, a certain level of decorum with regard to appropriate dress is the norm. The school now hosts a reception in the fall for parents in each division with faculty attending.

Parent involvement is welcomed. Parents with a particular skill or interest are invited to share it with the class. In one kindergarten class, for instance, parents were invited to celebrate the Japanese holiday "Girls Day" with rice cookies and tea.

Program: The Lower School consists of kindergarten through Class 3. Separation is handled gradually. By the second week the whole kindergarten group is staying until about 3 P.M. Monday through Friday. Parents had praise for the kindergarten teachers' warmth and skill. The days have a predictable structure, which gives the girls a sense of security: They know what to expect. Attention is paid to students' different learning styles. Although traditional in tone, there is a lot of creativity in the classroom. Art projects are used to enhance units of study, such as backdrops for the end-of-the-year play, often inspired by famous artists like illustrator Eric Carle. As one parent said, "These are sophisticated projects; there's no macaroni and glue here." Another commented, "It's very well rounded. Block building is an integral part of the kindergarten curriculum. One kindergarten class was building a mock version of Chapin, and the study extends to social studies interviewing members of the community. The Teacher's College Reading and Writing Project introduces kindergarten students to a balanced literacy program which continues through Middle School. Phonics are an important part of the program along with literature and comprehension.

Manipulative materials (Cuisinaire rods, blocks, etc.) and everyday experiences are used to teach math concepts. Girls go out of their homerooms for music, dance, science, computer and library, as well as physical education including gymnastics.

Spanish is offered three to fours times a week in Kindergarten through Classes I through III.

Classes I through III stay until 3:00 P.M. each day. The curriculum is a continuum, each year building upon previous experiences. In Class 1, the literacy program is balanced between learning comprehensive strategies and vocabulary. There is direct instruction in sounds, words, and learning how to be conversant in writing. Independent reading is required to foster the development of fluency and stamina. Much written work is published, bound and illustrated. Classes I through III girls participate in a strong writing program emphasizing creativity and clarity of expression as well as reading with an emphasis on critical inferential thinking and critical analysis called Writers Workshop.

Where possible, social studies are integrated with language and performing arts. Social studies in Class I focus on the study of the immediate school neighborhood and explore the needs of the community. Miniature models are created each year, complex architectural issues addressed, and block designs are most impressive.

Second graders learn about New York City both past and present.

161

Through classroom activities and field trips, they become familiar with the five boroughs, maps of the city and the NYC subway system. The unit on old New York focuses on Native America, the Lenape Indians and New Amsterdam.

In Class III the girls construct a geographical 'compare and contrast' multicultural project involving China, Kenya, India and Mexico which is integrated throughout the curriculum. There is a performance at the end of the year that blends many aspects of the year's study. Throughout classes in the Lower School, mathematics continues to be taught using an array of manipulatives and concrete objects, and focusing on basic operations and problem solving. The students practice many life skills such as measurement, time-telling and understanding money. Homework begins in Class I. Multiplication, division and fractions are studied in Class III. Technology is an integral component of the curriculum. Lower School students have weekly computer classes. Laptops are used in classrooms for graphing, digital storytelling, pod casts, Public Service Announcements about the environment have used iMovies. Science for Lower School Girls is held in their own special science lab once a week in kindergarten to three times a year by Class III. Recent experiments include watching chicks hatch, plants grow, building electronic and more.

As a school, Chapin is well-steeped in traditions, and publishes a small format Chapin green, 30-page handbook loaded with school traditions, and notes. Some traditions that persist in the Lower School are Teddy Bear Day, Field Day, Pumpkin Day, Holiday and Thanksgiving concerts, and community gathering.

Middle School at Chapin includes Class IV through Class VIII, where children are taught organization and study skills including how to read a text book, take notes, study for a test, and related skills. There's a daily schedule of varying subjects to foster a greater level of interdisciplinary work and projects.

Class VII is introduced to Shakespeare with *A Midsummer Night's Dream*. The study of a foreign language begins in Class V with French, Spanish or Chinese. Latin is introduced and required in Classes VII and VIII. Social studies units in Middle School cover U.S. geography and Native Americans, a study of ancient and medieval civilizations and American history. In Class VII there is an immigration project in which each student does individual research on a specific country.

Some science highlights include several classes at Chapin that work in the greenhouse and in Class IV students begin lab sciences. Class IV does a project on weather using Chapin's weather station.

Formal health education begins in Class I with a unit on nutrition. Class VI offers an introduction to biology that covers all the systems of the body, including reproductive, and the effects of drugs, alcohol and tobacco. Class VI's program revolves around the Laptop Immersion Program, becoming more sophisticated. Students lean to use technology as part of their daily classes in all subjects, including homework. At the beginning of Class VI, students go on a four-day marine biology and costal environmental studies trip to sea camp on Cape Cod. Spence also partners with select NYC boy's schools for evening social events.

Beginning in Class V girls go to nearby Asphalt Green for outdoor sports once a cycle. Field hockey, soccer, softball, track, lacrosse, and swimming are offered. Afternoon electives in physical education are available for Classes V–VII including fencing and gymnastics. Chapin girls are separated into the Green and Gold teams for intramural competition culminating in an entire day of competition at Bear Mountain in May known as Field Day. Interscholastic competition, which boasts over 30 teams in 20 or more sports, begins in Class V with gymnastics; in Class VI and beyond a multitude of athletic and fitness opportunities are available such as, soccer, track and swimming, and broadens in Class VII to include basketball, fencing and volleyball. The number of different sports offered and access to outdoor playing fields increases in the Upper School, and Chapin has several strong interscholastic teams.

Extracurricular activities in the Middle School also abound, including chess club, computer club, intramural and interscholastic sports teams, the literary magazine, readers' club art, drama, dance, music, debating and science. In addition, self-government begins in the Middle School.

The Upper School at Chapin consists of Classes VIII–XII. Chapin's Upper School remains a caring, close-knit community with a shift in ninth and tenth grades as some girls leave for boarding schools or coed day schools. The curriculum increases in rigor and there is a solid core curriculum. There are sixteen AP's offered, including art history, French literature, Calculus I and II and Physics. For Upper School students the Individual Study Option, Interschool courses and a residential term away (abroad to either Spain, France, Rome, Italy, Vermont, or Maine and faculty trips to India, China and Greece) add breadth as well as depth to Chapin's curriculum.

Multicultural perspectives are explored in the Class VII Asian and African History course which covers the cultures of Japan, China, India and Africa and the Americas. English students contrast and compare a Japanese novel to Shakespeare's *Romeo and Juliet*. There are a multitude of interesting electives offered in almost all disciplines.

The Upper School curriculum includes a Class IX unit that entails a three-day workshop on New York City, entitled "Urban Study." Class X attends an Interschool conference on environmental issues. Class XI travels to Washington, D.C., where they visit the Holocaust Museum in addition to the usual sites.

Physics, Chemistry and Biology are offered in the Upper School, with AP courses available for juniors and seniors. Students in the Upper School take Algebra, Geometry and Trigonometry with Calculus A and B offered to juniors and seniors.

In the Upper School, Chapin students continue active participation in studio art, dance, drama and music with opportunity for advanced work along with a wide variety of electives. For serious artists there is a portfolio course in preparation for the AP Studio Art Program, and there are courses in photography and multimedia studies as well. For drama students there is a playwright's workshop for Classes X-XII and a course called "The Uses of Enchantment." The Drama Club involves all areas of theatre production. A Choral Club performs at holiday time as well as throughout the year. Dance Club members choreograph and perform their works in an annual performance. Club Night is a unique tradition in the Upper School. The Halloween Club gives a party for the Lower School girls; Dance and Drama Clubs put on student performances at night; and Holiday Club in December provides an evening for students, faculty and parents to join in singing together.

Upper School girls can participate in the student Self-Government (established in 1909), Science Club, S.A.V.E., an environmental organization, Amnesty International, Volunteer Community Activities, the Cultural Awareness Project, Model U.N., French, Latin, Spanish/Latin American Club, Literary Magazine, Yearbook, and *Limelight*, the school newspaper.

One parent says, "The curriculum is geared for the above-average girl." A former teacher says that "honor, achievement and academic rigor are valued at Chapin and that adds up to competition." But nobody describes Chapin as a "pressure cooker." "Chapin never gives up on a child," one former teacher said. "People seem to hop out of the woodwork to help each other, there's lots of cooperation and teamwork." Individual attention and concern for the development of the individual are hallmarks of a Chapin education. One parent described Chapin as "the most well-rounded girls' school." Another parent said that "nastiness is discouraged, but cliques form early." One parent described a common scenario (seen in one form or another at all schools): "Cliques form between third and seventh grades. Seventh- and eighth-grade cliques form around physical development and looks and competition for clubs and boys." The parent of an alumna said that the girls "individualize their uniforms and can frequently be heard chatting away about the latest party." The net result of all this sociability is a boon for the school. Chapin's alumnae remain connected to the school long after they have left. The alumnae bulletin is bulging with notes and snapshots as if this was the largest extended family on the East Coast, and perhaps it is. It's no wonder that Chapin continues to enjoy great success in fund-raising.

Chapin is working had to overcome the White Glove image. (The school used to emphasize "good form" in everything from dress to term papers, an alumna recalls.) Today, the rigor of the curriculum and the variety of cultural perspectives cater to the interests of a more diverse student body. One parent said, "People don't know what a jewel Chapin is, except for the Chapin parent."

The day before commencement for the Middle and Upper Schools there is a final assembly at which awards are given for achievement in athletics, fine arts and academics. Chapin commencement is held at the school. The girls graduate as a class with no special recognition for any individual student.

Popular College Choices   Barnard, Brown, Cornell, Dartmouth, Duke, Emory, Harvard, Middlebury, Princeton, Stanford, University of Pennsylvania, Yale

Traditions   Fall Book Fair, Club Nights, Grandparents' Day, Lower School Halloween party, Holiday Program, Field Day, Chapin Spring Benefit

Publications   Upper School literary magazine: *The Wheel* (since 1917) Middle School literary magazine
Newspaper: *Limelight*
Computer news publication: *The Chapin Chip*
Yearbook
Alumnae Bulletin

Community Service Requirement   Community service is encouraged but there is no specific requirement

Hangouts   The purple chairs in The Annenberg Center for Learning and Research, student lounge, coffee shop on 84th Street and Second Avenue

The Children's Storefront

70 East 129th Street
New York, NY 10035
(212) 427-7900
website: www.thechildrensstorefront.org

Coed
Prekindergarten–8th grade
Accessible only at 70 East 129th Street

Kathy Egmont, Head of School

Birthday Cutoff   Children must be 4 by September 1st

Enrollment   Total enrollment: approximately 170
Preschool places: approximately 15
Graduating class size: 17

Tuition Range   Full scholarship

Financial Aid   100% of the student body

Endowment $3.5 million

After-School Program   After-school programs in music from 3:30 P.M. to 5:00 P.M.; 3:30 till 6 P.M. some Saturdays; free of charge

Summer Program   For Lower and Upper School students, a five-week academic summer program
Children's Storefront helps place children in summer camps

In 1966, The Children's Storefront was founded as a "grass-roots school" in a storefront on Madison Avenue. The school subsequently moved into four converted brownstones. The Children's Storefront is one of a few private schools that are tuition free. The Storefront receives the bulk of its funding from foundations, corporations and individuals. The Children's Storefront's annual fundraiser, A Night for Changing Lives, attracts many of New York's "A-list" partygoers. The school is accredited by The New York State Association of Independent Schools. There is a broad range of ability within the student body. Tracking students since graduation shows that 80 percent of Storefront students go on to graduate from high school, compared to 33 percent in the community at large. Average class size is fifteen, providing students with the attention they need to succeed. There is a waiting list of approximately five hundred students.

City & Country School

146 West 13th Street
New York, NY 10011
(212) 242-7802, fax (212) 242-7996
website: www.cityandcountry.org

Coed
Nursery–8th grade (ages 2–13; II-XIIIs)
Not accessible

Ms. Kate Turley, Principal
Ms. Elise Clark, Director of Admissions

Birthday Cutoff   Nursery II's must be 2 by September 1; October 1st is the cutoff for all other age groups

Enrollment   Total enrollment: 330
Nursery IIs places: 30
Nursery IIIs places: 14
Kindergarten (Vs) places: 8–10
Expanding to double groups for most other grades Graduating class 2009: 19

Grades   No letter grades; detailed narrative reports, at mid and end of year; parent/teacher conferences twice a year

Tuition Range 2009–2010 $15,400 to $30,100, nursery 2's, 4 days–8th grade
Additional fees: $500 new student fee

Financial Aid/Scholarship   20% of the student body receives partial financial aid

Endowment   The school has recently begun to build an endowment

Diversity   24% students of color; Early Steps, ABC, and Prep for Prep

After-School Program   Open only to City & Country students; an elective program that offers a variety of creative and recreational activities, including woodshop, library, art, science. a technology

program, and homework help, from 3:00 P.M. until 4:30 P.M. for 8–13 year olds that is included as part of the tuition;
Additional specialty classes for 4–7 year olds, with an early drop off at 8 A.M. option until 5:45; additional fee required. Specialty Add-Ins for IVs through XIIIs include Chinese, French, chess, majic, filmmaking, musical theater, hip-hop, and more; sixth through eighth graders can participate in an interscholastic sports program in basketball, volleyball, soccer and softball

Summer Program A six-week summer camp for 3–7-year olds from mid-June until the end of July
This program requires an additional payment

City & Country School, founded in 1914, is one of the oldest progressive elementary schools in the United States. Located on a historic block in Greenwich Village, the school occupies four adjoining brownstones on 13th Street and three floors in a brownstone on 12th Street; the brownstones are connected by courtyards that are used in the school's outdoor yard program.

Getting in: Gaining admission to the Nursery program is very competitive. Parents must submit an application in order to schedule a tour and information session, but may attend the open house before submitting an application. Kindergarten and first grade applicants have an in-house screening; ERBs are required for applicants for second grade and older, in addition to an in-house screening, which consists of a day-long visit with a group of peers. They are also observed by a group teacher and specialists. Younger children, Nursery through five-year-olds, come for a group visit (about an hour) and are observed at work and play in a classroom by teachers and the director of admissions.

Parents: The parent body runs the gamut from "corporate lawyers, bankers and doctors to writers, actors, and illustrators." What they have in common is that they want their children in "a quintessential progressive school."

Program: Visionary educator and founder Caroline Pratt believed children learn best through practical and meaningful experiences. According to the school's philosophy, they believe that an educator's greatest challenge isn't to teach children, rather to create an environment that keeps their curiosity in tact. From the earliest years, students work cooperatively with open-ended materials: blocks, water, paint, clay, and wood. Vs through VIIs plan their work as groups, which they sustain for a week or longer, creating cities with building blocks, wooden people, handmade signs and more. Care and respect is fostered through active participation in the C&C community in addition to other purposeful experiences.

Lower School classrooms have ample space and are equipped with an abundant supply of carefully chosen materials; these materials, along with teacher's guidance, promote children's active involvement and independence, creativity and cooperation. Children build a foundation in the academic disciplines of social studies, reading, writing, math and science. As children progress through Lower School, academic skills are taught more formally. Formal reading instruction begins in Kindergarten.

As a practical application of their academic skills and to develop social awareness, self-esteem and responsibility, older children participate in the Jobs Program—running the school post office or store, operating printing presses, working with younger children, writing and publishing the school newspaper. Each Middle and Upper School Group has a specific job to perform that helps the school community function smoothly. Because children are performing real jobs that meet real needs they develop a genuine sense of ownership and pride in their school community.

Trips to observe the community at work are an important part of the program. In the outdoor yards, students create their own play environment each day with large boxes, blocks, boards, ladders and sawhorses. Older groups use the yard for running and ball games and team sports. Students bring their own lunch, and milk is provided as is mid-morning juice and a snack.

Running parallel to the Jobs Program, group and individual research using primary and secondary sources, literature and trips rather than textbooks to study a civilation, time period, or major issue forms the core of the Middle and Upper School curriculum. This program is integrated with special subjects for the VIIIs through XIIIs. For example, a study of "living documents" of the Revolutionary period in American history is coordinated with the XIII's job of running the school newspaper. The annual IX's week-long country trip to Connecticut is a highlight. After studying life on the Oregon Trail, the students react to everything they have learned. They maneuver a covered wagon that they made, construct trailside rock-heated ovens, and make scientific observations about animal tracks. Parents say the trip, "really bonds the group; they come back changed."

Students three-years old and older participate in Rhythms (the music and movement dramatics program), and older children use the fully equipped woodshop, the art room, and music studios, the science lab and technology center. The music program includes singing and instruction in recorder and stringed instruments. Chorus and orchestra, art, filmmaking and podcasting are offered as electives in the upper grades. Spanish is taught beginning with the Xs and graduates often receive advanced placement in high school. From VII to XIII, all students spend a half-an-hour of independent reading in the library every day.

Parents whose children have been in the school for several years note several changes which indicate that City & Country is not the bastion of progressive education it once was: "Traditionally each class has a job in the school but because the school has nearly doubled in size in the last 10 years there is less opportunity for children to actually take part in running the school."

Most of all, C&C graduates learn to take responsibility, not only for their individual actions, but also for the community at large. With years of active decision-making and problem solving to support them, they meet life's challenges with optimism and compassion, allowing them to contribute positively and work collaboratively in any environment

Popular Secondary School Choices   Berkeley Carroll, Brearley, Fiorello LaGuardia High School of Music and Art and Performing Arts, Trevor Day School, Fieldston School, Friends Seminary, Packer Collegiate Institute, Bronx Science, Marymount, Dalton, Calhoun, Spence, Saint Ann's, Elisabeth Irwin, Horace Mann, Loyola, Marymount, Poly Prep, Regis, Stuyvesant

Claremont Preparatory School

41 Broad Street
New York, NY 10004
Tel (212) 232-0266
fax (212) 232-0284
website: www.claremontprep.org

Coed
3s program-12th grade (10th grade in September 2010)
Accessible

Irwin Shlachter, Headmaster

Uniform   A wide variety of school uniform options depending on the division; all school clothing is available from Lands' End; many items must bear the Claremont Preparatory School logo

Birthday Cutoff   Children entering the 3s program must be 3 by September 1st
Children entering the 4s program must be 4 by September 1st
Children entering the kindergarten program must be 5 by September 1st

Enrollment   Total enrollment: 510
3s program places: 36
Pre-kindergarten places: 50
Kindergarten places: 110
Graduating class size: Approximately 40 will graduate in 2013

Grades   Semester system for lower, middle and high school
Letter grades begin in 5th grade
Departmentalization begins in middle school

Tuition Range 2009-2010 $21,850 to $31,500, 3s program through 9th grade (at present)

Financial Aid/Scholarship   24% of the student body receives some form of aid

Endowment   N/A

After-School Program Open only to students from Claremont Prep; a variety of activities including swimming, sculpture and ceramics, dance, magic, rock band, yoga, jewelry design, Spanish culture, chess, woodworking, "silly" science lab, computer lab, piano, and more; all available for an additional fee

Summer Program Claremont Summer Camp offers swimming (Red Cross instruction), arts & crafts, karate, drama, cooking, music, sports, park outings, and theme days; for older campers Claremont offers week-long programs such as, Fine Arts Workshop, Music Camp, and Cooking Academy; an additional fee is required

Claremont Prep opened its doors in September 2005 at 41 Broad Street in the former Bank of America building in the heart of lower Manhattan's financial district. Claremont's 125,000 square-foot brand new space, can easily accommodate about 25 percent more students since the building has been completely transformed from a bank to a school and is growing organically and sensibly. The former "Broad Street Ballroom," now the school's auditorium, is equipped with theatrical lighting. The main entrance is flanked with a business-like security desk and velvet rope which exudes the formality of an office building, but once the elevator door opens, you are transported to a vibrant, school community in full swing. There are many state-of-the-art classrooms with motion-sensor lights, Smartboards, laptops, wireless Internet, "and the largest server farm of any school in New York City," according to the school's brochure. There is also a heated swimming pool, a beautiful library, art studios, a kiln, science labs, and a new cafeteria, called the Café, with a nutritionist/science/wellness teacher and several chefs, located where the bank's vault which used to stash cash, are also impressive features of the facility. The owner of Claremont Prep, Michael Koffler, has a sister nursery school on the Upper West Side, Claremont Children's School, that is not a feeder school to Claremont Prep. However, there are early notification privileges.

The current Headmaster, Irwin Shlachter, brings to Claremont many years of experience as head of a school. Formerly the Head of School at Rodeph Sholom School, Shlachter knows what works best both in terms of curriculum and administration. Mr. Shlachter describes Claremont, "as structured, and more traditional with a highly creative flair."

Getting in: A beautiful multi-sided aquarium greets applicants and their parents when the elevator door opens on the second floor at the admissions office. All of the fish have names and their own "fish doctor" on call.

Application forms can be downloaded or mailed. The deadline for applications is the end of the first week in December. After applying, children and parents are interviewed and tours can be scheduled either before or after applying and are also available in the evening as well as in the morning during spring. Younger children are interviewed in play groups, older applicants are interviewed individually and required to submit an essay. ERB test scores are required for all grades as well as previous school reports and/or other recommendations.

Parents: An eclectic mix from all over Manhattan, New Jersey and Brooklyn. "We are not a neighborhood school," I was told, but quite a few downtown families are naturally attracted to the proximity of the school. Enrollment for the early grades is strong. For example, in 2009-2010 Claremont enrolled five kindergarten classes of 15 to 18 children each. Claremont parents are dedicated to a partnership between home and school. They hold fundraisers and volunteer in a variety of ways. Naming a fish in the school's aquarium was a popular bid at a recent auction.

Program: Claremont Prep prides itself on it extremely small student/teacher ratio, about four to one, affording students whatever they need to succeed academically, creatively, socially and grow to be confident learners and members of a community. The school consists of three divisions, the Lower School, from the Three's Toddler Program through fourth grade; The Middle School, grades five through eight, and the high school, grades 9 through 12. Presently, Claremont has students enrolled through ninth grade and plans to hold its first commencement for the Class of 2013.

The Lower School program allows for individualized attention in a structured environment. The Threes have their own play area; they study the Middle Ages. All the basics are covered, each child or small group of children works in a myriad of ways to learn how to read, write, along with the fundamentals of basic math. Specials include all kinds of scientific, artistic and recreational opportunities in an age-appropriate supportive setting. "It doesn't matter what kind of a learner you are," explained one teacher. "There's lots of attention, there's no back of the classroom." The halls bustle, every classroom has tons of children's work displayed all over. Chicks serenaded by a nearby CD player were getting ready to hatch in one classroom, karate was being taught in another and an enormous igloo made out of empty gallon-size milk containers all painted yellow filled yet another. Foreign culture and language is introduced in kindergarten.

Middle School, grades five through eight, offer students the opportunity to challenge themselves in a variety of ways. Academically, classes are departmentalized but integrated and become more rigorous. There are solid core requirements in all disciplines and formal tests are given. Foreign languages includes French, Spanish and Mandarin, the goal is to prepare students for high school level foreign language classes. Independent learning is valued, but support is always on hand at Claremont. "We try to play to the strength of our kids," one teacher explains. There are four full-time, and one part-time learning specialists.

"Teachers throughout the school have careers not jobs and put in a lot of time," said one parent. "They are paid well and that gives them the opportunity and desire to put the time in."

The high school has just seen its first freshman class and is shaping up to be a fine program. Formerly from Dalton, Judith Sheridan, the new Head of Claremont's high school, brings her expertise in educating high school students at a sophisticated level to Claremont. Sheridan's goal, "To bring an advanced fluency regarding the 21st century's global imperative through language study, travel and technology." Since Claremont will not see its first graduating class until 2013, Claremont views its high school as a laboratory, with a supporting curriculum that rejects traditional dichotomies in favor of finding similarities between humanities and sciences. Like the Lower and Middle divisions, there will be support throughout the school year.

Participation in a variety of athletic and arts programs are required; the school teams are the Wolverines.

"What sets us apart from other schools," attests one parent, "is the individual teaching that creates a love of learning, and strong sense of self-esteem."

Community Service Requirement Community service is required; internships and volunteer opportunities are available in partnership with local community organizations and beyond

Publications School News: Weekly E-Blast, email updates for each division
The art and literary magazine of Claremont Prep: *Two Roads*
Weekly newsletters from teachers
Lower School Yearbook

Collegiate School

260 West 78th Street
New York, NY 10024
Tel (212) 812-8500 Admissions x552
fax (212) 812-8547
website: www.collegiateschool.org

All boys
K–12th grade
Accessible

Dr. Lee M. Levison, Principal
Mrs. Joanne P. Heyman, Director of Admissions and
Financial Aid

Uniform   Kindergarten and Lower School: long pants and a collared shirt
Middle and Upper School: grades 5–12, collared shirt and tie, long pants, shoes or sneakers

Birthday Cutoff   It is recommended that boys be 5 by the start of Kindergarten

Enrollment   Total enrollment: approximately 640
Kindergarten places: approximately 45
5th grade places: approximately 2–3
6th grade places: approximately 4-6
7th grade places: approximately 4–6
9th grade places: approximately 6–10
Graduating class size: approximately 54

Grades   Trimester system (Lower and Middle School), Semester system (Upper School)
Grades Kindergarten–4: detailed anecdotal reports and conferences Letter grades begin in 6th grade
Departmentalization begins in 5th grade
First final exam is given in 7th grade

Tuition Range 2009–2010 $33,400, Kindergarten through 12th grade

Tuition at Collegiate includes lunch, books, class overnight trips, and most additional costs, but not athletic clothing or special functions There is an alternative payment plan through Smart Tuition

Financial Aid/Scholarship   Approximately 20% of the student body receives financial assistance

Endowment   Approximately $62 million

Diversity   Approximately 25% children of color
32 Prep for Prep students enrolled as of Fall 2009; most students enter in either sixth, seventh or eighth grades;
Collegiate enrolls students from Early Steps, A Better Chance (ABC), The Albert G. Oliver Program, and TEAK Fellowship
JAMAA: an organization for students families, alumni and faculty of color founded in the 1960s
Collegiate Teaching Institute for prospective teachers of color

Homework   Grades 1 and 2: ½ an hour reading every night
Grades 3 and 4: approximately 45 minutes plus reading
Grades 5 and 6: approximately 2 hours
Grades 7 and 8: approximately 2 ½ hours
Grades 9 through 12: 2–3 hours

After-School Program   In-house after-school activities program available for Kindergarten–Grade 6. Collegiate boys participate in various sports programs; athletic teams practice after school

Summer Program   Two-week June basketball clinic for Lower and Middle School boys
For older boys there are exchange programs in Europe, China and Latin America

Collegiate is the oldest independent school in the United States. The school was established in 1628 by the Dutch West India Company and maintains a continuing relationship with the Dutch Reformed Church. Collegiate's strength is an emphasis on classical education combined with modern innovations. Collegiate is a well-rounded, academically rigorous school with a superior college placement record.

Collegiate has had a long-standing relationship with the West End Collegiate Church. In 1940 the church and school separated but they still share some facilities. The "Moving Up" ceremonies for the Lower and Middle School are held at the West End Collegiate Church, as is graduation. There is a school chaplain who is also an Upper School advisor, Religion Department Head, and community service coordinator. The holiday program, held in the church, includes various religious traditions. Seventh grade students study world religions. In the Upper School, students must choose two three-credit religion courses.

All Collegiate students benefit from a series of renovation and building projects completed over the years. In 1990, the school added a fabulous new gym and weight room, two new art rooms, a black box theater, a photography lab and a music room. In September 1997, Collegiate opened a kindergarten in the West End Plaza building of the school. Two spacious classrooms with an adjoining block/project room provide space for academic centers, computers, creative movement, music, blocks and art projects. In the same year, science laboratories were installed for Lower and Middle School students. In 1998, a roof-top play area opened, the school's dining facilities were expanded, a two-story Middle School center was completed and state-of-the-art biology, chemistry and physics laboratories were built for Upper School students.

Getting in: The application fee is $50. Parents are encouraged to tour the year before their sons will enroll in kindergarten. Once parents have applied, they bring their son to the school. Kindergarten applicants visit in small groups with members of the faculty. Middle and Upper School applicants have interviews and guided tours of the school. Parents of applicants are interviewed on an individual family basis. There is a policy favoring siblings and legacies but admission is not automatic. Is there a typical Collegiate Boy? An alumni said, "He is self-confident, slightly preppie, a social, smart kid."

Parents: The parent body at Collegiate runs the gamut: Academics, artists, writers, professionals, musicians, and some Wall Street types mingle comfortably in what most say is an intellectual atmosphere. About half come from the East Side and half from the West Side. "It is a fun loving group, easy to connect with," said one parent. Another told us, "The parent body at Collegiate is tremendously diverse and not stuffy; cocktail parties might be held in an apartment in the Village with people eating cross-legged on a futon or in a Park or Fifth Avenue apartment." Jewish parents have long been comfortable at Collegiate. There are many Jewish legacies attending Collegiate and school is closed on the major Jewish holidays. Parents Association meetings are scheduled on the school calendar and all parents are invited to attend.

Program: Academically, the early years at Collegiate are "challenging, yet comfortable." Learning is developmental and low-key. A former Lower School teacher said the style of the school "is not extreme, not too traditional or informal, but they've borrowed what's best and held onto the things that have worked." Throughout the kindergarten and Lower School there is the understanding that boys develop at different rates. Table groupings in classrooms are informal; no rows. The heterogeneous classrooms (approximately 20 boys in each with one teacher and a full-time assistant) often break into small groups for activities. There is an eclectic approach to reading instruction: some boys come in reading and some don't, it's not an admissions requirement. There is recognition of different learning styles.

First grade homework is approached with the attitude that parents are partners. Parents are encouraged to come in to the classroom to share their skills and talents, or to simply read to the boys during library time.

Lower School boys leave their homerooms to go to specialists in art, music, physical education and science. Kindergarten boys usually have science in their project room while all Lower School students go to a specially designed Lower School science lab. Through fourth grade there is a teacher and an assistant for each class. All Lower School students have access to computers in the classrooms. The boys have regularly scheduled classes in the Lower School technology lab. The full-time Lower School technology coordinator works closely with teachers to support computer-related activities. In the Lower School, boys learn keyboarding, basic computer skills and begin to use computers as tools to create documents and multimedia presentations.

In the early grades reading and math are "geared to the individual." The Fisher Landau department consisting of learning specialists provides support and enrichment.

In social studies, third graders study immigration and learn about the Dutch settlers of New Amsterdam. In April and May, the Lower School takes part in an interdisciplinary unit focusing on a common topic of particular interest such as rivers, islands, stories, fabric, structures, oceans or treasures. The music program at Collegiate is very strong; renowned pianist Emanuel Ax was a former trustee and parent of an alumnus. Lower School boys have music twice a week. In fourth grade the recorder is introduced; in fifth and sixth grades students

179

study a string instrument. Each year students are given an instrument for use at school or practice at home. On our tour we saw eight boys playing their violins in a practice room. Private and semi-private instruction is available and music theory is taught. Third and fourth graders may choose to join the Lower School chorus. Collegiate students have participated in instrumental and choral performances at Carnegie Hall on numerous occasions. Eighth graders are introduced to music technology and composition. The boys explore music and creativity through the use of computers and synthesizers.

In fourth grade the work load is stepped up and letter grades begin in sixth grade. Parents stressed, however, that "Nobody is pressured at Collegiate, the boys are encouraged to do their best."

The Middle School at Collegiate consists of grades five through eight. According to parents, Middle School demands a greater amount of independence. In fifth grade, departmentalization has begun. Fifth graders get lockers; desks are still organized in groups, not rows. There are regular forty minute periods. The Middle School technology lab is easily accessible and often used. Technology skills are put to use as boys write papers, examine data and learn to use digital information sources for research. Students use computer-generated graphic materials in oral presentations in many of their classes. Fifth graders select either French or Spanish which they can take through high school. They can also begin Latin in eighth grade.

Beginning in fifth grade, students are given long term assignments. Students learn to plan their weeks and organize their time. At Collegiate, students really know how to think. Readings include *The Ancient Greece of Odysseus, Beowulf the Warrior, Love that Dog* and selected Irish folktales, myths and legends and extend to *Brave New World* and *The Merchant of Venice*. "My fifth grader was asked to write a paper about one of Robert Louis Stevenson's books from the point of view of a minor character," a parent said. Another fifth grade assignment was to write a piece of historical fiction. One student wrote a piece on a Vietnamese teenager and the assignment was graded by both the history and English teachers.

Fifth through eighth graders take regular tests during the school year. At the end of seventh and eighth grades there is a formal exam period and study and organizational skills are reinforced.

The social studies curriculum begins in the Lower School with the study of families and communities, and expands in the upper grades to include the wider world. Fifth graders study ancient civilizations and read Greek myths and English folktales. Sixth graders study the

Middle Ages, the exploration of the New World and the cultures of the Americas and American colonial history. Seventh graders focus on American history from George Washington to the present. Eighth graders study World History (Asia, Africa, Islam and Europe). Research papers and projects are completed in all Middle School grades. Chinese is introduced in fifth grade with Mandarin Chinese and includes language, customs, traditions and legendary stories and songs. French and Spanish are also explored in earnest through a variety of materials that include language skills, and literature. Students can continue studying Mandarin and/or Chinese culture through high school.

There is a non-academic activities program for Middle Schoolers "to broaden and enrich the boys' experience." Course offerings include: community service projects, computer, photography, drama, student government, Middle School newspaper, literary magazine, and excursions away from school to take advantage of the urban setting.

Experience in public speaking is gained through weekly assemblies, morning meetings and many opportunities to perform in dramatic and musical productions. One trimester of drama is required in seventh and eighth grades. Arts for grades seven and eight includes the opportunity for the boys to play in a chamber music group, participate in the Middle School Chorus, study photography, produce dramatic pieces and learn musical composition using computerized synthesizers during the year.

Summer reading is required for grades five through nine. Most boys purchase their books at the Paperback Book Fair held in the Spring. They also gather books at the Annual Book Festival organized by the Parents Association in the fall. Guest authors often include Collegiate parents and alumni. Sixth graders produce their own anthology of original literature. Grades six through eight take a three-day trip to locations of interest. Sixth graders visit an environmental study center, and seventh graders begin the school year with a three day trip to Frost Valley. The eighth graders end their year with a trip to Washington, D.C.

Human Sexuality, an eight-week course is taught to Middle School boys and provides a forum for discussing sex, sexuality, reporoduction, birth control, and sexually transmitted diseases. Boys read *The New Teenage Body Book* and engage in discussions about behaviors, attitudes and values relating to sex and sexuality.

Interscholastic sports begin in seventh grade in a wide variety of sports; participation is stressed over competition. After spring break, eighth graders can sign out for lunch and join their older peers at "Big Nick's Pizza." After school the courtyard handball court is the social gathering spot.

Upper School at Collegiate consists of grades nine through twelve. The Upper School curriculum, according to a trustee and former PA president, is both "traditional and innovative." The school is not rigid in its approach to education, though the backbone of the curriculum is classical. There is an academic core program with electives offered in eleventh and twelfth grades. Some readings focus on the Classics. Other perspectives are explored in courses such as: PlayProduction: Performance III, Acting for Stage and Film, West African Drumming, Exploring Modernism through Art and Music, Irish Literature, The Craft of Poetry, The Marriage Plot: the Nineteenth Century European Novel, and Twentieth Century Japanese Fiction. In math and science, AB and BC Calculus, Statistical Modeling, Environmental Issues and Astronomy are among the courses offered. The high school course guide and syllabi mirrors that of most liberal arts college's freshman and sophomore years.

Parents say there is an emphasis in all grades on good writing and research skills. A former PA President told us that Verbal SAT scores are consistently high because of the emphasis on language arts and the academic core program. There is no summer reading list for grades ten through twelve. Summer reading is encouraged for pleasure at all grade levels.

The Technology Department offers an expanding program in computer and technology education and there are numerous opportunities for students to use computers in conjunction with course work in all disciplines. An academic local area network connects computers in the computer labs, the library, the science department and classrooms throughout the school. Access to the network allows students to "plug-in" to the many resources available through the system, including the Internet, the library catalog and reference materials.

In addition to the yearly course offerings, Collegiate students can design an Independent Study course in an area of interest, taken in addition to the minimum course load. A senior project in an area of the student's choice (often some form of internship) can be undertaken in the last semester of the senior year if all other requirements are completed.

"The faculty at Collegiate is extraordinary," says an alumnus. A parent said, "They are a very senior faculty. Teachers average ten to twelve years of experience and three-quarters have advanced degrees." There is an assistant teaching program in the Lower School in which less experienced teachers work with a mentor, eventually becoming head teachers. A big incentive to keep faculty is housing provided in a building connected to the school. A former PA President said, "Collegiate has one of the lowest tuitions yet offers the highest remuneration for independent school teachers which is why it keeps and attract good teachers." The faculty is part of the larger Collegiate community: there is a parent/faculty chorus which performs at Upper School events.

Student government at Collegiate consists of three representatives from each grade. The Middle School student government meets regularly and plans student programs and special events. Upper School student government has tackled furnishing the student center, finding summer jobs for students and relaxing the dress code.

Theater continues to be a strength in the Upper School at Collegiate. Upper School students put on two to three plays per semester, both in the school's two hundred and sixty-seven seat theater auditorium and in the large "black box" theater.

Clubs at Collegiate are popular. The Model U.N. Club, CENIC (environmental club), chess club, Asian Cultural Society, the Science Olympiad Team, the Debate Team, and JAMAA, an organization for students, families, alumni and faculty of color are among the more active ones.

There is a community service requirement at Collegiate of one hundred credit hours, twenty of which must be done outside of school. Programs include opportunities such as tutoring and working at the West End Avenue Collegiate Church soup kitchen, or volunteering at various museums or hospitals throughout the city. There are special food drives each year and the proceeds are donated to various community programs, such as winter coat drive, Project Cicero Book Drive, Clean-up of Riverside Park, Can-a-Day Food Drive, Publicolor (painting walls in public schools), NYC Special Olympics, and 'ol faithful, Trick-or-Treat for Unicef. In-house tutoring performed at Collegiate is also a way to fulfill the requirement. A number of juniors join the Peer Leadership program after completing a course in Group Dynamics, which is designed to develop basic counseling techniques.

The atmosphere at Collegiate is shaped by the interaction of the student body and a sense of community within the school. In the Upper School, as far as contact between grades, one alumnus said, "There's sports, the drama program, clubs and chorus. It's too small a school for hazing." "Of course, you can only get a Collegiate varsity jacket if you play on a varsity team," an alum mentioned. The Dutchmen's colors are orange and blue, the same as the the Knicks and the Mets. Collegiate's biggest rivals are Trinity, Poly Prep, Riverdale and Fieldston. The traditional Friday night basketball games are popular. Collegiate also has a championship cross-country team that runs in Riverside Park as well as championship teams in basketball, track, wrestling and soccer.

A recent alumnus told me that more important than the traditions themselves is the sense of success you get at Collegiate: "When you've been there a long time, you begin to think 'I can do anything.' If anything, Collegiate boys spread themselves too thin." Another alumnus said, "Athletes are also actors or musicians too."

The school stresses values, particularly integrity. "They are sticklers for honor and principle; competition is stressed in a healthy way. But it's tough and demanding," according to an alumnus. Collegiate is structured but students may choose from a growing number of electives from ninth grade on.

Collegiate enjoys great success at college placement. The school provides a highly personalized process. Since the graduating class usually numbers about fifty, it not difficult to know each boy; each senior takes control of his own college search in an independent fashion and is encouraged to go beyond the obvious in the quest for the best match.

There are no academic prizes at Collegiate. Seniors with outstanding grades are inducted into the Cum Laude Society (the secondary school equivalent of Phi Beta Kappa). The Collegiate faculty and graduating class vote for the Head Boy each year, a senior who shows a combination of leadership, sportsmanship and citizenship.

There is a genuine school spirit at Collegiate demonstrated at class dinners, the holiday assembly and at Moving Up Day. One parent said, "They all sing the school song and you cry no matter how many times you've seen it." A traditional graduation ceremony is held in the West End Collegiate Church. Cap and gown are worn and the alma mater is sung.

Popular College Choices Yale, Harvard, Brown, Dartmouth, Princeton, University of Pennsylvania, Columbia, Wesleyan, Williams

Traditions Library Week, Parents Association Book Festival, Paperback Book Fair, 2nd grade trip to Manhattan Country

School Farm, 3rd grade trip to an outdoor environmental education center, 7th grade trip to Frost Valley, 8th grade trip to Washington, DC, 10th grade Interschool trip to Frost Valley, Lower and Middle School Field Day, 5th and 6th grade music evenings, Grandparents and Special Friends Day, Upper School Community Service Day, Senior Project Presentation Day, Senior Holiday Breakfast, Moving Up Days for Lower and Middle Schools, Athletic Banquet, graduation at Collegiate Church, alumni film festival, reunion and alumni receptions

Publications   Newspaper: *The Collegiate Journal* (monthly)
Yearbook: *The Dutchman*
French publication: *Charabia*
Spanish publication: *La Herencia*
Literary magazine: *Prufrock*
Science and Technology publication: *Technically Speaking*
Opinion publication: *Issues*
Lower School: *Lower School News*
Middle School literary magazine: *Jabberwock*
Collegiate Magazine, Newspaper: *The Collegian*
Parents Association: Newsletter

Community Service Requirement   Grades 9–12: 100 credits by graduation (40 minutes–1 hour 5 1 credit)

Hangouts   Collegiate cafeteria (the menu is in French, Spanish and English), the courtyard, library, Upper School student center, technology labs and Platten Hall lobby

Columbia Grammar and Preparatory School

5 West 93rd Street
New York, NY 10025
(212) 749-6200
website: www.cgps.org

Coed
Pre-kindergarten–12th grade
Grades 5–12 accessible

Dr. Richard J. Soghoian, Headmaster
Ms. Simone Hristidis, Director of Admissions (Pre-K–12)

Uniform No torn jeans, sweatpants, T-shirts with inappropriate messages, tank tops, cutoffs, boxers, gym shorts or bicycle pants

Birthday Cutoff Children entering Kindergarten must be 5 by August 1

Enrollment Total enrollment: 1195
Pre-kindergarten places: 22
Kindergarten places: 30–40
6th grade places: 10
9th grade places: approximately 25-30
Graduating class size: approximately 113

Grades Semester system
Letter grades begin in 7th grade
Departmentalization begins in 5th grade
First final exam is given at the end of 7th grade

Tuition Range 2009–2010 $33,040 to $34,990, pre-kindergarten–12th grade
There are no additional fees
A Tuition Refund Plan and a Student Accident Reimbursement Plan are available

Financial Aid/Scholarship 19% of the students received aid totaling $4.4 million

Endowment $25 million

Diversity   17.8% students of color PreK–12,
53% of the families of color received aid in 2008/9
MECA, Multi-Ethnic Cultural Awareness Club
23 Prep for Prep students enrolled as of Fall 2009
Parent Diversity Committee

Homework   Kindergarten: none
1st: 20 minutes
2nd: 30–45 minutes
3rd, 4th: approximately 1 hour
5th–8th: 1½–2½ hours
9th–12th: approximately 3 hours

After-School Program   CGPS After-School Program for grades
K–6 offers a variety of creative and recreational activities until
4:30 P.M.; extended day program available until 6 P.M.; additional fees are required

Summer Program   CGS Summer Camp: for Pre-kindergarten–2
from the end of school until the end of July, staffed by CGS
teachers, an additional payment is required

Columbia Grammar School was founded in 1764 and functioned
as a feeder school for King's College (later, Columbia University).
Now CGPS graduates go on to a much wider range of universities and
colleges. CGPS became a nonprofit school in 1941 and merged with a
nearby girls' school. Since 1981, CGPS has been guided by Richard J.
Soghoian, who holds a Ph.D. in philosophy from Columbia University
and is also an International Fellow at the School for International
Affairs. His expertise is manifested in the innovative social studies, history
and geography programs throughout CGPS. Dr. Soghoian guided
the school through quite a few major construction projects and has
been at the helm while several new buildings/brownstones have been
added that now serve the entire school community, including a state-
of-the-art 200-plus seat theater, computer and science labs, at least
five art studios with photography and filmmaking equipment, a third
library, a gym, and additional academic areas. Moreover, the school
purchased a brownstone down the block to house admissions, administrative
offices and development. Even though individual class sizes

have grown, with eighteen to twenty students per class, individual attention is still a hallmark of CGPS.

Columbia Grammar offers a well-rounded but structured program for able students. The Grammar School is now composed of pre-kindergarten through sixth grade. The Prep School consists of seventh through twelfth grades.

The Director of the Lower School, Stanley Seidman, was formerly head of Dalton's Lower School. Parents say Seidman is well-liked, knows all the children's names and is very accessible. Parents say they feel free to contact the teachers at any time. Teachers respond to parents throughout the day via email or a phone call.

Getting in: The application is very straightforward. There are one or two essay questions. The ERB/ISEE is required. All applications for kindergarten and first grade must be filed by mid-November. There is one open house where prospective parents meet grammar school teachers and admissions staff. Once an application has been filed, parents are taken on a more extensive tour of the school while their child is being interviewed (a small group interview of four children at a time, which lasts about one hour during which the child is observed by the Director of Admissions as well as admissions personnel). After the tour, parents meet with Dr. Seidman and Ms. Hristidis over coffee. Parents say that the admissions process at CGPS is low-key and comfortable. "They are really interested in the child, not scrutinizing the parents," I heard. CGPS has not gone to its wait list in several years. What are they looking for? Hristidis told me, "A bright child who can handle an enriched curriculum, eager to learn; nice, well adjusted children; we're not looking for a type, a range of children would do well here but they must be academically inclined."

Prospective applicants to the Preparatory School attend one of several afternoon meetings or morning coffee chats in which the program is described followed by a tour. Tours are given by current Prep students. The application deadline is also usually mid-November.

For ninth grade, the primary goal according to Hristidis, "is to enroll kids from schools that end in eighth grade like Town, Rodelph, Grace Church, Allen-Stevenson and Bank Street." She warns parents seeking to move kids from rigorous schools like Dalton, Horace Mann or Riverdale, to a school with softer academic expectations, that CGPS isn't the place. "Kids must be exemplary candidates in every way," she asserts.

The typical CGPS student? "This is not a jock school," said one parent. "The typical student usually has some artistic bent." "The atypical student," one parent said, "is pushy, snotty or overly competitive." Plus now that CGPS is growing, there are students who are getting more involved in a wide range of athletics.

Parents: The parent body at CGPS consists of many professionals. There is an equal division between West Siders and East Siders. There are a number of Parent Association events such as the Skating Party, Theatre Party and Spring Benefit. They are fun, low-key events. At the annual holiday concert "First Noel" as well as "O Chanukah" are sung. "What you see is what you get," says one parent with two children at CGPS. "There are absolutely no surprises."

Program: The school provides a very informative handbook for each division (Lower and Upper). Parents say CGPS is supportive about separation when school actually begins.

All students have a well-rounded schedule, which includes a strong swimming program (required for grades pre-kindergarten through fourth grade and optional for fifth grade.) Kindergartners swim twice a week for forty minutes plus art, music and academics.

Presently, the Grammar School (composed of pre-kindergarten through fourth grades) is housed in five interconnected brownstones on West 94rd Street connected to the original school building on West 93rd Street (now housing grade four). Children and adults develop strong legs because of the many stairways in the school. The classroom space is long, with windows at either end, but well laid out and bright. There is a courtyard play area for recess. Parents say that the kindergarten teachers are warm, and make learning fun, although by third grade they get more serious. "The children respect the teachers," a parent commented.

Throughout the Grammar School learning is viewed as a progression, especially in math and reading. The brochure says: "Each grade's work builds on the work of previous years." Individual rates of learning in math and reading are accommodated. Wherever possible, art is coordinated with work in other subjects in the Grammar School. Pre-kindergarten, kindergarten and 1st grade have two teachers and one associate teacher. For second and third grades there are two teachers for approximately twenty to twenty-two children. Although it is considered a "structured school," the teaching at CGPS is flexible, "using a variety of approaches and techniques." Parents praise the well-paced reading program. In kindergarten reading readiness is the focus; in first grade, it incorporates phonics, whole language and guided reading techniques. Math instruction in kindergarten stresses experiential learning through the use of manipulatives and games.

There are at least two computers in all of the classrooms, and many are equipped with Smartboards. Each class in pre-kindergarten through second grade attends the computer lab for two projects over the course of the year. Third graders attend to the computer lab once a week, fourth grade twice a week and fifth grade three time a week.

The extensive music program draws from the Kodaly and Orff as well as other methods. Second graders learn to play the recorder. Instrumental instruction begins in fourth grade and students are given an instrument to take home. Opportunities to perform include the third- and fourth-grade choir, a recorder ensemble for second and third graders, a string ensemble and a chamber music ensemble for more advanced students. In fourth grade students pick one instrument for further study.

The social studies curriculum for pre-kindergarten through fourth grade begins with families and community and broadens to include a study of ethnicity and immigration in second grade, Native Americans are the subject in third grade, explorers and Colonial America in fourth. Fifth graders study the Revolutionary War, Western Expansion and the Civil Wars. They use primary sources and read Early American folklore. Sixth graders study ancient civilizations and the Middle Ages and write a research paper. The Writing Workshop is a standard part of the curriculum in which students practice the steps of good writing (see Glossary, p. 58, *supra*). Fifth and sixth graders also take public speaking, engage in debates and practice speech writing.

The approach to science in the Grammar School "is firmly experimental and based on the scientific method." Environmental awareness begins as early as first grade with a discussion about how waste leaves Manhattan island. First graders study endangered animals; second graders learn about the water cycle and testing; third graders study the northeast woodlands. fourth graders travel to Nature's Classroom, an environmental study center in Connecticut. Fifth and sixth graders engage in a hands on, guided discovery program based on the scientific method of problem solving

Parents say that by third grade the academic pace picks up and the work gets much more serious. Extra help is readily available. Foreign language study is offered after school.

In mathematics, the focus is on problem-solving skills. There are enrichment topics in each grade. In fifth grade these are palindromic numbers, tangrams and hieroglyphics. Other enrichment projects include curve stitching, M.C. Escher's tessellations, and participation in the Math Olympiad.

Reports and grades come home twice a year. The anecdotal reports in the Lower School are extensive and detailed. In addition, there is a checklist in each subject area showing that the student is either "progressing well," "developing" or "needs strengthening."

If a child has a learning difference, CGPS will "provide some degree of professional skills remediation on a temporary basis." CGPS also has a highly specific and intensive in-school treatment of learning disabilities called the Learning Resource Center, staffed by ten highly trained professionals. The program is limited to forty students, grades kindergarten through twelfth, who are otherwise fully mainstreamed students. There is a significant additional cost. This program is an in-house program only. No outside applicants are admitted.

For physical exercise students play in the courtyard, on the roof turf playground or go to Central Park, which is located only a block from the school, weather permitting. There is a rooftop play yard for fifth and sixth graders. Physical education is required in all grades. Intramural and interschool sports begin in fifth grade. After-school sports are available. A Field Day with games is held at the end of the year for each division.

The Prep School (grades seven through twelve) is on a semester system. Grades are issued quarterly, there are two parent conferences and two narrative report cards. The school day begins with a ten minute homeroom period and is divided into forty minute periods, ending at 2:55 p.m.

The building at 36 West 93rd Street houses grades five and six as well as seven through twelve. It is bright and spacious, with a special area for the arts: photo lab, filmmaking, jewelry-making and so on. The "underground" theatre holds 150 but is mainly used by Grammar School students. Stagecraft models (made by students) on display in the lobby are wonderful.

In seventh and eighth grades students are required to take English, science, social studies and math as well as art, music, computer and PE. Foreign language study begins with a two month sequence in each of five languages: French, Spanish, Latin, Japanese and Mandarin. In eighth grade students choose one of these languages for continued study.

Seventh graders are ready to think critically and express themselves clearly and sensitively on issues of social relevance. In seventh grade, students study Ancient and Medieval Civilizations, as well as themes of prejudice, tolerance and freedom. Readings include *Inherit the Wind* and *To Kill a Mockingbird*.

In grade eight, Global History covers The Emergence of the Modern World.

In grades nine through twelve students are required to complete four years of English, and social studies, as well as three years of math, fine arts, including two semesters of either theater art or music history and two years of science. A foreign language must be studied through the end of eleventh grade. Other requirements include a course in computer literacy (there are two computer labs, with Macs), two of three offerings in the history of art, theater or music, and a community service requirement of one hundred hours to be completed by the end of the senior year. Electives are available in all the major subject areas. Six courses are the normal course load, except during the senior year when only five are required. Students can arrange independent study projects in their final semester.

Ninth and tenth grades are assigned to full year English classes. In ninth grade, the class addresses the fundamental human theme of coming of age and exposes the students to a wide range of literature. In tenth grade the course focuses on the fundamentals of good writing, as well as a selection of British and American literature. Eleventh and twelfth graders choose from a variety of electives but they must take at least one course in each of the following: British literature, American literature, and pre-twentieth century literature.

When asked about a multicultural curriculum at CGPS, Dr. Soghoian responded that "CGPS has always emphasized Africa, China, Japan and South America on an equal footing with the study of Europe in the preparatory school program." CGPS also uses its extensive assembly program to emphasize multicultural performers and themes.

The history sequence reads like a description of a college history program. Students in ninth study American History, in tenth grade they study Global History, including European history from Greek and Roman times to the French Revolution and continuing through the Reactionary Era, Imperialism, World Wars I and II, and the Cold War. Juniors and seniors are required to take four semesters of history including at least one U.S. history course and one non-U.S. history course. Juniors and seniors can choose from electives such as economics, philosophy, the Holocaust, and a course taught in conjunction with Tufts University, as well as AP courses in comparative government, modern European history, and U.S. government.

Calculus BC and AB (college calculus and preparation for the AP exams) are offered by the math department, and graphing calculators are used in the calculus classes. The science department offers AP biology, chemistry and physics as well as electives in astronomy, genetics, electronics, human evolution, and a three year research course.

There is a great range of choice in the arts at CGPS. Photography, drama and filmmaking are popular. The ceramics room is full of inspired and beautiful work ready to be fired in the kiln. Wood shop and jewelry-making/metal smithing areas are busy places too.

The Prep School has its own Winter and Spring Concerts, (choral and instrumental) and a three day Arts Festival. There are several major theatre productions each year and at least one musical.

The student government, with elected representatives from each grade, helps coordinate activities such as the annual Field Day and fundraising for various causes. Clubs include Amnesty International, Jazz Band, Acting Troupe, Book Club, Film Appreciation, Guitar Club, MECA (the multicultural awareness group), Model U.N., Model Congress, and Environmental Awareness.

About 60 percent of the high school students participate in a varsity sport. The gym is large and cheerful with wooden bleachers. At the end-of-the-year Sports Award Banquet the year's outstanding teams and coaches are recognized and individual achievement is honored. CP has strong teams in soccer, cross-country and varsity basketball. There are trophy cases in the school lobby.

Moving Up Day at CGPS reinforces the feeling of a warm community. It is a special day when all the students from pre-kindergarten through twelfth grade, faculty and staff gather together in the gym to share awards for academic excellence, citizenship and character, success in sports and so on. Songs are sung and class banners are handed down from one class to another to signify graduation.

Alumni speak about fond memories of CGPS: "Reunions hold good memories," "CGPS was a little more laid-back and less pretentious than some of the other schools and we all did well there."

Popular College Choices   Emory, University of Wisconsin, Boston University, Brown, Middlebury, Northwestern, University of Michigan, Tufts, Cornell, Columbia, Vassar, University of Pennsylvania, University of Southern California

Traditions   Grammar School Science Fair, Earth Day, Field Day, class dinners, Holiday Concert, Skating Party, theatre benefit, Winter Concert, Spring Concert, Instrumental Concert, 4th-grade trip to Nature's Classroom, Spirit Week, Spring Benefit, The Reading Club, Operation Santa Claus, Sports Award Banquet, MECA (Multicultural Awareness) Dinner, Prep School Research Symposium, Moving Up Ceremony, Young Alumni Reunion

Publications   Alumni magazine: *Columbiana Today*
Literary, news and art magazine: *CPJ* (Columbia Prep Journal)
Yearbook
Newspaper

Community Service Requirement   Grades 9–12: one hundred hours, cumulative

Hangouts   McDonald's, deli around the corner

Convent Of The Sacred Heart

1 East 91st Street
New York, NY 10128
(212) 722-4745
website: www.cshnyc.org

All girls
Pre-kindergarten–12th grade
Accessible

Dr. Joseph J. Ciancaglini, Head of School
Ms. Jacqueline A. Casey, Director of Admissions

Uniform Pre-kindergarten and Junior Kindergarten: gray smock jumper, gray corduroy pull up pants or navy pants (no denim) can be worn in colder weather

Kindergarten–Grade 4: gray smock jumper, white blouse with McMullen collar and red trim, white anklets (warm weather), red long-sleeved mock turtleneck shirt and medium gray knee highs (cool weather); red-and-white-check pinafore worn every day, navy stretch shorts worn every day under gray jumper

Grades 5–7: embroidered cotton short sleeve polo shirt; embroidered or non-uniform white, cotton short or long sleeve collared shirts, white turtlenecks, or a white blouse are also acceptable; logo-free shirts are preferred; no logos larger than a quarter in size; the shirts must be long enough so they can stay tucked into their skirt, or when not tucked in, that midriffs are not revealed when hands are raised; gray kilt, medium gray knee socks or white anklet socks; red, cable cardigan sweaters are required and worn in chapel and special assemblies

Grades 8–12: pleated blue skirt or khaki flat front pants in fall and spring; pleated plaid skirt or black pants in winter; shirts, sweaters, sweatshirts, fleeces must be solid, no stripes, text, patterns, or images are allowed; acceptable colors are white, navy, royal blue, light blue, black and gray; shirts must have a collar; shoes may be any color, but have a black sole; flip flops and boots are not permitted; black, white or navy plain tights permitted, but no patterns; socks also must be solid, and either white or black, navy or light blue or gray; plain footless tights are allowed and must be worn to lower calf or ankle

Birthday Cutoff   Pre-kindergarten 3s applicants must be 3 by July 1st before entering
Pre-kindergarten 4s applicants must be 4 by September 1st before entering
Children entering kindergarten must be 5 by September 1st

Enrollment   Total enrollment: 670
Pre-kindergarten 3s places: 16
Kindergarten places: approximately 54
Graduating class size: 50

Grades   Semester system
Letter grades begin in 5th grade
Departmentalization begins in 5th grade
First final exam is given in 8th grade

Tuition Range 2009–2010 $17,530 to $33,985, Pre-kindergarten 3s–12th grade

Financial Aid/Scholarship $2.85 million (13% of the operating budget)

Endowment $36 million

Diversity   27% students of color; CSH admits students from Early Steps, Teak Fellowship, DeLaSalle, and Prep for Prep
Women of Proud Heritage (founded 1991)
Women's History Assembly

Homework   1st and 2nd Grades: 20 minutes, plus an additional 30 minutes of reading
3rd Grade: 30 minutes, plus an additional 30 minutes of reading
4th Grade: 45 minutes, plus an additional 30 minutes of reading
5th–7th: 2 hours
8th–12th: 2–4 hours

After-School Program   All Lower School (Kindergarten–4th Grade) after-school programs require an additional payment; the programs offered vary from season to season and include athletics, arts and crafts, and an assortment of other activities; students in Kindergarten through 4th Grade are also eligible to participate in the extended day program which cares for the children from the end of the school day until 5:45 P.M., but not for kindergarteners on Fridays; Middle School: All Middle School students (Grades 5 through 7), can participate in after-school electives; the cost for these electives is included in the tuition; choices include a variety of recreational, creative and educational activities Upper School: Junior Varsity and Varsity interscholastic athletic competition in the Athletic Association of Independent Schools of New York City and the Ivy League, clubs, publications, and other groups also meet after school

Summer Program   Creative Arts Summer Program: a multi-arts summer program for boys and girls ages 6–15 (junior program for ages 6 and 7) offering instruction in art, drama, film, computer, science and athletics; all-day arts festival at conclusion of the program; an additional payment is required (limited financial aid is available)

———

Chartered by the International Society of the Sacred Heart in 1881, Convent of the Sacred Heart is the oldest independent girls' school in Manhattan. Sacred Heart is housed in two magnificent land-marked buildings—the former Otto Kahn and James Burden mansions. The winding marble staircase leads from the vaulted lobby to bright and spacious classrooms as well as banquet hall and ballroom in the manner of Versailles, complete with tapestry and marble. The ballroom was a wedding gift to Adele Burden née Sloane (great-granddaughter of Commodore Cornelius Vanderbilt) and the scene of many splendid parties and dances in the 1890s. Today the ballroom is used for Sacred Heart functions, dance classes and assemblies, and is rented out on the weekends for corporate and charitable events and weddings, providing the school with additional income.

Sacred Heart is an independent Catholic girls' school that is neither cloistered nor parochial in its outlook. Sacred Heart is governed by a lay board of trustees and Dr. Ciancaglini is the second lay head of the school. Approximately one-third of the students have a mixed religious background. As one parent said, "It's a Christian school because Sacred Heart stresses how you lead your life—there is an emphasis on ethics."

The idea of social service is built into a Sacred Heart education. The catalog states: "A primary aim of a Sacred Heart education is the development in each individual of a personal faith that impels to action." All schools claim to care about every student as an individual; at Sacred Heart, parents say, "They really mean it." Service begins with age appropriate projects in the lowest grades and continues through the Upper School where Sacred Heart has led other city students in the Conference on Homelessness and intensive summer service programs.

Sacred Heart has enjoyed a decade of enrollment growth. Additional sections have been added in most Lower School grades, facilities have been upgraded, technology has been integrated into the curriculum; amenities have been added including a lunch program and cafeteria/dining room, weight-training room and exercise studio, automated library accessible via Internet, new science labs, upgraded existing libraries, a new theater, and renovated classrooms. Additionally, Sacred Heart just purchased a three-story 35,000 square-foot building on East 91st Street that will house a state-of-the-art athletic complex.

Off campus, Sacred Heart is experiencing a historic expansion of its recreational programs and has joined the Black Rock Forest Consortium providing access to a forest and an environmental sciences center shared with several other independent schools. Sacred Heart has also endowed lanes at the Asphalt Green Aqua Center and it is one of the seven schools pioneering the renovation of sports fields on Randalls Island. Sacred Heart has committed to an extensive athletics rentals program to supplement its capabilities and 80% of the students participate in one or more junior varsity or varsity teams, often bringing home the championship trophies.

Getting in: Parents should contact the Admissions Office or go onto the school's website (www.cshnyc.org) to request a viewbook and application. The largest points of entry are pre-kindergarten, kindergarten and ninth grade. The application fee is $65 and the application asks for parents' education and employment. After applying, parents come for their tour and interview on the same day. Brick Church, Park Avenue Christian, Episcopal, West Side Montessori, International Preschool, and St. Thomas More Nursery School are all considered "feeders" to Sacred Heart. The admissions office is sensitive to the needs of parents: "They are very courteous," one parent said, "and particularly accommodating to families from abroad." "When you're accepted at Sacred Heart you're accepted as part of a large international family," said a parent. Another parent said she found Sacred Heart's geographical and ethnic diversity "with a lot of families from

Europe and Latin America," refreshing after her daughter's homogeneous nursery school.

Parents: Sacred Heart parents say that social competition is negligible. They don't need to dress up to pick up their daughters at school. Parents are considered partners in their daughters' education. Newsletters are sent home three times a year. Communication from teachers, the PA, and administration is frequent. There is a new parents' cocktail party and family dinner held in May for incoming families, as well as a welcoming party in September. The Parents Association consists of officers, school representatives and class representatives and hosts an annual spring meeting and cocktail party and the annual auction or benefit fund-raiser and family events. Other Parents Association functions include Christmas caroling, tree lighting and sale (neighbors are welcome) at which you can buy your tree as well as the ornaments and have a picture taken with Santa Claus by the Otto Kahn fireplace outside the former dining room where Enrico Caruso once sang.

Program: At a recent Upper School open house, five elements of a Sacred Heart education were delineated: 1) faith: You will learn "what you are going to be and give in this world"; 2) academic challenge: Sacred Heart's academic program will impart a love of learning and enable each girl to become an independent thinker and grow in her own particular gifts; 3) social awareness: Everyone does service at Sacred Heart, and "we do not count hours" and the school has regular all-school service days, during which the entire community, including alumnae, get involved in a service project; 4) growth as a community: There is a strong relationship between faculty and students, and a diverse student community; 5) personal growth: To recognize your strengths, gifts and limitations, "you come as you are and are loved into being the very best that you can be." A Lower School parent said that what she likes best about Sacred Heart is that the head of school and the heads of the divisions "have a real concern for each and every family—people are what matters."

Religion and social service go hand in hand at Sacred Heart. According to the brochure, the "basic intent of the Lower School religious program is to build in each student a positive sense of herself in relation to God and to her community." Ethics and spirituality are stressed—the basic premise is "you have a friend in God." There is Mass once a week in the beautifully appointed chapel and parents are always welcome. In Middle School "the link between faith and action is forged by social action activities that reach out to communities beyond the school." Middle School service projects include working in a day care center and participation in walkathons, God's Love We Deliver (meals delivered to AIDS patients) and Amnesty International. In the Upper School community service is coordinated through the campus ministry and the Student Activities and Service Program. Students are expected to volunteer on a regular basis in a social service agency outside of school, keep a journal and share their experiences in a weekly meeting. Students in Class Ten must complete a final project in which they examine a social issue in depth through academic research and field experience.

The Lower School at Sacred Heart is composed of grades prekindergarten through grade four. In Lower School, the girls wear the signature Sacred Heart uniform: a gray jumper with a red-checked pinafore (both machine washable). Each Lower School girl has an "Angel" or "Big Sister" to guide her. The fourth graders are partners with seniors in the Upper School and Middle School girls read weekly to Lower School children. There are three kindergarten classes of approximately seventeen children each and two teachers in each classroom (plus a rabbit). Beginning in kindergarten the following subjects are taught: language arts, math, science, social studies and French or Spanish. Students meet weekly for religion, art, music, library, gym and drama/movement. There are formal as well as informal assembly presentations. Exercise is taken on the two play terraces, which have views of the reservoir, or in Central Park across the street.

Parents say academics in the Lower School consists of "good old-fashioned teaching combined with some of the newer methods" and "there's a lot of structure." Conferences are held twice a year but parents say you can schedule one any time if necessary. A tone of "warmth and acceptance" prevails along with academic expectations. Director of Admissions Jackie Casey describes Sacred Heart as "not overly pressured, but everyone is expected to do serious work." The mother of a third grader concurs: "Sacred Heart is competitive but each girl is encouraged to do her best." Collaborative learning is emphasized in the early years, and there are no individual desks until third grade.

The reading program begins in kindergarten and becomes more formal in Class One. Phonics is taught as an essential reading skill along with creative writing, Writers' Workshop, whatever works. If a student is not progressing well she will begin working with a reading specialist. There is individual as well as small group instruction and basal texts are used. Girls are taught to experience mathematics "as an integral part of everyday life" through cooking, manipulatives and math games. For example, to learn the value of a million, one class is collecting and counting tea bag tags. The project is on display in the classroom.

Lower School science makes frequent use of technology, emphasizes the skills of observation and investigation. There is a two-day field trip to an environmental center in fourth grade. The social studies curriculum begins with a study of the students' own families, then extends to a study of the community. Students in Class Three research topics such as the rain forest or deserts. Class Four studies Early Explorers and American History.

Art is integrated into the science and social studies curriculum in many ways. Students in Class Two pick an animal to study and model it in clay, then the entire class works together to create a Calderesque circus from wood, wire, foam and fabric. Students in Class Three made "incredible" papier-mâché vegetables in art and studied the growth of plants from seed through maturation in science. Fifth graders studying antiquity created a museum of ancient cultures.

Drama and movement activities are "designed to enhance the students' understanding of dance as a means of communication and expression." By Class Four the girls create and perform their own original dance/drama pieces.

Technology is integrated into the classrooms and curriculum, and there are Smartboards in nearly every classroom. Formal computer instruction begins in first grade. The classes are team taught by a computer specialist and the classroom teacher and use multimedia CD-roms and related software. Fifth graders work with lego logo, a robotics application, and by sixth grade students and teachers use Hyperstudio to create multimedia research projects.

A team of Lower School psychologists and learning specialists give additional help where necessary. Project Charlie, an anti-drug program that focuses on self-esteem, is taught in the Lower School. A comprehensive health program which focuses on nutrition begins in second grade.

Birthdays in Lower School are special because the birthday girl can wear a party dress, bring in cupcakes or another sweet and can donate a book to the library in her name. Another fun event in Lower School is the Halloween costume party. The Lower School Christmas Pageant "can make you weep" it is so beautifully produced, parents say.

Middle School at Sacred Heart consists of Classes Five through Seven. All six Middle School homerooms are located on the fourth floor. Each new Middle School student has an "angel" for the first weeks of school. New students and their angels are invited to school for a luncheon and orientation day the week before school begins. Flexible ability grouping in mathematics begins in Class Six. The core curriculum is English, math, science, social studies, and religion. French and Spanish are offered in the Middle School, and students are required to take one year of Latin. Students say there is an increased workload in Class Six and the development of good study skills is emphasized.

Art continues to be integrated with the curriculum at many levels. Students in Class Six studying Medieval and Renaissance Europe create family crests and banners, work on tapestry projects and make stained-glass windows. The study of South America in Class Seven is supplemented by the creation of relief sculptures and the study of pre-Columbian art.

The Middle School elective program is a required weekly enrichment elective. Among the choices are sports, drama, literary magazine, photography, ice skating, swimming and ceramics.

There is a Middle School musical production in the fall as well as smaller productions in the winter and spring. Other highlights include the Class Seven father/daughter volleyball game, the pancake breakfast and the mother/daughter liturgy.

The Middle School has its own student government, a Committee of Games, that oversees the sports competition between the Green and Buff teams. There is also a Big Sister Program. Each class takes an overnight trip, which is coordinated with the curriculum. Class Five travels to Mystic, Connecticut, sixth graders to a Pennsylvania Renaissance Faire and seventh graders to Plymouth, Massachusetts.

Beginning in Middle School and continuing through Upper School, academic achievement awards are given to students who maintain an A average for the year in four or more academic subjects. At the end of the year there is a Sports Banquet to honor athletic achievement.

The Upper School at Sacred Heart consists of Classes Eight through Twelve. Class Eight is a transition year at Sacred Heart. In Class Nine there is an influx of new students from parochial and independent schools in the New York City area while some of the students who have been at Sacred Heart since pre-kindergarten or kindergarten opt to leave for a coed or boarding school. Incoming ninth graders have an overnight immersion program and each new student in the Upper School has an "angel" for the first weeks. Upper School students at Sacred Heart say they feel they have more opportunity to take risks and to be more articulate in an all-girls school. (But the school continues to be strict about skirt length.)

Students say that the academic expectations are high—Sacred Heart was recognized by the U.S. Department of Education as a National School of Excellence. "The teachers work you hard, and honors courses are pushed," they say. The sense of community continues in the Upper School: "It's not so competitive because we're all friends and we help each other." There has been an enormous change in the emphasis on the sciences in the past four years—now 90 percent of the students take an advanced science course during their senior year. Students take six or seven academic subjects in Classes Eight through Ten and add electives in Classes Eleven and Twelve. A former Parents Association president told us, "The Upper School is rigorous but there is a lot of support." The study of religion includes textual study, literary exegesis, historical background, comparative religions, ethics and philosophy. In the eleventh grade the interdisciplinary approach culminates in a thirty-page baccalaureate level thesis and oral presentation of a topic combining Christology and the Arts. Recent topics have included examinations of the films of Fellini, the music of J.S. Bach, and Beguin lace makers.

Because the Upper School is small, the teachers know each girl very well. Teachers are approachable and there are peer tutors.

There is an intensive five-year writing program in the Upper School and students become familiar with all literary genres. Students are expected to write well in all disciplines. In Class Nine there is an interdisciplinary social studies and English project that produces *Medieval Magazine* and culminates in a banquet. Juniors and seniors can choose from courses in Asian and African-American literature. The Memoirs course examines feminist thinking through the stories of women in a variety of cultures. For "New York City in Literature," students read the work of an author (such as Edith Wharton, who lived in New York City) and visit his or her home and/or sites in the novel.

Students who excel in mathematics can take calculus AB and BC. Members of the Mathematics Club compete with other Catholic high schoolers in the tristate area.

The school has a standing research internship program at Rockefeller University where several girls study each year. Students have also interned at the Museum of Natural History, the New York Academy of Sciences, the Cooper Union Engineering School, the Columbia Science Honors Program and the U.N. A lab science research internship is available to students in eleventh and twelfth grades. Interns spend six hours a week in a laboratory and write a research paper.

The art department has been expanded in recent years.

In May there is a three-week Festival of the Arts when students celebrate their accomplishments in many areas. Artwork is on display throughout the school, and there are dance recitals, as well as performances by the handbell choir and the Speech and Drama Clubs.

Many of the extracurricular activities in the Upper School are coed. There are Upper School dances in September and at Christmas each year, and Sacred Heart students can audition for roles in the Collegiate, Regis and Browning schools' plays and musicals. At Sacred Heart the drama department produces one-act plays or Shakespeare in the fall and a musical in the spring in which boys play some parts. There are also Service Days together with neighboring boys' schools.

Students can also join the Interschool Orchestra or the Sacred Heart Handbell Choir.

Other extracurricular opportunities include student government, Peer Support, Archeology Club, Drama Club, Environmental Club, yearbook, literary magazine, newspaper and Women of Proud Heritage. Sports are popular and plentiful: There are eighth grade teams, intramural clubs and eight varsity sports. Two of Sacred Heart's chief competitors are Trinity School and Brearley.

Sacred Heart students in Classes Nine through twelve can participate in the exchange program at other Sacred Heart Schools either here or abroad. Students have studied in France, Belgium, Spain, California and Louisiana.

College guidance begins in Class Nine, and there are assemblies with alumnae. Students say that because the teachers know and remember them so well it is easy to get recommendations. A young woman, a senior, who came to Sacred Heart from a public school, says she "holds school dear, it has molded me into what I am."

Popular College Choices Columbia, Georgetown, Harvard, Middlebury, Princeton, University of Pennsylvania, Vassar, Yale, Boston College, Cornell, University of St. Andrews

Traditions Big Sister/Little Sister Cookout, used uniform sale, class coffees, Middle School Mother/Daughter Liturgy, Upper School Mother/Daughter Tea, Senior Mother/Daughter Breakfast and induction into the Alumnae Association, tree sale and caroling party, Christmas Pageant, Father/Daughter Dinner Dance, Dad/Daughter boat cruise, Black History Month (February), Women's History Month (March), Ring Day, Sacred Heart Feast Days, First Communion, Confirmation, May Festival of the Arts, Spring Book Fair, Grandparents' Day, archeology trip, class nine Blairstown trip, class eleven retreat, Upper School service trip in March, Sports Banquets, Senior Dinner Dance, alumnae mothers lunch, Senior cut day, Spring Street Fair, Prize Day, Homecoming

Publications   Newspaper: *Spirit*
Upper School Literary magazine: *Zenith*
Yearbook: *Cornerstone*
Women's issues: *Women of Proud Heritage*
French Literary Magazine: *Sous Presse*
Middle School Literary Magazine: *Millenium*
Annual report
Parent/Alumnae Newsletter
Alumae Magazine: *Les Amies*
Visual Arts Magazine: *Iris*
Spanish Literary Magazine: *A Toda Vela*
Science Magazine: *Catalyst*

Community Service Requirement   Each student is expected to give of herself to the school community and to the community at large—hours are not counted

Hangouts   Jackson Hole (hamburger restaurant), Pintaile's Pizza

Corlears School

324 West 15th Street
New York, NY 10011
(212) 741-2800
fax (212) 807-1550
website: www.corlearsschool.org

Coed
Nursery–5th grade
Not accessible

Ms. Thya Merz, Head of School
Ms. Saphiatou N'Jie, Director of Admissions

Birthday Cutoff   Children entering Nursery 2's and 3's must be no younger than 2.6 years-old by September 1st Children entering Pre-kindergarten/Kindergarten (4's/5's) should be no younger than 4 years-old by the end of August

Enrollment   Total enrollment: 150
Largest point of entry is 2.6/3s
Kindergarten places: varies from year to year
Graduating class 2009: 13

Grades   Detailed anecdotal reports

Tuition Range 2009–2010 $17,500 to $25,975 2.6 year-olds through 5th grade
Additional fees: $600 building fee; reduced to $360 for a second child in the school

Financial Aid/Scholarship   30% of the student body receives some form of aid

Endowment   None
Each family makes a non-interest-bearing loan; there is a 3-year staggered payment system for this loan

After-School Program   Child care available after school, Monday–Friday until 5:45 P.M.
Corlears After-School Specialty Program is open to Corlears

students only; weekdays from 3:15 P.M. to 4:15 P.M.; an additional fee required; activities include music, drama, sports, gymnastics, chorus, Spanish, cooking, technology

Summer Program Science Camp: four weeks from mid-June to the end of July for children ages 3 through 8; children explore scientific themes such as energy, animals, dirt and water as well as taking part in recreational and creative activities, swimming and trips; an additional payment is required

---

Corlears was founded in 1968 on the Lower East Side and moved to West 15th Street in 1971. The school is described by families as a "small, nurturing, neighborhood school." The facility spans three townhouses, and has expanded to include a 5th grade. There are well-equipped classrooms, an art room, wood shop, library, two gyms and a lovely play yard. Classrooms are integrated throughout the buildings. Children bring their own lunches

Getting in: Admission is based on interviews with parents and play-dates with other children with at least three other prospective students of the same age group, and available school records.

Program: The program is designed to be supportive and fosters a genuine love of learning and life-long problem solving skills, specializing in the education of children in the early years.

Spanish, art, music, movement, physical education and library supplement the program.

Developmental stages and individual learning styles are respected. Computers are not integrated into classroom work until the 6/7s or 1st and 2nd grades. Although computers are not a major focus in the younger student's classrooms, they are used more frequently as students get older. There is an extensive counseling placement program including a Director of Placement who assists fifth grade graduates and their families with entrance to ongoing schools.

The Dalton School

108 East 89th Street
New York, NY 10128-1599
(212) 423-5200, fax (212) 423-5259
website: www.dalton.org

Coed
Kindergarten–12th grade
Accessible (4th through 12th grades)

Ms. Ellen Stein, Head of School
Dr. Elisabeth Krents, Director of Admissions, Kindergarten–12
Ms. Eva Rado, Director of Middle School/High School Admissions
Ms. Jacqueline Katz, Assistant Director of Admissions,
Kindergarten–12

Birthday Cutoff   August 31st; Children must be 5 for kindergarten

Enrollment   Total enrollment: 1300
   Kindergarten places: approximately 93
   Graduating class size: approximately 100–115

Grades   Semester system
   Letter grades begin in 8th grade
   Full departmentalization by 6th grade
   First midterm and final in 9th grade

Tuition Range 2009–2010 $34,100 Kindergarten through 12th
   grade
   No additional fees other than minimal PA and activities fees

Financial Aid/Scholarship   Approximately 20% of families receive
   some form of financial aid
   $6.5 million available

Endowment   Approximately $45 million

Diversity   Approximately 35% children of color
   351 Prep for Prep students enrolled as of fall 2009
   Affiliated with Early Steps Program, TEAK, A Better Chance,
   Albert G. Oliver Scholarship Program for children of color, Faculty

Diversity Committee, PTA Diversity Committee; Full Time Diversity Coordinator, Affinity Groups, Mentoring Program for students, S.E.E.D. Program

Homework   Kindergarten: none
1st: none
2nd: 15 minutes of reading nightly
3rd: 45 minutes plus reading (not on weekends)
4th–6th: 1–1½ hours
7th–9th: 2–3 hours
10th–12th: approximately 3 to 4 hours a night

After-School Program   The Dalton Serendipity Program: a variety of creative and recreational activities including computer, foreign language instruction (including French, Spanish, Chinese, and Japanese), newspaper, opera, ballet, cooking, cartooning, sports and games; an additional payment is required; Kids Club: after-school care daily on premises until 5:45 P.M.; Middle School After School Program; an additional payment is required
The Dalton Chess Academy for all age students
Interscholastic athletic competition, clubs and committees for Middle and High School students

Summer Program   Summer camp for Lower School students, open to children from other schools; an additional payment is required

––––––––

Since its founding in 1919 by visionary educator Helen Parkhurst, The Dalton School's mission has been the improvement of education. Dalton is often described as having "one foot in traditional education and one foot firmly planted in the progressive movement." Known for inculcating independence of thought combined with intellectual rigor and for having a plethora of innovative programs with an emphasis on the use of technology to enhance education, The Dalton School serves as a model for other schools around the world and Dalton clones can be found in England, the Netherlands, Australia, the Czech Republic, Chile, China and Japan. Dalton is a famous school well known for its philosophy and is historically rich in people and programs.

The foundation of a Dalton education is still the Dalton Plan which is not as complicated in actuality as it appears in writing. It consists of The House (the home base for each student); The Assignment (the work: a type of contract between student and teacher); the Laboratory (one-to-one or small group sessions between student and teacher that augment classroom work). Dalton is unique in that Lab time is built into each teacher's schedule and students say that teachers are very accommodating and Labs often take place on the same day they are requested. Throughout the First Program and the early years of Middle School, the House Advisor is also the classroom teacher. House groups change each year and are composed of students of the same age until high school. Then there are mixed grade levels in each group and these students remain with the same House Advisor for four years. The role of the House Advisor is to act as an advocate for each child and as the key contact person for parents with the school. The Assignment is a document created by the individual teachers that covers a period of time and details the academic expectations in a unit of study. It is introduced in the First Program (Lower School) and increases both in scope and rigor through Middle and High School.

Getting in: Dr. Elisabeth Krents, a Dalton alumna with a doctorate in Education, is the Director of Admissions for kindergarten through twelfth grade. Parents describe her as "knowledgeable, enthusiastic and warm." She brings a welcome professionalism to the process. Parents interested in learning more about the school can attend spring tours conducted by Elisabeth Krents and/or the admissions staff, or attend open houses at both the First Program and middle and high school in the fall before applying. Dalton takes a close look at parents to make sure they have a clear understanding of the school's philosophy and to assess their values. For First Program applicants, Dalton requires both a parent tour and a meeting with Elisabeth Krents or another senior admissions staff member. Children are either interviewed at Dalton in small groups or observed in their nursery schools. Letters of recommendation from those who really know the applicant are optional. Don't waste time with letters from every celebrity or politician you ever met unless they really know your family or your child. This is true of admission to Middle and High School too.

In the two upper divisions, Dalton is looking to admit students who seek an extremely challenging academic environment that also stresses a deep appreciation for the visual and performing arts. Once an application is received, prospective students and their parents are invited for an individual family tour given by a member of the faculty or a senior. The tour is followed by a class visit for the student and a meeting with Eva Rado for the parents. Applicant families get a chance to meet Dalton students, teachers and administrators at each visit.

Beginning with admissions and extending throughout the school, Dalton doesn't merely pay lip service to all kinds of diversity. The school prides itself on its inclusiveness providing an afterschool program for children whose parents work, as well as diversity literacy training, parent and student support groups and a superb mentoring program that pairs high school students of color with successful professionals of color. These high school students, in turn, mentor younger students coming up through the Middle School and in First Program. High school students join with the PA Diversity Committee to organize the First Program, Multicultural Festival featuring, art, food, music and storytelling, A three division PA Diversity Committee exists to deepen the community's understanding of the school's commitment to diversity.

Dalton's recent strategic plan, guiding the school's goals for the next decade emphasizes the need to develop cultural fluency in its students.

What is Dalton looking for? Elisabeth Krents told me "We are trying to get away from the myth that there is a 'Dalton type' of child. We look for all kinds of children. Helen Parkhurst's goal was to have a community of different individuals and to educate every type of child, preparing each for the real world. We want to admit students (and families) who reflect the diversity of the real world and that means geographic, socioeconomic, racial and religious diversity." Parents say that eccentricity and varied ethnicity are valued. The 2009 First Program is composed of about 35% children of color and of children from all over the city. One does not have to be a genius to be accepted to Dalton; a former admissions director told us they look for "the child who is not just a sponge, but who will contribute." Dalton has a policy of preferring, but not automatically admitting, siblings and children of alumni. Dalton will accept an "at risk" child and does mainstream children with moderate disabilities provided they can keep up academically. But, be aware that an assertive child will do best here.

Parents: The school views parents as partners in the education of their children and they are invited to be involved in many different ways: There are committees that focus on ethics, gender, community service, the Book Fair, safety, and children's entertainment. Ongoing parent dialogues are conducted at the First Program. Kindergarten to grade 12 parents are invited to "Rap Sessions," meetings for parents and administrators to discuss developmental and social issues.

Dalton's glamorous, materialistic image of the 1980's is no longer as accurate. In the past, students had been labeled "spoiled." Years ago a student described the problem as particularly acute in Middle

School "where students are not as considerate of one another as they could be" but this has changed somewhat over the years. Values education is at the top of the school's agenda. The school works hard to embed Service Learning Projects K through 12 as well as to include conversations about ethical issues in classes with their teachers (despite novels or other propaganda to the contrary). Neighborhood committees made up of families of all different grades get together during the year for social events, as well as to discuss topics relevant to their community.

Dalton parents have created an extensive internship program for students. Opportunities include working as an intern in the sciences, arts, publishing and politics. Recently, a Dalton student researched patterns behind information in the brain, which led to his becoming a semi-finalist in the Intel Science Talent Search.

Dalton parents are generous in their financial support of the school. A capital campaign funded major improvements in the school's facilities. A 32,000 square foot Physical Education Center was constructed at 200 East 87th Street with a spectator gym (the basketball team is a strong draw) and other amenities. A floor was added to the top of the 89th Street building that houses a visual arts center with seven skill studios. An 8,000 square foot science center was built increasing the space allocated to the science program by 25%. Recent renovations include updating the Martin Theater as well as construction of the state-of-the-art Performing Arts Center which augments the other arts facilities.

Program: First Program (affectionately known as Little Dalton) consists of kindergarten through third grade. It is housed in three interconnected townhouses on East 91st Street. Recent renovations added 2,000 square feet of instructional space to the school which includes a science center plus a spacious commons area used by all the grades. The children still find Little Dalton "cozy" and move about the building freely.

Ellen Stein, a Dalton alumna, and former vice principal at Friends Seminary, was the Director of the First Program for six years and is now Head of School, after serving for two years as Associate Head of School. Parents speak highly of her commitment to ethics and the establishment of a strong sense of community in the school. "While Dalton is noted for its individualization, we also want to develop children's senses of their responsibility as members of the school and to the community at large." Janet Shaw, a gifted administrator and well-respected educator, is the Director of the First Program.

After Ms. Shaw's arrival parents noted that the First Program tightened the kindergarten through third grade curriculum to create a more even balance between rigorous skills and "process learning."

Academics are approached in a structured but relaxed setting. In kindergarten the school becomes acquainted with a child's learning style. Instruction is individualized, some parents say "to a fault." While the day is highly organized, children are encouraged to proceed at their own pace within the context of curricular goals for the year that are consistent across the grade levels. "The children learn how to think, how to take risks and how to make mistakes," according to a parent. Children are not expected to read by the end of kindergarten but if they do, individualized work is planned for them. Careful attention is paid to the placement of each student with the right teacher and right class.

From the very beginning of the learning process at Dalton, young students are actively and creatively involved in what they study. Dalton is historically known for its strength in the arts which are integrated into the curriculum. Dalton's First Program is based upon a social studies "core" where language arts, math, science, music and art are directly related to the core study. Second graders focus on New York City. The children create a model city which reflects what they have learned about city needs and urban design. They write and revise written reports about landmark buildings on the computer. In music classes the children put their own city poems into song and in art they paint murals of city scenes. In science class while studying animals, specifically birds, they dissected owl pellets classifying the excreted bones and formed hypotheses about what type of prey the owl had consumed. In addition, second graders created their own multi-media magazine on the theme of "diversity in the city." One class photographed neighborhoods, buildings and faces, another class focused on jobs and workers, interviewing parents in their workplaces and analyzing the data they collected, creating graphs (and posting data on the Internet). Another class concentrated on schools, foods and neighborhoods.

Former art teacher Sheila Lamb, a Dalton institution and "Artist in Residence," has guided the creative work of First Program students for over thirty years. Every child is treated like an artist. The approach at Dalton is to be with the children with their imaginations and nurturers of their visual language. First Program art integrates all forms of arts and crafts. Creativity carries over to other students as well. Examples of this include third grade students grinding lapis and malachite to paint their own illuminated manuscripts as they study the Middle Ages in social studies. Other third graders try on costumes borrowed from the Costume Institue at the Metropolitian Museum of Art as part of the research to determine how the clothing British colonists wore might have contributed to the failure of the Jamestown colony. Second graders learn about geometry after studying the work of Frank Lloyd Wright, and calculate the area of his home using blueprints. Dalton remains innovative in its commitment (both financial and philosophical) to technology and education and in many ways, physical classroom boundries can seem to no longer even exist at the school. Under its new lab for teaching technology, faculty have designed projects and curricula that use advanced multimedia technology. Online management systems are utilized and all Dalton Assignments at the Middle School and High School are posted. According to a former headmaster, technology does not replace traditional educational methods: "It allows us to deliver the Dalton Plan more powerfully than ever and is consistent with Dalton's individualized approach, sense of community and mission to prepare students for life after Dalton. Technology shifts education from adults giving answers to students seeking answers to their own meaningful questions." However, with respect to the high level, competitive and intellectual expectations, not all students thrive here and extensive private tutoring can be necessary.

Walking through the halls one can see kindergarten children making their own interactive counting slide shows. First graders are blogging with children from England and India as the Dalton students and those from abroad review American, British and Indian books, discussing and coming to an understanding of different cultures. Fourth grade students post written work and have Newbury authors respond to their blogs.Sixth grade students can be observed being introduced to history and scientific principles through simulated excavations of Assyria and Greece. High school students participate in advanced astronomy simulation, and English students explore the ideas of Shakespeare's *Macbeth* through online resources, including digitized versions of scenes from the play by three different repertory companies.

Specialists enrich the Dalton experience. It's a school with an Archeologist in Residence who spends six weeks with each third grade class excavating a dig set up in the backyard. Children also sing with a Composer in Residence who writes lyrics and music tied into some of the curriculum topics they are studing. Sixth graders participate in the Archaeotype program, "a computer-based, integrated curriculum unit" developed by Dalton faculty in which they examine artifacts from ancient Greece and Assyria, conduct their own research and discuss their findings. It is also the only school in the city to have special lecturers who teaches Dalton classes at the American Museum of Natural History. Chess is taught in kindergartners through second grader by an experienced chess master.

There is roof time for the younger children to stretch their limbs as well as their minds here. In addition to daily play on the two play roofs and at the gym several times a week, beginning in second grade students use Dalton's impressive Physical Education Center located on East 87th Street. Children are bussed to and from the center.

At the end of third grade the children at Little Dalton pass through the arch during the traditional Arch Day Ceremony in June and move on to Big Dalton. Before they do, each makes his or her own colorful ceramic tile that is permanently mounted in a hallway of Little Dalton. The transition to Big Dalton seems to be an easy one since the children have frequently visited "Buddy Houses" and attended a variety of events at the ivy-covered 89th Street building.

In Middle School, fourth and fifth graders are taught in self-contained classrooms in which the House Advisor teaches most subjects. Departmentalization begins in sixth grade and all students in sixth through eighth grades are taught math, social studies and English by a core group of three teachers who work together. The core groups make Big Dalton seem small and provide a comfortable transition to the more demanding high school. Each core teacher is an advisor and each student has a sense of belonging to a particular core. Students are placed in different core and House groups every year. Individual differences in levels or skills are recognized by grouping within the classroom, by the individualized assignments and by the enrichment and support provided in the classes and in Labs.

Student life at Dalton's high school is informal. There are no bells and the dress code is relaxed. "There's a small grunge element," said a student. Starting in late spring ninth grade students can sign out and leave school during a Lab period. Students who serve as peer leaders or peer tutors are involved with faculty in programs for incoming freshmen. A parent told us, "They do a superb job to ensure that the transition is smooth."

There is no Dalton "type" per se; there are jocks and artists and techies, and cliques form around interests. There is a strong drama group, a newspaper group, and athletic teams. Dalton students embrace technology and communicate through Forum, an active e-mail message system. Amusing top ten lists are popular; students also discuss community and current events online. With a focus on ethics in place, students pay more attention to how they treat one another, including keeping the cafeteria clean.

Service Learning is one avenue for teaching ethics and values and it is integrated into the curriculum at every grade level. Service Learning projects occur throughout the year: making bread for a homeless shelter to distribute, or First Program parents and children getting together to decorate bags for the God's Love We Deliver Program for homebound patients with AIDS.

Third grade students founded the Human Rights Club whose mission is to acknowledge and support human rights both locally and globally. Over thirty third graders as well as Middle Schoolers and those in high school are interested in being socially active and creating positive change For example, a former Dalton student, a son of a Kenyan activist who was a member of Parliament, maintains close contact with Club members about serious economic and environmental problems in Kenya. The club is raising tuition money for Kenyan children so they may continue their education beyond elementary school. Children become actively involved in current global challenges such as sustainability and the issue of Fair Trade practices.

In the high school, Service Learning is required and viewed as an opportunity for students to learn through interaction with the world beyond the school. One of the longest standing among the city's private schools, the service program encourages students to assume an active civic role. Students must complete four projects during their high school years, each being a sustained, meaningful commitment to one agency or cause that provides a valuable service to those in need. Dalton's recent strategic plan, guiding school goals for the next ten years, emphasizes the need to develop cultural fluency in its students. Students work with such agencies as the Youth Service Opportunity Projects, the East Harlem Tutoring Program, where children are tutored both in and outside of school, the Burden Center for the Aging, and Public Color, where students paint public schools and community centers.

The Dalton Lab for Global Citizenship provides the launching pad for numerous initiatives. These include a two-week trip for language immersion in Beijing, a student exchange and faculty collaboration as well as service learning at Raffles Junior College in Singapore, an online course and exchange with high school students in The Hague, and alliances with schools in India, Turkey, Spain, France and

Argentina. Additionally, Dalton sponsors service learning trips to Mexico and Costa Rica.

Dalton students are politically savvy. During the war in Iraq, they held town meetings, and during the presidential election, students had an electoral college discussion and expressed their views through political videos, radio ads and cartoons. Dalton students do not shy away from open and difficult discussions concerning race and gender. There are diversity groups such as: DAALAS (Dalton Alliance of African-American, Asian and Latino Students) and the more inclusive group, Another Perspective, which includes students of all backgrounds and ethnicities. A discussion might be sponsored by Another Perspective, GLASS (gay, lesbian, and straight students) or Gender Issues or Human Rights or by the Exploration Committee and speakers are invited to address the students in groups both large and small. Environmental issues are important to the community and a seminar on sustainability was recently conducted. Student government instituted a recycling program and convinced the cafeteria to stop using styrofoam products.

In general, teachers are addressed formally (Mr. Smith, Mrs. Brown) but it depends on the teacher. Students describe the staff as "relaxed, intense, knowledgeable." And because of Lab time, students have the opportunity to develop close relationships with their teachers. Dalton nurtures its faculty providing some of the highest salary and fringe benefit programs offered by the independent schools. The school takes special pride in recruiting and retaining a talented, caring and charismatic faculty. Faculty are encouraged to take advantage of sabbaticals, travel grants, workshops and funded summer curriculum grants. Among members of the high school faculty are published historians, philosophers, writers and artists. They can be characterized as committed to creating a classroom environment that challenges students to pose compelling questions and to analyze and interpret texts and data. In addition, during Lab, when students work one on one with faculty, the faculty validates students' academic work and their creativity in a tutorial mode. Students emerge as independent and confident thinkers.

Dalton's requirements and course offerings in the high school seem quite traditional in scope. Freshmen, sophomores and juniors have to take at least five major courses. Core courses are English, history, languages, math and science. Students take elective courses as juniors and seniors. A junior can choose among five different courses in American literature, each with a different focus and reading list. A

217

senior can choose among such humanities courses as "Asian Literature: East Meets West" and "Postmodern America," or "All the News That's Fit: The Press and the Public Interest." AP courses were recently eliminated in favor of enriched courses created by Dalton's faculty that provide students with in-depth study of all subject areas in a creative and analytical way so students can take, and do well on, AP exams and learn more.

Personal exploration is also provided in Lab throughout the students' years and particularly in the high school as students become increasingly independent learners. "It's not an easy school to go to," said a junior, "because you can't squander your free time—you do have to go to Lab." The Assignment might be a month-long project; for instance, students studying the pre-Civil War years might write a newspaper typical of the period.

In keeping with the emphasis on creative expression and intellectual pursuit, many students elect to produce senior projects in which they demonstrate their abilities to work as visual and performing artists, historians, scientists and writers. Recently, a senior initiative program, promoted through the student government, was established. During the final month of senior year, students focused on scholarly, creative and service learning work and presented their results to an audience of faculty, students and parents.

At Dalton, there is support and encouragement for students seeking their own personal vision in the arts. Whether developing an energetically choreographed piece set to hip hop, studying the complexities of a Schubert Mass, designing an original set for Stephen Sondheim's *Company*, or studying life drawing for three consecutive years, a Dalton student is guided by professional artists who are committed to teaching. One student described his experience this way, "If you're interested in a certain area, you are given a great deal of support and encouragement to pursue it in depth." According to a senior art teacher, "The skylit art center is a place where everyone uses every inch of space for the creation and consideration of art."

Dalton students display an array of musical gifts. There are two orchestras for the Middle and high school, a chamber music ensemble, a percussion ensemble, and a jazz-rock ensemble; and chorus. And all groups perform at the Annual Spring Concert.

While Dalton high school students are serious in their endeavors and ambitions, they also embrace opportunities for poking fun at themselves and the school community. A humor magazine, *Liquid*

Smoke and Phase, a student cabaret replete with spoofs, give the students an avenue for expressions of irreverence.

Dalton's logo shows a child confidently leaving a mother's embrace. After thirteen years of self-discovery and academic adventure, Dalton's graduating seniors sing the words of the school motto: "Here we have learned to go forth unafraid."

Popular College Choices   Brown, Harvard, Cornell, Yale, University of Pennsylvania, Johns Hopkins, Dartmouth, New York University, Wesleyan, Amherst, Williams, Vassar, Oberlin, Kenyon, Hamilton, Emory, Colby, Bard, Barnard, Columbia, Duke, Washington University, University of Wisconsin, Tufts, Boston University, George Washington,

Traditions   Greek Festival, Candlelighting, Arch Day, Dance Theater Workshop Performance, Spring Concert, parent discussion days, annual trips beginning in Little Dalton and throughout Middle School, First Program Multicultural Festival, school street fair on 91st Street, high school prom

Publications   Monthly student newspaper: *The Daltonian*
Literary Magazine: *The Blue Flag*
Middle School Literary Magazine: *The Dalton Paw*
Art, Photography: *Fine Arts Magazine*
Public Affairs Journal: *Macrocosm*
Science publication: *Quantum Leaps*
Ethics publication: *Voices*
Yearbook

Community Service Requirement   Four approved projects during high school

Hangouts   Starbucks, Stargate, The Bagelry, the gym

The Dwight School

291 Central Park West
New York, NY 10024
(212) 724-2146 ext. 1
website: www.dwight.edu
e-mail: admissions@dwight.edu

Nursery Division
Woodside Preschool
Trump Place
140 and 160 Riverside Boulevard
(West 67th Street)
New York, NY 10069
(212) 724-2146 ext 0
e-mail: admissions@woodsidepreschool.org

Coed
Pre-K–12th Grade
Not Accessible

Mr. Stephen H. Spahn, Chancellor
Dr. Blake Spahn, Associate Headmaster
Ms. Chris Allen, Director of Admissions, Preschool
Ms. Alicia Janiak, Head of Admissions, K–12; Kindergarten Dean
Ms. Marina Bernstein, Head of Admissions, K–12
Ms. Alyson Waldman, Director of Admissions,
Grades 6 through 8, Admissions Administrator, grades K-12

Uniform   A uniform is not required for the Woodside Preschool, but polo shirts are encouraged
K–8 boys: khaki or navy tailored trousers, turtleneck, long-sleeved or short-sleeved polo shirt or sweater with Dwight crest.
K–8 girls: tan or navy jumpers, skirts, or trousers, white collared shirts or sweaters with Dwight crest
9–12 boys: collared shirt with tie, solid color polo shirt, or solid color sweater with solid color pants
9–12 girls: collared button-down shirt, solid color polo shirt, or solid color sweater with solid color pants or skirts

Birthday Cutoff   Children entering Preschool must be 2-years-old by September 1st
Children entering Kindergarten must be 5 by September 1st

Enrollment: 700
    Preschool enrollment: 200
    Lower Division (Grades K–5): 140
    Upper Division (Grades 6–12): 360
    Preschool places: 80 K places: 40
    Ninth grade places: 35-40
    Graduating class approximately 75

Grades Trimester system
    In grades Pre-K–5th, parents receive extensive narrative written
    reports; middle and upper school reports also include teacher
    comments in addition to self-reflections Formal letter grades
    begin in 6th grade
    Departmentalization in science, math and foreign languages
    begins in 6th grade
    First final exam is offered in 6th grade

Tuition Range 2009–2010 $11,400 to $33,800, Preschool through
    12th grade
    Additional fees for registration, graduation and support activities
    range from $900 to $1500
    A tuition payment plan is available for families

Financial Aid/Scholarship $1,600,000 in financial aid is available
    13% of students receive some form of financial assistance

Endowment $8 million

Diversity 30% students of color, approximately 40 countries are
    represented in the student body; 20% of the teaching faculty is
    international; the International Baccalaureate (IB) is offered to
    students ages 3 through 18
    English as an Alternate Language (EAL) instruction is available
    Dwight has an expanded language program offering French,
    Latin, German, Spanish, Italian, Japanese, Hebrew and Chinese
    In 2009, Dwight established the first Sino-American program within
    a Provincial school in Beijing; Dwight also helped found a boarding
    program, Dwight International School on Vancouver Island

Homework K: 15–20 minutes
    1st and 2nd: ½ hour

3rd and 4th: 45 minutes
5th and 6th: 1 hour
7th and 8th: 1½–2 hours 9th–12th: 2–3 hours

After-School Program Parents should check to see if one of Dwight's After-School Programs is open to students from other schools

Grades Pre-K–6: Spanish, creative and recreational activities for an additional fee

Grades 7–12: there are approximately 40 clubs and activities including, Model UN, student council, The Green Team, Peer leaders, Honor Council, Young Writers Society, Jazz band, Photography, Mock Trails, Drama, Music, Studio Art, Science Club, Boxing, Workouts, Dance, Yoga, SAT Prep; Middle School offers junior varsity sports including, fencing, soccer, tennis, golf, lacrosse, volleyball, basketball, track, baseball, and cross country

Summer Program Woodside Summer Camp runs from mid-June through mid-July. The Dwight School Summer School Program is designed for students who seek to accelerate in a specific subject or require work on study skills; the program begins in mid-June. Additionally, The Dwight school runs summer leadership trips. In recent years, students have traveled to Arizona, Peru, Australia, India, Sudan, China, Tanzania, and Saudi Arabia to build houses, schools, and work on environmental projects; the new Dwight facility on Vancouver Island, Canada offers further environmental studies in the densest rain forest in the world

---

The Dwight School was founded in 1872 as an academy of classical studies, became coed in 1967 and added a London campus, The North London International School, in 1972. The Woodside Preschool campus was opened in 2005. Dwight merged with the Anglo-American International School in 1993 and offers three International Baccalaureate (IB) programs. The Spahn family has had a long association with both schools. Stephen Spahn, the chancellor of The Dwight School, attended Anglo-American and his father headed that school for more than thirty years. The Dwight School retains its identity as "a small traditional school" while adding the international elements of the Anglo-American School following the International

Baccalaureate Curriculum from pre-kindergarten through twelfth grade. The Dwight School also offers a fully mainstreamed program for children with mild learning differences called the Quest program.

The Dwight campus occupies four buildings: a five story building on 89th Street, two joined brownstones on 88th Street, a facility on Central Park West, and the Preschool through Kindergarten division on Riverside Boulevard. In addition to classrooms, these buildings contain a photography darkroom, two computer centers, a theater space, art room, and four gymnasiums. The new nursery school has 10 large classrooms, two indoor play areas and an outdoor recreation area. The school has recently added a new library and student center, additional technology space, and new science labs. A new recreational rooftop allows for science, art, and other outdoor activities. The school has also acquired the adjoining brownstone to the main building and plans to add 10,000 square feet of new space. A new 3,000 square foot kindergarten center will open in September 2009.

With students and faculty from over forty nations, the school has a unique social as well as academic environment. Internationalism has been a natural part of the curriculum for many years. Students learn that there are many ways to celebrate and observe holidays. One of the highlights of the primary school is the annual holiday show. Each grade selects a country (often the country of origin of a classmate) and celebrates the country's most important holiday. Middle and Upper School students attend and some are involved in production and musical elements.

The Dwight School is one of the few New York area schools to offer the International Baccalaureate diploma. As described in the school's brochure, "eleventh grade students may enroll in this challenging curriculum in six subjects requiring solid academic skills and the ability to think clearly and communicate effectively. The IB curriculum is a deliberate compromise between the specialization required in some national systems and the breadth preferred in others." Foreign students planning to return to their countries of origin are often required to have passed the "bac." The IB program is acknowledged as an excellent preparation for the more competitive U.S. colleges and can often represent a year's college credit.

Perhaps the most intriguing innovation is the school's creation of a non-profit organization based at Dwight, The Institute for Civic Leadership (ICL). The goal of ICL is to encourage civic action and greater cross-cultural awareness among teens from public, private and parochial schools. The school has successfully run the "Dare to Dream" conferences each year, inspiring hundreds of high school students to reach out and participate in meaningful service projects.

Presently, the ICL has expanded its program and works with student leaders from forty other schools. During the summer, ICL sponsors school building programs in Costa Rica, Kenya and India.

The school believes that everyone has the capacity to excel at some endeavor. The inquiry-based curriculum that Dwight has used in the Lower and Middle Schools for over twenty years, relates to Dr. Howard Gardner's theories of "Multiple Intelligence." (See Glossary *supra*, pp. 56 and 57). The Dwight School appreciates the differences in students' learning styles and interests.

In addition, the low student/teacher ratio of 12 to 1 allows for small classes and individual attention. Faculty create many of the imaginative programs that prepare students to think critically while demonstrating common sense, the ability to work with others and manage time, people and information.

"Any child can succeed with a properly designed program," attests Mr. Spahn. "We can take virtually any college preparatory youngster, motivate him, provide positive reinforcement and transform him into a serious and enthusiastic learner." There is constant communication between the school and the families. Mr. Spahn really means it when he says, "We welcome input from parents. We have an open door policy." Parents say the warm, dedicated faculty come in early and leave late—new challenges are there when needed. Student progress is monitored through standardized tests including the SATs. Grades are given on most work in the upper houses (grades). Parents meet with teachers two times a year, and in individual conferences when requested.

By focusing on a student's strengths, transfers to Dwight get better grades, and acquire improved self-esteem and develop their talents. A student who transferred into Dwight from Dalton said, "At Dwight teachers and peers give you lots of attention; everybody knows your name. Dwight has a traditional curriculum. They don't offer as many courses, but there is more structure." One mother said her daughter went from "just keeping up" at her old school to "doing very well at Dwight." The amount of homework was the same, about two to three hours, but she made honor roll. "She got so much out of it," says her mother, "real values and friendships." One parent whose child had a vision problem said it was handled so that her child never felt bad about herself.

Getting in: The Dwight School and Woodside Preschool offer Evening Open Houses in the fall. Parents and students have an opportunity to meet faculty and learn about the school. Once an application is filed the admission's staff arranges an interview and tour and the child's current transcripts, standardized test scores, teacher recommendations are requested. Parents say the setting is relaxed, friendly and professional. Applicants for grades 1 through 12 have a one-on-one interview. Applicants for Preschool and Kindergarten visit in groups.

Program: Dwight is described as "a family school" with many siblings in attendance. The preschool program utilizes the Primary Years Program (PYP) of the International Baccalaurate as well as other creative and developmentally appropriate early childhood methods from around the world. Spanish is taught to all children ages 2 to 4. The Lower School is small; all of the primary schoolchildren know each other and the teachers. However, the teachers are addressed formally as "Mr. Jones" or "Miss Smith." In the after-school clubs a first grader can get to know a fourth grader. Because reading and math are taught on an individual basis, a child can advance at his or her own pace.

Perhaps the most distinctive feature of The Dwight School, in the words of a student, is that "there is no norm here." The student body is composed of children from diverse cultural, religious and geographic backgrounds. There is also a broad spectrum of academic ability at Dwight: a talented and superior group of international students who take advantage of a well-arranged EAL (English as an Alternate Language) program and the opportunity to take the rigorous International Baccalaureate; average students taking the program, all of whom show significant improvement because of the baccalaureate's flexibility; and students with mild learning difficulties who are taking regular college prep with the support of the Quest program. There is a positive emphasis on differences. But all see themselves as part of the school.

The Quest program was started in 1976 to provide high ability children with additional support, structure and skill-building so that they could participate in a challenging college preparatory curriculum. All Dwight students are expected to develop a solid foundation of basic skills but the teachers at Dwight understand that children learn differently. Quest teachers provide extra support outside and within the classroom allowing students to be part of the group. The Dwight School reserves a limited number of places per grade for the Quest program and parents must pay an additional fee for Quest program specialists. A parent said, "The teacher-student relationships are very personal and caring. The individuality of the students is stressed."

Parents say that the program instills confidence: "My child thinks that he's a good learner now," said one parent. Parents also says that the program instills confidence, reports are elaborate and informative, (include over thirty categories). Parents also learn the results of special testing in speech, reading and hearing.

The Quest program can serve students with mixed abilities; for instance, one student who is in the Quest program for science takes the International Baccalaureate course in history. Quest teachers also provide enrichment in English during the schoolday. Foreign students taking English as a second language often need assistance in certain subject areas.

The Timothy House students (grades K–5) play in Central Park or the gym every day. Reading is taught using an individualized eclectic approach. The philosophy of the lower school, along with the Primary Years program (PYP) of the International Baccalaurate curriculum fosters a blending of challenging approaches and traditional methods. A combination of literature, phonetics and basal readers is used through third grade. First graders use invented spelling but the work I saw on display was corrected. Spanish and Chinese language instruction begins in kindergarten. Small daily reading groups are designed to explicitly improve reading comprehension, decoding, and encoding skills. Students also participate in "Writer's Workshop." Writing is integrated into all areas of the curriculum: The study of math incorporates traditional numeracy, mental math, and mastery of applications of probability, statics, spreadsheet analysis, graphing and problem solving skills. In addition to science and social studies reports, daily diaries are kept. Timothy House provides for the study of other foreign languages; technology is used as a learning tool.

Lower School students participate in library, art, music, drama, and dance classes. Physical education classes stress teamwork, coordination and sports around the world. Aditionally, Lower School students visit the American Museum of Natural History, the Bronx Zoo, Liberty Science Center New York Hall of Science, The Metropolitan Museum of Art, The Children's Museum, MOMA and Ellis Island. Students in the last year of PYP or 5th grade, venture out on an exchange program with Dwight's sister school in London, North London International School.

Dwight's Middle and Upper Schools are divided into three houses. Each house has its own Dean. The first class period is a House Community or Advisory meeting. Dwight's continuing IB program challenges students through their Middle and Upper School years connecting critical and reflective thinking to what's going on in the real world.

Bentley House is composed of grades six through eight. Average class size is fifteen to eighteen students. Students are offered a mixture of a structured curriculum with challenging group and individualized interdisciplinary skills. Dwight's teacher's continue to inspire students. Study skills are taught in all grades. Students learn how to prepare for tests and quizzes. (Spahn says that when handwriting is a problem, the student can write on a computer and the ideas flow.)

Weekly advisory groups address issues in a smaller setting. Bentley House students study English, social studies, arts, foreign languages, math, sciences, technology, health, and physical education. English classes focus on writing, grammar, and reading. Students take supplemental writing classes in essay writing, and an additional math class that reinforces numeracy and problem solving. Electives include, chorus, art, photography, drama, community service, journalism, dance, Latin, jazz, chamber music, and student government.

Franklin House is composed of grades nine and ten, and Anglo-House, grades 11 and 12. The Upper School delivers a core curriculum of academic interdisciplinary subjects plus community service, social education, goal-setting and environmental awareness. All students learn to use technology for online research, collaboration and learning. The school is vibrant; walking around the halls you hear students and teachers in discussion on topics of environmental, political and economic concern. Teachers challenge their students to think outside the box. All 10th graders prepare a Personal Project, under supervision, but on any topic of their choice. Approximately four-fifths of the junior and senior class takes the full IB Diploma Program, which provides in most cases, provides for college credit. Students also have the option to participate in film, theater, art, music, photography, digital media, computer programming, and design technology classes.

The Dwight Athletic Department focuses on how to live a healthy and happy life through exercise and competition. Attitudes, sportsmanship, and mental skills are stressed. Dwight's athletic program has produced elite athletes in tennis, basketball, fencing, judo, sailing, swimming, squash, and ice skating. Recent championships have been claimed in soccer, basketball, baseball, tennis, volleyball, and track. In 2008-2009 the boy's junior varsity and varsity basketball teams won the ACIS League and playoff Championships, and the girl's varsity basketball team won the GISAL championship. Students can play on middle school junior varsity or varsity teams. Lacrosse has recently been added to the afterschool program.

Popular College Choices Brown, Columbia, Cornell, Dartmouth, Bowdoin, Boston University, Harvard, George Washington, Princeton, Georgetown, University of Michigan, Northwestern, NYU, Skidmore, Syracuse University

Traditions La Guardia History Research Paper Competition, Art Exhibition, Camerer Essay Writing Contest, Shakespeare Monologue Competition, Doris Post Oratory Competition, Spring Benefit and Auction, assemblies with guest speakers, Spirit Day, Model U.N., Spring Arts Festival, Head Boys and Girls, Honor Council, Green team

Publications Yearbook
Dwight School newspaper: Dwight Chronicle
Alumni magazine: Dwight Today

Community Service Requirement All students in grades Kindergarten through 8th are encouraged to engage in meaningful community service and learning activities; Dwight has a community service requirement for all students in grades 9-12 as part of the IB Program; Dwight has won major international awards for building schools in the developing world; students are encouraged to participate in projects that they are passionate about, including those associated with the American Museum of Natural History, Yorkville Common Pantry, UNICEF, New York Cares and various environmental organizations

Hangouts Jackson Hole, Columbus Café, Bella Luna, Pizza Pete's, Starbucks

The Ethical Culture Fieldston School

The Ethical Culture Fieldston School encompasses four divisions: Ethical Culture, Fieldston Lower, Fieldston Middle, and Fieldston Upper School. Each division has its own principal; there is a central Administrative Council, consisting of the head of school, the principals and the heads of centralized administrative offices.

Ethical Culture School

**33 Central Park West
(at 63rd Street)
New York, NY 10023
(212) 712-6220 (main number)
(718) 329-7575 (admissions)
fax (212) 712-8441
main website: www.ecfs.org**

Fieldston Lower School

**Fieldston Road
Bronx, NY 10471
(718) 329-7310 (main number)
(718) 329-7313 (admissions)
fax (718) 329-7337**

Fieldston Middle and Upper School

**Fieldston Road
Bronx, NY 10471
(718) 329-7300 (main number)
(718) 329-7575 (central admissions number)
fax (718) 329-7337 (Fieldston Lower and Ethical Culture
admissions)
fax (718) 329-7302 (Fieldston Middle and Upper admissions)**

Coed
Pre-kindergarten–12th Grade

Elevator at Ethical Culture
Fieldston Lower and Fieldston Middle and Upper, partially accessible

Joyce Gregory Evans, Interim Head of School
Taisha M. Thompson, Director for Enrollment Management and
Financial Aid
Elka Rifkin, Principal Ethical Culture
Ms. Jocelyn Gooding-Smith, Admissions Ethical Culture
Mr. George Burns, Principal Fieldston Lower
Ms. Rita McRedmond, Admissions Fieldston Lower School
Dr. John Love, Principal Fieldston Upper School
Dr. Luis Ottley, Principal Fieldston Middle School
Carson Roy, Admissions Fieldston Middle and Upper School

Birthday Cutoff   Children entering pre-kindergarten must be 4-years-old before September 1st
Children entering kindergarten must be 5-years-old by September 1st

Enrollment   Combined enrollment: 1686
Total enrollment Ethical Culture: 448
Total enrollment Fieldston Lower: 273
Total enrollment Fieldston Middle: 388
Total enrollment Fieldston Upper: 577
PreK places at Ethical Culutre: 36
PreK places at Fieldston Lower: 18
Kindergarten places: approximately 36 at Ethical Culture and 18 at Fieldston Lower
Middle 6th grade place: 25
Fieldston Upper 9th grade places: 35
Size of graduating class: approximately 135

Grades   Semester system
Scheduled parent-teacher conferences pre-kindergarten through Form VI (12th grade)
Kindergarten–6: detailed anecdotal reports and checklists of skills
Letter grades begin in Form I (7th grade)
Forms I-VI (Grades 7–12): letter grades with teacher's comments; no final exams in Form III (9th grade), limited final exams given in Forms IV-VI (Grades 10 through 12)

Tuition Range 2009–2010 $34,045 pre-kindergarten through grade 3; $32,195 for grades 4 and 5; lower school students are provide with books, supplies, and lunch; $34,045 Middle and Upper school (grades 6 through 12), additional fees for books, supplies, and other course-related expenses are approximately $500 to $800; lunch and the yearbook are included

Financial Aid/Scholarship The Ethical Culture Fieldston School has one of the largest financial assistance programs of any independent day school in the country. $8.6 million was granted in 2009–2010
22% of the students school-wide receive some form of financial aid
Monthly payment plan with no interest charges available to all enrolled families

Endowment $44 million

Diversity 23% students of color throughout ECFS
Approximately 20-25 Prep for Prep students are enrolled at Fieldston
Fieldston enrolls students from the Early Steps, Albert G. Oliver, and A Better Chance, and Pan Asian Alliance programs among others
Multicultural Committee for parents and faculty at all campuses, student clubs include: S.U.M.E. (Students United for Multicultural Efforts), Asian Alliance, Diaspora, Gay/Straight Alliance, Interfaith, Social Justice Club, Gender Studies, Roundtable, Model United Nations and World Awareness Club

Homework Kindergarten and 1st: no homework
2nd: varies from 10 minutes to 1½ hours and 15 to 30 minutes reading
3rd and 4th: varies from 15 minutes–one hour plus additional 1½ hour of reading each night
5th, 6th: 1–2 hours
7th and 8th: no more than 3 hours
9th–12th: 2-3 hours a night

After-School Program At ECS and Fieldston Lower: after-school program for pre-kindergarten–5th with some mixed-age groups;

selections include sports, dance, music, martial arts, shop, cooking, drama, arts and chess (for fun) for an additional payment; classes meet from 3:30–5 P.M., Monday through Thursday; Friday after-school programs begin and end earlier; drop off and extended hours options at EC and Fieldston Lower; "Good Deeds Bandits" for Grades 1–2, and "Cookies and Dreams," for Grades 3–5 at EC introduce children to community service; Before School Music at EC is small group instruction in instrumental music for Grades 4–5 6th, 7th and 8th: intramural sports, extracurricular clubs, Middle School newspaper and musical
9th–12th: interscholastic sports, extracurricular clubs, newspapers, literary magazines and yearbook, two theatrical productions, jazz, chorus, and orchestra and several student-written and produced plays

Summer Program   Weeks of Discovery: at EC, winter vacation and June Weeks: a variety of creative and recreational activities, pre-K–3, are offered for an additional payment
Media Arts Camp: a June weeks program at Ethical Culture: Lego building programming and web design and animation are offered for Grades 3–8, for an additional payment
Weeks of Adventure: a June weeks program at Ethical Culture, for an additional payment; Fieldston Sports Camp at Riverdale campus; all sports/learn to swim program for Kindergarten–6th grade, for an additional payment; Fieldston Outdoors Camp: for ages 5-12, at Riverdale Campus full activities including swim instruction; focus on nature, environment and Hudson River region; trips; head counselors are experienced teachers, an additional payment is required; Fieldston Enrichment Program (FEP): A four-week program on the Fieldston campus for public school students in grades 7–8, beginning in July, offering rigorous academic classes and team-centered recreational activities; field trips, students who complete the program are invited back for school year Saturday sessions
Young Dancemakers Company: a tuition-free project for public high school students, performances are open to the public and the schedule is posted on the school website

The Ethical Culture Fieldston School was started in 1878 by Felix Adler, the founder of the Society for Ethical Culture. The school was tuition free only until 1890, but continues to follow many aspects of Adler's original vision of active learning. The school has always been diverse ethnically, racially, and financially. In ECFS's recent strategic plan, the school restated its commitment to the original mission of the school: to ethical education as a foundation, to diversity in all its manifest aspects, and to being a "beacon for progressive education." A recent capital campaign has added a spectacular, completely green, new Middle School building, a collegiate-level athletic complex, a various other significant upgrades to the school's vast facilities. In 1994–1995 an agreement was reached separating the schools from the Society, but ECFS continues to offer nonsectarian ethical training beginning in second grade. ECFS backs up its values with financial support and personal commitment. The school gives out more financial aid than most other independent day schools in the country.

Today many schools boast about "educating the whole child"; it is in vogue to have a child-centered curriculum. The Ethical Culture Fieldston School has been doing this from its inception, and is way out front in developing an integrated curriculum that emphasizes experiential learning. Children are active participants in their education here.

Getting in: Don't be intimidated by the imposing turn-of-the-century stone edifice on Central Park West; Ethical Culture (EC) is a warm and friendly place. One parent described the admissions process at ECS as "humane." All applicant families go to Fieldston for interviews; Ethical Culture schedules tour dates for parents of applicants for pre-kindergarten and kindergarten. Applicants for grades other than pre-k and kindergarten meet with an administrator at Ethical. Two model classrooms are designated for groups of up to six children to be observed and interviewed. There are two interviewers who are part of an admissions team composed of experts in early childhood education and teachers. Extensive reports are written about each child, roughly 1-2 page narratives and a 2-page checklist. There is a $60 application fee.

Parents must apply before scheduling their parent tour and separate playgroup interview for their child. The interviewer asks, "Who's ready to come and play?" "Whose name begins with A?" and so on. After some leg hanging, all the children go off to play while the parents tour, (typically in groups of about 12 parents), the Middle and Upper schools and ask questions of the admissions personnel and/or parent guides.

What are they looking for in a candidate? A child who feels good about him/herself, who is enthusiastic, who enjoys being part of a group (there's an emphasis on collaborative learning). The child should enjoy his visit. The admissions staff really looks at all the measures of a child to make sure they have an accurate picture of each applicant. After admissions decisions have been made, the wait list is active. There is no typical student, but one parent said the children are "bright, and laid-back yet outgoing."

Parents: The parents are "a low-key mix" of West and East Side professionals, artists and media people, very few celebrities, but most lack "the pretentiousness you find at other schools," parents say. There is an acknowledged association between Ethical Culture, liberal thinking and progressive education.

There are many opportunities to socialize, and interesting lectures and discussion groups are offered for parents on child-related, topics such as learning styles and parenting issues. Class dinners are potluck, usually held at the school. Social competition is minimized and celebrity parents (there are a few) enjoy their anonymity. Parents get involved in the school in the early years and stay involved. Parent volunteers help with awards dinners, book sales and weekly lower school bulletins, for instance. Here, you can have lunch with your child (K–2). School events include plays. concerts, picnics in the park, carnivals and auctions. Birthday parties run the gamut.

Program: An awareness of ethics is implicit from the moment children begin their Ethical Culture Fieldston education. Formal ethics instruction begins in second grade with community responsibility and decision-making. The emphasis is on ethics in action. The million-penny drive began as a math exercise at Fieldston Lower, then quickly expanded to include participation in the yearly Penny Harvest. Community service is part of the ECFS experience, from fifth grade editors assisting first grade authors to Fieldston high school students giving a party for a local community center.

One parent described her daughter's move from nursery school to Ethical as a "warm to warm transition." Pre-kindergarten and kindergarten separation is handled gradually; parents can stay for the first week if necessary. There is a staggered schedule. Under the guidance of two full-time teachers, children often work on group projects. For instance, the kindergarten creates a school-wide post office each year, complete with student designed stamps and mailboxes, with daily pick up and delivery of internal mail.

In kindergarten, children begin going out to specialists in half groups but are not fully departmentalized until sixth grade. Most "specials" (library, movement, music, computer, science, social studies, workshop and so on) are taught by the specialist in half classes. The other half of the class either attends another special class or remains in the classroom, allowing the core teacher to work with small groups in math and writing.

Parents say there's a new emphasis on building a collaborative approach between child/faculty and parents, as well as a greater openness at EC. The most noticeable change is improved articulation of the curriculum through the grades. The emphasis is still on full mastery and competence with awareness that children work at different paces. "The focus is still on what's developmentally appropriate," with much "horizontal enrichment."

During the elementary years, students learn how to gather, organize, analyze, evaluate and communicate information. The work load increases appropriately as children are guided toward internalizing the learning process and becoming independent learners.

Ethical Culture has resisted pressure from high-powered parents to "hurry" the curriculum. Departmentalization doesn't begin until fifth grade, and no final exam is given until tenth grade. (Most schools start these in seventh grade.) Parents say, "Children at Ethical Culture develop a positive attitude about learning, which prepares them for the academically demanding high school." Proof that children with different learning styles can find success here is that more than 95 percent go on to the Fieldston School, which is considered a "very selective" high school. It is one of the three "hill" schools (along with Riverdale Country School and Horace Mann School) located in Riverdale, New York, just north of the city proper—a twenty-minute drive that might take forty-five minutes at some hours.

Every activity in the Lower School is coed. No basal textbooks are used in the first years. Homework is given in appropriate amounts, not as busywork or evidence of academic rigor. Some parents, who grew up in schools that stressed rote memorization and drill, are a little perplexed by these methods and a commonly voiced concern is, "Is my child learning enough?" They can be reassured that in addition to early childhood readiness assessments, teachers' own assessments throughout the grades drive their instruction.

While there is a definite curriculum for each grade, Ethical's developmental approach to learning anticipates that not everyone will get to the same place at the same time. Emphasis is placed on conceptual development in tandem with building skills in reading, writing and math." Because the program is responsive to children's needs and interests, it varies from year to year. Most of the children will learn to read in the first grade. From pre-kindergarten on, you see words all over the classroom. There is mixed-ability grouping throughout the school and at various times throughout the week students break into half groups. Ethical Culture and Fieldston Lower each have math specialists who work in the classrooms and coordinate the programs. The math specialists hold workshops for parents throughout the year.

Ethical Culture has three science centers; one is a fully equipped laboratory with sinks, microscopes and computers. Wherever possible, science is hands-on and the scientific process is stressed: collect data, analyze it, construct a hypothesis, test it, reach a conclusion. In one classroom the students were studying the use of earthworms for indoor composting. In grades kindergarten through third, there is a deliberate effort to integrate science into the broader curriculum. Fifth grade students track hurricanes on the computer and work in coordination with the science and shop teacher to make simple machines—robotics. ECFS enhanced the level of technology in the classrooms, establishing common areas for the use of technology, and creating "libraries without walls," i.e., information network accessibility to and from classrooms, homes, major universities, as well as the Library of Congress. There are many Smartboards in every division. Each of the school's divisions has a Technology Integrator to the curriculum. In grades 4 and 5 children are introduced to Ethics of the Computer, logo, use of spreadsheets, databases, word processing, graphics, web pages, and on-line and multimedia presentation tools.

The library at EC is equipped with laptops and a wireless network. Schoolwide, ECF has an extensive network that encompasses libraries, classrooms, and computer labs. A new technology plan is being implemented that will, among other improvements, provide wireless access throughout the campus. The school's website is highly interactive and is an essential conduit of information between the school, its immediate community, and the world outside.

Ethical says it educates the "whole child," bringing out his or her natural creativity and encouraging its expression. The creative arts are considered intellectual disciplines; it follows that the arts at Ethical are strong. Four full-time art and workshop teachers are available at EC; there is an art studio with a pottery center equipped with a kiln. Art is integrated into the curriculum at many points. "Social Studies Workshop," a hands-on program relating to the social studies core, includes woodworking, sewing and cooking.

A hallmark of education at the ECS is an integrated curriculum, with subject areas overlapping in many different ways. Creativity and writing ability are also fostered. These elements combine in dramatic play. As part of the kindergarten curriculum, children learn that people live in communities, including the home, classroom, school, as well as the larger world. They interview people who work in the school about their jobs, from the principal to the head of facilities.

Critical thinking skills are emphasized from early on. A fifth grade class studying Greek myths switched the gender roles—Hercules became a she—and there was much discussion about the implications. There are many ways in which students are asked to examine the underlying assumptions about our culture. A parent told us that when a student brought in a Barbie doll for a model science fiction project the class got into a discussion about cultural artifacts: If Barbie were found by an advanced civilization, what conclusions would be drawn about our civilization?

Ethical has two recently renovated full-size gyms: the sixth-floor gym, which is large enough to be subdivided, and a lower level gym with an overhead track. The gym program stresses individual skills development, games and sportsmanship. Ethical makes use of its location next to Central Park in many ways. The park is used as a laboratory and playing field, and of course, the children get to play in the snow and mark the change of seasons. There are no competitive sports in the Lower School, the goal of athletics is to learn how to get along as a corporative team.

Manhattan parents should note that while Fieldston Lower, a second ECFS elementary division located in Riverdale, primarily serves families from Upper Manhattan, all sections of the Bronx, Northern New Jersey, Riverdale and Westchester, almost 40% of its students travel from Manhattan. Touring parents smell scents of freshly cut wood from the woodshop where Fieldston Lower students enjoy building all kinds of things out of wood until at least fourth grade. Groups of roughly 11 children visit the woodshop at a time; kindergarteners come in groups of four. The lovely campus and outdoor play areas, and the teaching of its "core" curriculum are prominently on display for parents who are interested in this unique program. Daily schedules are posted, following are some examples of the subjects Fieldston Lower uses in constructing the core curriculum. There is an exposure to Spanish throughout the program, and although there is not any formal instruction, groups meet daily. Laptop trolleys along with a Technology Integrator transport laptops to classrooms and work with students to coordinate units with teachers. And, fourth and fifth graders work with two specialists in the math/science room twice to three times each week. First graders become experts in North American bird life. Third graders enact the lives of the Northern Woodland Indians who once inhabited the school's site. Fourth graders study colonization, make furniture and barn structures and take a trip to Harriman State Park, stay overnight at Plymouth Plantation and visit Sturbridge Village for a view of farming. Fifth graders have a medieval fair; one class built a model cathedral and played roles in the social hierarchy of the time. The old cafeteria serves as a student commons, off which is a bridge to the new Middle School.

Like its hilltop competitors, Riverdale Country and Horace Mann, Fieldston has built a new Middle School building, adding new athletic facilities and making renovations that will include more space for the performing arts as well as various other areas.

Two green roofs, easily visible from the old gym, now a new cafeteria, represent much of what Fieldston has built since the last edition of this guide—one building is the school's brand new, bright, LEED-certified green Middle School for students in grades six through eight, the other an incredible, state-of-the-art athletic center. Designed by renowned architect Cooper Robertson, the Middle School's main entrance, a glass tiled wall, is welcoming and defines the new Middle Division. The mixed plants (herbs and perennials) and sedum, on the roof are the product of a "Green Dean" along with a plant ecologist from Columbia University. A model showing the anatomy of a green roof is prominently displayed at the entrance to the roof. Students help with the various plantings on the roof of the Middle School. Excess water from the roof is stored in the basement and used for irrigation throughout the property.

The Middle School curriculum moves students from concrete to abstract ideas through a variety of experiences such as lectures, small group activities, experiential learning, and individual and group classrooms presentations. The Middle School's overarching concept is "the culture of cooperation," which guides the community in its behavior, decision-making, and planning.

The Middle School's academic program helps students develop the skills they need to investigate, research, write, compute, and problem-solve. Visual arts, music, and performing arts are essential components of the program. I saw a slew of sixth graders working on computer-generated Warholesque self-portraits which adorn the halls

238

of the building. Each course is designed around an essential question, and teachers look for natural connections between courses. For example, in eighth grade history, students explore the overriding question, "Whose story is it?" Ethics is taught as a classroom subject. Physical education meets daily. Each grade also has its own Academic Center, dedicated to creating opportunities for students and faculty to work closely together in developing projects, programs and ideas. The Academic Center has faculty offices located off the center affording easy access to students. The Middle School also builds community through a variety of extracurricular activities; there are many Middle School sports teams, student clubs, a middle school newspaper, and a Middle School yearbook, *The Milestone,* which made its debut in 2009, with the theme, "Going Green." Not surprising for students who spend their days in a building with low-flush toilets and waterless urinals.

Fieldston is "a big school that seems small." In good weather, the grassy quad surrounded by fieldstone buildings is full of students. But the "Senior Grass" is not to be trod upon by underclassmen/women. The Tate Library is an award-winning facility (students say it's the best of the three "hill" school libraries) with over 40,000 volumes, an on-line catalog, multiple databases, media center and classrooms. Unique to Fieldston is a state-of-the-art print shop where everything from invitations to personal notepads are printed. In the spirit of founder Felix Adler, who believed in learning by doing, Fieldston is the only school that produces its own school publications from composition to final product. There are no bells, dress is casual and students seem relaxed. Sophomores can leave school grounds during "frees" and lunch. College preparation does not begin in earnest until the second semester of junior year.

Fieldston's course guide is clear, descriptive and informative. The curriculum is broad, with electives that reflect a diversity of interests in the student body. Requirements are similar to those of the other independent high schools: a minimum of five academic courses per semester, with more elective choices as the students progress. Ninth graders have electives in language, arts and science. By junior year students can choose electives in English, math, history, language, science, visual arts, performing arts or computer. Seven year sequences are offered in Chinese, French, Spanish, and Latin, beginning in sixth grade. Conversational Spanish is part of the EC and Fieldston Lower experience. Courses are offered in Modern and Ancient Greek as well as Mandarin Chinese and Spanish for Native Speakers. An ethics course is required each year in Forms I through IV (grades 7–10); juniors and seniors must take a one semester course in ethics. Advanced electives are offered in all disciplines, and are so strong that Fieldston has discontinued the standard AP curriculum, a decision encouraged by colleges, parents, and faculty.

Two programs that typify Fieldston's unique approach to learning are "the summer reading book" and "awareness days." The summer reading book is tied into a theme, such as "global studies," "science and math," or "social justice." In the fall, a student/faculty group plans an entire day of activities related to the book and if possible, the author's visit to the school. Recent books were Kurt Vonnegut's *Slaughterhouse-Five*, Jose Saramago's *Blindness* and Ken Kesey's *One Flew Over the Cuckoo's Nest*.

"Awareness Days" address relevant political or social themes—Presidential elections, or global economics—through a day-long line-up of speakers and workshops.

Although independence is fostered in the high school, support is always available. Fieldston has a well-developed advisory system. Each grade has a dean who stays with them until graduation. A tenth grader said that she could talk to her advisor about anything and that students feel "the administration is on your side." Respect for individual learning styles continues at Fieldston, and the Learning Center helps students with individual learning differences. There are centers for writing, history and math, where English and history teachers and peer instructors are always available. Students can also meet with teachers during free periods. Outside tutors are recommended if necessary but in the words of one student, "Most people don't hire a tutor unless it's a desperate situation." Students say that although a lot is expected of them and they work hard, homework is not oppressive. One student said she has friends who are "drowning in work" at other schools.

Elective choices in English include, "Film and Literature," "Social and Political Issues in Literature," "African-American Literature," "Russian Literature" "Women and Literature" "Dramatic Literature and Theatre" and "Shakespeare." Course offerings change annually.

History in Middle School focuses around an essential question each year. In seventh grade, for example, students explore cultural anthropology and ask: why do societies change? History survey courses in ninth and tenth grades provide a solid footing for later electives, which include: "The U.S. Since 1945," "Modern Architecture,"

"The Middle East," "The History of Technology, and "History of the Working Class."

There is a six-year unified mathematics sequence culminating in an Advanced Calculus course. There are many offerings in computer science.

At Fieldston there is a continued commitment to the artistic development of the students. As at Ethical and Fieldston Lower, the arts at Fieldston are considered an essential part of the curriculum and the offerings are extensive. Sixth graders begin with a visual arts sampler. In tenth, eleventh and twelfth grades a visual arts major is available. Elective offerings include "Ceramics," "Life Drawing" (with live models), "Creating from the Keyboard," "Architecture" and "Photography." Fieldston's Graphic Communications Department, based in its print shop, offers electives and a major for grades 10–12.

Music opportunities abound, from curricular to extracurricular activities, from classical music to jazz; there is an electronic recording studio. Dance at Fieldston is considered a key part of the performing arts program. In addition to modern, jazz and ballet, electives include "Multicultural Dance." There are numerous opportunities to perform: The dance company tours and there is an annual dance concert with student choreography.

Students who like drama can take advantage of a well-developed theatre program. There is a theatre minor or major for juniors and seniors. There are six student-directed shows every year, plus one major drama (an original production one year, and a classic the next), and a musical, (*The Pajama Game* one year). Students can take a course in stagecraft and practice their skills in the Alex Cohen Memorial Theatre. The drama and dance groups tour elementary schools. All sixth graders must study a musical instrument or sing in an ensemble. Small group and ensemble instruction is available.

In addition to arts there is a full athletic program, with 65 different teams. The fabulous new athletic center boats a collegiate sized trophy case with hundreds of awards and trophies, a double size/two gyms, and a fitness center that rivals a five-star health club. Fieldston has a three season interscholastic sports program for eighth graders. Ninth through twelfth graders have a full interscholastic sports schedule, including strong teams in girls' field hockey, tennis and volleyball; coed cross-country, boys' basketball, baseball, football, lacrosse, and soccer. Additionally, the school has four tennis courts, a weight room and a gorgeous, bright, six lane swimming pool. There is a healthy competitive spirit. One student said, "At Fieldston team sports are for fun; at Riverdale and Horace Mann they're out for blood." That doesn't mean Fieldston doesn't play to win. In recent years, the girls' volleyball team was the Independent School Athletic League champions, girls' tennis was the Prep League champion. The baseball team won the Ivy Prep League Championship. Basketball games always draw good crowds. During football season the school mascot, the Eagle, walks around campus. Homecoming is a major event at Fieldston. First there is a pep rally the day before big games, which besides football include soccer, volleyball and field hockey.

Over the past five years, a student fashion show, with student's own designs made out of non-fabric materials has become a big hit. I saw dresses made out of Metrocards, an Obama for President campaign sticker dress, a Tic Tac dress and a dress made out of paint chips. Red carpets and runways are set up in the gym, there's music and photographers but no awards.

Student government is the PAC or Principal's Advisory Committee, a longstanding organization that meets regularly to discuss academic and social affairs. One year students initiated a program to get teachers to bring a mug from home instead of using Styrofoam cups. The money saved was donated to a charity to benefit the environment. PAC also deals with social aspects of life at Fieldston and the bolstering of school spirit. PAC organizes the annual fall barbecue and Fieldston Awareness Days that raise community awareness of the school's mission and goals. In addition to PAC there is STS, a student-to-student counseling program. In the high school there are electives in ethics including an advanced course in peer leadership and peer mentoring.

Tolerance and respect for difference are at the heart of Fieldston, and by and large relations between different groups are harmonious. One student said, "Fieldston is a lot more politically correct than other schools; I've become a lot more aware here."

There are over forty clubs at Fieldston that vary from year to year, depending on the interests of the student body. An activity period is built into the school day so that students can participate in a club and perform in a school play or compete in interscholastic sports. Some clubs are the ever-popular Amnesty International, Social Justice Watch, Environmental Club, and S.U.M.E. (Students United for Multicultural Education).

John Love, Fieldston's principal, said, "The ECFS mission to provide a humanistic, ethical and progressive education really is present in the day-to-day life of the school. ECF attracts and nurtures people who question, think and aren't afraid to act."

Parents say that ECFS is not merely a college preparatory school, but that Fieldston prepares students to be citizens who are analytical thinkers, creative problem solvers, lifelong learners and agents of positive change in the world. Apparently the colleges agree; Fieldston students are accepted at a range of colleges and universities including the big Ivies—one recent year ten students went off to Yale.

Popular College Choices   Brown, Carleton College, Columbia, Cornell, Dartmouth, George Washington, Harvard, Oberlin, NYU, Northwestern, Skidmore, Stanford, University of Chicago, Washington University, University of Wisconsin-Madison, Vassar, Wesleyan, Yale

Publications   Yearbook: *Fieldglass* (since 1929)
Newspaper: *The Fieldston News* (since 1929)
Monthly parent newsletter: *Field Notes*
The Middle School yearbook: *The Milestone*
Literary magazine: *Litmag*
Alumni magazine: *The ECF Reporter*
Student community service magazine: *Community Server*
Student visual arts magazine: *Eagle Eye*
Alternative student literary magazine: *Maverick*
Student history magazine: *The Fieldston Historical Review*
Student on-line young women's magazine: *Roxine*
Faculty newsletter: *Fieldston Performing Arts Newsletter*
Many of ECFS's publications are printed at Fieldston's own printing press.

Community Service Requirement   60 school hours or 120 summer hours beginning in 9th grade; academic community service courses are offered

Hangouts   The Quad, Student-Faculty Center, Form Dean's offices, Riverdale Diner (if you have a car), the cafeteria for breakfast

The Family School

Dag Hammarskjold Plaza
323 East 47th Street
New York, NY 10017
(212) 688-5950, fax (212) 980-2475
website: www.familyschools.org
e-mail: famschool@aol.com

The Family School West

308 West 46th Street
New York, NY 10036
(212) 688-5950, fax (212) 980-2475

Coed
Toddler (18 mos) through 6th grade
Not accessible

Mrs. Lesley Nan Haberman, Headmistress, Founder and Director of
Admissions

Birthday Cutoff   Children entering the Toddler Division must be
18 mos by September 1
Children entering kindergarten must be 5 by December 31st

Enrollment   Total enrollment: 210
Toddler places: 60 (18 mos–3 years)
Family School West places: 40 (2.6–6 years)
Pre-Primary places: 80 (3-6 years)
Elementary places: 30 (6–12 years)
Graduating class size: varies; 10-20

Tuition Range 2009–2010 $9,500 to $16,800 (2 half days) Toddler
Program–Elementary Program
Additional payment is required for children with special needs
who require additional support

Financial Aid/Scholarship   On an individual basis

Endowment   None

After-School Program Monday through Friday, 3:00–6:00 P.M., supervised homework time and a variety of recreational and creative activities for an additional payment; winter and spring recess programs are also available

Summer Program Weekly camp program from mid-June through the end of August, 8:30 A.M.–6:00 P.M.; a variety of recreational and creative activities and academic maintenance, weekly field trips and instructional swim.

———

Founded in 1975 by the current Headmistress and Director of Admissions, Lesley Nan Haberman, The Family Schools are members of the American Montessori Society. The Family Schools offer an eclectic Montessori environment, a comfort to those who think of pure Montessori as too rigid. All of the teachers are certified Montessori teachers and traditional Montessori materials are used in the classrooms. Children are placed in heterogeneous mixed age groupings, also characteristic of the Montessori approach.

Getting in: All candidates are informally interviewed and invited to spend time in a classroom. Applicants to kindergarten and above are required to take the ERB.

The Family School was founded as a nursery school, added a toddler and elementary school program, and now serves children through twelve years of age. The Family School is housed in a bright, up-to-date (and meticulously clean) building adjacent to the Japan Society. The school has a state-of-the-art auditorium/gym but children also play outdoors on Dag Hammarskjold Plaza. Toddlers play in an attached backyard/playground.

Children bring their own bag lunch and parents take turns providing snacks and flowers. The Family School West serves twenty-eight children (ages 2½ through 6) in a one room school house, the former gym of a Lutheran Church with its own backyard.

As its name suggests, The Family School is an inclusive, nurturing, warm community. The students come from all parts of the city. Some parents commute to work in the neighborhood. The school also has a limited program for children with special needs, some of whom receive additional support services.

In a pre-primary classroom (ages three to six) each day begins with the morning circle. Children then choose materials and work either independently or in small groups with their teachers. Areas of study include sensorial, language, math, music, art, foreign languages, chess, martial arts, violin, yoga, drumming, cultural arts and practical life. Examples of the children's work adorn the walls of the school. In the Elementary Program, (ages 6-12), children continue learning in a practical context (for example using math manipulatives) and begin to move toward the understanding of abstract concepts. Reading is taught using several methods with a phonetic base. Students can move at an advanced pace, emphasis is placed on personal responsibility. Additionally, Elementary school students can participate in swimming, the Stock Market Game, The Global Citizenship Action Project, and an annual Spring Camping Trip to the Adirondacks.

Parents receive written narratives twice a year and the ERB is offered each fall and spring. The school-parent partnership is an essential component of the Family Schools' experience and parent-teacher conferences are held three times a year. Families are encouraged to share special talents and interests with students.

Traditions   Grandparent's Day, Nanny's Day, May Day, Holiday Programs and Family Fied Day

Popular School Choices   Brearley, Browning, Dalton, Convent of the Sacred Heart, Dalton, Friends, Nightingale-Bamford, Riverdale, St. Davids, Spence, Town, UNIS, and various public school programs.

Friends Seminary

222 East 16th Street
New York, NY 10003-3703
(212) 979-5030, fax (212) 677-5543
website: www.friendsseminary.org

Coed
Kindergarten–12th grade
95% accessible

Robert Lauder, Principal
Harriet Burnett, Director of Admissions

Birthday Cutoff   Children entering kindergarten must be 5 by September 1
Children entering Grade 1 must be 6 by September 1

Enrollment   Total enrollment: 700
Kindergarten places: 43
Grade 6 places: 18
Grade 9 places: 27
Graduating class size: approximately 65

Grades   Semester system
Lower, Middle and Upper Schools: conferences and written reports Letter grades begin in Grade 9
Departmentalization begins in Grade 5
Final exams begin in Grade 7

Tuition Range 2009–2010 $31,940, Kindergarten–Grade 12
Additional fees: Building and Technology fees, PTA dues, Accident Insurance, Beverage Plan, lunch, (required in kindergarten-Grade 8 and optional in Grades 9–12, approximately $2,300)

Financial Aid/Scholarship   23% of students receive some form of financial aid

Endowment $8.4 million

Diversity   28% students of color
Friends participates actively in and enrolls students from Early

Steps, Prep for Prep, The TEAK Fellowship Program, Albert G. Oliver, and ABC (A Better Chance) scholarship programs
Friends receives foundation grants to support diversity
CARE (Cultural Awareness Reaching Everyone) is a student-run organization that "takes an active role in discussing and educating the community about cultural diversity"
Office of Diversity Divisional coordinators supervised by the Director of Diversity; Office serves as a liason for both students and parents; provides a forum for issues of concern
A school-wide Peace Week and an Upper School student led Day of Concern are held each year. Recent topics include: In the Presence of Justice: The Politics of Peace, Environmental Stewardship, A Pathway to Peace, Nonviolence in the Age of Terrorism, Iraq beyond the War, Day of Wealth and Poverty Education
Student committee on gender issues
Alumni Peer Mentoring Program and Student Peer Mentoring through the Diversity Office

Homework   Begins gently in Grade 1
Grades 2–3: 20–30 minutes per night
Grade 4: ½–1 hour per night
Grades 5–6: up to 1–1½ hours per night
Grades 7–8: up to 2–2½ hours per night
Grades 9–12: 3 plus hours per night

After-School Program   Early Bird Program: (Lower School) 8:00 A.M. to 8:45 A.M.
Friends After Three Program: Monday through Friday for Lower and Middle School; creative and athletic activities from 3:00 P.M.–4:30 P.M. with extended day coverage available until 5:30 P.M. each day; the above programs require an additional fee; the library is open until 6:00
Athletics: Team Sports, Grades 6–12

Summer Program   Summer Friends: A seven-week program in June and July, open to 3 to 13-year olds from all over the city, offering a variety of recreational and creative activities; The Friends Summer Institute, open to students in Grades 5–12 offering courses in SAT prep, academic subjects, and creative arts

Friends Seminary, the oldest continuing coeducational day school in New York City, is hardly the most traditional. Friends is distinguished by its Quaker heritage. Founded in 1786, Friends is under the care of the New York Quarterly Meeting of the Religious Society of Friends. Friends provides a value-based, academically challenging program informed by the Quaker values of simplicity, peace, integrity, community, equality and sustainability. There is a Principal rather than a Headmaster.

In 2003, Robert "Bo" Lauder became the thirty-fourth Principal of Friends Seminary after several years at Sidwell Friends in Washington, D.C.. With a handshake and a smile, Bo greets students and parents in the morning setting the tone for community and accessibility.

Academically, Friends challenges its students to stretch themselves as they engage in the learning process. The academic program begins gently and, age appropriately becomes increasingly rigorous. A former Parents-Teacher Alliance president told us: "Friends is not a socially competitive school but Friends does create competitive students."

Getting in: Parents are invited to tour Friends before making application to the school. For kindergarten and Grade 1, groups of six students meet with two teachers for one hour during which time each family has a twenty to thirty minute interview. Friends is a very popular choice city wide—not only for those who live downtown. Admission is competitive. It is the school's policy to give priority consideration to qualified children of members of Quaker Meetings. Qualified siblings and children of alumni are given priority consideration as well. Admission, however, is not automatic; one parent told me her daughter was deferred a year even though she had an older sibling at Friends. There is a wait list.

Parents: Parents talk about the family feeling at Friends. One mother described the school as "a community of shared values. Everyone is on a first-name basis." There is a program for new families called the Parent Connection to help new parents get involved in the school. Parents say there are definitely more working mothers than not. Fathers are very involved in the school; in fact, several fathers serve as class representatives and pick up their children at day's end. In response to the changing needs of two-career families, Friends provides programs before and after school and during vacations.

Socially the parents are very low-key; there is a form of reverse snobbery: "Downtowners don't flaunt," says a parent.

The Friends Spring Fair is an annual event made possible through the efforts of hundreds of parents and students. In addition, there is an annual benefit and class potluck suppers. Many Friends parents remain involved long after their children have graduated. Because it is a Quaker school, raffles and games of chance are prohibited.

Friends parents feel they have a voice. Throughout the year the PTA sponsors dialogue meetings for each division of the school. Examples of topics discussed include: seventh graders and their need for independence, the role of the advisor, substance abuse and conflict resolution. The PTA has organized a PTA-community service partnership in which parents and students work together in support of a specific community service project.

Program: "Quaker philosophy permeates the school and after you've been there a while you recognize it," said one parent. Service learning is a priority in kindergarten through Grade 12. Walking through the hallways you might see tenth graders working with first graders; fifth graders helping in the library, and parents working with students of all ages in workshops to decorate bags for God's Love We Deliver. Recent service learning projects include Kids Helping Kids, Project Clean, Civil Rights Project, HELP Dinner, Dark Day, AIDS Walk, Pennies for Peace, and Lower School Bank Street-Head Start partnership.

Quaker Meeting is the heart and soul of the school. Meeting is a time for students and teachers to come together in silent reflection, and if moved to do so, share thoughts and feelings with their community. In Lower School, a few moments of silence takes place in the classroom during the beginning of circle time. Once a week, Lower School students go to the landmarked meetinghouse, for silent Meeting. Both Middle and Upper School have Meeting four times a week. In Middle School, Meeting always begins with ten minutes of silence, followed by announcements, assemblies and so on. In Upper School, students have silent Meeting twice a week for twenty minutes, while the two other weekly Meetings focus on relevant issues and school business. The mother of a fifth grader says, "Everybody thinks that because Friends is a Quaker school there are hours of silence, but that's not so; Meeting is a quiet time to come together, discuss the day, and to hear announcements." A former PTA president said that "even the shy child will speak out and feel comfortable at Meeting." Parents always are invited to attend Meeting.

The Lower School focuses on academics as well as children's emotional and developmental needs. Friends recognizes that young children learn at their own pace and that the development of self-esteem early on will lead to future success. Lower School placement is considered carefully at Friends. Teachers know their students well and consider a variety of factors before making placement decisions. A father told me that his children's reports were "wonderfully detailed with a huge space filled with comments."

Parents say the emphasis at Friends is on learning process; learning how to learn. "Students don't just memorize the date of a battle but rather what really happened at the battle," said one. "Learning is an ongoing process," said another. "My daughter's teacher said, 'Just because you turn it in doesn't mean it's over.'" Students may not realize that when they are measuring and baking, they are using math and language arts. This integrated approach to education in the Lower School is becoming the norm among most independent schools.

The Lower School classroom is a "combination of teacher-directed instruction and self-directed exploration and learning." Children spend time working in groups toward a common goal (collaborative learning), as well as engaging in their work individually. In the younger years, teaching is hands-on whenever possible; no one approach to teaching reading is used because teachers consider the approach that is best for each child. Students use math manipulatives as well as workbooks. Computers are in every classroom to support the curriculum. Spanish and French are introduced in Grades 3 and 4. In social studies students begin by looking at themselves and their families, widening their perspective to include the city, the country, and the world of other cultures. Lower School children at Friends leave their classrooms for science, art, music, library, physical education, dance, and drama.

Middle School consists of Grades 5 through 8. Middle Schoolers hang out in the courtyard, cafeteria or library, not in the hallways. The head of the Middle School, Ben Fussiner, joind Friends in 2007. His easy-going manner, sense of humor and sensitivity to the needs of this age group make him both approachable and well-liked. Each Middle School Day starts with Meeting, and Quaker values permeate school-life. Each student from Grades 7 through 12 has an advisor for academic guidance and also as a liaison between home and school. Students and parents say that the workload increases in fifth grade and again in seventh and ninth grades. In fifth grade departmentalization begins. Concrete work (including plenty of homework) is given "and the kids crave it," one mother said. A parent said, "The kids are more comfortable and really show progress quickly and early in the year." Math for fifth and sixth graders is grouped by homerooms with sub-groups based on ability. One mother said her daughter started to slack off and wasn't keeping up with her math work. The teacher discussed the problem with the student before it became a pattern, and she got back on track without her parents having to worry. Math enrichment is available for students who are more advanced in math.

Beginning in Grade 5, students have increasing opportunity to make choices for themselves in the areas of foreign language and performing and visual arts. In Grades 5 and 6 students choose French or Spanish. In Grades 7 and 8, students are required to add two years of Latin.

Literature, grammar, and good writing are emphasized in English. Eighth graders have weekly writing assignments using analytical and creative skills. Topics in Social Studies begin with the study of ancient civilizations in fifth grade and progress through Medieval and Renaissance History in sixth grade, including the history of civilization in Africa or the Americas. Seventh graders study the American Constitution and Government, African-American History and "The Immigrant Experience." Eighth graders focus on world history.

The Middle School science program is comprehensive, beginning with a hands-on general curriculum for Grades 5 and 6 encompassing areas of Life, Earth, and Physical Sciences. In Grade 7, students concentrate on Earth Science and Ecology with an added introduction to Chemistry. In Grade 8, Biology is introduced. Middle Schoolers also take a Health and Wellness course that examines the physical changes and social issues of adolescence.

The arts program at Friends includes both two- and three-dimensional offerings as well as many performing arts courses. In addition to two art studios, the Seegers Arts Center houses a photography lab, a fiber optic arts room and an art gallery. Seventh and eighth graders can take art electives. Under the direction of Jennifer Fell Hayes, an award-winning playwright, the Friends Seminary drama program features three major theatrical productions annually. Recent productions include: *The Sound of Music, Pippin, Twelfth Night, The Hobbit,* and *Peter Pan.* In addition, drama electives are available to students in seventh through twelfth grades. Theatre is performed in both the Meeting House and in the new "black box" theatre.

In Middle School, each day begins with Meeting, and Quaker values continue to play a central role in school life, particularly regarding discipline. Each student from seventh through twelfth grade has an advisor who offers curricular guidance and who is an advocate in matters of discipline and emotional support.

The Middle and Upper School music program at Friends is focused in two areas: classical and jazz. Students can also choose from a range of electives including chamber music, instrumental music and vocal jazz ensemble, wind ensemble and instrumental instruction. Students can learn an instrument in fifth grade; jazz instruction begins in seventh grade. Bob Rosen, Friends' jazz impresario, exemplifies the private school teacher who not only teaches but does. Mr. Rosen is a jazz clarinetist, saxophonist, composer and conductor. He arranges for Friends students to jam with noted jazz musicians: Each year, students perform in concert.

Remarkably, for an urban school downtown, Friends fields 26 sports teams in Grades 6–12. Accomplishments include league tournament championships and state invitationals. In 2006, the Boys Varsity Basketball team won the Class "C" state tournament. The spirit in which teams conduct themselves in competition is particularly valued. Many parents apply to Friends because of the unique brand of sportsmanship displayed when their current school's competed against Friends.

Athletics at Friends is competitive. In Grades 9–12, there are varsity and some junior varsity teams in soccer, basketball, softball, baseball, volleyball and tennis as well as coed teams in squash, track/cross-country and swimming. (One seventh grade boy said he longed for football.)

President Theodore Roosevelt, an alumnus, would be pleased to note the school-wide emphasis on experiential education. The Wilderness and Outdoor Adventure programs at Friends begin in kindergarten with apple picking and become more sophisticated in the Middle and Upper Schools. First and second graders make their own maps of their routes from home to school and go to a nature study workshop. Third and fourth graders go to a nature center for outdoor education programs. Middle Schoolers also travel outside the city to learn mountain climbing and rappelling. Upper School students take backpacking trips, go sea-kayaking, learn telemark and cross-country skiing, and master rock-climbing skills.

A substantial number of new students enter Friends in Grades 6

253

and 9. "Friends is an easy school to start," says the mother of two. "There are many new kids and there's an enormous effort to be welcoming." Current Upper School students mentor ninth graders. Ninth graders and above can leave school for lunch or relaxation in adjacent Rutherford Place (but have to sign out first).

The Upper School, Grades 9–12, is a rigorous program. Minimum requirements for graduation include four years of English, three years of history and math, two consecutive years of French, Spanish, Arabic or Latin, a minimum of two years of laboratory science, and twenty-seven hours of community service per year. Advanced Placement courses are given in most disciplines. If a student is interested in pursuing an AP course and if there are not enough students to form a full class, a teacher will mentor that student so he/she can sit for the AP exam. In addition, Friends has a relationship with New York University, enabling qualified juniors and seniors to take courses for high school credit free of charge.

In September 2008, The Chapman Academic Center was opened for students in Grades 7 through 12. The Center offers additional opportunities for students to work individually with a teacher in the Humanities, Math or Science departments. It is staffed from 7:30 A.M. until 4:30 P.M.

One Upper School parent commented that the Upper School course offerings looked like a mini-college catalog. For example, English electives include "Tragedy and the Limits of Language," "Homer's *Odyssey* with Joyce's *Ulysses* and Walcott's *Omeros*," and "Major Novels of Gabriel Garcia Marquez." Choices in history include "Poverty in the United States," "Ethnic NY: Historical and Contemporary Perspectives," The Making of the Middle East: Islam and Modernity, and "International Relations: Modern Africa."

Friends has made a serious commitment to technology. There are two computer labs, and iBooks and SmartBoards in some classrooms, a foreign language lab in addition to classroom computers. The entire school is networked. Students interested in media can take advantage of the outstanding Chapman Media Center which houses a screening room with editing capability.

Upper School students participate in several international and national study programs including School Year Abroad, in France, Spain and China, and another semester at St. Stephen's School in Rome, The Mountain School, High Mountain Institute, Maine Coast Semester, and The Network of Complementary Schools.

Service learning is a cornerstone of the kindergarten through

Grade 12 program. In the Upper School, The Social Action Committee "informs on issues and activities of community and global concern." Friends students volunteer to help the less privileged or donate time to Amnesty International, "Children of War" or to an environmental group. Friends students are not afraid to speak up and speak out. They are socially aware and committed to service. A father of two children at Friends told us, "The philosophy of the school prepares children to deal with the outside world. They become independent and self-assured."

The centerpiece of the Friends graduation is Quaker Meeting. One parent said that out of the silence of the Meeting "the students speak with remarkable self-possession; some of their speeches are political and some are nostalgic." There are no caps and gowns.

Popular College Choices Brown, Yale, University of Pennsylvania, Northwestern, Cornell, Colgate, Oberlin, Wesleyan, Haverford

Traditions Quaker Meeting, nature and wilderness trips, Friends Spring Fair, Book Fair, potluck suppers, concerts, God's Love We Deliver bag decoration workshops, Lower and Middle School Field Days, Halloween Party, drama, concerts, and musical theater productions

Publications Literary magazine: *The Magpie*
Yearbook: *It's Simple* (2009)
Middle School newspaper
Upper School newspaper: *The Oblivion*
Photography journal: *Exposures*

Community Service Requirement Kindergarten–Grade 8: performed within the school; Grades 9–12: performed within and outside of school
Grades 7–8: minimum of 15 hours, within the school
Grades 9–12: minimum of 20 hours, outside of school, 7 hours in school service
Grade wide service projects for ninth and tenth graders are required

Hangouts Mariella's Pizza, Joe Jr.'s Coffee Shop, Gramercy Coffee Shop, Stuyvesant Square Park

The Geneva School of Manhattan

583 Park Avenue
New York, NY 10021
(212) 754-9988
fax (212) 754-9987
e-mail: Admin@genevaschool.net
website: www.genevaschool.net

Coed
Preschool–8th Grade
Not accessible

Mr. Scott Parson, Director

Uniform   Girls wear a plaid jumper or navy skirt, a white blouse, and a navy cardigan sweater with the school logo. Boys wear khaki pants, white shirt, and a navy cardigan sweater with the school logo.

Birthday Cutoff   Children entering preschool must be 2½ by September 1st, Children entering kindergarten must be 5 by September 1st

Enrollment   Total enrollment: 130
3 year old places: 20
Pre-K places: 16
Kindergarten places: 18
Approximately half of the student body enters after Kindergarten

Grades   Parent conferences and progress reports six times a year. Progress reports are issued three times per year. Letter grades begin in 4th Grade. The standardized tests are given each year in the Spring.

Tuition Range 2009–2010 $11,750 to $18,250, Preschool 2½'s through 8th grade
Additional fees are approximately $200

Financial Aid/Scholarship   Available upon request

Diversity   Approximately 25% students of color

After-School Program Diverse recreational programs and Geneva Conservatory of Music are available

Summer Program In development

The Geneva School of Manhattan was founded by a small group of Christian parents and educators who wanted to provide a classical education based on Christian tenets. Inspired by Dorothy Sayer's essay, "The Lost Tools of Learning," parents, foundations, and private individuals funded the school named after Geneva, Switzerland, the center of the Protestant Reformation in the 1500s. The school opened in 1996–97 with pre-kindergarten through first grades and is growing.

A Christian-based independent school, the first in Manhattan, is likely to appeal to many parents who now home-school their children and to others who want a correlation between their faith and their children's schooling.

Getting in: A personal interview, ERB assessment, and a screening test, administered by the school, are required. The school has a non-discriminatory policy but parents must sign a statement of faith and a statement of cooperation. (The school will discipline children but corporal punishment is not permitted.) The registration form asks parents to describe their children, hobbies, and sign a "statement of faith'" and answer the question, "Please give a short explanation with regard to your understanding of a Christian education."

Parents: All parents are required to volunteer at the school. Parents are also involved and participate in the school-wide prayer ministry, plan field trips, and other extracurricular activities and special events.

Program: The school "teaches the truth from the Bible," including creationism. But according to a staff member, "Our school doctrine is not specifically in support of the fundamentalist movement." According to the school's literature, the educational program is founded on the principles and values set forth in Scripture. The Geneva School will revive the educational style that uses the classical "trivium," a three phase model that corresponds to the different phases in child development.

The Geneva School's distinctive characteristics include: 1) curriculum based upon the Bible as God's Word; 2) Classics taught as enduring works of excellence; 3) rigorous academics and small classes; 4) emphasis upon languages with foreign language instruction beginning in pre-school; 5) disciplined and nurturing Christian faculty; 6) involved parents who volunteer time and talents; 7) affordable tuition based on financial need.

The preschool program provides three- and four-year olds with cognitive, language, motor and social skills. Children learn English and conversational French, math, science, art, Bible and music.

The Lower School offers students in kindergarten through fifth grade a deeper understanding of God, along with basic academic skills in a literature-based program. Subjects are taught in a traditional way, the focus is on phonics, penmanship and formal grammar.

Students in Upper School, grades six through eight, take language, math, science, history, Bible, Latin, and fine arts. Readings stress the Classics, all students must read Homer, Virgil, and Dante, among others.

Popular Secondary School Choices   Bard High School, Birch/ Lenox, Bronx High School for Science, Browning, Brooklyn Tech, Catherdral, Chapin, Columbia Prep, Convent of the Sacred Heart, Deerfield, Dwight, Fordham Prep, Hewitt, Horace Mann, Kent, Loyola, Poly Prep, Spence, St. Georges, Stuyvesant High School, York Prep

Grace Church School

86 Fourth Avenue
New York, NY 10003
(212) 475-5609, fax (212) 475-5015
e-mail: mhirschman@gcschool.org
website: www.gcschool.org

Coed
Junior Kindergarten–8th grade
Accessible

Mr. George Davison, Head
Ms. Carol Collet, Head of Upper School (Grades 5-8)
Ms. Barbara Haney, Head of Lower School (Grades 1-4)
Ms. Cheryl Kelly, Head of Early Childhood (Junior Kindergarten and
Kindergarten)
Ms. Margery Stone, Director of Admissions

Uniform: A generous dress code that includes four different styles
and colors in tops and bottoms; items vary depending on the
vendor; the Parents Association also runs a sale of gently worn
school-wear

Birthday Cutoff   Children entering junior kindergarten should be 4
by September 1
Children entering kindergarten should be 5 by September 1
Children entering first grade must be 6 by September 1

Enrollment   Total enrollment: 417
Early Childhood Division (Junior Kindergarten and Kinder-
garten): 78
Lower School (Grades 1-4): 174
Upper School (Grades 5-8): 165
Junior Kindergarten places 30
Kindergarten places: 15
Graduating class size: approximately 43

Grades   Semester system
Junior Kindergarten through Fourth Grade: detailed reports
Letter grades begin in 5th grade with comments

Departmentalization begins in 5th grade; parent/teacher conferences twice a year (fall and spring) for Lower School; one fall parent/teacher conference for Upper School families

Tuition Range 2009–2010 $30,900, Junior Kindergarten–8th grade Additional fees: for Parents Association Dues $100 Trip fees in Grades 5-8: $500-$575

Financial Aid/Scholarship   23% of the student body receive some form of aid

Endowment   Approximately $18 million

Diversity: Approximately 25% of the student body is diverse Grace enrolls students from more than 100 different nursery schools and children from Early Steps, Prep for Prep, Boys Club and many other schools

Homework   Junior Kindergarten and Kindergarten: once a week, plus children bring select items to and from home and school to show responsibility
Grade 1-4: 30 minutes to 1 hour
Grades 5-8: 1-2 hours

After-School Program   The Grace After-School Program (GASP) is open to Grace students; Monday–Friday until 5:30 P.M., students take classes and participate in a variety of age appropriate activities such as, cooking, fencing, Mandarin, chess, gymnastics and more; there are after-school playgroups, all for an additional payment, financial aid is available

Summer Program   June School is a week-long program starting after graduation available to students entering Junior Kindergarten through Grade 5; activities include bowling, swimming, music art, gym time, and computers; an additional payment is required for June School, financial aid is available

Grace Church was founded in 1894 as the first Choir Boarding School in New York City. Coeducation at Grace Church began in 1947. Well-located in the hustle and bustle of Greenwich Village, the school occupies nine adjoining landmarked Gothic buildings and is a popular choice for many downtown and even some uptown families. Extensive recent renovations honoring the school's Gothic architecture have taken the facilities to a new level and blend amazingly well with the original buildings affording much light and space.

The school is traditional and follows a structured curriculum. There is a dress code, although pretty flexible, and teachers are addressed formally ("Mr. Smith," "Miss Jones"). A vestige from the school's founding, Grace's ethics and religious program remains committed to educating its students in spirituality, life skills and service learning. There's weekly chapel services led by the school's chaplain. Chapel services have a broad appeal, are inclusive and reflect the school's diverse community.

The school has a greatly enlarged library with state-of-the-art computer catalog, over 14,500 books, a reading room, and research facilities. The school is filled with the latest in technology, Smartboards and laptops are available in almost every classroom, two computer labs, a computer center. All classrooms, and the library are connected via a wireless network with Internet access; e-mail links the entire community.

The arts center has two art studios, a sculpture studio, studios for digital arts, ceramics, a music room, dance and drama studio, and digital technology lab integrating computers with the arts. There is a separate play roof for the younger children in addition to a new full-sized bright gymnasium, a smaller gym/auditorium, and spacious courtyard, and dance studio. Central Park's fields, Chelsea Piers, and a neighborhood indoor swimming pool are used to augment the physical education program. Dining is family-style in the school's brand new cafeteria. The daily menu offers not only a hot lunch in a variety of cuisines, vegetarian options, and a salad bar, but is also is nut-free.

Getting in: After submitting an application, parents must call to schedule a tour and interview. ERBs and reports from current schools or programs are required for admissions as well as an interview. Junior Kindergartners, Kindergartners and first graders are interviewed in small groups. For specific admissions information check the school's website or call (212) 475-5609 ext. 104.

Parents: Grace parents are an eclectic mix of downtown professionals. The community's diverse and inclusive and parents play a major role supporting the school. The Parents' Association sponsors a book fair and an annual Scholarship Benefit Auction and volunteers in many other ways, such as chaperoning field trips, and helping out in special classroom celebrations and more.

Program: Grace Church School has three divisions: The Early Childhood Division: Junior Kindergarten and Kindergarten; Lower School: grades one through four; Upper School: grades five through eight. The youngest children, in Junior Kindergarten and Kindergarten begin the school day when they enter a separate door into their own area of the school which fosters a feeling of ownership of their space, which includes an outdoor playground and gym. "We're our own little entity," explains, Cheryl Kelly, Head of the Early Childhood Division."

Technology training starts in Kindergarten with age-appropriate software and by the time students reach eighth grade they are able to create websites and are well-versed in various computer languages. First graders are integrated gradually into the Lower School. Class sizes are small, there's plenty of individual attention, and the feeling throughout the Lower School is intimate and warm.

Not only because Grace has a pool of creative people as part of its community—as parents, teachers, and educators—but because the school highly values the arts, there are plenty of opportunities for students in every grade to engage in a variety of dramatic, theatrical productions, choral groups, visual arts (painting, drawing, sculpture, ceramics, and digital art), instrumental music, and dance programs. Grace stages many productions throughout the year.

A choice of French or Spanish is offered in third grade. Latin is offered starting in seventh grade. Students who choose not to take Latin may take an arts course instead.

The Grace International Exchange Program (for an additional cost of $3,500; financial aid is available), offers students a chance to learn about different cultures, culminating with reciprocal visits and home stays in France or Spain.

The point of the exchange program, according to George Davison, Head of Grace, "Is to get kids out of their American minds."

Popular Secondary School Choices: independent day schools including, Trinity, Dalton, Riverdale, Horace Mann, Friends, Packer-Collegiate, Poly Prep, Berkeley Carroll, Chapin, Marymount, Browning, Collegiate, and Spence. Boarding schools include, St. Paul's, Deerfield, Lawrenceville, Groton and Andover as well as the specialized New York City high schools

Traditions: Grace has almost 50 traditions, such as, Special Chapels, Thanksgiving, Christmas Pageant, Martin Luther King

Celebration, Graduation, Holiday Shopping, Math Breakfast, Diversity Dinner, Medieval Day, Art Expo, Book Buddies, New Parents Dinner, DISC Field Day, Family Community Service Day, Latin Feast

Publications   Lower School *Times*
Grace Church School *News*
Grace Church Literary Journal: *The Scribbler*

Community Service Requirement: The school chaplain oversees several community service and life skills projects including environmental projects on sustainability, ethical consciousness and social responsibility.

Hangouts   Italian ices cart in front of school; PIE pizzeria

The Hewitt School

Middle and Upper School (Grades 4–12)
45 East 75th Street
New York, NY 10021
(212) 288-1919
Admissions: (212) 994-2597
website: www.hewittschool.org
Not accessible

Andrew J. McKelvey, Lower School
(Grades K–3)
3 East 76th Street
New York, NY 10021
Admissions (212) 994-2597
Accessible

All girls
Kindergarten–12th grade

Ms. Joan Z. Lonergan, Head of School
Ms. Martha Hirschman, Assistant Director of Admissions

Uniform   Lower School: Hunter green and navy plaid jumper; a white blouse, tights or socks and sensible, non-skid shoes
Middle School: a Hunter green plaid kilt, a white blouse, tights or socks and closed low-heeled shoes with non-skid soles. Casual options for both Lower and Middle School include uniform slacks, skirt, and a variety of uniform shirts, blouses, and sweaters. Sneakers can be worn
Upper School: Navy or khaki cotton or corduroy pants; navy, khaki or plaid A-line skirt; polo shirts and turtlenecks. Seniors have a dress code that specifies appropriateness

Birthday Cutoff   Children entering Kindergarten must be 5 by September 1 of their kindergarten year

Enrollment   Total enrollment: 514
Kindergarten places: 50
Average graduating class: 32

Grades   Semester system
Letter grades begin in 5th grade

264

Semester exams begin in 7th grade
Narrative reports and checklists twice a year for all grades

Tuition Range 2009–2010 $34,950 to $27,500, Kindergarden–
12th grade, includes lunch and books

Financial Aid/Scholarship $2.5 million

Endowment   Approximately $10 million

Diversity   21% of the student body

Homework   Kindergarten: reading for 20 minutes with an adult
Grade 1: 15 minutes, plus 15 minutes reading
Grade 2: 30 minutes, plus 15 minutes reading
Grade 3: 45 minutes, plus 15 minutes reading
Grades 4 and 5: 45–90 minutes including reading
Grades 6 and 7: 1½–2 hours per night
Grades 8 and 9: 35 minutes per subject per night
Grades 10–12: 45 minutes per subject per night
In Middle and Upper school, no more than two tests are sched-
uled per day.

After-School Program   Hewitt AfterNoon (grades K-3) Monday
through Friday, from dismissal until 4:30 P.M.; an optional program of supervised fun, and educational experiences in art,
chess, Mandarin, science, swimming and yoga; Hewitt Academy
(Grades 4 through 7), Monday through Friday, from dismissal
until 4:20 P.M.; an optional after-school program that offers a
series of classes designed to spark the imagination and deepen
the enjoyment of the arts and sciences; programs may include
ceramics, chess, computer animation, photography, and Science
Olympiad

Summer Program   Summer Magic: a three week camp in June
from 9 A.M. to 3 P.M.; The program provides activities and
courses in dance, drama, soccer, basketball, science and technology, mosaics, drawing, painting, and trips to the Central Park
Zoo, Bronx Zoo, and the New York Hall of Science

The winding staircase and floral wallpaper lined with class pictures of girls in white dresses holding bouquets harks back to the 1920s, when the school was known as "Miss Hewitt's Classes" and educated the daughters of the city's socially prominent families. In the eighty-plus years since then, Hewitt has evolved to meet the needs of modern young women. As the smallest of the girls' schools in Manhattan, Hewitt "offers an academic environment that meets the strengths and challenges of each girl, all within a safe atmosphere," explained one former Head of School. As new Head of School, Joan Lonergan, takes the reins, Hewitt has just completed a long range strategic plan that examined and reaffirmed everything about the school and provided clarity about the future. There are steering committees and Board retreats, and a community retreat with parents and students. The school now offers a rigorous academic program as well as a supportive environment.

Hewitt is situated in two townhouses, the facilities include technology labs and stations, a dining room, performing arts center, administrative offices, and a newly renovated library media center. A connecting wing through the buildings provides space for music rooms, a counseling office, science labs and a darkroom. The new McKelvey Lower School building provides developmentally appropriate libraries on each floor, science exploration, a music room, art studio, a dining/multipurpose room, a fiber-optic backbone, streaming videos, a lap top program with infrastructure, blogs, electronic library catalogue, LCD projectors, document cameras, professional quality photography, and wireless access points for technology.

Getting in: Applications are available and can be submitted the day after Labor Day; they are located on the school's website and may be submitted on-line.

For the Lower School, a member of the admissions staff contacts the family to schedule three appointments once an application has been received. These appointments include an interview and tour for parents, attendance at a conversation with the Head of School, and a playdate for the child. A member of the admissions staff conducts this playdate for four applicants at a time to assess each girl's readiness for kindergarten. For Middle and Upper School, the family is contacted to arrange a family tour and interview for both parents and the applicant once an application has been received. During the visit, a student tour guide introduces the family to the school's program and facilities. A member of the admissions staff interviews the family; the student also meets with a relevant division head or the Academic Dean. In January, the Middle and Upper School candidates and their parents are invited to an admissions evening at which the Head of School, members of the administration, the college counselor, and a panel of students speak about the Hewitt experience.

A parent said, "Hewitt lacks some of the social crustiness of the other girls' schools"; Hewitt is "definitely nurturing and traditional, with a less aggressive atmosphere than some other places. They play down competition but there are prizes and awards." One mother said her "tomboy/nonconformist child fits in just fine at Hewitt." Many parents describe Hewitt as "a very comfortable environment."

Parents: Although many mothers and fathers work outside the home, parental involvement is encouraged. One parent describes the Hewitt atmosphere as "small, cozy and inviting; you never feel out of place. You can be there as much as you want." The Parents Association is active; there are many social and fund-raising events throughout the year. Some highlights are the Book Fair, a Parent Book Club, the Spring Benefit, and Lower School party.

Program: The Lower School at Hewitt consists of kindergarten through third grade. The kindergarten is a full-day program. A parent said that Hewitt girls are very busy after school; she has to book play dates at least three weeks in advance because girls are enrolled in ballet, swimming or religious classes.

Hewitt offers a low student/teacher ratio providing each girl with easy access to teachers and frequent communication with parents. There is a school-wide dedication to supporting each girl. Hewitt has an integrated curriculum including reading, writing, literature, math, science, social studies, art, music, dance, foreign language and physical education. Academic subjects are introduced in kindergarten and are built upon in developmentally appropriate ways in the succeeding years. French and Spanish are introduced in kindergarten through songs, games and activities that foster conversational language skills. There are computers in the kindergarten classrooms and computer instruction in the computer lab. Hewitt has laptops in its High School, training for teachers, and all of the classrooms are wired for LCD's. The computer labs were recently renovated with help from a $50,000 Edward Ford Foundation Grant.

Individualized attention is a hallmark of instruction at Hewitt. The teacher-student ratio at Hewitt is high. The majority of the faculty hold advanced degrees. Students learn at their own pace and teachers pay careful attention to different learning styles. There is individual as well as small-group instruction in writing and reading.

Math is taught with manipulatives like unifix cubes and games that develop a strong number sense. There's no one way to do something. "There are a lot of creative children here," says an admissions officer. One mother said that her daughter, who has musical ability, takes private lessons at school and was encouraged to write a song that she'll sing with her class.

The Lower School, kindergarten through third grade, is furnished with tables in clusters, to encourage collaborative learning. Beginning in kindergarten, all girls take both French and Spanish simultaneously. By second grade there are weekly spelling tests. Lower School parents receive narrative reports and checklists twice a year; there are individual conferences in fall and spring. Assemblies begin with the pledge of allegiance. In special assemblies the author of a children's book might speak, or a dance or musical group might perform.

Parents say at Hewitt, which is committed to single-sex education, "there is an implicit validation of female values." One mother praised the emphasis on women in society.

Middle School at Hewitt, composed of grades four through eight, emphasizes study skills, organization, and leadership. The girls have advisors they meet with for morning announcements who monitor each student's program. Departmentalization begins in fifth grade and is completed by seventh grade. Girls continue to study a full schedule of subjects including English, history, math, science, computer, French or Spanish (with the addition of Latin in eighth grade), studio art, drama, music and gym.

The focus of the integrated curriculum is on humanities and American History. Strong emphasis is placed on the spoken and written word. Grades seven and eight are combined into a mini- division within the Middle School to provide a gradual transition into the Upper School. There is an emphasis on math and science in the Middle and Upper Schools.

The Middle School has its own student council, clubs and its own literary magazine, *Enterprise*.

The High School at Hewitt is composed of grades nine through twelve. There is a focus on independent thinking, and a solid core curriculum. Students have faculty advisors that work with the same families for the four high school years. A minimum of five to six academic subjects per year is required but most girls take five major subjects and choose from numerous electives, like, Film, the New York Art World, astronomy, genetics, Women in Literature, Comparative Religion and the Holocaust. Three lab sciences are required as are four years of English and three years of math, history and foreign language. There are a significant number of AP classes offered, impressive since Hewitt is so small. In addition, the school offers an Upper School laptop computer program that gives students universal access to a completely wireless network that accesses the Internet and many other resources. The school provides relevant online links, and homework assignments are also posted online.

There are several dramatic productions a year, at least one of which is performed in conjunction with boys from other independent schools. Many students participate in the production, either as cast or crew. The arts and music program includes music study, a handbell choir, instrumental music, a chorus, ceramics, and studio art. There are also some interesting coordinating electives in the arts, such as Advanced Studio Art, Film Studies, and Chamber Choir. All teachers in the Hewitt Creative Arts department are themselves professional artists.

Clubs at Hewitt include: International Thespian Club, Latin Club, Animal Rights Club, ACTION; French Club, Future Problem Solvers, Junior Statesmen of America, Science Olympiad, Memory Project, Art Club, Students Against Destructive Decisions, Gay Straight Alliance, Model UN, Photography Club (LOMO), Pen Pal Club, Book Club, Student Council, Math Counts, Science Olympiad, Hewitt Goes Green, and Model Congress.

Senior privileges include using the front staircase, the "Senior Stairs," instead of the back stairs and a four-week, year-end independent project with an individual faculty advisor. Eleventh and twelfth graders can leave school with parental permission.

Community service is an integral part of the Hewitt experience. Beginning in Lower School, there are many opportunities for students to volunteer. Hewitt families participate as a team in the Breast Cancer Walk for the Cure in Central Park, collect cans of food for the Yorkville Common Pantry, coats for New York Cares, and books for book drives. The school also has a Community Service Day in which the entire community perform "good works" where Hewitt volunteers can be found working for a wide variety of organizations including habitat for Humanity, hospitals, and social service agencies.

Hewitt has teams in volleyball, badminton, basketball, soccer, track & field, cross country, swimming and tennis. There are also intramural sports clubs and junior and varsity sports teams. Hewitt is the only girl's school with a crew team.

Commencement exercises at Hewitt are traditional. The seniors wear white dresses, gather onstage and are joined in the processional by their kindergarten little sisters. Faculty members and trustees who have daughters graduating are allowed to present diplomas.

Popular College Choices Boston University, Colgate, Connecticut College, Cornell, Harvard, Johns Hopkins, Duke, Vassar, University of Michigan, University of Pennsylvania, University of North Carolina, NYU, George Washington

Traditions Arts Festival, Book Fair, Grandparents' Day, Thanksgiving Assembly, All School Holiday Concert, Model UN trip to Washington, Achievement Assemblies, senior projects, Ms. Hewitt's Birthday Celebration, Senior Prom, Senior Staircase, Lower School Valentine's Day Breakfast, Blue/White Competitions, Susan D. Komen Race for the Cure, Community Service Day, Family Community Service Day, Lower School Halloween Parade

Publications Upper School newspaper: *The Hewitt Times*
Middle School literary magazine: *Enterprise*
Art and Literary magazine: *The Venturer*
Photography magazine: *Perspicacity*
Yearbook: *Argosy*
School magazine: *The Hewitt Anchor*
School newsletters: *Hewitt Happenings*

Community Service Requirement Community service begins in lower school in a variety of ways and extends to the upper school with a twenty hour yearly requirement; in addition there are two family service days a year

Hangouts La Viande Coffee Shop, 3 Guys Coffee Shop (both on Madison Avenue)

Horace Mann School

Horace Mann Nursery Division
55 East 90th Street
New York, NY 10128
(212) 369-4600

Horace Mann Lower Division
4440 Tibbett Avenue
Bronx, NY 10471
(718) 432-3300

Horace Mann Middle/Upper Division
231 West 246th Street
Bronx, NY 10471
(718) 432-4000
e-mail: admissions@horacemann.org
website: www.horacemann.org

Coed
Nursery–12th grade
Accessible for Nursery Division and Middle/Upper Division
Not accessible for Lower Division

Dr. Thomas M. Kelly, Head of School
Dr. David Schiller, Head of Upper Division
Ms. Robin Ann Ingram, Head of Middle Division
Ms. Wendy Steinthal Head of Lower Division
Ms. Lisa Moreira, Director of Admissions and Financial Aid
Mrs. Patricia Yuan Zuroski, Head of Nursery Division

Birthday Cutoff   Children entering nursery 3s must be 3 by September 1
Children entering Kindergarten must be 5 by September 1

Enrollment   Total enrollment nursery–12: 1,756
Total enrollment nursery division: 148
Kindergarten places: 35
Total enrollment Lower Division, grades Kindergarten–5: 460
Total enrollment Middle and Upper Division, grades 6–12: 1,150
Graduating class size: varies, from approximately 170 to 175
Horace Mann also has a Kindergarten with two classes of up to 21 children located in Riverdale, serving families from Riverdale, Westchester, the Bronx and New Jersey

The sixth grade admits 50–55 new students and is often the largest point of entry

Grades Trimester system
Kindergarten–3: detailed anecdotal reports, conferences and checklists; check, check-plus or minus grades; weekly quizzes
Letter grades begin in 4th grade, and anecdotal reports continue
Departmentalization begins in 4th grade, is completed by 5th grade
First final exam is given in 7th grade

Tuition Range 2009–2010 $24,440 to $34,050, nursery 3's–12th grade
Additional fees for books, transportation and lunch, approximately $1,100 to $3,000

Financial Aid/Scholarship Over 7 million dollars is awarded annually for financial aid
There are 12 named scholarship funds in the Upper Division

Endowment Approximately $68.5 million

Diversity Horace Mann enrolls Prep for Prep, Early Steps students, and Oliver Program students; participates in TEAK, Reach, Early Steps, KIPP, and No Seeds and hosts Summer on the Hill
The Union is an organization of students of color at Horace Mann
There is a parent support group

Homework Kindergarten: reading with an adult
1st grade: Worksheets, always due on Wednesdays and Fridays
2nd: 4 times a week, 10–15 minutes in the beginning of the year going up to 20 minutes, 2 worksheets per night
3rd and 4th: 30–45 minutes a night
5th: 1 and ½ hours a night
9th: 2–2½ hours per night
10th–12th: 50 minutes per subject per night, approximately 3 to 4 hours; more time is required for studying for exams and long-term projects

After-School Program For grades K–5 in Riverdale: a variety of recreational and creative activities; an additional payment is required
Upper Division: 40–70 clubs, which vary from year to year depending on the interests of the student body
Competitive sports in the Ivy Prep League and various other leauges

Summer Program   Six weeks of courses for credit or review for Horace Mann students and new students; many summer camp programs available

———

"Harvard man" is what many parents are wishing for when they enroll their three and four-year-olds at this very selective school. If you have a vision of your youngster in a crimson uniform cavorting on a grassy field with the best and the brightest, then this might be the right place. (HM's colors are crimson and white.) And, as at an Ivy League campus, most of the old stone buildings at Horace Mann High School are named after former headmasters and founders: Tillinghast Hall, Van Alstyne Auditorium, Pforzheimer Hall, the Loeb Reading Room, the Prettyman Gymnasium.

The school opened two new buildings in 1999: a new Middle School building for grades 6 through 8 and an Arts and Dining Center serving grades 6 through 12. These buildings highlight the Middle Division programs, increase student and public spaces, focus on art and music offerings, and make the existing T1 Internet and WAN accessible from every classroom.

In September 2002, Tillinghast Hall reopened after undergoing a sizable renovation that included the addition of three computer labs, a foreign language technology lab, thirty-two classrooms with wireless internet access, and a new addition that houses the Katz Library and the Loeb Reading Room, the 650-seat Alfred Gross Theater, dance studio, black box theater, and state-of-the-art theater scenery shop with a hydraulic lift that serves both as an orchestra pit and as an elevator to convey sets and equipment to the stage.

It is somewhat ironic that this prestigious private school is named after a man known as the father of public schools. Horace Mann actually had nothing to do with this namesake. According to HM's history *The First Hundred Years*, it was founder Nicholas Murray Butler who chose the name because "at the time it was the only household name in American education." Blessed with strong leadership through the years, HM has served as a model for both public and private schools, combining the traditional and the innovative, and has always encouraged physical hardiness as well as academic rigor; the faculty boasts holding among the most PhDs of any private school in the country.

Originally coed, except for a forty-year hiatus when the campuses were separate (under Inslee "Inky" Clark), Horace Mann readmitted women in 1974. Along with Clark, Dr. Mitchell Gratwick, HM's head for seventeen years, left an indelible stamp on HM: "High standards, conservative values and innovative methods." Gratwick was a founder of the AP program and acquired the John Dorr Nature Laboratory, two strong components of the HM experience.

HM uses the building-block approach to learning: "Each step leads to the next." This philosophy is carried all the way through HM, ultimately leading to preparation for advanced college study. HM's bottom line: With superior preparation, a good measure of ability and the willingness to work like an ox, a student can achieve excellence here.

Horace Mann Nursery Division was originally established as a service for the children of alumni "who wanted to start their offspring in a Horace Mann system." It is located in a tight but tidy converted coach house on 90th Street between Madison and Park. There is no indoor gym but children use a rooftop playground or a yard for at least an hour a day and go to Asphalt Green once a week. Classrooms are colorful and well ordered—if crowded—reflecting a structured but stimulating "hands-on" curriculum. The school houses a new studio that features the Reggio Emilia curriculum. The staff psychologist is available to parents for consultation. All the head teachers have a Masters in Education.

Getting in: You must apply to the Nursery Division (HMND) when your child is two and a half years old. Getting in at the nursery level is far easier on the parents because the ERB is not required for admission at that time. However, there is a caveat. At the age of three there is really no way of knowing if your child will be able (or willing) to keep up with the high expectations and the work required later on. Also, potential learning differences that might be picked up by the ERB are not apparent. I know too many parents who boasted about their children getting into HM Nursery only to have to tutor them extensively after school or (like one parent we know) over the entire summer. Parents may have to consider a change of school by third grade because a child is falling behind. It is not that HM weeds out children. The school is prepared to give as much support as is needed but there is a process of self-selection.

Applicants to Lower, Middle and Upper Divisions come to campus for a student and parent interview. Tours are led by student "ambassadors." Applications should be filed by December 1st and must be completed by January 15th. Families who request an application are invited to fall open houses. The ratio of applicants to places at the kindergarten and nursery levels is about ten to one. It's easier to get into HM at sixth or ninth grade.

The relocation of the sixth grade to the Middle School campus has led to a significant change in Middle School Division admissions. At present HM enrolls approximately 50–55 new sixth graders and 15 or fewer seventh graders. The Director of Admissions says the transition resulted in four applications for every place in sixth grade and more than six applications for every seventh grade opening.

The Upper Division enrolls approximately 35 new students each year in ninth grade with eight applications for every place and receives 30–40 applications for five tenth grade places. Few openings are available for eighth and eleventh grades.

Kindergarten applicants may be observed at their nursery schools if there are many children applying from those schools, but all children are observed in a group interview at HM in the afternoon (1:30 or 3:30). "By kindergarten," one interviewer said, "it doesn't bode well if a child doesn't separate well in the interview."

Some entering students don't know how to write their names while some come in reading. But by the end of kindergarten most kids have "cracked the code." Formal instruction begins in first grade, and reading is expected to be well under way by second grade. "The curriculum in the early years is geared to the readiness of the children," states the brochure. There is a strong emphasis on basic skills balanced with new techniques and tools. Experiential learning is stressed, and computer, chess and other learning games are introduced. There is a resource room with six computers for kindergarten. One parent praised the fact that here children "capture the enthusiasm for learning young." During the second half of the year kindergartners travel up to Riverdale to get acquainted with the elementary school campus. (I suggest that parents applying to the Nursery Division take a tour of the Elementary Division, because before you know it your child will be up in Riverdale.)

Parents: The Nursery Division is homogeneous. Parents describe it as predominantly Jewish and financially mixed. One said, "I thought the parents would be a lot hipper." There is a very active Parents Association. One mother recalls attending her first parents' meeting thoroughly underdressed. Where do many families go on weekends and vacations? "You know," said one parent, "it's the triangle: the Hamptons, Florida, Vail." But parents report that once they reach Riverdale the school community is more mixed. Communication with the parents is frequent, and there is a Parents Association newsletter. Nursery Division parents can be class representatives and they may also serve as elected members on the Horace Mann Board of Trustees.

Since the Elementary Division, located in Riverdale, is "no one's neighborhood school," communication between home and school is very important. Teachers often call and chat with parents. There are many student-teacher conferences.

Program: Horace Mann is very honest in acknowledging that this school is not for everyone. The Director of the Lower School explains, "There is a quick pace with lots of enrichment." Most children thrive on the stimulation—the classrooms are buzzing with activity and the students are clearly engaged. The PA president said that the school "breeds independence." At the beginning of third grade a letter is sent to parents urging them not to help their children with their homework, and parents must sign it. Parents may only suggest, "Try this or that." The Lower School Director stresses that Horace Mann is supportive and committed to each child. "Yes, there is a lot to do but the children meet the challenge," she says. "This is a school for children who really like to learn." There is a real emphasis on teaching study skills and on learning how to be a student. One parent summed up the issue of competitiveness at HM astutely: "It's not that the school or the kids are necessarily so competitive; it's the high-powered parents behind them." The same can be said for all the top tier schools in New York City.

The Elementary Division has large open areas, although there are no "open classrooms." Some of these large areas are shared by four classes, with cubbies in the center. Some classes have two sections, one for reading lab or language arts, one for math. Formal reading instruction begins in first grade with an eclectic approach. There are three reading specialists and a communication skills specialist. Emphasis is placed on the writing process. HM children are tested for reading each year and there is a full reading lab.

HM is known for having strong math students. There are many classroom projects: The computer program begins in kindergarten. Elementary students have computer lab at least once a week for forty-five minutes. Beginning in fourth grade, they learn word processing and keyboarding; in fifth grade, graphics and programming. By fifth grade almost all of the students use a computer at home.

When the Middle Division at HM was established, faculty prompted a re-evaluation of the Middle School curriculum. Now, there is increased emphasis on interdisciplinary works and team teaching at the sixth, seventh, and eight grade levels. Students have more choices to make and more accountability, including the introduction of "free periods." One Lower School PA president explains: "It's wonderful for the sixth graders to experience the independence and increased responsibility that comes with the Middle School environment. Until my older daughter started seventh grade I didn't realize how much they crave that sense of freedom."

There are three art teachers on staff. The Art Enrichment Program is an enhancement to the Lower School curriculum. Using a variety of media (painting, collage, papier-mâché, ceramics, metal tooling and felt appliqué) students create two and three dimensional forms to go with a topic being studied in English, reading, social studies or science. Students from first grade through fifth work to create individual as well as large group projects. The completed work is often used as a learning tool or teaching aid in the classroom.

Foreign language study begins in first grade. First graders take both French and Spanish. In second grade students choose French or Spanish for the remainder of the Lower School. In eighth grade students can elect Latin, German, Spanish, French, or Japanese.

Parents of active children will be glad to know that there is time for physical exercise: In first through fourth grades, gym meets four times a week in a huge gymnasium. Fifth graders have gym four times a week. Students use a playground and the AstroTurf field year-round, and can use the tennis courts and pool at the upper division.

Special trips: Fifth graders take a three-day trip to Washington, D.C.; all second, third, fourth and fifth graders spend time at the John Dorr Nature Lab.

Programs are held at the John Dorr Nature Lab for incoming sixth and incoming seventh, eighth, ninth, and tenth graders for orientation and exploration, which includes the Searchers program, an adapted Outward Bound program.

The Upper Division: Now the group increases, is larger and more diverse (26 percent are children of color), "large enough to be happy as they grow and change." In general "students respect the school" and enjoy the freedom of an open campus. There are no bells, and teachers are addressed formally.

Dr. Thomas Kelly is HM's ninth Head of School. Dr. Kelly had been superintendent of the Valhalla Union Free School District in Westchester. Colleagues feel Dr. Kelly's experience in the public sector has brought a fresh perspective to the post. They admire his energy and enthusiasm for the job.

In preparation for the challenge of the upper grades, students who need review attend the six-week summer session. Seventh and eighth graders also take mandatory life skills courses. Readings include *Inherit the Wind*, *Things Fall Apart* and *Ishi: Last of His Tribe*. Students gain experience in creative and critical writing. Eighth graders celebrate "Pi Day" (on 3/14 of course) and build solar houses which are tested for temperature and heat retention on the football field on a cold day.

Historically HM has been strong in English and history, and HM's science labs are also state of the art. Approximately four out of ten faculty members hold Ph.D.'s and the chemistry department has three research-quality labs. The science library and resource room has six microcomputers and is often open for independent study. Science teachers are very accessible to students with an interest in advanced study.

The course catalog says that most of the eighth grade courses are equivalent to ninth grade courses at many high schools. And even the introductory courses move along at quite a clip. One alumnus said, "It was like going to college before college." In keeping with Dr. Gratwick's legacy, HM was a pilot school for the AP program, and HMHS offers more AP courses than any other school, including AP Psychology, AP Latin: Epic Poetry and AP Economics. The math department offers AP Calculus AB, AP Calculus BC Honors, and Probability, Statistics and Social Science. English courses stress the classics but there are interesting electives in Memory and Identity, Heros and Heroines, and the works of Toni Morrison.

One Horace Mann and Ivy League alumna says, "Academically there's lots of freedom and choices but there are no gut courses at HM; no course can be blown off." The average grade is a B, which, one student boasts, "would be at least a B+ anywhere else." One HMHS student says, "Some people work hard for grades, and some people work harder for excellent grades." "It's as hard to get an F as it is to get an A" is also heard. Testing is so frequent (quizzes every week, exams every other), "you always know how you're doing." What is not listed in the catalog is the advanced level of maturity and independence required of students at HMHS, qualities already ingrained in students who came up through the HM system. The pressure is real, but one student said, "It's mainly self-inflicted." Yet another student told us that "teachers go to extremes to make the homework challenging." All homework requires a lot of time and thought, and one student said that he might blow off homework in one subject to study for an exam in another but if he missed two nights of homework assignments, he would fall behind.

Some students thrive under pressure and rise to the challenge of the competitive atmosphere, like the young woman (a HM "lifer" who had been at HM for thirteen years) who took three AP courses, did four hours of homework a night and still managed to watch her favorite TV shows. The minimum amount of homework is three to four hours each night, more on weekends. "This school makes you hungry," a student told us. "You get used to working hard and getting what you want, and you take that with you." One private school advisor tells families who are considering a most demanding school like Horace Mann to consider their family lifestyles. Some students will be able to accompany the family on weekend ski trips and still get their work done (one student trains for competitive ski racing). Others will be hitting the books in the lodge.

Contrary to popular belief, students at HM do support one another. There is a peer leadership training program and a student tutorial program, and most evenings HM students spend lots of time on the phone or on-line discussing homework or exams.

Does this leave time for extracurricular activities? One student put it this way, "If you want to be in a play or a sport and you don't mind sacrificing that time, then you do your work when you get home." Still, extracurricular activities are encouraged even for kids who aren't excelling academically. The Lower School Director explains, "Because the academics are so challenging, it's even more important for students to pursue their other interests. We want every student to experience successes, to explore abilities in and out of the classroom."

The community service requirement also contributes to personal growth. One alumna told me that HM helped her find a job as a counselor at a summer camp for homeless children and she then returned for four consecutive summers and found it an invaluable experience.

HM students are far from one-dimensional math nerds, as evidenced by the variety and number of their extracurricular activities. Every year there is a huge musical, and three smaller plays are put on annually. HM produces more than a dozen publications. Students can choose from up to seventy clubs in any given year. Popular ones include The Union (formerly the Joint Minority Coalition), which is open to everyone, political clubs (there is a Young Republicans of HM Club), the East Wind, West Wind Asian Club, Glee Club, Model U.N., Junior Statesman Club (debating) and a Shakespeare Club. The Glee Club and Chamber Chorus are very popular; they have made their own CD and traveled to Europe and the Middle East.

Students do have a voice in setting policy affecting student life at HM through the governing council, comprised of twenty-four students and fifteen faculty members who are elected annually. There is an annual tenth grade health survey (anonymous), and students are required to take health courses. In 1997 the Governing Council passed the Teacher and Course Evaluation Bill. The Council spent three meetings debating the document, which called for written evaluations by the students twice a year. The bill compelled the school faculty and administration to pass a similar resolution, making teacher and course evaluations a reality.

They say that Harvard is tough to get into, but easy to stay in; HM is tough to get into and tougher to remain in, but there is no question that the child who stays the course at HM will receive a superior, accelerated education. One alumna told me, "Horace Mann's great strength is it instills good work habits and is superior in college placement: HM goes above and beyond to get you into one of the colleges of your choice." It's prep for success. If your child makes it through, maybe you'll get to the Harvard-Yale tailgate picnic after all.

Popular College Choices   University of Pennsylvania, Cornell, Yale, Columbia, Brown, University of Wisconsin, Harvard, Tufts, George Washington, Amherst, Williams, Princeton, Dartmouth, Barnard, Duke, Johns Hopkins, Stanford, University of Chicago, Washington University, Syracuse, Northwestern, Hamilton, Carnegie-Mellon, Colgate, University of Michigan, Georgetown

Traditions   The Buzzell basketball game (vs. Riverdale), Senior Absurdity Day, Holocaust Remembrance Assembly and Martin Luther King Assembly, East Wind–West Wind Dinner (Asia Night), Service Learning Day (sponsored by HMS CCVA, Center for Community Values and Action), Lower School Caring in Action Day

Publications   Yearbook: *The Mannikin*
Newspapers: *The Record*
Literary magazine: *Manuscript*
Prose literature: *Legal Fiction*
Science magazine: *Spectrum*
Math magazine: *Mantissa*
Sports: *The Lion's Den*
Journal of opinion: *Outlook*
Multicultural paper: *The Drum*
Photography: *Insight*
Movie/Theater Review: *The Cinemann*
Alumni publication: *Alumni Bulletin*
Student Opinion Journal: *The Horace Mann Review*

Community Service Requirement   80 hours in grades 9–12; special activities in grades 6–8
Student Voluntary Service Organization

Hangouts   Riverdale diner, the library or cafeteria, The BBQ or the field outside on nice days

La Scuola D'Italia G. Marconi

Preschool and Elementary
12 East 96th Street
New York, NY 10128

Middle and High School
406 East 67th Street
New York, NY 10021
Main number: (212) 369-3290, fax (212) 369-1164
e-mail: secretary@lascuoladitalia.org
website: www.lascuoladitalia.org

Coed
Pre-kindergarten–12th grade
Not accessible

Dr. Anna Fiore, Head of School
Mrs. Pia Pedicini, Vice Principal and Director of Admissions
Mrs. Maria Alaimo Cinquemani, Preschool Coordinator
Mrs. Aimee Felton Freedman, Elementary School Coordinator
Mrs. Augusta Fleischer, Middle School Coordinator
Mr. Michael Prater, High School Coordinator

Uniform: Girls: White blouse/shirt/turtleneck, navy blue skirt/ trousers, navy blue cardigan or blazer, navy blue or white socks or tights, blue, black or brown street shoes Boys: white shirt/short sleeved polo shirt or turtleneck, a conservative tie, navy blue or gray trousers, navy blue cardigan or blazer, navy blue or gray socks, blue, black or brown street shoes

Birthday Cutoff Children entering at the nursery level must be 3 and toilet-trained by December 31
Children entering kindergarten must be 5 by December 31
Children entering first grade must be 6 by December 31

Enrollment Total enrollment: 250
Pre-Kindergarten 3/4's places: 34
Kindergarten places: 20
Graduating class size: 10-20

Tuition Range 2009–2010 $19,600 for all levels
Early registration available for Middle and High School

Financial Aid/Scholarship 12% of the student body receives some form of aid

After-School Program A variety of offerings from grades Pre-kindergarten through 12th including, arts and crafts, piano and music lessons, Italian Club, English and Italian language homework help, creative movement, soccer; for Middle and High School students, journalism and film making are offered; from September through May; an additional payment is required

La Scuola D'Italia G. Marconi, of New York was founded in 1977 by the Italian Ministry of Foreign Affairs and is dedicated to Guglielmo Marconi, the inventor of the wireless. Although the school was founded to meet the needs of Italians living in New York City, a groundswell of American families have enrolled. The bilingual curriculum is rooted in the European classical tradition. The school is bilingual—it is a good idea to be fluent in both English and Italian—and bicultural and offers supplemental classes in both Italian and English as second languages. The main building is housed in a historic building, once a private mansion, on East 96th Street. La Scola's Middle and High School are located on East 67th Street. Both buildings offer state-of-the-art facilities.

La Scuola is recognized by the Italian Ministry of Education and chartered by the Regents of the University of the State of New York as a private, independent American school.

Getting in: Applicants and their families are invited to an open house in the fall. The process also includes interviews and an assessment of previous school reports. La Scuola does not require applicants for grades pre-kindergarten through 9th to know Italian before enrolling. Applicants for ninth grade and above are required to have an intermediate level of Italian.

Parents: La Scuola parents run the complete gamut—-from contractors' children to Cipranis—and they meld without much notice. Fund-raising is low-key but vital to the life of the school. The school seeks and welcomes parents who want to get involved in school projects and special events such as organizing the annual gala and forging relationships with various cultural institutions and organizations that benefit the school community. Some La Scuola families participate in the Columbus Day Parade, and Italian Language Week in October.

Program: The curriculum at all grade levels is taught in both Italian and English, and students must become fluent in at least one of these two languages. The program offers a liberal arts curriculum that includes math, science and in-depth study and appreciation of American, European, and Italian civilizations and cultures along with a classic academic curriculum.

There is total immersion in Italian from the outset, but fluency in Italian is not a prerequisite for admission. Bilingual instruction in English and Italian begins in Pre-kindergarten. In Pre-kindergarten and kindergarten children follow the best of Italian educational practices. The Reggio Emilia philosophy also known as the "5 Fields of Experience" are integrated into a pre-academic, life skills, boundary setting preschool program. The Elementary Program, Scuolos Elementare, grades 1 through 5, is structured, and follows both Italian and New York state guidelines. Specials include art, drama/musicals, reading and writing assignments, art, photo and film reviews as well as visits to museums and historical sites.

The Middle School program, Scuola Media, grades 6 through 8, focuses on liberal arts, math and natural and physical sciences. Both European and American cultures are explored. French is introduced as a third modern language, along with American History, social studies, geography, art, music, physical education and the ways to use computers effectively. Various cultural projects are conducted throughout the year with a number of Italian institutions in New York and overseas.

La Scuola's High School, or Liceo, follows Howard Gardner's theory, *Five Minds for the Future.* Academic skills are honed along with character development, in a supportive environment. The program offers a balance in the classics and humanities with math and science. The humanities program is integrated where possible throughout the four years in English, Italian, Latin, literature, geography, history, philosophy, art, art history, law and economics and physical education. Additionally, the sciences and math are also emphasized.

Class size is small, there is lots of individual attention, exchange programs abound and change from year-to-year, but many are Italian-based. By the end of senior year, all students are required to take the Italian Ministry of Education State Exam, the Maturita, an equivalent of the International Baccalurate.

Graduates Columbia, NYU, Universita Bocconi (Milan, Italy), Boston University, Bristol University (England), Oxford University (England), SUNY Binghamton

Publications Weekly Newsletter: *Friday memo*
Newspaper *La Scuola Times*, an on-line students journal
Yearbook

Little Red School House and Elisabeth Irwin High School

Lower and Middle Divisions
272 Sixth Avenue
New York, NY 10014
fax (212) 677-9159

Upper Division
40 Charlton Street
New York, NY 10014
(212) 477-5316 (main number), fax (212) 675-3595
website: www.lrei.org

Coed
Pre-kindergarten–12th grade
Accessible

Phil Kassen, Director
Barbara H. Scott, Director of Admissions

Birthday Cutoff   Children entering pre-kindergarten must be 4 by September 1
Children entering kindergarten must be 5 by September 1

Enrollment   Total enrollment: 575
Pre-kindergarten places: 30
Kindergarten places: 50
Graduating class size: approximately 45

Grades   Semester system in Middle School; Trimester system in High School
Letter grades begin in 6th grade
Departmentalization begins in Middle School

Tuition Range 2009–2010   Approximately $30,000 to $32,000 Pre-K–12th grade

Financial Aid/Scholarship   28% of the student body receives some form of aid

Endowment   Approximately $2 million

284

After-School Program   All programs are for LREI students

The Early Bird Program: for 4–13 year olds, 7:45 A.M. to 8:30 A.M. The general after-school program is divided into three age groups: four-year olds–1st graders, 2nd–4th graders, and the Middle School group; the program runs from 3–6 P.M., Monday through Friday, and includes a structured variety of creative and recreational activities

The Enrichment Program also runs from 3–6 P.M. Monday through Friday, includes weekly classes such as Art in Motion, Flamenco Dance, woodworking, ceramics, Mandarin Chinese, karate, dance, theater, super sports, chess and parent classes in yoga and pilates

The Instrumental Program includes private instruction in such instruments as flute, saxophone, piano, guitar, voice and drums

Summer Camp Program   Open to children from other schools, the traditional Day Camp is offered for age 3.5 through 14; the camp includes age-appropriate activities including arts & crafts, drama, recreational sports, swimming and field trips; also offered are specialty camps such as, Musical Theater, Robotics, and Creative Writing. Camps run from mid-June through July; an additional payment is required

---

Little Red School House and Elisabeth Irwin High School (LREI) was founded in 1921 by Elisabeth Irwin. Working closely with such luminaries of the progressive movement as John Dewey, William Heard Kilpatrick and Lucy Sprague Mitchell, Ms. Irwin set up a "model school" within New York City's public school system with an emphasis on experiential (or active) learning. She eventually moved the program out of the public schools. Ms. Irwin selected students she thought reflected the diversity of New York City and aimed for a school with an exceptionally involved parent body. Today, faculty, parents and students remain active in the school.

In the early 1930s, Ms. Irwin moved the school to Bleecker Street and Sixth Avenue, where it has grown. A second site was acquired on Charlton Street, a few blocks away, when the high school grades were added in 1941. Its facilities include a cafeteria, a library and technology center, and Middle School classrooms, including a sky-lit art studio. The high school's extensive renovations include a library, a performing arts center, a media lab, classrooms and a lobby. Facilities in all three divisions have undergone recent renovations. The High School has also undergone a major expansion.

Getting in: The ERB is required for admission to grades four through twelve. All applicants and their families tour the school and are interviewed.

Parents: LREI parents are active in the school. The PA sponsors a Book Fair, a Literary Evening, and auctions in the spring, among other educational and community events.

Program: Little Red and Elisabeth Irwin is proudly celebrating its 80th anniversary and maintains a progressive approach which nurtures both intellectual rigor and a genuine joy of learning. The school retains its original emphasis on experiential and collaborative learning, and a commitment to diversity—both in the student population and curriculum. During the 1960s the "Red" in the school name supposedly implied sympathy for the leftist viewpoints. Today, LREI remains an activist school, with many students impassioned about human rights, but as an institution the concern is with critical thinking.

True to its mission as a model school, LREI provides an atmosphere in which innovative teaching thrives. The faculty create exciting curricula which can then be replicated in other schools. Frequent field trips provide experiential learning opportunities. Third and fourth grade students spend four days on a working farm. Social Studies in the Lower School begins in the classroom and moves to the neighborhood, extending to other areas of New York City. Specialists in science, math, visual arts, music, woodworking, Spanish, library and technology also work with students through project-based activities.

The school is composed of three divisions. Lower School: four year olds through fourth grade; Middle School: fifth through eighth grades; High School: ninth through twelfth. A hot lunch is provided for all grades. Formal foreign language instruction begins in the fours with Spanish; in fifth grade students may choose between beginning French or continuing Spanish. Mandarin Chinese is added in High School.

At LREI the classes are small and the student teacher ratio is approximately seven to one. Classes are structured but informal; almost everyone is on a first name basis. Formal reading instruction begins in first grade. A student's progress is constantly being assessed, and teachers are able to address each child's progress in kindergarten and first grade by working in very small groups. There is always a reading teacher along with the classroom teacher in every Lower School classroom during reading time. There are rigorous academic expectations while allowing for plenty of creative expression. Community service is a requirement beginning in the Middle School.

Parents say that LREI has always been in the forefront of innovative education. "Elisabeth Irwin has taught my son to solve problems and think through issues. Yet at the same time it has encouraged him to take risks regardless of the outcome," said a parent. Essentially it provides a very comfortable learning environment with a solid academic foundation: "The day is tightly structured without being constraining; one subject flows into the next"; "The Gestalt at a school has to be right for learning and at Little Red, it is." A teacher at LREI told me "Their first priority is to really love and care about the kids . . . they feel it is their responsibility to find a way so that each child can grow and be challenged."

The High School and Middle School each perform one musical and one drama production every year. Drama in the Lower School is usually something that grows out of the classroom curriculum. At LREI the classroom meeting is a long-standing tradition, as is the assembly program. Guest speakers address a range of topics. Student representatives organize and run Middle and High School assemblies. Every class in the school is paired with a buddy class in another division. They meet informally during the year to read together, as well as for special days, such as Poem in Your Pocket Day, Founders Day and Field Day.

The Lower School Thanksgiving Assembly is a tradition that reflects the sense of community at LREI. The room is decorated with a beautiful display of autumn cornucopia and corn stalks. The children and teachers sit in chairs and on the floor and there is a big basket in the middle. Representatives from each class get up and read a poem and put something they've made—cornbread, for example—into the Thanksgiving basket (the gifts are donated to the needy.) One of the faculty talks about the origin of the Thanksgiving tradition and they sing a Native American song. "It was not a spectacle for the parents, it had real meaning and was very moving," said a participant.

In Middle School, classes continue to focus on inquiry and investigation and students are called to use authentic materials and assess them. In math and science classes, students experiment with computer-based and robotic simulations, sensors, graphing calculators and tablet PCs. In humanities classes, students work with primary source documents and challenging texts and write for a variety of purposes and audiences. In all grades, the visual, musical and performing arts are integrated with the core social studies curriculum. In addition seventh and eighth graders take a performing arts elective. In their humanities curriculum, fifth and sixth graders study ancient civilizations through the expert lens of the anthropologist and archeologist and explore the ideas of and medieval societies and the Middle East.

Seventh and eight graders engage in a two-year study of United States history that examines history as a contested narrative through the lens of "cultures in contact." Through in-deph readings, role plays and simulations, students examine the founding principles of the Constitution and consider the role that power, politics and key social justice issues have played in defining our nation's history. Key events like the Egyptian Tomb, the Greek festival, the Medieval Pageant, the Colonial Museum, Constitution Works, the Science Exploration and week-long trips to Colonial Williamsburg, Washington D.C., Spain and France serve as important focal points for student learning.

In depth High School classes are combined with frequent field trips. Courses are interdisciplinary and organized around real-world themes, issues and problems. Ninth and tenth grade science classes integrate biology, chemistry and physics. Ninth grade World History class focuses on the central theme of social justice and the development of a global understanding of human rights. Ninth grade English places a particular emphasis on the structure and development of the essay, while reading world literature. In tenth grade, the emphasis in history is on the Constitution and the early national period, with a focus on expanding people and the economy. Tenth grade English also examines the various literary movements in America and the pivotal historical moments from which they emerged. This course builds on the essay writing, research, interpretive and analytical skills learned in ninth grade. All eleventh graders study the history of New York City. Juniors and seniors have extensive elective choices in most subject areas including Art and Politics, Toni Morrison, Classic American Literature, Latino/a Literature: voices of the 20th and 21st Century, Dante's *Comedy*, *Girls Gone Wild*, Gender and Madness in Dramatic Texts, Writing Workshops in everything from playwriting to creative short fiction and memoirs, science and math. Students who are in good academic standing may petition to include an Honors Project in any subject are in the schedule. Juniors and seniors are eligible to take courses at NYU. The Senior Project includes extensive research and an internship; assessments include exams, written assignments, exhibits, portfolios, and research projects.

Lower School students have physical education three times a week in a new physical and performing arts room. Younger children play on the school's rooftop playground. Older students use the Houston Street playground down the block for recess. Competitive sports begin in Middle School. Fifth and sixth graders have intramural sports and seventh and eighth graders compete against other schools. The High School offers track and field, cross-country, volleyball, soccer, basketball, softball baseball, tennis, and golf teams. The PE program offers yoga, dance, aerobics, karate and personal training.

Popular College Choices   Barnard, Brown, Columbia, Cornell, Oberlin, NYU, Vassar, Wesleyan, Williams

Traditions   Weekly Assembly Program, Buddy classes, Division and class trips, Book Fair, Halloween Fair, Arts Auction Literary Evening, Poem in Your Pocket Day, Founders Day, The Coffeehouse, High School Jazz Ensemble Community Service Round Table

Publications   Yearbook: *Expression*
Literary Magazine: *i.e.*
Newspaper: *The Charlton Label*
Lower School yearbook: *Really Red*
LREI newsletter (three times a year)
Weekly parent blogs

Community Service   Community service is a requirement in all three divisions of the school. Lower School students hold food and clothing drives to help support families in need. Middle and high students work in local soup kitchens, clean up the neighborhood and participate in such events as the AIDS Walk; high school students run the Community Service Roundtable, a student-driven "foundation," which identifies and awards grants to various worthy causes, volunteers for activities and service organizations in the community. The Roundtable consists of an advisory group composed of parents and friends of LREI. Additionally, high school students work with Amnesty International educators and policy experts to enhance their understanding of global social justice and human rights issues. The group writes letters, sponsors assemblies and one of the annual Coffeehouses

Hangouts   Student lounge, Pizza Box, In the Black Coffee Shop

Loyola School

980 Park Avenue
New York, NY 10028
(212) 288-3522
website: www.loyola-nyc.org

Coed
9th–12th grade
Not accessible

Rev. Stephen Katsouros, S.J., President
Mr. James Lyness, Headmaster
Ms. Lillian Imbelli, Director of Admissions

Uniform Dress code consists of blue blazer with Loyola patch for all students. Boys: collared shirt, tie, slacks. Girls: collared blouse, skirt or slacks. No jeans, T-shirts or sneakers

Birthday Cutoff None

Enrollment Total enrollment: approximately 200
Graduating class size: approximately 50

Grades Semester system
Numerical grades for exams and report cards; letter grades for progress reports

Tuition 2009–2010 $27,000, 9th through 12th grades; additional fees approximately $1,000

Financial Aid/Scholarship Approximately 30% of the student body receives some form of financial assistance

Endowment $8.5 million

Diversity As one student said: "Loyola has a very diverse group of students from different walks of life. When the student body comes together a very special atmosphere is created."

Homework Approximately 2½–3 hours per night

After-School Program Extracurricular activities and clubs meet after school and during a mid-day period set aside for this purpose in a six-day cycle; choices include arts, speech, debate; varsity and junior varsity teams compete in the Independent School Athletic League, the Girls Independent School Athletic League, and the New York State Association of Independent Schools Athletic Association

Summer Program   None

Loyola School was founded in 1900 by Jesuits at the request of parents who wanted a Catholic alternative to non-sectarian prep schools. At that time the school was "up in the country," but featured the most up-to-date classrooms in the entire city. It became coed in 1973. Loyola School is the only independent coed Jesuit high school in the New York tri-state area. Loyola combines Jesuit traditions with a strong college preparatory program. The school's motto, Ex Fide Fortis, means "From Faith, Strength." The school is governed by a lay board of trustees and has been named a School of Excellence by the U.S. Department of Education.

The school is housed in an imposing stone building at Eighty-third Street and Park Avenue. In September 1996, Loyola completed a half-million dollar renovation of the fourth floor. This expansion allowed the school to enlarge its science and computer labs. Over the past five summers, Loyola School has undergone a complete floor-by-floor renovation of all classrooms, science and computer labs, and administrative offices. This renovation also included the complete overhaul of the 100-year-old chapel, which revealed a beautiful arched Venetian-inspired mosaic. Loyola has one of the largest professional-sized air-conditioned gymnasiums in the city. Such home court advantage has long fostered award-winning basketball and volleyball teams.

Getting in: Applicants and their families may RSVP to one of three information sessions held throughout the fall. Parents can also schedule tours for a morning when school is in session, or spend a day shadowing a student. Applicants are evaluated on the basis of their academic and personal qualifications. Admissions requirements include: a transcript from the current school, a personal interview, two letters of recommendation, and one of three standardized tests, the ISEE, SSAT, or HSPT which is scheduled once a year for applicants and is included in the application fee. All tests are viewed equally. Applicants are encouraged to spend a day visiting classes.

Parents: A "New Parents" evening is held in the fall of the freshman year, an opportunity for parents to socialize and to familiarize themselves with their child's daily life. Parent-teacher conferences are held four times a year and either a written report or an estimate is sent home approximately every six weeks. There is an active Parents Association that publishes a newsletter.

Program: There is a warm and friendly family atmosphere at Loyola. As one student said: "At Loyola, they care about us as students and as teenagers getting through today's world." Every student has a faculty mentor who assists with student's academic, spiritual and extracurricular options.

Loyola's goals are to promote religious, intellectual, cultural, social and physical growth in every student as well as a concern for social justice. "Jesuits are known for being very independent," I was told. While many students are Roman Catholic, a variety of faiths are represented. According to the school, Loyola's philosophy is: "Strong faith must be founded on a solid understanding which extends to theology classes, where knowledge rather than belief is stressed." The curriculum in religious studies is complemented with a program of retreats, and each morning, before classes begin, optional Mass is available in the chapel.

The core curriculum consists of four years of theology, English and physical education; three years of history, math and foreign language; three years of science, one year of speech, composition skills, art history, computer, health and music history. Writing skills are stressed; freshmen are required to take seven periods a week in English and composition skills.

Students may take elective courses in art history, art studio, computer science, writing fiction, poetry, discrete mathematics, Latin, modern drama, modern American fiction, film study, chorus, ensemble, modern British and American poetry, philosophy in literature, global perspectives, political science and economics. French, Spanish, and Latin are offered. Advanced placement courses are offered in American history, European history, biology, physics, calculus, computer science, English, French and Spanish.

Loyola students excel in speech and debating, and there is a trophy case filled with the forensic and debate clubs' winnings. Loyola often places first in the small school division for State Championships. The school competes successfully in many local, regional and national competitions.

There is a large art studio and students work in many mediums including drawing, pastels, prints, watercolors, and oil painting. Students' musical activities include solo, ensemble instrumental and choral performances. "The Loyola Players" perform a drama and or comedy in the fall and a musical in the spring. Recent productions include, *Dead Man Walking* and *Once on this Island.*

The elected student government is an integral part of school life at Loyola. Representatives help plan school dances as well as address student's issues. The volunteer service program, whose motto reflects the Jesuit motto, "Men and Women for Others," provides opportunities for students to help others.

During Spring Break, in addition to the annual ski trip to either Utah, Colorado or Wyoming, students have the opportunity to participate in an annual trip to Europe with teachers and classmates. Recent trips have included Greece, Turkey, Austria, and Germany. Seniors may also attend a Habitat for Humanity service trip to Belize during the summer after graduating.

The athletic teams at Loyola are competitive. For boys, sports teams include junior and varsity soccer, basketball and baseball. Girls teams include volleyball, basketball, softball and coed varsity track and cross country. In a recent year the girls were finalists in the GISAL volleyball championship. The girls varsity softball team was season champion in GISAL. In recent years the boys' varsity basketball, soccer and baseball teams won championships. A professional quality gym, paddle tennis courts, and a fully equipped fitness room are also available to students.

The school has a cafeteria that serves a hot lunch daily. Beginning in ninth grade with parents' permission, students may leave for lunch.

Popular College Choices Amherst, Brown, Boston College, Columbia, Georgetown, Holy Cross, Loyola College, New York University, Princeton, Wesleyan, Williams

Traditions Freshman/Senior Night, Junior Talent Night, Family Day, Fall/Spring Drama Productions, Christmas Concert, Awards Convocation, Sports Night, Sophomore/Junior Semi-Formal, Senior Prom, Senior Trip to Italy

Publications Newspaper: *Blazer*
Literary Magazine: *The Lit Mag*
Yearbook

Community Service Requirement There is a four year Christian service requirement. Choices include: annual school-wide service projects at Thanksgiving, Christmas, and during Lent, which provide food, clothing, toys and monetary donations. Students also tutor underprivileged children, visit shut-ins, prepare and deliver meals to an SRO and to the homeless, work in metropolitan area hospitals, and help senior citizens. In addition to community service, students also volunteer in the weekend homeless shelter at St. Ignatius Loyola Church.

Hangouts The Commons, Ray Bono Pizzeria, the steps of the Metropolitan Museum of Art, Loyola Café and Senior Section

Lycée Français de New York

The French Baccalaureate School

505 East 75th Street
New York, N.Y. 10021
(212) 369-1400 fax (212) 439-4200
website: www.lfny.org
e-mail: admissions@lfny.org

Coed
Nursery–12th grade
Accessible

Mr. Yves Thézé, Head of School
Boualem Maizia, Deputy Head and Director of Secondary School
Vannina Boussouf, Director of Primary School
Martine Lala, Admissions Director

Uniform   All students have a dress code: white blouse and grey skirt or trousers

Birthday Cutoff   Children entering at the pre-nursery level must be 3 by December 31; at the nursery level they must be 4 by December 31 Children entering kindergarten must be 5 by December 31

Enrollment   Total enrollment: 1,376
Nursery places: 46
Pre-kindergarten places: 76
Kindergarten places: 105
Graduating class size: approximately 100

Tuition Range 2009–2010 $19,000 to $23,000, Nursery–12th grade; additional fees for registration enrollment and for new students, $3,200; tuition payment plans are available

Financial Aid   Approximately 25% of the student body receives some form of aid

After-School Program   After-school program for nursery and elementary only; activities such as dance, French, theater, art, karate, judo, private music lessons, soccer, fencing, rollerblading, gymnastics, flute, chess club and supervised homework study time are offered; an additional payment is required

Summer Program   Weekly sessions from June 22–July 24; Full day sessions only; all activities are conducted in both French and English; each group participates in a daily French course. There are trips to museums, parks, and the zoo

———

Founded in 1935 by a group of French and American individuals, the Lycée Français de New York offers a traditional French education as well as an English/American Social Studies program. At least fifty nationalities are represented in the student body. The dual approach produces bilingual students, proficient in both English and French, who have a deep understanding of European and American cultures. "Here we are not just French students," wrote one student in the Memory Book. "We are part of an international community. We live together and we share our experiences, our cultures."

The firm that planned the Clinton Library designed the school's new spacious facility which has central offices, a cafeteria, a gym, and many new classrooms and labs, an atrium, computers, and state-of-the art technology. The buildings rise above a beautifully landscaped courtyard in two separate five-story towers, one for the Lower School, the other, for older students. Three full-lot floors connect these towers and act as the coeur, or heart, of the Lycée. The entire school uses the two libraries—both have wireless Internet access—the cafeteria and gyms, which unite the school's community. There's a large roof-top play area for younger students.

Upper School students have their own spacious art studio, science labs. Both Lower and Upper schools have classrooms equipped with Smartboards.

Getting in: Applicants to nursery through fifth grade are admitted on a rolling basis that includes interviews and school records. Applicants to the secondary school (sixth grade through terminale—twelfth year) must take an entrance examination unless they are transferring from an accredited French School (in France or elsewhere). The admissions office recommends that applications be submitted early in the fall.

Program: The Lycée is accredited by the French Ministry of National Education and by NYSAIS. No knowledge of the French language is required for nursery through kindergarten, (though recommended for kindergarten). The tone is decidedly traditional; there's a dress code/uniform that consists of familiar grey and white school attire. Students in grades one and above should have a working knowledge of the French language. Bilingual instruction is given in nursery and kindergarten. By first grade, French is the main language of instruction except for English, American literature, civics, and history, and other foreign languages. English as a Second Language (ESL) classes are available for non-English speaking students. Specialized teachers work with non-French speaking students in small group settings for at least one year. Mandarin is mandatory in Grades 3, 4, and 5.

Middle School consists of grades six, seven, eight and nine. Students take classes in math, science, geography, French, English, art, music, computer science, and physical education. Each subject is taught in French by specialists. In sixth grade, students choose a third language; choices include German, Italian, Spanish and Mandarin. An introduction to Latin and Greek is optional in seventh and ninth grades.

By the end of ninth grade, students are expected to take a French national exam called the Brevet des Colleges, which measures and evaluates a student's knowledge of French, math, history and geography.

By the last two years of Upper School, grades ten, eleven and twelve, students must choose a "major," in either Literature and Languages, Economics and Social Sciences, or Mathematics and the Sciences." Because of an accelerated curriculum, a high school diploma may be awarded to students after eleventh grade. All students are required to continue to the end of terminale and take the French Baccalaureate. The Lycée also offers students the option of taking the International Option of the French Baccalaureate (OIB) which allows for more writing, English and Social Sciences as well as a French-American Baccalaureate. Advanced Placement (AP) exams are offered in French (many ninth graders qualify), English, and Geography.

Popular College Choices   Brown, Cornell, Dartmouth, Duke, Harvard, MIT, Princeton, Tufts, Stanford, University of Chicago, University of Virginia, Yale, University of Quebec, McGill; Graduates also enroll in the "cours preparatoire" system before attending the "grandes écoles" of France, including Ecole des Hautes Etudes Commerciales, Ecole Polytechnique, Ecole Normale Superieure, Institut d'Etudes Politiques; European Universities include Université de Paris La Sorbonne and the American Business School in Paris

Publications: LFNY Magazine
The Lycee (in both English and French)

Lyceum Kennedy

225 East 43rd Street
New York, NY 10017
(212) 681-1877 fax (212) 681-1922
website: www.lyceumkennedy.org
e-mail: Info1@lyceumkennedy.org

Westchester Campus:
Cross Road
Ardsley, NY
Tel (914) 479-0722
Nursery–5th grade
e-mail: Info2@lyceumekennedy.org

Nursery–11th grade
Partially accessible

Ms. Kelsey Maples, Admissions Coordinator
e-mail: info1@lyceumkennedy.org

Birthday Cutoff Children entering preschool must be 3 by the start of school

Enrollment Total enrollment: approximately 150

Tuition Range 2009–2010 Approximately $18,600 to $23,400, nursery through 5th grade

After-School Program A daily program for children in grades nursery through 6th, from 3:30–5:30 P.M.; extracurricular activities are taught by specialist teachers in French and English, art, computers, theater, dance, martial, arts, photography, cooking and other activities

---

Founded in 1964 as a French International School that offers a French immersion program, Lyceum Kennedy boasts a diverse, multicultural, international community. According to the Head of School, Yves Rivaud, "We have 150 students representing 25 nationalities and more than 20 languages spoken." The school enrolls both French and non-French speaking students from around the world.

The school is small with only one classroom per grade, and the student-teacher ratio is low. All students take American and French tests and exams at both the elementary and secondary levels.

All subjects are taught with a dual approach to language that combines the flexibility and creativity of the American system with the more rigorous French method.

The Ardsley campus also offers the same bilingual program and educational philosophy for younger students, 3 to 11-years of age.

Mandell School

128 West 95th Street
New York, NY 10025
(212) 222-2925
website: www.mandellschool.org
e-mail: admissions@mandellschool.org

Coed
Nursery 2s-8th grade
Accessible

Gabriella Rowe, Head of School

Uniform None for toddlers through Pre-Kindergarten; Junior Kindergarten through eighth grade all students wear school colors, either green, gold or white; Lands' End provides uniform

Birthday Cutoff Children entering the 2s program must be 2-years-old by October 1st
Children entering the 3s program must be 3 by December 15th and toilet trained
Junior Kindergarten is for children who have summer birthdays that make the September 1st cutoff but who are not quite ready for a full kindergarten program
Children entering Kindergarten must be 5 years-old by September 1st

Enrollment Total enrollment: Approximately 430, increasing to approximately 620 by 2015
Nursery 2s places: 80
Nursery 3s places: 10-12
Kindergarten places: Approximately 15-25

Grades: Trimester system
Letter grades begin in fourth grade
Parent/teacher conferences are held three times a year from Junior Kindergarten through eighth grade; portfolio based interim reports are provided at the end of the school year; formal final reports provided at the end of the school year; parent/teacher and student conferences are available for fourth through eighth grade as needed
Departmentalization begins in fifth grade

Tuition Range 2009-2010 $11,400 to $29,500, Nursery 2s through 8th grade

Financial Aid/Scholarship   20% of the student body receives some form of aid; recently $650,000 was awarded in aid

Endowment   N/A

Diversity   Approximately 40% of the student body is diverse. Mandell enrolls students from Early Steps

Homework   Begins in Junior Kindergarten with one "home-study" project per trimester
Kindergarten: 15-20 minutes of parent assisted reading each night plus reading science journal entries two nights each week, as well as one "show and tell" item each week
First grade: 30-40 minutes of reading and math homework; weekly journal entries and a "Scientist of the Week" presentation each trimester
Second through fourth grades: 45-60 minutes plus reading
Fifth through eighth grades: 60-90 minutes, Monday through Thursday, and 90-120 minutes over the weekend

After-School Program   "Firefly," Mandell's after-school program offers a variety of activities; extended day is also offered Monday through Thursday, an additional fee is required, financial aid is available

Summer Program   For Nursery 2s through Kindergarten children from Mandell only; an Arts and Science camp is open to children from other schools, priority is given to Mandell students; a summer teaching program for Mandell graduates and high school students from other ISAAGNY schools

-----

The Mandell School was founded in 1939 as a neighborhood nursery school by Max Mandell, the current Head of School's grandfather and a deeply committed community minded pioneer in early childhood education. A large photograph of Max Mandell graces the school's lobby. Since Mandell's founding, both Gabriella Rowe and her mother, Barbara Rowe, have grown the school into not only a top-tier nursery school, but are in the process of adding an elementary division which is currently serving students through first grade. The school offers a homey, warm environment, but is decidedly traditional, structured, academically rigorous, diverse, and offers a strong teaching staff. Gabriella Rowe grew up on the two floors above the school, and she attests, "That feeling of home has been shared by many hundreds of Mandell children."

Mandell has several locations depending on the division. The youngest children are housed on West 95th Street, older nursery and pre-kindergarten programs are housed on West 96th Street, and junior kindergarten through eighth grade will be housed in a 60,000 square-foot facility on Columbus Avenue between West 97th and West 99th Streets.

In September 2010, the new building opens its doors; inside as well as outside everything is a green as the school's color. All rubber flooring is from recycled materials, there's a planting garden, a cafeteria, solar panels, greywater systems in the bathrooms and a vegetable garden on the terrace, and naturally, a green wall. Hot lunch is provided for students who stay a full school day, and of course there is always something green (or red or orange) on each plate every day. Children are expected to clean up after lunch, making sure they separate the liquids, scrap food, and paper products into different garbage cans.

Getting in: For the Toddler program, parents should go the Mandell School website (www.mandellschool.org) on the first working day after Labor Day beginning at 9 A.M. to request an application. All applications are emailed and should be returned as quickly as possible. "Messengers, overnight delivery and personal drop-offs" are recommended in the admissions instructions. Hence, receipt of an application does not insure an interview, as appointments are allocated on a first come first serve basis. After an application has been processed, a person from the admissions office will call to schedule a group tour for parents and an interview. Interviews and tours are offered between late October and January; both parents are expected to attend both the tour and interview and have an opportunity to speak to a member of the parent body. A member of the Mandell staff interviews parents and children for approximately half-an-hour. For applicants to kindergarten and first grade, applications can be emailed beginning in late-August, and must be completed and mailed or sent overnight or dropped off, along with a $60 application fee to the school. The admissions process consists of four steps: 1) the child's play date/group meeting for half-an-hour with the Director of the Preschool Program;

2) a one-on-one parent meeting with the Admissions Director; 3) a parent tour given by a current Mandell parent; and 4) attendance at a Mandell Town Hall Meeting with the Head of School. All applicants are required to submit test results from the ERB if applicable, along with previous school program, day care or parenting program reports. Both parents are expected to attend all admissions meetings, tours and interviews.

Parents: It comes as no surprise that parents are an integral part of the tightly woven fabric of Mandell's community. Parents volunteer their time tirelessly and enthusiastically; there are over 20 different parent-led committees, and a Parents Association president who oversees a dozen or more fund-raising activities, such as, an on-line auction, book fair, family music event and more, held throughout the school year. Mandell publishes a handbook of quotes from parents, teachers, and students, past and present. "Mandell has a very special place in our hearts," one parent said. "The friendships our children and we as parents have made at Mandell will be with us for the rest of our lives."

Program: From the earliest years at Mandell the concepts of good citizenship, academic preparedness and parental involvement define the school's program. One example of good citizenship at Mandell is the choice of materials used for the school's expansion. All flooring, paint, and finishes are as eco-friendly as possible and classrooms are equipped with occupancy sensors and carbon dioxide sensors to limit the use of lights and cooling.

The school consists of four divisions, The School for Toddlers, the Pre-School Division, the Elementary Division and the Preparatory Division. In the 2s program, children are guided through a smooth transition from home to school; the 3s program stresses community and collaborative learning along with block building, story time, art projects, puzzles, manipulatives and skill work. The 4s and 5s are divided into sections based upon age and ability and along with daily jobs, academic work begins in earnest. Curriculum themes are largely based on social studies units and include art projects, science experiments, math surveys, phonics games, pattern block designs and by kindergarten reading. According to one kindergarten teacher, "It is kindergarten and they are really, really ready to read," she explains. Composition books and lined paper for writing are used for learning word families and children begin personal journals listing members of their family. There are clipboard surveys that bolster math skills as well as social skills. All students from junior kindergarten through eighth grade have mandatory music and drama classes. Third and fourth graders take stringed instruments, and in the school's new black box theater all children from junior kindergarten through eighth will participate in at least one full theatrical production each year.

Foreign language begins in kindergarten with American Sign Language; first through fourth grades both have French and Spanish; fifth through eighth grade students have the option to continue either French or Spanish and all take Mandarin.

"Home-Study" projects start in junior kindergarten when parents or caregivers are asked to visit a chosen stop on the NYC subway map, collect artifacts, and make a poster-board presentation to the class about their trip. This is part of a larger unit on the study of NYC.

Students in the elementary division continue to learn independently and collaboratively to develop critical and analytical academic skills as well as sportsmanship, community service, and social awareness. Recently, a first grade class sponsored a mission to an orphanage in the Dominican Republic. Teachers, parents and children accompany a planeload of aid and begin a year-long relationship constructing a project with children at the orphanage. Homework help is available after school as well as during the school day.

Mandell plans to offer the same type of challenging yet supportive program through its pre-preparatory division along with a variety of core academic, elective classes and athletic activities affording graduates entry into the best private and public schools.

Traditions   Kids Grow New York, Moving Up Day, Teacher Made Holiday Gifts

Publications   School News: *Mandell Citizen*
Parents Association Publication: *PA Post*

Community Service Requirement   Community service at Mandell is mandatory; in kindergarten, students volunteer for Kids Grow New York (website: www. kidsgrowny.org), a project that relates to Green Spaces in New York in some way; teachers and staff work with students throughout the year on their projects

Manhattan Country School

7 East 96th Street
New York, NY 10128
(212) 348-0952, fax (212) 348-1621
website: www.manhattancountryschool.org
e-mail: mcs@mcs.pvt.K12.ny.us

Coed
Pre-Kindergarten–8th grade
Not accessible

Dr. Michèle Solá, Director
Ms. Lois Gelernt, Director of Admissions

Uniform   None

Birthday Cutoff   Children entering the 4/5's must be 4 by October 31 of the year for which they are applying

Enrollment   Total enrollment: 190-195
4/5's places: 19
Graduating class size: approximately 20

Grades   Detailed anecdotal reports
Three parent conferences required per year
No letter or number grades in the Lower School (through 4th grade); Effort is graded in the Upper School
Departmentalization begins in 5th grade and is completed by 8th grade

Tuition Range 2009–2010 $28,500 to $32,500, 4/5's through 8th grade
All parents pay according to family income on a sliding scale. The maximum compares to full tuition at other schools
Fees are included in the tuition
Parents can pay tuition on a monthly basis; there is a 25% deposit required when contracts are signed

Financial Aid/Scholarship   Approximately 70% of the student body receives some financial aid

Diversity   55% of the student body is diverse

Endowment $8 million

After-School Program   A variety of creative, academic, and recreational activities. MCS After-School Program meets Mondays–Thursdays from 3:00 P.M. until 5:30 P.M. for 4 year olds to 8th graders, an additional payment is required

Homework   Nursery and K—None
   1st grade: Once a week, 30 minutes
   2nd: 30 minutes, 3 times a week
   3rd and 4th: 45 minutes, 4–5 times a week
   5th and 6th: 1–1½ hrs per night
   7th and 8th: 2–3 hrs per night

Summer Program   Three-week summer farm camp program in the Catskills; for 20 children age 9 and up; open to students from other schools; an additional payment is required

---

In 1966, Manhattan Country School was founded by Augustus and Martha Trowbridge, on Manhattan's Upper East Side, in an elegant private landmark building designed by Ogden Codman. Manhattan Country School's origins are deeply rooted in the social and ideological principles of the Civil Rights Movement. Its commitment to equality, social justice and cultural diversity are at the center of its curriculum. MCS has achieved what many independent schools with far greater endowments and financial aid claim is their goal: a truly diverse school. Over fifty percent of the student body and faculty are people of color. There is a unique tuition/scholarship program at MCS. The school is a recipient of a private family foundation grant to develop a gender-equity curriculum.

   Getting in: All parents applying to MCS should visit the school as a first step in the admissions process. From mid-September until mid-December, tours are held during the school day. Additional tours are available in May. Parents of children applying to Pre-K through first grade should attend a tour before December. In the fall, an evening open house is held at the school. Parents who have requested admissions materials prior to October will automatically receive an invitation.

For applicants from pre-kindergarten through first grade, MCS does not require the ERB test. However, if the test is administered MCS should receive a copy of the test results. Children are observed and asked to play games, draw or do a puzzle at the group interviews. For applicants for second grade and above, ERB test results are required, as well as the applicant's school report and an interview. "Most importantly, we're looking for a good match, families that are comfortable with a diverse community," attests the Director of MCS.

Parents: Parents at MCS, as well as parents of alumni, are active fund-raisers for the school. They help organize many events throughout the school year. The parents of each class are responsible for one event, a total of ten in any given year. These include: Farm Festival, Grandparents' Day, Spring Benefit, Dr. Martin Luther King, Jr. Commemorative Walk, and Farm Outing Day. There are many opportunities for parents to come together with the faculty and administration, to discuss common issues relating to education and child development. Parents Association Meetings are well attended and committees meet regularly.

Parents are an integral part of the social studies curriculum. The 4/5's class make "home visits"; the 7/8's study their families in depth for one semester; the sixth grade invites parents and other relatives to share their histories as part of their study of the Civil Rights Movement. Teachers at MCS welcome the opportunity for parents to share stories and talents and accompany students on class trips. Parent-teacher conferences are held three times a year, and parents may meet more often if there's a need.

Program: The Lower School at MCS is composed of six mixed-age groupings from 4/5's through 9/10's. The Lower School groups span two overlapping age levels. These mixed-age groupings offer flexible academic and social placements for children and enable the school to meet the developmental needs of each child. Within this framework, a grade level for each student is designated by the school. The average class is eighteen, but many classes are taught in smaller groups of eight to ten students. Each of the four youngest classes has a head teacher and an assistant, as well as student teachers, in most classrooms throughout the school. One parent recounts, "To me the most important characteristic of MCS is the deep respect shown to students and their individuality. In this school community, students learn to value themselves along with their peers. The artificial barriers that schools routinely set regarding the teaching experts and the learners are less visible in the MCS environment. Everyone is learning and everyone is teaching."

The core curriculum at MCS is its social studies program. It allows the school to apply its multicultural perspectives and fosters positive social values. In the Lower School, social studies is integrated into all areas of the classroom through graphs, geography and mapping, creative writing, literature, drama and art. In the Upper School, social studies and history follow a chronological organization. Students refine research skills, and learn how to write formal research papers, as well as point-of-view essays.

Formal reading instruction begins in the 5/6's class. In small groups, (approximately half the class), students have reading and writing times. MCS takes into account that children learn to read in a variety of ways, and the teachers use many materials, including basal readers, structured phonics materials and literature. For students who need reinforcement, a reading specialist works in the classroom with small groups of students. If additional support is needed, a student will work with the specialist in another room. If a tutor is recommended, the school will work together with the student's tutor to help meet the student's needs.

The school considers Spanish to be an essential component to the multicultural experience at MCS. Beginning with the four-year-olds, Spanish is taught at every level in mixed-age groupings. Signs throughout the school are written in Spanish. The Lower School Spanish program is culture-based and integrated into the classrooms. The Upper School Spanish program is textbook based and prepares students for the New York State Proficiency Exam in Spanish.

The Upper School at MCS is composed of grades five through eight. Departmentalization begins in fifth grade. Fifth and sixth graders study English, social studies and math with their group teacher. Specialists teach Spanish, science, art, music, shop and physical education. In seventh and eighth grades, students are divided into two mixed-age homerooms, and each student is assigned a faculty advisor. Classes for seventh and eighth grades are fully departmentalized.

The math program follows four fundamental themes: making sense of data, patterns and predictions, numbers and number sense, and geometry and spatial sense. In the Lower School, math is integrated into the children's daily activities and manipulative materials are used. Upper School students follow a common text.

MCS has taken a hands-on approach for the science curriculum.

Teachers and science consultants make use of Central Park as a nature laboratory. Students learn to use the scientific techniques necessary for accurate observation, problem-solving and recording. Classrooms have work areas for experimentation, science displays, and science libraries. A goal of the science program is to instill a critical understanding of the ethical questions surrounding scientific issues.

MCS is wired for Internet access and classrooms are networked. Beginning in the second grade, students have computer and Internet access available in their classrooms. Fifth through eighth graders must complete a four-year computer literacy course and older children are offered electives in computer graphics and design and computer classes. An after-school computer class is offered to the 4/5's through fifth grades.

Computer use is directly related to the curriculum. For example, the seven- and eight-year-olds host their own website on Mammal Study; the eight- and nine-year-olds communicate via e-mail with Native American students in New Mexico; shop students use AutoCAD to design woodworking projects, and the fifth grade writes and formats the school newspaper.

Art, music and drama enhance the curriculum. Art is required of all students through sixth grade; seventh and eighth graders must meet a combination requirement in the arts, with additional electives available in each subject.

Upper School classrooms also contain Smartboards. All students have weekly library classes. The library hosts presentations by visiting authors, such as Jamaica Kincaid, Milton Meltzer, Brian Pinkney and Vera B. Williams. It is also where class plays and family story-telling gatherings are held.

Children in the 4/5's through 7/8's have daily outdoor activities at a nearby playground or in the meadow at Central Park. There are structured group activities with a physical education teacher once a week either in the school's music room or in the park. The 8/9's through eighth grade have outdoor time in Central Park three times a week and a structured physical education class twice a week at the 92nd Street Y. There are elective classes in soccer, track, basketball, softball, and tennis for older students.

MCS owns a small working farm, located on 177 acres in the Catskill Mountains in Roxbury, New York. Students with their teachers, begin going to the farm in the spring of their 7/8's year. By fifth grade, they have three week-long trips a year. The farm acquaints students with a self-reliant way of life. "One of my favorite times was at the farm. My farm education gave me an appreciation for a completely different lifestyle, as well as teaching me various things like milking cows, tapping trees, creating textiles," says an alumna. The farm program leads to six graduation requirements: to milk a cow; to plan and cook an evening meal for the entire class and to bake bread or another yeast dough product without adult assistance; to identify birds, plants, animals and their tracks; to describe the life cycle of one animal; to produce an original textile from fleece to a finished garment, artifact or material; and to participate in a "town meeting" on an environmental issue. One graduate recounts, "Looking back at my years at MCS, I realize that I loved everything about it. At the time I remember feeling that the school was so small and undeveloped. However, MCS had everything I needed. The diverse community and the close relationships with my teachers were experiences that I would not have gotten anywhere else."

Graduates: About half go on to the specialized or alternative public high schools; half go on to the independent schools including Riverdale, Fieldston, Friends, Dalton, Calhoun, Trevor Day; one or two students attend boarding schools such as Andover and Suffield Academy

Marymount School of New York

1026 Fifth Avenue
New York, NY 10028
(212) 744-4486, fax (212) 744-0163
website: www.marymount.K12.ny.us

All girls
Nursery–12th grade
Accessible

Ms. Concepcion R. Alvar, Headmistress

Uniform   Lower School—Fall/Spring: blue cord jumper, white short-sleeved blouse, navy blue blazer or sweater. Winter: navy blue jumper, white or red turtleneck, navy blue sweater or blazer; pants option
Middle School—Fall/Spring: blue cord skirt, white short-sleeved shirt or blouse, navy blue blazer or sweater Winter: plaid or gray skirt, white turtleneck blouse, navy blue blazer or green sweater
Upper School—Fall/Spring: blue cord skirt, white, black, gray, pink, or navy blue short-sleeved shirt and sweaters or navy blue blazer. Winter: plaid or gray skirt, white, black, gray, or blue turtleneck/blouse and sweater or navy blue blazer; pants option

Birthday Cutoff   Children entering at the nursery level should be 3 years old by August 31
Children entering kindergarten should be 5 by August 31

Enrollment   Total enrollment: 570
Nursery places: 24
Kindergarten places: approximately 25
Graduating class size: approximately 48

Grades   Semester system
Letter grades begin in Class V. Grades are distributed each semester; interim reports are given in November and March at parent-teacher-student conferences twice a year
Departmentalization begins in Class VI

Tuition Range 2009–2010 $19,595 to $34,000 Nursery–Class XII; includes fees for books and activities and lunch fees for kindergarten through Class VII

311

Financial Aid/Scholarship   Approximately $2.5 million dollars is available in financial aid/scholarships to those who qualify
Approximately 25% of students receive some aid

Endowment   N/A

Diversity   Approximately 26% students of color; Marymount enrolls Prep for Prep students
32 nationalities are represented
Cultural Awareness Club, Diversity Committee, Bias Awareness Training, Jazz Festival, Harambee Night, International Week, Monthly Culture Celebrations, Senior Class trip to the U.S. Holocaust Memorial Museum, Class VII study tour in Paris, Class VIII European sports tournament, Marymount Singers European Concert Tour, China 2000 Program, Exchange programs with other Marymount schools in London, Los Angeles, Paris and Rome; variety of conferences including: Asia Pacific Americans Youth Association, Diversity Awareness Initiative for Students, NYSAIS Diversity, NAIS-People of Color/Student Diversity Leadership

After-School Program   Marymount's after-school program for K–III requires an additional payment
After-School Activities Program: for grades kindergarten through Class III, Monday–Thursday until 4:30 P.M., Fridays until 3:30 P.M.; a variety of creative and recreational activities
Classes IV through VII offer a variety of sports and clubs throughout the year including a musical dramatic production, spring concert, student government, instrumental recitals, award-winning literary magazine
Supervised Study Program, Monday–Thursday until 6:00 P.M. for Kindergarten through Class VII

Summer Program   Marymount Summer Program Day Camp: coed, ages 3.5 to 5 years-old open to students from other schools; five weeks, mid-June through July; a variety of creative and recreational activities; Performing Arts Camp: coed, ages 5 to 13 years-old, acting, improvisation, dancing, singing, and set design; the program culminates in the production of a full-scale musical; Science/Technology Camp: coed, ages 5 to 12 years-old, exploration in science and technology centers, field trips; team sports and swimming are part of both programs

The Marymount School of New York was founded in 1926 as part of an international network of twenty-one schools directed by the Religious of the Sacred Heart of Mary. The founder, Mother Butler, believed that women should be leaders in society and that, "the world never needed women's intelligence and sympathy more than it does today." The school became independently incorporated in 1969, and is a current member of the Annual Implementation Committee of the Marymount International Network of Schools.

The Upper and Lower Schools are housed in three adjoining Beaux Arts mansions on Fifth Avenue, part of the Metropolitan Museum of Art landmark district. The breathtaking ballroom on an upper floor serves as an auditorium, lunchroom and gymnastics/movement room. The Middle School is located at 2 East 82nd Street, a completely renovated six-story turn-of-the-century townhouse. Sixty-six percent of the student body is Catholic and thirty-two different nationalities are represented. Headmistress Concepcion Alvar attests, "Spiritual values, community service and liturgy are the moral thread that binds the school." Chapel service, held once a week, may be conducted by students of any faith. Students attend Mass at least six times a year. Students can participate in an exchange program with other Marymount Schools such as Los Angeles, London, Paris or Rome.

Getting in: Parents can inquire any time on the website or by phone. Applications and other admissions materials are also available on the school's website or by regular mail at the start of the admissions season in September. An Upper School Open House is held in the fall. Families may tour the school before applying. Spring and fall tours are offered. In Middle and Upper School, applicants and their parents are interviewed together. For Lower School, the Director of Admissions interviews the parents, and the applicant is interviewed on a separate date. ERBs are required for 4-year-olds and above. The school says it "thoroughly considers the unique qualities of each applicant including academic curiosity, humor, diligence, and sensitivity."

Parents: The parent body includes business people, artists, academicians, engineers, doctors, lawyers, researchers, educators, bankers, civic leaders and government officials. Parents are an active and integral part of the school. They give tours as parent ambassadors, volunteer to read to children, accompany classes on field trips, etc. Activities sponsored by the Parents Association include parent meetings, the annual benefit, Christmas Fair, Book Fairs, the Skating Party, the Parent/Daughter Book Club and others that strengthen school-family ties. Parents and alumnae give career seminars and offer their places of work for senior internships.

Program: The Lower School is composed of nursery through third grade. The average student/teacher ratio in the school is 1 to 7. There are two sections of nursery, one in the morning and one in the afternoon. An optional afternoon session is available for pre-kindgerten students who are ready for a full day for either two or five afternoons a week, Nursery through Class I have head teachers and assistants. Classes II and II are team taught. The program is structured and traditional, but aims to be creative, integrated and dynamic. Organized learning centers are equipped with hands-on, interactive materials that encourage experimentation and collaboration. Specialists in math and language arts work closely with teachers to develop different learning strategies and or groupings to best meet student's needs.

Science and technology education starts at the nursery level. Beginning in nursery school, Lower School students learn in the state-of-the-art science and technology laboratory with its child-size tables and stools. The school also has specialists in art, music, science, computers and physical education.

Marymount has a unique relationship with the nearby Metropolitan Museum of Art, ranking first among all city schools in the use of the museum as a learning resource. Other city resources that the school uses as classroom extensions: the United Nations, Ellis Island, the Stock Exchange, the Central Park Zoo, the Metropolitan Opera, Lincoln Center, Sloan-Kettering Research Labs, the Staten Island Observatory, American Museum of Natural History, the Rose Planetarium, the Frick, Guggenheim, and El Museo Del Barrio Museums and various galleries and museums.

Each Lower School student has a big sister in the Middle or Upper School. This bond is strengthened throughout the year by trips, special events and collaborative academic projects. The recent project on water has been installed at the United Nations as part of their "decade of water" celebration.

According to the brochure, in Middle School, grades four through seven, "Each student is encouraged to develop and pursue areas of interest, to think honestly and critically about the world around her and to acquire a sense of social responsibility in school, at home and in her community." The integrated core curriculum gradually increases in the degree of departmentalization at each grade level. Research and study skills, with a focus on time management and organization, are emphasized.

French, Spanish and Latin are introduced in Middle School, and there is a Class VII study tour to Spain and France. A leadership training program begins in seventh grade. Speech, debate and drama

314

are incorporated into the program and students participate in weekly assemblies, chapel services and an annual drama production.

Marymount School integrates technology into the curriculum creatively, and appropriately. Technology provides multiple tools for gathering data, sharing information and completing assignments. The school has over 400 computers and numerous servers that are all networked—wired and wireless—on a dual platform system. All computers have direct access to the Internet via a T-1 connection. Students collaborate on curricular-based projects, master software, learn to use the Web for information, research, communication and publishing, and master a variety of computer-related materials such as scanners, digital cameras and digital probing equipment. Students' videoconference with other schools in the Marymount Network and produce a web-based Weekend Weather Forecast.

All staff and Upper School students have their own e-mail accounts and all syllabi are on-line; on-line courses are offered to Upper School students. Lower and Middle School students have class accounts that are under a teacher's supervision. There's a laptop program in art, library, science, and the entire middle school. Computer clusters are available for independent work, as well as "Smart" classrooms for group work, two computer centers for one-on-one computer work, and "one computer" classrooms for demonstrations and introducing new topics. Students in Class VII explore a variety of technology applications in Tech Lab. Class XI take a Computer Science course, and Class XII studies Advanced Programming. Robotics is covered in Class III and IV, while Scratch Programming is taught to Classes VI and VII.

Upper School students take three years of laboratory science and ninety-five percent elect a fourth year of science. AP courses are offered in chemistry, biology, physics, statistics, calculus AB and BC, English, French, Latin Literature, Spanish, Spanish Literature, United States History, Portfolio Drawing, and Design and Art History.

The Upper School consists of grades eight through twelve. In addition to French, Latin or Spanish students may choose to take Greek as a second language. Graphing calculators, computers, Smart-Boards, blogs, wikis, pod casting, and other technological tools are used frequently throughout the curriculum. The ninth grade team-taught Integrated Humanities Program links interdisciplinary themes in English, history, art history, religious studies, and studio art. Students visit the Metropolitan Museum of Art at least once a week. In the spring, seniors begin a four-week internship program, sponsored by institutions in the city, alumnae, parents, and friends, during which they are exposed to a wide range of careers. Students take four years of religious studies including World Religions, Social Justice, Hebrew and Christian Scriptures and Ethics. New Upper School Electives include, economics, music history, classical Greek, History of Theater, studies in Africa, South America, the Middle East, and modern China.

Hybrid on-line courses are also offered in Atmospheric Science, Multimedia Applications and Programming Languages.

With the Director of College Counseling, seniors take part in a weekly senior career seminar hosted by alumnae who discuss their lives and work, as well as college placement.

All Marymount students are encouraged to participate in a variety of extracurricular activities, and they can select from a wide range of sports and clubs. Clubs include three publications, the Finance Club, Simply Shakespeare, Philosophy Club, Set Design and Tech Crew, Forensics, Model UN, Mock Trial (finalists for the 2009 Mock Trail Championship), Art Club, Student Government and more. Fourteen team sports are offered, including swimming, field hockey, tennis, golf, and fencing. In addition to varsity sports there are six junior varsity teams and Class VII/VIII teams.

At weekly assemblies, students make presentations and gather to hear various speakers address the school community. The alumnae sponsored Vincent A. Lisanti Speaker Series has brought in well-known speakers such as Pulitzer Prize winning author Jhumpa Lahiri, *Washington Post* foreign correspondent Robin Wright, the HIV/AIDs Prevention Organization's founder Sr. Tribebemaco, Athlete Tegla Laroupe, bioethicist, Ronald Green, nanotechnologist, Dr. Susan Arney, African-American painter, Philomena Williamson, and Sr. Helen Prejan, author of *Dead Man Walking*.

Each year students from classes nine through twelve spend time at retreats. Ninth grade students travel to Frost Valley to bond as a class, sophomores focus on community service, juniors on leadership and seniors on ethical values/transition into colleges and careers. All students participate in community and school service. Students in tenth grade are required to contribute forty hours of volunteer service at hospitals, schools or agencies in New York City as part of their Social Justice class. Lower and Middle School students visit senior citizens and participate in fund-raisers and holiday food drives. Students volunteer as student ambassadors, office assistants and peer tutors.

Federal Judge Katharine Sweeney Hayden, Class of 1959, described her experience at Marymount: "We were always encouraged to express ourselves! We read and read and learned to absorb, synthesize and digest large amounts of material. As a lawyer and judge, I draw upon the benefits of my Marymount training every day."

Popular College Choices   Barnard, Boston College, Boston University, Brown, Columbia, Connecticut College, Cornell, Dartmouth, Fordham, Harvard, University of Virginia, New York University, Notre Dame, Duke, Tufts, University of Pennsylvania, Vassar, Georgetown, Holy Cross, Wellesley, Loyola College, Princeton, Wesleyan, Villanova, Yale

Traditions   Founder's Day, Father-Daughter Square Dance, Vespers, Christmas Fair, Christmas Pageant, Lessons and Carols, Family Ice-Skating Party, Grandparents and Special Friends Day, the Book Fair, New Parents Reception, Field Days, Upper School retreats, Family Picnics, Athletic Awards Ceremony, Spring Benefit, Junior Ring Day, Alumnae Reunion, 100 Nights Senior/Faculty Dinner, Parent/Daughter Book Club, RSHM theme of the year, Senior Appreciation Week, Pre-season sports camp, Lower School Choral Concert, Instrumental Concert, Parent/Daughter "Light Up Your Mind" STEM (Science Technology, Engineering and Math) Project

Publications   Student Newspaper: *Chez Nous* (Middle School), *The Joritan* (Upper School)
Student Literary Magazine: *The Muse*
Yearbook: *The Marifia*

Community Service   Community Service is required of all students. Opportunities include participating in service trips to places like New Orleans, and Jamaica, taking part in New York Cares Day and the Achilles Club; visiting the elderly at the Mary Manning Walsh Nursing Home and the Kateri Residence; and sponsoring food and toy drives for the families of New York's Incarcerated Mothers Program and fund raising for sister schools in Zimbabwe, and Ronald McDonald House. Community service activities are coordinated through Campus Ministry, one of the largest student clubs at the school; students volunteer as student ambassadors, office assistants, and peer tutors; Class X contributes 40 hours of service as part of a social justice course; proceeds from dances, and local coffee houses support causes

Hangouts   Amity Coffee Shop, Metropolitan Museum of Art steps, Marymount teahouse, CitiMarket, Dean and DeLuca

317

Metropolitan Montessori School

325 West 85th Street
New York, NY 10024
(212) 579-5525, fax (212) 579-5526
website: www.mmsny.org

Coed
Pre-kindergarten through 6th grade
Accessible

Ms. Mary Gaines, Head of School
Mr. Bob Reveri
Ms. Jeanette Mall, Admissions Director

Birthday Cutoff   Children entering Pre-kindergarten must be 2.9 years old by September 1

Enrollment   Total enrollment: 200
Pre-K and Kindergarten places: 25–40
Kindergarten places only: as available
Graduating 6th grade class size: 10–15

Grades   Parents in the Primary level observe in classrooms and meet with teachers twice a year Lower Elementary and Upper Elementary parent/teacher conferences once a year and as needed; beginning in Extended Day, all parents receive a year-end detailed written report that describes their child's educational, social, and emotional development; letter grades begin in fifth grade

Tuition Range 2009–2010 $24,000 (primary half-day)–$29,700 (elementary)
New students registration fee: $1,500 paid upon enrollment

Financial Aid/Scholarship   13% of the annual budget is allocated to financial aid

Endowment $3 million reserve fund

Diversity: Approximately 30% of the student body is diverse

Homework   1st grade: 20 minutes three times a week
2nd grade: 30 minutes three times a week

3rd grade: 45 minutes three times a week

4–6th grades: 1½–2 hours four times a week

After-School Program A variety of activities before and after school: the before school program, from 8 A.M. to 9 A.M., offers physical education, art, and chess; after school offerings include strings, drama, chess, soccer, art, and study hall; a Clubhouse program that operates until 6 P.M. is also available daily; there is an additional charge for all programs

Summer Program None

___

Metropolitan Montessori School, formerly St. Michael's Montessori, was founded in 1964 and took its name from its previous location in St. Michael's Church on West 95th Street. In 1996, this popular nursery and elementary school moved 14 blocks south into a stately red brick building in the heart of the gentrified West Side. Located in an extensively renovated 1865 carriage house, London plane trees frame the stone and glass entrance of the building which once belonged to William Randolph Hearst. The building provided the growing school with an additional 5,000 square feet of space. Characteristic of this nurturing school, when digging the foundation for the new building they took great care to preserve two one-hundred-year-old London plane trees that grace the entrance.

Getting in: After submitting an application, parents tour the school. Tours are given twice a week in the mornings, followed by a question and answer period with the Admissions Director and the Coordinator of the Primary program. Children also come for a half-hour afternoon visit of a few children with a teacher in a Primary classroom. ERB testing is required for applicants to kindergarten through third grades. Students of color constitute approximately 20% of the school.

Parents: MMS parent body is "an eclectic mix of families from the Bronx to Chelsea, but most families are from 10023 to 10025 zip codes," explains the school's Director of Admissions. Parents are friendly, welcoming, and low-key. Each class has a parent-hosted cocktail party in the fall and MMS hosts a new parent evening in the spring where parents see classrooms and meet their child's teachers.

Program: The brochure states that "While educational method and classroom materials are firmly rooted in the philosophy of Dr.

Maria Montessori, the school addresses the unique issues and concerns of today's children." There are Montessori materials in carefully planned classrooms, and parents are pleased with the way the school imparts the academic groundwork necessary for later learning.

Mixed-age groups of children remain in the same classroom for three years, starting in Primary and continuing through the Lower and Upper Elementary programs. The school has four Primary classrooms for ages three, four, and five; three Lower Elementary classrooms for first through third grades; and two Upper Elementary classrooms for fourth through sixth grades.

In Primary, materials cover a full range of Montessori curricula, including language, math, art and culture, sensory development, and practical life skills. As children get older, materials are supplemented with a large array of resources and learning tools. The youngest children either work independently or with an older child who shows them how the materials are used. As children develop they begin to work collaboratively.

In Upper Elementary, they are ability grouped. Children in grades one through six keep journals for all subjects and continue working in them as they move up through the school producing a visible record of their academic progress. All students learn the fundamentals: math, grammar, spelling, and other disciplines. Grammar is taught through the use of symbols; it looks difficult but most children have achieved mastery by third grade. Attention is paid to individual development within a group setting and students are ability-grouped for every subject. For instance, a first grader might be reading at a fourth grade level, a sixth grader might be doing seventh grade level math. There are clear curriculum guides for each grade level, and a syllabus, that is supplemented with guest speakers and field trips around the city and region.

Starting in kindergarten, children meet with specialty teachers for French, Spanish, art, music, physical education, science, health and library. Strings instruction begins in first grade. Students begin using computers for word processing in fourth grade. Upper Elementary performs a play or musical every year.

MMS's Learning Center is staffed with a full-time psychologist and teacher who consults on a regular basis with the teaching teams, reviews teaching and student issues, plans and delivers individual and group remediation in coordination with teachers and parents, and coordinates the use of outside learning consultants and psychologists.

Popular Secondary School Choices Metropolitan Montessori graduates attend various public and private schools including Allen-Stevenson, Brearley, Bronx Science, Browning, Buckley, Calhoun, Chapin, Collegiate, Columbia Grammar, Dalton, The Delta Program, Fieldston, Friends, Horace Mann, Hunter, Little Red/Elisabeth Irwin Nightingale-Bamford, Marymount, Riverdale Country, Sacred Heart, Spence, Stuyvesant, Hunter, Saint Ann's, Sacred Heart, Town and Trinity

Traditions Fall Parent Social, Back-to-School Picnic, Spring Benefit

Publications The Messenger Newsletter; Primary Newsletter, MMS *Yearbook*

Community Service Requirement Service and respect is an important component of a Metropolitan Montessori education; the school raises money for its sister school, the Central School for Tibetans in Chauntra, India, as well as for other groups the children choose.

The Montessori School of New York International

347 East 55th Street/Sutton Place
New York, NY 10022
(212) 223-4630; fax (212) 644-7057

105 Eighth Avenue/Park Slope
Brooklyn, NY 11215 (718) 857-3341

55-30 Junction Boulevard
Elmherst/Queens, NY 11373
(718) 857-3474
website: www.montessorischoolny.com

Coed
Nursery 2s through 8th Grade
Not accessible

Mrs. Hannah Sinha, Director
Ms. Donna Thomas, Admissions

Birthday Cutoff: Children must be at least 2.0 years-old by the start of school; December 31 for Elementary grades

Enrollment: 100

Grades: Montessori checklists and anecdotal progress reports as well as standardized testing

Tuition Range 2009-2010: $10,000 to $15,000, Nursery 2's through 8th Grade; tuition varies depending on session

Financial Aid: None available

Endowment: None

After-school Program: Extended care available until 6 P.M.; for MSNY students only; additional fees for swimming, gymnastics and other activities

Summer Program: MSNY is open all year; summer registration is by the week; open to children from other schools; weekly themes include art and science projects, field trips, swimming, horseback riding, dance, drama, assemblies, end-of-camp talent show, academic tutoring and test prep for children ages 4 through 14

Founded in 1969, The Montessori School of New York now has three locations all offer a solid Montessori program. Classrooms are equipped with a full array of Montessori materials and equipment. Ages span roughly two years in each class, yet every class is small, and individualized attention is given to each child.

Getting in: check the school's website for specific information; siblings and international students are given priority.

Parents: According to the school, "The parent body is a complete cultural mix, an unpretentious, intimate group."

The program explores a variety of cultures through designated study units. Ethnic days and traditions are celebrated that reflect the school's diverse population. Children learn foreign language, either French or Spanish, as well as traditional basic skills through Montessori materials. Swimming lessons are given once a week, and children participate in two theatrical performances each year. There is a warm nurturing, secure atmosphere that permeates throughout the school.

Elementary students take public speaking, take on leadership roles and responsibility of various school events such as Fairs and the Senior Lunch.

The Nightingale-Bamford School

20 East 92nd Street
New York, NY 10128
(212) 289-5020 (main number), Admissions: (212) 933-6515
fax (212) 876-1045
website: www.nightingale.org
e-mail: admission@nightingale.org

All girls
Kindergarten–12th grade
Accessible

Ms. Dorothy A. Hutcheson, Head of School
Ms. Margaret Metz, Director of Admissions

Uniform Each division has a dress uniform designated for formal occasions detailed in the school's handbook; everyday wear for Lower School: navy or blue plaid tunic with several options of white collared shirts with navy piping or white turtleneck; navy sweatpants on cold days, plain navy cardigan, plain white ankle-length socks with navy piping, navy knee socks, navy tights; kindergarten girls may wear white tie sneakers, grades I-IV navy or brown leather tie oxfords or tie athletic sneakers
Middle School: navy skirt, gray or uniform blue plaid (no shorter than 5" above the middle of the knee), white blouse or turtleneck, white ankle socks, white or navy knee socks or navy tights or Nightingale yoga pants underneath skirts; Nightingale uniform sweater or Nightingale sweatshirt; athletic sneakers only, no slip-ons, yoga shoes, or "Chuck Taylor" Converse sneakers; minimal jewelry, one bracelet, watch, button or stud earrings, no makeup
Upper School: navy, gray or blue plaid uniform skirt (no shorter than 5" above the middle of the knee), solid-color collared shirt, including polo shirts, turtlenecks, and man-tailored shirts; Nightingale sweatshirt or any solid color sweater; solid-color ankle or knee socks or peds, solid-color tights; low-heeled or flat shoes or sneakers; no boots, clogs, or sandals all shoes must have closed toe and back

Birthday Cutoff Girls must be 5 years old by September 1

Enrollment Total enrollment: 560

Kindergarten places: 42–44
Graduating class: approximately 40–45

Grades Semester system, K–IV detailed narrative reports and checklists; comments continue through upper grades
Letter grades begin in 5th grade
Departmentalization begins in 5th grade
First final exam in 7th grade

Tuition Range 2009–2010 $33,725 to $34,350 all inclusive, kindergarten–12th grade; optional fees include Parents Asssociation dues and a yearbook fee; a Tuition Refund Plan is available

Financial Aid/Scholarship 33% of students receive some form of aid $3.2 million was budgeted for financial aid in 2009-2010

Endowment $50 million

Diversity 26% students of color, NBS enrolls students from Prep for Prep, TEAK, The Oliver Program and ABC (A Better Chance) among other programs; C.A.F.E.: Cultural Awareness For Everyone (school multicultural club that meets biweekly) sponsors assemblies, dinners, evenings with faculty advisors playing an integral role; parents and students of C.A.F.E. hold meetings and discussions; oversees a series of multi-cultural events throughout the school year
Faculty Diversity Committee; The Community Life Task Force, a group initiated by the board of trustees that develops programs that strengthen the Nightingale community including alumnae, trustees, parents, faculty, and staff; the school also has a Director of Community Life and Diversity who oversees these groups and their programs and is open to suggestions

Homework Lower School families are expected to read aloud with their children from kindergarten on, a half hour a night reading or being read to by the child.
Kindergarten: weekends
1st and 2nd: ½ hour
3rd and 4th: 45 minutes
5th and 6th: 1½–2 hours with built-in study hall during the school day

7th and 8th: 2½ hours
9th–12th: approximately 45 minutes per subject a night (with one homework-free subject per night); weekly assignments are given to encourage long-term planning

After-School Program   Hobbyhorse: coed, a variety of recreational and creative activities for kindergarten through Class IV until 6 P.M.; boys from St. Bernard's Schools also participate; 12–15 courses are offered including gymnastics, drama, dance, chess, fencing, tennis, swimming, cooking, magic, knitting, photography, computer; an additional payment is required; junior varsity and varsity sports for Middle and Upper School girls, NBS participates in interscholastic athletic competition and also the 12-team Athletic Association of Independent Schools including badminton, basketball, cross country, indoor track, lacrosse, soccer, softball, swimming, tennis, track and field and volleyball; the NBS gymnasium is usually open every Saturday for "pick-up" games and practices and Nightingale girls can participate in Saturday sports at St. Bernard's School
Special interest clubs include, Art Board, Asian Culture Club, a capella groups, community service board, debate club, EARTH Club, Gospel Choir, Drama Club, Human Rights Club, Model UN

Summer Program   Sunny Days Program: coed, a June program for children ages 5–12 from 8:30 A.M. to 3:00 P.M.; trips, arts and crafts, swimming, computer, cooking and so on; open to children from the community; an additional payment is required

---

The Nightingale-Bamford School began with classes held by Miss Nightingale in 1906. In 1919 Miss Nightingale was joined by Maya Stevens Bamford and together they founded The Nightingale-Bamford School in 1920. The school has central air conditioning, state-of-the-art science labs and a hi-tech theater/auditorium, a photo lab, three computer labs and a new cafeteria. "Formal, but not rigid, for very bright girls who know where they stand; not overly competitive," is the way one mother describes the school.

Traditional in the early years, Nightingale offers more choices later on. There is a conscious attempt to avoid gender stereotyping, while still instilling the social graces. They've struck a nice balance—keeping the best of the old while incorporating the new. "Academic rigor with a soul," says one parent.

Only the sixth head in the history of the school, Dorothy Hutcheson was preceded by the formidable Mrs. Edward McMenamin, who reigned for twenty-one years. "Ms. Hutcheson, now the senior head amongst the girls' schools, can be warm, accessible and fun and also strict and firm. She listens to and also takes action for the students," a senior said. Ms. Hutcheson knows each student by name and often greets them and shakes their hand as they enter the blue doors in the morning. A ninth grader told me, "Ms. Hutcheson cares and is very open to new ideas and suggestions. It's good to be able to tell her the way we feel." A full-time working mother, Ms. Hutcheson has already made her refreshing presence known in other ways too. She accepted the Student Government's proposal to add pants to the dress code (after allowing female faculty members to wear pants). She re-established the Senior Independent Study project which allows qualified seniors to drop some of their required courses and pursue in-depth a topic of their choosing. There is great emphasis on integrating technology into the classroom. " Nightingale's time to gather by division, a time to reflect, to make announcements, and to discuss issues of moral and ethical concern, was formerly known as "Prayers." By renaming it "Morning Meeting," which more accurately describes it, Ms. Hutcheson has shown that she is not afraid to break with tradition.

Getting in: One parent described NBS's application process as "warm and welcoming." Parents can arrange for a tour before applying. When the application is received, parents are given an appointment for a tour and an interview with a member of the admissions staff. On another date kindergarten applicants will have a group interview with Lower School teachers while their parents meet with Ms. Hutcheson or the head of the Lower School. Middle and Upper School girls take their tours with student tour guides. (Significant points of entry in addition to kindergarten are seventh and ninth grades.)

Individual interviews with a member of the admissions team or a division head are required. Girls do placement work during a separate testing visit held after school or on a Saturday morning. If admitted, girls and parents are invited to re-visit and spend time in the school. There are welcome parties for all new students and parents in the spring and early fall. A great deal of care is given to having families make a smooth transition to Nightingale. Preference is given to siblings and legacies, but they are not automatically accepted, and an active wait list is maintained after admissions decisions have been made. No letters of recommendation are required or desired as part of the process. Admission is based on the right academic match, not the correct social connections, they say. Nightingale has made a major commitment to diversity, and enrolls girls from a range of socioeconomic, ethnic and geographic backgrounds.

A mother who eventually chose NBS said that she "couldn't sit up straight enough at some of the other schools," and while she noticed "a lot of scarves on the parents at other girls' schools," she was impressed by "the sensible shoes" she saw at NBS.

Is there a typical student? It depends on whom you ask. According to one parent, "She has blond straight hair, uses little or no makeup and carries an L. L. Bean bookbag." Yet another parent told me the typical student is "earnest, engaging, vibrant and aware," referring to an Upper School student she felt exemplified NBS qualities. A tenth grader said "We are smart, involved in the life of the school and have learned to speak with confidence." Obviously!

A parent told me that NBS delivers "a ton of nurturing." She felt her daughter walked the line between "funny and fresh." Since it sometimes seems that outgoing girls receive the most attention, it was refreshing to see that Nightingale awards the Molly Hemmerdinger Scholarship Fund, in memory of Molly Hemmerdinger, "for support of a shy student with hidden potential." An NBS mother with two daughters at the school said she feels the school "is making little Eleanor Roosevelts out of the girls: self reliant, inner-directed and well versed." A father said, "They learn to be independent, to do for themselves." He also believes there is a hidden agenda, to teach the girls the social graces. He also said he thought "Nightingale makes feminists of the fathers."

Parents: The parent body is diverse and varies from class to class. "There are lots of mixed [religion] marriages," said one parent. Jewish and Christian holidays are observed. "When you give at Nightingale, you receive," said one parent. "It's good to be an involved parent and make yourself known." One father who admits he always shaves before attending a school event or dropping off his daughter, yet describes himself as "one of the youngest and loosest" parents there, said he enjoys serving on "Daddy Patrol" (safety patrol) and walking his daughter to school with other Nightingale fathers and daughters.

A mother remarked, "As a parent of color in the school, I wanted to be vigilant, vocal and visible. Nightingale has welcomed me and my daughter fully and made us feel comfortable and I've loved the C.A.F.E. dinners and volunteering for various committees."

The Parents Association plays an integral role in the life of the Nightingale community by providing communication among parents, staff, administration and faculty and by supporting the school. Many parents volunteer their time and talents for school activities and events such as Grandparents Day, Father-Daughter breakfast, programs on parenting, Safety Patrol and the Book Fair. Other ways that parents are involved include speaking to classes and assemblies, asking friends with special areas of expertise to share them at school, inviting students to visit them on the job, singing at an all-School concert, performing in or helping with costumes and make-up for an all-School play, chaperoning class trips, volunteering in the library and cooking or baking for class get-togethers. In addition, the Parents Association sponsors the fair, a "Fathers Who Cook" dinner, and other major fundraising events to benefit the scholarship fund. There are other outings, including family picnics and skating parties. The Parents Association meets monthly to discuss issues of general interest; meetings are scheduled at convenient times for working parents. Nightingale's Speaker Series is one of the best in the city. The series is sponsored by the Parents Association and seeks to address issues concerning girls' intellectual, social, and emotional development. Recent participants include Reverend Debra Haffner, author of *From Diapers to Dating: A Parents Guide to Raising Sexually Healthy Children;* well-known nutritionist Joy Bauer; physician and medical journalist Dr. Holly Atkinson; Nightingale parent, Dr. Richard Haass, president of Council on Foreign Relations; and Catherine Steiner Adair, author of *How to Counter the Culture: the Challenge of Raising Healthy Girls.* The public is invited to attend these lectures, an example of the Nightingale's sense of community extending beyond the schoolhouse. Parents also publish a very helpful monthly newsletter, *The Nighthawk*, which includes calendars, updates on what is going on throughout the School, and thoughts from Dorothy Hutcheson, the Head of School.

Program: A great deal of care and intelligent planning has gone into the facilities and curriculum at Nightingale, taking into account much research into how girls learn. The rooftop playground is completely modernized with an emphasis on play that strengthens the upper body, an area where girls are traditionally weak. Math and science are taught by hands-on methods. Girls use math manipulatives and play math games.

The Lower School consists of grades Kindergarten through Class IV. Teachers in each grade are responsive to the differences in rates of social and emotional development and different learning styles. The program includes reading, English, math, history, and geography, and all of them incorporate use of computers. Other Lower School faculty members, specialists in their fields, teach science, music, art, library and physical education. Faculty members engage students in an integrated curriculum involving a number of hands-on activities insuring that each student learns how to learn in an increasingly systematic way. There is attention to individual learning styles and learning how to think independently and deductively. Basic skills are taught systematically, and content is a vehicle that enforces basic skills.

Art and music are integrated into the curriculum. There are museum trips and visits to other local points of interest.

Girls are expected to read every night. There is "daily practice in oral and written communication." A parent told me that her third grader has reading and writing homework every night.

Music appreciation classes are offered at many levels. Each class presents musical performances integrated with other studies.

The Middle School is composed of Classes V through VIII and addresses the special needs of early adolescents. As girls grow academically and developmentally, Nightingale offers broad opportunities to sample many kinds of activities. The academic program includes study skills and organizational skills needed for success in the upper grades. Classes are small and structured, girls are taught how to listen, follow directions, use computers and technology to produce independent research projects. Daily, before and after school, "labs" are available in every academic subject for students who request extra help or choose to explore a subject in greater depth. Every Middle School class has a homeroom with two teachers who are available throughout the day. An advisory system provides each student in Class VII an added opportunity to meet in a small group once a week and encourages a sense of community. In addition, each Class VII and VIII student meets with a learning specialist to help foster a better understanding of each girl's learning style. Art, drama and music focus on creative expression, physical education promotes fitness, skills, and sportsmanship. Clubs are another outlet of individual interests and talents. Trips augment the program at every level.

In the Upper School the curriculum is rooted in the liberal arts in preparation for college and life-long learning. Girls study English and math and establish a strong foundation in history, science and at least one foreign language. As a general rule, students take five courses each year, electives are offered in English, history and science. While many describe Nightingale as rigorous, no parent or student described it as a sweatshop either.

Grades are compared but not posted. The average grade is a C, one student said. Many teachers seem to go at the pace of the smartest students. Nightingale facilitates the seamless integration of technology into the curriculum. At Nightingale the goal is to have every teacher in every subject be fully capable of using technology to augment the best methods of instruction. Off-campus or study abroad options include a Swiss Semester in Zermatt, Ascham in Sydney, French exchange in Paris, Spanish exchange in Barcelona, St. Paul's exchange in London, The Maine Coast, The Island School, School for Ethics and Global leadership, Mountain School, Rocky Mountain Semester, Diocesan School, Upper School Chorus trips to Italy, Spain, Austria and Czechoslovakia, a Latin study trip to Italy, and London trip for all of Class IX.

Socially, one student noted, there was a definite popular group, and because the school is so small, it can be quite obvious. But a ninth grader said she had made "friendships that will last for life" at NBS and the "family-like environment makes learning more bearable and enjoyable." On the subject of single-sex education, one ninth grader told us, "You won't get distracted by a guy you like, it's easier to focus on schoolwork. On the other hand, it can be very hard to feel comfortable around boys because you don't get to spend much time with them." There are ample opportunities, however, for coed experiences through Interschool activities. At a recent open house an eleventh grader commented: "I came to NBS from a downtown coed school in ninth grade and I thought I'd really miss boys. Instead, I feel liberated. I don't have to worry about distractions during classes and I've kept my old friends who are boys and made new ones through Interschool activities."

Community service is a requirement in the Upper School; twenty hours in school and twenty hours outside of school are mandatory, plus twenty hours in an activity of choice. A student said, "Community service is stressed." NBS girls are very concerned about their community and participate in a variety of service activities.

Popular clubs in the Upper School include C.A.F.E: Cultural Awareness for Everyone, and the Gender Issues group. Other choices include the Drama, Dance and Glee Clubs, Interschool plays and musicals, student government, yearbook, newspaper, literary magazine, and Environmental Club.

Nightingale alumnae feel a strong connection to the school. "During a recent visit last spring I was pleased by the friendliness, the familiarity of the uniforms, and the sense that Nightingale is still a superior learning environment and a safe haven in a frenetic city," said an alumna. According to a mother, "Nightingale is a traditional community where people really care about each other, the girls are well mannered and well behaved . . . there are high expectations and they measure up from day one."

Popular College Choices   Harvard, Brown, Cornell, Vassar, Wesleyan, Yale, Dartmouth, University of Pennsylvania

Traditions   All-School Fair (proceeds support the Scholarship Fund), Big Sisters/Little Sisters, singing holiday songs before winter break; the Daisy Ceremony for Class IV; Moving Up Ceremony for Class VIII, Upper School Honors Assembly; Upper School Athletic Awards dinner; Class VII Gilbert and Sullivan production; Class VIII Shakespeare play with Allen-Stevenson; Field Day, Cum Laude, and other weekly assemblies with a mix of prominent speakers and student-led discussions; Winter Concerts, Dance Concert, Homecoming, The Father/Daughter breakfast; Grandparents and Special Person Day; Book Fair, Auction

Publications   Middle School literary magazine: *Out of Uniform*
Upper School newspaper: *Spectator*
Upper School literary magazine: *Philomel and Phunomel*
Upper School Current Events Journal: *Time Regained*
Alumnae magazine
Yearbook
Monthly parents newsletter: *Nighthawk*

Community Service Requirement   Upper School: 20 hours in school, 20 hours of service in the community, and 20 hours in an activity of choice

Hangouts   The Upper School terrace, Jackson Hole Burger Restaurant, Ciao Bella, senior lounge, Student Center

The Packer Collegiate Institute

170 Joralemon Street
Brooklyn, New York, NY 11201
(718) 250-0200, fax (718) 875-1363
website: www.packer.edu

Coed
Nursery–12th grade
Not accessible

Dr. Bruce Dennis, Head of School
Ms. Denise DeBono, Director of Admissions, Preschool and Lower
School
Mr. Jason Caldwell, Director of Admissions, Middle and Upper
School

Birthday Cutoff   Children entering at kindergarten must turn 5 by
August 31
Children entering first grade must be 6 by August 31

Enrollment   Total enrollment: approximately 980
Kindergarten places: 25
First grade places: 10
Ninth grade places; 30
Graduating class size: approximately 80

Grades   Semester system:
K–4, detailed anecdotal reports and checklists
Letter grades begin in 5th grade; in addition, detailed anecdotal
reports are sent twice a year

Tuition Range 2009–2010 $19,485 to $28,620 Nursery 3s–12th grade
Additional fees: under $300 for books (5th–12th grades only)

Financial Aid   32% of students receive some form of tuition assistance

Endowment $18.5 million

Diversity   32% children of color; Packer enrolls students from Prep
for Prep, The Oliver Program and students from other diversity
programs
Packer Collegiate has a Diversity Committee and full time Diversity Coordinator

Homework   Kindergarten and 1st grade: none
2nd grade: formal homework begins; the amount varies up to about 30–40 minutes per night
3rd and 4th grades: 1 hour, each school night
5th and 6th grades: 1–2 hours
7th and 8th grades: 2–3 hours
9th–12th grades: 3–4 hours

After-School Program   Packer Plus is open to Packer Collegiate students only in kindergarten through 8th grade; a variety of creative and educational activities from 3:15 P.M. until 6:00 P.M.; for an additional charge
Packer Plus Courses are offered on a trimester basis and meet from 3:30–4:30 P.M. for eight weeks; extracurricular clubs and activities; Junior varsity and varsity athletic competition

Summer Program   Summer Camp: open to children from other schools; mid-June through the end of July; an additional payment is required

---

Founded in 1845 as the Brooklyn Female Academy, and endowed by Harriet Packer, The Packer Collegiate Institute is the oldest independent school in Brooklyn and was the first to offer higher education to young women. It became coed in the early seventies. Packer's architecturally unique landmark building boasts many beautifully renovated and connected new spaces that include a new Middle School, an Atrium, Commons, Arts Center, music rooms, theater with retractable seating and tons of classrooms and more. In addition there is an elegant chapel with a 1906 Austin organ and nine Tiffany stained-glass windows. Chapel attendance is required once a week at which social, political, environmental and ethical issues are discussed. Packer also has an outdoor play area known as "The Garden." The style of the school is informal and there is no dress code. Hot lunch is available for grades three through twelve only.

Packer's diverse student body represents the five boroughs of New York City and the outlying metropolitan areas. Approximately 55% of Packer's Upper School students live in Brooklyn and 40% live in Manhattan. Parents say a distinct feeling of community exists among children of all ages and backgrounds and the faculty.

Getting in: Open houses are offered throughout the fall so prospective parents can tour the facilities and talk with students, faculty and administration. For pre-kindergarten through fourth grade applicants,

Packer requires a completed application and fee with school and teacher evaluations when appropriate. Pre-school candidates, ages 3, meet in small groups, 4- and 5-year-olds, meet individually and in small groups. Applicants to kindergarten and first grade are interviewed and evaluated at the school to assess their aptitude and learning style. Candidates for grades 2 through 4 are interviewed at the school and tested at the ERB. Applicants for grades 2 through 4 also spend a day visiting a Packer class. Applicants to K through 4th grade are required to submit ERB test results; and applicants to grades 5 through 12 have a personal interview and must submit previous school records, two teacher evaluations and results of the ISEE or the SSAT. There is a sibling and legacy policy for qualified candidates, but admission is not automatic. The main points of entry to the school are in kindergarten and ninth grades.

Program: The Lower School at Packer emphasizes an interactive, individualized, developmentally appropriate approach. Reading is taught using eclectic methods. "We use a wealth of materials to accommodate the variety of learning styles so characteristic of young children."

The Middle School at Packer begins in fifth grade. Students have one extended core class in English and history and another in mathematics and science. Computer, music, dance, theatre, chorus, gym and health round out the curriculum. All fifth graders must take a course called Frameworks which reinforces good study habits and skills such as note-taking, test-taking, research and so on. In sixth grade, some students, upon recommendation by their teacher, continue to build skills in a course called Language Extensions, with the expectation that they will begin foreign language in seventh grade. All other sixth graders begin study of a foreign language in French, Latin, or Spanish.

In seventh and eighth grades, the program is fully departmentalized. There are competitive sports teams and a variety of extracurricular activities from which to choose. Throughout Middle School homeroom teachers and advisors stay in close contact with both students and their families.

The laptop program provides all students in grades 5 through 12 with a varied grasp of techology and it's use. Packer has a wireless network and "Smart" classrooms.

Each Middle and Upper School student has an advisor who is a teacher in the school. The Peer Support program involves juniors and seniors who are selected to attend a leadership training seminar preparing them to meet with freshmen in small groups throughout the year to discuss their transition to high school.

In the Upper School, the freshman year is built around a study of major literary works. A collaborative program that involves faculty from the

English, History, and Arts departments integrates the study of ancient civilizations through the Middle Ages. Freshmen also take a rigorous year of conceptual or computational physics, foreign language and mathematics. The interdisciplinary approach continues in the sophomore year as students study The American Experience from historical, literary and artistic perspectives. Chemistry, foreign language and mathematics complete the academic program. Students in their junior and senior years have many electives from which to choose, including AP courses in 17 areas. A junior year English course, biology, and Modern European History are requirements. The average class size in the high school is fifteen, but the student-teacher ratio is 8 to 1, and the advisee to advisor ratio is 10 to 1.

Graduation requirements include four years of English and physical education; three years each of foreign language, mathematics, history, and sciences; two years of electives; two years of arts; one year of Health; and 45 hours of school and community service. Older students can participate in independent study, Senior Emphasis Program, Maine Coast Semester, High Mountain Institute, or a Cultural Exchange Program. Most seniors also use the second semester to work on a senior thesis.

Offerings in the arts are broad and include visual arts, photography, computer graphics, modern dance, orchestra, brass, choir, woodwind ensemble, jazz band and women's ensemble.

Clubs and organizations available to students include Amnesty International; Brothers and Sisters; Chorus (the Packer Chorus has been on two European Tours during the past four years.); Debate; Mock Trial; Model Congress; Multicultural Student Association; Drama Club, SAFE (feminist club); Packer Civil Liberties Union and the Social Action Committee; Student Government; and various school publications. There are numerous athletic teams in Middle and Upper School, including a Middle School coed soccer team, girls' volleyball, gymnastics, basketball, and softball, and boys' soccer, basketball, baseball, volleyball, tennis and squash.

Popular college choices   Brown, Harvard, Yale, Cornell, Wesleyan, Vassar, Dartmouth, Columbia, Connecticut College, Oberlin, George Washington, University of Chicago, Middlebury, Haverford, NYU

Publications   Art and literary publication: *Packer Current Items*
Yearbook: *The Pelican*
Newspaper: *The Prism*

Community Service Requirement   45 hours in the Upper School (9th–12th), tenth grade service project at a day care center, senior center, or soup kitchen

Philosophy Day School

12 East 79th Street
New York, NY 10021
(212) 744-7300, fax (212) 744-5876
website: www.philosophyday.org
email: secretary@philosophyday.org

Co-ed
Nursery (2.11 years old through 11 years old)
partially accessible

Mr. William Fox, Headmaster
Ms. Katherine Kigel, Director of Preschool Admissions

Birthday Cutoff   Children entering nursery school must be 2.11 years old by September 1
Children entering kindergarten must be 5 years old by September 1

Enrollment   Total enrollment: 140
Graduating class size: Approximately: 5-10

Grades   Anecdotal reports and checklists starting in kindergarten

Tuition Range 2009–2010   Approximately $15,000 to $22,000 Nursery–11-year-olds

Financial Aid/Scholarship   Approximately 25% of the student body receives some form of aid

After-School Program   Extended day available for students grades Kindergarten and above; an additional fee is required.

––––––

The Philosophy Day School is part of a worldwide group of associated schools that share the same values. The oldest of these is the St. James School in London, founded in 1975. The choice of name reflects a recognition of "the needs and traditions of America" according to the school's literature. The school building is an elegant landmark limestone townhouse which houses The School of Practical Philosophy in the evening. William Fox, the school's headmaster, was affiliated with the St. James Independent School before coming to New York.

Getting in: The school hosts an open house in the fall. After applying, parents tour and meet with the director of admissions. Applicants are interviewed on a separate date; the ERB is required for kindergarten. Siblings receive admissions priority.

Program: Like The Ark Nursery School, now under its aegis, The Philosophy School is closely connected to The School of Practical Philosophy (a non-profit organization chartered by the Board of Regents of the State of New York). According to the brochure, The School of Practical Philosophy "draws upon the timeless teachings of both Western and Eastern traditions to discover the unifying principles that underlie human existence, the emphasis is on the practical application of these teachings."

The Early Childhood program is half-day, Nursery and kindergarten have afternoon sessions.

Philosophy Day emphasizes learning through play incorporating the NAEYC's Best Practices. Beginning in kindergarten, students learn the eighteen virtues over a two year cycle. Topics include goodness, compassion, honesty, loyalty and truthfulness.

The teachers at the school are all members of The School of Practical Philosophy: "All teachers have attended the School's teachers group for many years studying both teaching and their particular subject."

Many subjects are taught in separate boys and girls classes in the belief that boys and girls learn better when taught separately. The student/teacher ratio is about 7 to 1. Small group learning blends with large group activities where students can explore different dynamics.

The school offers students such traditional subjects as reading, writing, mathematics, science, history, Latin and Spanish as well non-traditional studies: philosophy, scripture, and Sanskrit (the oldest extant language known to man and a model for the study of language in general.) The development of strong language skills is emphasized, with particular care given to the clear development of speech. Students examine the universal themes and principles found in the world's great philosophic and religious traditions in weekly philosophy classes.

Central Park is used for recreation and exercise. Additionally, frequent trips to nearby Museum Mile's exhibits are used as resources.

Popular secondary school choices   Nightingsle-Bamford, British American School, St. Joseph's (York and First Avenues), York Prep, Public Schools, including Robert Wagner

Traditions   Philosophy Day, Speech Day, Penny Harvest, Festival of Lights, Book Fair, Holiday Concert, Field Day, Awards Day

338

Poly Prep Country Day School
Coed
Nursery–12th Grade
Partially accessible

Poly Prep Lower School
50 Prospect Park West
Brooklyn, NY 11215
(718) 663-6003
website: www.polyprep.org
(Nursery–4th Grade)

Lawrence Donovan, Interim Head of Lower School Division
Pat Montero, Director of Lower School Admissions

Poly Prep Middle and Upper School Divisions
9216 Seventh Avenue
Brooklyn, NY 11228
(718) 663-6060
website: www.polyprep.org
(5th–12th Grade)

David B. Harman, Headmaster
Lori W. Redell, Assistant Head of School,
Admissions and Financial Aid

Uniform: There is a dress code for fifth through twelfth grades.

Birthday Cutoff Children entering nursery school must be 2.3 years
old by September 1
Children entering kindergarten must be 5 years old by September 1

Enrollment Total enrollment: 1001
Nursery–4th grade: 213
Nursery places: 25
K–4th grade places: 15
5th grade places: 20-25
6th grade places: 34

9th grade places: 35–50

Graduating class size: Approximately 120

Tuition Range 2009–2010 $9,050 to $30,250, ½ day Nursery–12th grade

Additional fees: lunch fee for grades 5th–12th approximately $950; bus transportation for students from Manhattan, Staten Island, Brooklyn and Queens is provided at no extra charge

Financial Aid/Scholarship $5.2 million awarded; 28% of the student body receive aid

Diversity   Poly Prep enroll students from Prep for Prep as well as other scholarship programs

After-School Program   Lower School, arts, sports, languages, electives program, Monday–Friday for K–4th grades, an additional payment is required; for grades 5th–12th, instrumental music, theater, debate, dance, extracurricular activities and clubs, Varsity and Junior Varsity athletic competition

Summer Program   Day Camp, Performing Arts Camp, Sports Camp, Science Camp and Computer Camp; from the end of June until the beginning of August; open to students from other schools; an additional payment is required

---

Founded in 1854, as part of the Country Day School Movement, Poly Prep has been located on a twenty-five acre campus in the Dyker Heights area of Brooklyn since 1917. The Lower School historic, land-marked building or "castle" is located in a Park Slope mansion that has recently been updated with a $20 million dollar addition adding classroom space, a gymnasium, dance studio and dining hall. The expansion was awarded the Lucy G. Moses preservation award by the New York Landmarks Conservancy and is the first LEED-certified (Leadership in Energy and Environmental Design) school in New York State. Children learn within the community by visiting neighborhood shops, bakeries and doing mapping exercises; they also enjoy playtime in nearby Prospect Park. The Middle and Upper School campus boast a state-of-the-art science building dedicated to lab science, a recently renovated 360-seat theater, an indoor playing swimming pool and athletic complex including lighted athletic fields, tennis and squash courts, dance studios, and a Mondo Track.

The school is becoming increasingly popular and admissions are competitive.

Approximately 25 percent of students in grades five through twelve come from Manhattan and approximately 12 percent are from Staten Island.

The school's motto, Virtus Vitrix Fortunae, or "Hard Work Conquers the Vagaries of Fortune" is as relevant now as it ever was. It's one of my favorite school mottos. Poly Prep is diverse—children of color represent almost a third of the student body.

Getting in: Parents may tour the school, meet faculty and ask questions before applying, but call early as tours fill fast. For children applying for nursery, pre-kindergarten and kindergarten, parents are asked to send a copy of the child's birth certificate. Separate appointments for interviews will be scheduled for parents and children after applications are received. ERB testing or the SSAT is required for admissions. Check the school's website for specific admissions information.

Weekly chapel meetings for the entire school are held in the Memorial Chapel on the Bay Ridge campus that was built in the early 1900's.

The Lower School curriculum draws on both traditional and progressive teaching methods. For example, second graders learn about symmetry by playing symmetry games, and studying symmetry and symbolism in Native American art and constructing Kachina dolls.

Writer's Workshop starts in third grade and by fourth grade students are analyzing chapter books and strengthening vocabulary by studying common Greek and Latin roots. Math starts with an exploration of patterns and shapes in kindergarten and extends to finding perimeter, volume and area by fourth grade.

Middle School at Poly, grades five through eight, is a blend of a classic and traditional curricula presented in a progressive, interactive way. Students take English courses that stress critical reading and writing, math is focused on problem-solving. An accelerated program is offered to students through the first two years of high school. The scienes and American History round out the curriculum.

Kingdoms and Cultures, and Journeys, French, Spanish and Latin are offered. Art, computers and technology are thoughtfully integrated into the curriculum.

The High School offers a rigorous program with breadth and

depth, with support and structure. Students are required to take classes in all disciplines, but opportunities are available to study a specific subject in depth with a large range of elective courses. There's an advisory/dean program that starts in Middle School and extends through High School where every student has at least one and sometimes two advisors or deans. Poly is a proponent of the AP program and offers AP courses in almost every discipline. Each year Poly honors students who receive National Merit Scholarship awards based on PSAT scores. Poly has relationships with foundations that subsidize travel and allows students to act as ambassadors, not just tourists. Global education is a priority not only within the curriculum and community, but via a broad range of travel experiences from two-week trips to a full-year abroad. Students have traveled to Japan, India, Argentina, France, Turkey, Greece, Cuba and Italy.

Popular College Choices   Amherst, University of Pennsylvania, Boston College, Johns Hopkins, Brown, Duke, George Washington, Georgetown, Harvard, Haverford, Middlebury, Muhlenberg, Vanderbilt, Williams

Professional Children's School

132 West 60th Street
New York, NY 10023
(212) 582-3116, x135 Admissions answer line,
x112 Admission Director
website: www.pcs-nyc.org

Coed
6th–12th grade
Mostly accessible

Dr. James Dawson, Head of School
Sherrie Hinkle, Director of Admissions

Birthday Cutoff   None; applications are accepted at various times during the year

Enrollment   Total enrollment: 190
6th grade places: 10-15
Graduating class size: variable, from 45–60

Tuition Range 2009–2010 $29,655 6th grade–12th grade; $32,500 new 12th graders
Additional fees for books and supplies total approximately $600

After-School Program   Extracurricular activity groups are formed if there is enough interest in the student body

Summer Program   None

———

Professional Children's School was founded in 1914 as an academic program for children appearing in vaudeville or on the Broadway stage. Today, Professional Children's School is the only fully accredited independent school providing a college preparatory curriculum for children actively involved in the performing and visual arts as well as competitive sports. (It is to be distinguished from LaGuardia High School for the Performing Arts, one of the New York City specialized public high schools, depicted in the movie *Fame.*)

Applicants must have a serious interest in the arts/sports and academic ability—no auditions are required for acceptance. A transcript, personal interview, standardized testing, teacher references, and a visit complete the application process. About 40 percent of the student body receives partial financial aid.

Students follow a regular school day but the periods are slightly shorter. The school day ends at 2 P.M. so that students can go on to professional activities.

A Guided Study Program is available for students whose professional commitments keep them away from the classroom for an extended period.

According to James Dawson, Head of PCS, approximately 95% of Professional Children's School graduates apply to colleges and/or conservatories for immediately after graduation on a full or part-time basis; "while some defer their matriculation, many apply or reapply later after a professional career."

Popular College Choices   Barnard, Bowdoin, Brown, California Institute of the Arts, Carnegie Mellon, Columbia, Dartmouth, Johns Hopkins, Juilliard, Middlebury, NYU, Princeton, Sarah Lawrence, Skidmore, SUNY, Vassar, Wesleyan, Yale

Rabbi Arthur Schneier Park East Day School

164 East 68th Street
New York, NY 10065
(212) 737-7330
fax (212) 639-1568
website: www.parkeastdayschool.org

Coed
2s–8th grade
Accessible

Rabbi Arthur Schneier, Dean
Ms. Barbara T. Etra, Principal
Mr. Andrew Butler, Assistant Principal
Mrs. Debbie Rochlin, Director of Admissions; Early Childhood
Director
Dr. Sherry Wiener, Director of Student Services

Uniform: Kindergarten through grade 8 students wear a school uniform; children in nursery wear comfortable clothing of their choice

Birthday Cutoff   Children entering at the nursery level must be 2 by August 31
Children entering kindergarten must be 5 by December 31

Enrollment   Total enrollment: 350
Graduating class size: approximately 25

Tuition Range 2009–2010 $4,100 to $23,100 Early Childhood Program through 8th grade, additional fees: $300 for 2s to $1,800 for 8th grade
Financial Aid is available

After-School Program   "Act Two," for Park East students only; an extracurricular after school program that offers a variety of creative and recreational activities; an additional payment is required

Summer Program: Summer camp is available for children ages two- to four-years old, and is open to children from other schools; a summer high school prep program that focuses on language arts and math is available for Park East students entering 8th grade; an additional payment is required

———

The Park East Day School was founded by the famous human rights advocate, Rabbi Arthur Schneier.

Park East's newly renovated eight-story school building includes state-of-the-art classrooms with Smartboards and interactive whiteboards, a science laboratory, computer center, art studio, library, auditorium, cafeteria, gym and outdoor playground. The program combines Jewish traditional religious values with a demanding secular curriculum. General studies and Judaic studies are taught thematically; all learning is interdisciplinary, and centered around Jewish holidays, Shabbat, Israel, and the calendar. Children celebrate Shabbat and holidays with music and art, cooking, baking, and dramatic play. Students learn about Israel in a variety of ways, including, torah stories, famous places, holidays, fairs, and charity drives.

Getting in: Students come from diverse Jewish backgrounds. ERB testing is required for admission to kindergarten and above. Admissions decisions are based on an application, observation of the children, an interview with the parents and ERB test results.

Program: The Early Childhood and Nursery programs are nurturing, child-centered and non-competitive. The program takes a balanced and nurturing approach to children's social, emotional, behavioral and cognitive needs.

The Lower School program is geared to the individual child's readiness and includes beginning reading and personal writing, collaborative learning, problem solving and critical thinking skills. Students study math, science, social studies, and language arts. Technology is used as a tool for learning on a daily basis, and students can take electives in chess, music, art, dance, computers, library and gym. In kindergarten, first and second grades, students learn sight words and study phonics and word problems, draw, and use invented spelling; each child progress at their own pace.

In grades three through five, writing skills are honed, research skills learned, ideas organized, and written communication clear and crisp.

Reading comprehension and writing are continually cultivated, and according to the school's Assistant Principal, "a love of reading and writing at every age," is one of the school's goal for its students.

The Middle School, grades six through eight, are tough. The focus of the program is to prepare students to succeed in prep school. The curriculum is rigorous and interdisciplinary combining general and Jewish studies, taught in Hebrew and in English.

Advanced reading and writing, social studies, and gifted programs in math are available. Sports teams and extracurricular activities include, math and science teams, chess club, soccer, yoga, swimming and basketball.

For the oldest students, Judaic studies is a deeper, richer discovery of Jewish identity and heritage. The study of the Hebrew Language, Torah, Talmud, and prophets emphasizes history and tradition, and a focus on Israel, both in terms of history and modern cultural connections. Middle School students take an additional class in Jewish History, with one year focusing exclusively on Zionism. Special guests include Rabbi Schneier himself, as well as several of his colleagues—ambassadors, religious leaders, and UN representatives to discuss topics such as religious freedom, and human rights, among other issues of global importance.

A hot kosher lunch is served beginning in kindergarten. Kindergarten students eat lunch with their teachers in their classrooms. First through eighth grades eat together in the school cafeteria.

Class size from first grade through eighth grade averages 15 students. Beginning in first grade, students have a dual curriculum, with part of the day devoted to secular studies and part of the day devoted to Hebrew/Judaic studies. Formal Hebrew instruction begins in this year. Students are introduced to Hebrew grammar and vocabulary, Jewish culture, Torah, prayer and holidays. Both boys and girls participate equally in prayers. Thematic studies (Holocaust, immigration and the history of modern Israel) are integrated throughout. The curriculum is supplemented by trips to museums, Jewish theatre productions, and the study of Jewish authors. There is weekly instruction taught by specialists in science, computer, library, art, chess, gym and music.

Students who show proficiency in math receive enrichment several times a week. Park East students have the opportunity to participate in city, state and national math and chess competitions throughout the year. Students with a special interest or proficiency in English are enriched with in-depth assignments. Beginning in third grade students can attend a weekly book discussion club moderated by one of the teachers. There is a learning center staffed by a specialist for students who need strengthening in Hebrew, reading and mathematics.

The artist-in-residence program exposes students to various facets of the arts. Guests have included a classical pianist, a songwriter, a radio announcer, an actor, a stamp collector, an opera singer, a cellist and a designer. Literary Week, in November, is a school-wide celebration of books. Lecturers have included publishers, book designers, authors and illustrators.

A spirit of community is reinforced through various school assemblies such as the Biography Fair for grades 3 through 5, the first grade Siddur play, the second grade Chumash play and the Science, Math and Technology Fair presented by students in grades 1 through 8.

Extracurricular activities include: Chess, science, computer, painting, museum club, basketball, creative writing, cooking, costume design, team sports, softball and mathematics.

Popular Secondary School Choices   Graduates attend a variety of NYC private and specialized public high schools; recent choices include Ramaz, Abraham Joseph Heschel, Solomon Schecter High School, Dalton, Horace Mann, Columbia Grammar and Prep, The Lab School, Eleanor Roosevelt High School, Bronx Science, Stuyvesant

Traditions   Annual Purim Carnival, Chanukah party, Literary Week, Sukkoth dinner celebration, participation in the Salute to Israel Day Parade, Student Art Exhibit

Community Service Requirement   Park East students are encouraged to participate in a wide-range of community service activities such as visiting nursing homes, helping to support synagogues on the Lower East Side, organizing coat drives, collecting Passover foods for Project Dorot, and entertaining the elderly during holidays

Ramaz

Early Childhood Center and Lower School
125 East 85th Street
New York, NY 10028
(212) 774-8005 ECC
(212) 774-8010 Lower School

The Rabbi Haskel Lookstein Middle School
114 East 85th Street
New York, NY 10028
(212) 774-8040

The Rabbi Joseph H. Lookstein Upper School
60 East 78th Street
New York, NY 10021
(212) 774-8070
website: www.ramaz.org

Coed
Nursery–12th Grade
Accessible

Rabbi Haskel Lookstein, Principal
Ms. Judith Fagin, Head of School
Ms. Laurie Bilger, Dean of Admissions

Birthday Cutoff Children entering at the nursery level must be 3 by August 31
Children entering kindergarten must be 5 by August 31

Enrollment Total enrollment: 1,055
3's places: 45
Kindergarten places: 20
9th grade places: 50-60
Graduating class size: approximately 100–110

Tuition Range 2009-2010 $18,100 to $22,100, nursery 3s–12th grade
The Ramaz Foundation is a fund for financial aid; additional fees for registration, lunch, student activities, and educational materials, range approximately from $5,700 to $7,600

349

Financial Aid/Scholarship   30% of the student body receives some form of financial aid

Endowment $13 million

After-School Program   Lower School: a variety of creative and recreational activities until 5:00 P.M.; an additional payment is required
Upper School: a variety of creative and recreational activities until 6:00 P.M.; there is an additional charge for most programs

Summer Program   None

Ramaz is an Orthodox Jewish day school founded in 1937 by the late Rabbi Joseph H. Lookstein. The initials (in Hebrew) of the rabbi's name make up the acronym that is the school's name. Ramaz is committed to modern or centrist Orthodox Judaism. Applicant families may also be "conservative and committed" but all families keep kosher homes. The school has a fully renovated top-of-the-line Middle School on East 85th Street. Formal Hebrew language instruction begins in first grade. Ramaz offers an extremely rigorous program throughout all grades and many students take a gap year in Israel after they graduate.

Half of the school day is devoted to Judaic studies and half the day is devoted to the general studies curriculum. Although all classes are coed, the sexes are separated during morning and afternoon prayers. Ramaz has a dress code and a kosher hot lunch is served.

Popular College Choices   Barnard College, Columbia University, Cornell, Harvard University, New York University, University of Pennsylvania, Yale, Princeton, and Yeshiva and Stern Colleges of Yeshiva University, University of Michigan, CUNY, Emory, Maryland, Johns Hopkins, Brandeis

Regis High School

55 East 84th Street
New York, NY 10028
(212) 288-1100, fax (212) 794-1221
website: www.regis-nyc.org

All boys
9th–12th grade
Not accessible

Rev. Philip G. Judge, S.J., President
Dr. Gary J. Tocchet, Principal
Mr. Eric P. DiMichele, Director of Admissions

Birthday Cutoff   None

Enrollment   Total enrollment: 531
9th grade places: 135
Graduating class size: approximately 125–130

Tuition   None: all students receive tuition-free scholarships and pay
only laboratory and activity fees of approximately $550

After-School Program   A variety of extracurricular activities until
5:30 P.M.
Varsity sports competition in the Catholic High School Athletic
Association

Summer Program   None

———

Regis High School was founded in 1914 by the Society of Jesus as
a tuition-free school for Catholic boys. Regis High School is sustained
through the original bequest of a generous parishioner of the Church
of St. Ignatius Loyola as well as contributions from alumni.

Regis High School is highly selective. Only baptized Catholic
eighth grade boys may apply. Regis does not accept transfers. The
admissions process is rigorous: Applicants must score in the ninetieth
percentile and above on standardized tests and have an outstanding
elementary school record. In addition, students must sit for the Regis
scholarship examination. Semifinalists are interviewed by faculty and

alumni, and approximately half of this group is selected for admission to Regis. Financial need is one factor in the admissions process.

Regis offers a traditional liberal arts curriculum. The pace is accelerated, and the work load and expectations are most demanding. Four years of theology are required as well as participation in community service projects, liturgies and religious retreats. Catholic holidays are observed.

The average combined SAT score for the Class of 2009 was 2130.

Popular College Choices   Harvard, Columbia, Cornell, Fordham, Georgetown, Yale, NYU, Johns Hopkins, Williams, Princeton, Holy Cross, Boston College, Notre Dame, Villanova

The Riverdale Country School

Middle and Upper School or Hill Campus
5250 Fieldston Road
(at West 253rd Street)
Riverdale, NY 10471-2999
(718) 549-8810, fax (718) 519-2795
website:www.riverdale.edu

Lower School or River Campus,
Spaulding Lane (between Independence and Palisades
Avenues)
Riverdale, NY 10471
main number (718) 549-7780, fax (718) 432-4793
admission (718) 432-4782 fax (718) 432-4794

Coed
Pre-kindergarten–12th grade
Not accessible

Mr. Dominic A.A. Randolph, Head of School
Mr. Kent Kildahl, Head of Upper School
Mr. Milton Sipp, Head of Middle School
Mr. Sandy Shaller, Head of Lower School
Ms. Jenna R. King, Director of Middle and Upper School Admission
Ms. Sarah Lafferty, Director of Lower School Admission

Uniform   Lower School: casual and neat, turtleneck, shirts with collars, no logos, no white T-shirts
Middle and Upper Schools: appropriate attire

Birthday Cutoff   Children entering pre-kindergarten must be 4 by September 1
Kindergarten: Children entering kindergarten must be 5 by September 1

Enrollment   Total enrollment: 1,080
Lower School: 375
Middle School: 230
Upper School: 475
Kindergarten places: 44
6th grade places: 30–35

9th grade places: approximately 45
Graduating class size: approximately 110–115

Grades   Semester system
Kindergarten–5th: detailed anecdotal reports and checklists
Letter grades begin at the end of 5th grade
6th–12th: grades with comments twice a year; grades alone twice
a year
Modified departmentalization in 4th–5th grade
Full departmentalization by 6th grade
First midterms and finals begin in 7th grade

Tuition Range 2009–2010   Approximately $30,000 to $31,500,
pre-kindergarten–12th grade
Riverdale has a monthly payment option and a quarterly payment
option running from June to March
Extended repayment plan (educational loan)
Tuition refund plan (insurance)
Busing from Manhattan is approximately $3,800 for Lower School
students, approximately $2,500 for Middle and Upper School stu-
dents

Financial Aid/Scholarship   Approximately 20% of students receive
some form of need-based tuition assistance
$5.5 million available

Endowment   Approximately $31 million

Diversity   20% children of color
Riverdale enrolls students from The Oliver Program, and Prep for
Prep as well as other diversity programs
Lower School multicultural literature program at all grade levels
Riverdales offers a school-wide Community Development Team
that addresses issues of diversity within the Riverdale community;
this includes sponsoring celebrations, provoding on-going support
for students and their families, and support to the administration
and faculty; The Community Development Team is composed of six
people, three on each campus; among other esponsibilities, members of the Lower School Community Development Team facilitate
a support group for students of color in grades pre-k through 5

Homework 1st: 15 minutes, Monday through Thursday
2nd and 3rd: 30–40 minutes, Monday through Thursday
4th: 45 minutes–1–1½ hour, Monday through Friday
5th and 6th: 1–2 hours a night
7th and 8th: 2–2½ hours a night
9th–12th: average of 3½ hours per night; more for those taking
many APs, assume 40 minutes per subject per night
In addition, parents of young children in Lower School are
encouraged to read to their children every night; there is a Lower
School recommended reading list

After-School Program Riverclub: For grades Pre-K through 5th;
3:35–4:45 P.M., Monday through Thursday, 2:45 to 3:45 on
Friday; a variety of creative and recreational activities for an addi-
tional payment; transportation home is available
Grades 7–8: intramural and interscholastic sports
Grades 9–12: interscholastic sports, theatrical productions

Summer Program The New Heights Program: a privately funded
5-week-long program (established in 2007) that prepares 90 talented Middle School students from the inner city for competitive
high schools; it is tuition-free and taught by Riverdale High School
students as well as college students under the guidance of two
directors and several other teachers
Summer camp: 7 weeks, for ages 6–11; sports, nature and creative
activities; for an additional payment; Riverdale also offers a Students Athlete Summer Academy that combines athletics and academics; the program features a 50-50 content of classroom and
outdoor/recreational/athletic programs; such as basketball training
with an expert coach, or an opportunity to work with a teacher to
develop academic skills

After coming upon an intoxicated schoolboy in the street in
New York City in the early 1900s, Riverdale Country School's
founder, Frank Hackett, decided to found a school in the countryside,
far from the degrading influences of city life and offering abundant
opportunity to play in the open air. Hackett coined the term "independent school" to distinguish his school from the "hoity-toity private

355

schools." From the outset, Hackett had a vision of a "world school" with an "international curriculum."*

Today RCS offers a strong community with a diverse population. RCS welcomed Dominic A.A. Randolf in 2007. He took over from John R. Johnson, who had been Headmaster for ten years. Mr. Randolf, served as Assistant Headmaster at The Lawrenceville School, is a British/American who holds degrees in Education from an American university and in English Literature from Harvard.

The curriculum is grounded in liberal arts basics. Parents say academic expectations are high and many types of students can find success here, but they must be committed to doing the work that is expected of them. Moreover, gaining admission to RCS has become increasingly competitive. "It happened because we've worked hard, and continue to work hard, to balance our strong academic program with a genuine understanding of developmental issues. We have a well articulated academic program and an integrated ethics and values program called C.A.R.E. (Children Aware of Riverdale Ethics) package and we're fortunate to have a beautiful campus which we use both recreationally and as part of our academic program. We're a school that never stops refining itself," says Sandy Shaller, Head of RCS's Lower School.

The Lower School consists of grades pre-kindergarten through fifth. At RCS's Lower School "There really is no typical student. Sixty per cent of our students come from Manhattan. The others come from The Bronx, Westchester or Northern New Jersey." One parental concern is that a car is necessary if you send your child here. Not true. Parents can easily find a ride to Riverdale for Parents' Night, two conferences, one music program, three parenting evenings and one play (in each grade), the Academic Fair, Book Fair and the carnival. RCS's Middle School consists of grades 6–8; Upper School is grades 9–12.

Getting in: Respect and consideration for the individual is a hallmark of RCS, beginning with the admissions process. RCS is one of very few schools to grant each Lower School applicant a one-on-one interview with either the Director of Admissions or one of her assistants. Continued interest in the Lower School by an ever-increasing number of qualified applicants has made it more difficult than ever to be accepted at RCS. Children who are shy in a group of strangers have nothing to fear here. "We don't have a mold that children must fit

*The Quickened Spirit, by Allen Hackett (The Riverdale Country School, New York City, 1957), p. 51.

into," says a member of the admissions staff. The mother of a girl who transferred from a single-sex school said, "My child has never been negatively typecast here."

Cake, cookies and hot coffee greet you on the morning of your tour, and it will not count against you if your spouse cannot make it, and please don't brag about your many accomplishments.

Admission to the Upper School is also competitive. The RCS Upper School admissions staff are personable and friendly and offer students and parents a one-on-one interview with either the Director of Middle and Upper School Admissions, or one of the associates. "Careful attention is paid to making sure that RCS is the right personal and academic fit for each applicant," says Ms. King, Director of Middle and Upper School Admissions. Once admissions decisions have been made, RCS maintains a small selective wait list.

Riverdale's pre-kindergarten program, at the River Campus, is helpful for parents of children with borderline birthdays and parents who know from the start that they want to send their children to Riverdale.

Parents: There isn't a typical student, nor is there a typical parent at RCS. Many types can feel comfortable here. The class cocktail party might be held in an apartment on Park Avenue or on Riverside Drive. "There may be more than quite a few parents who don designer labels, but there are still those who prefer clogs," one parent said after attending myriads of school functions. Parent involvement is welcomed and parents can volunteer to go on class trips, work in the library or help teach computer. Communication between teachers and parents is just a phone call away, and one parent said her children's backpacks are always full of correspondence from Riverdale. One mother said, "A note came home the first day homework wasn't done." The school's bus service says they will drop off homework at your door "every day if necessary" if your child misses school (Lower School only).

Program: The Hill Campus serves grades six through twelve, the River Campus serves pre-kindergarten through fifth grade. At the Lower School learning is more experiential; the Middle and Upper Schools are more traditional and structured.

Each morning as the younger children arrive at the River Campus, Sandy Shaller, Head of the Lower School, is there to greet them. He knows every child (and nearly every parent) by name, and is involved in almost every aspect of the Lower School. Parents say, "Mr. Shaller *is* the Lower School." Almost all prospective parents have a chance to ask

Mr. Shaller questions about RCS, either when they tour or certainly after acceptance. Mr. Shaller teaches a class a day. At the Spring Carnival, with booths operated by each class relating to a theme, Mr Shaller is always present and often surprisingly costumed for the event.

An architecturally eclectic group of buildings make up the River Campus. One building is a three-story, twelve-classroom building with a 6,000-square foot gymnasium (designed by an alumna whose children have all attended RCS's lower school). The Perkins Building houses an auditorium, library, classrooms, administrative offices and science resource room. The Junior Building contains admissions, the cafeteria, a computer complex and music classrooms. The Senior Building (Arts Building) houses two art studios, special music classes and support services. In addition, there are four tennis courts, a soccer/football field, an environmental education area, patios and a well-designed play area. The River Campus is large enough to accommodate all these facilities in one place, and intimate enough to feel like a community. Children have the freedom to jump rope, build a snowman, enjoy the playground or throw a football at recess, depending on the season. Students are not allowed to wander around the River Campus alone; they are always well supervised, particularly at busing time.

Like a traditional elementary school, RCS has recess (formal recess ends after third grade), three gym periods each week and a health class. "It's an intense day and at recess there is an explosion of energy. It's a country campus and we use it." says Mr. Shaller. Each grade puts on a music and drama performance and there are bi-monthly assemblies where folk songs are occasionally sung. Pre-kindergarten and kindergarten at Riverdale stress readiness and provide individualized attention. Classes in pre-kindergarten through second grade all have a head teacher and an assistant teacher. There is traditional circle time, along with job charts and journal writing with invented spelling. Since the school is in a country setting, much attention is paid to the study of nature and environmental issues. For example, every Lower School student gets seed pots and plants them in the wetlands area and has a hands-on opportunity to work in a garden with plants. Pre-kindergarten and kindergarten children have garden plots where they plant flowers and vegetables as part of the spring science program. Nearly every kindergarten and first grade class has a pet: guinea pigs, turtles or fish. Math instruction is hands-on in the early years. One mother came in to make pizza for a kindergarten math project that included grating the cheese and measuring the circumference of the pizza (she brought her own homemade sauce).

By first grade, formal academics are introduced and the teachers have serious expectations. For those who need strengthening there is the Small Group Reading Program. In first grade there are daily homework assignments four times a week. The Lower School administers the ERB's standardized tests that measure academic skills.

There is ability grouping for reading in grades 1–5, and ability grouping for math in grades 2–5 that continues through Middle and Upper School. Foreign language is introduced in third grade. Writing is stressed in all subject areas, and creative expression is encouraged. The Lower School has its own publication called the *Rivulet*. In fifth grade, students pick topics and learn how to research and write term papers. The first final exam is given in sixth grade.

Many class trips are scheduled, including a train trip for kindergartners up the Hudson for a picnic lunch. All grades make use of the city's resources, museums, and art opportunities. Art, music, foreign language or science teachers accompany trips to integrate their areas of expertise with the classroom teachers'.

Fifth graders are introduced to independent research through an inquiry-based research project. Students are taught how to refine their topic, take notes, isolate facts on index cards with titles, write outlines, and produce a final documented paper. Modified departmentalization begins in fourth grade but is not complete until sixth.

Computer study at Riverdale is strong. The use of the Internet is curriculum driven and is primarily for educational purposes. An "Acceptable Use Policy for Technology and Computer Networks" is sent to all Riverdale families to inform parents of possible issues concerning the use of this technology. For parents who aren't as computer savvy as their children, RCS provides parents with on-line (Internet) and off-line (books, videos, etc.) materials, a Parents Association course on computers and technology, and a list of books that offer guidance to new users. All members of the administration, teachers, Middle and Upper School students have e-mail addresses. Lower School students do not presently have e-mail accounts, but e-mail can be sent through their teachers.

There are computer labs on both campuses. RCS has a technology staff of at least six trained profesionals who run the computer science department and provide information on the use of computers. "Technology is a powerful tool. At Riverdale our curriculum drives technology, not the reverse," says Mr. Shaller in describing the Lower School's integration of computers and academics. RCS offers four computer science courses—Introduction to Technology is a required course for all seventh and tenth graders—including two AP courses. The computer and the Internet are helpful tools, but they should be used appropriately. "Children have a great deal of exploration to do away from the illuminated screen," says Mr. Shaller.

When asked what values are stressed at RCS, many parents and students said "teamwork," both on and off the field. One student described Riverdale as "a healthy environment that promotes community feeling." In 1989 the RCS Lower School Student Council created C.A.R.E. (Children Aware of Riverdale Ethics), a program that emphasizes problem-solving strategies, respect for differences and consideration for the feelings of others. The official C.A.R.E. song was written by a former Lower School drama teacher and it evokes the spirit of the program in an entertaining way. This sense of consideration and caring extends to the larger community as well. Each year, Lower School students hold a walk-a-thon to benefit a designated charity.

There is positive interaction between the grades at Riverdale. Friendships between children in different grades begin on the bus ride to school, and also through various planned activities. All upper grades are buddied with younger grades. Fifth graders prepare the Holiday Feast with pre-kindergartners, second and fifth graders work together on a butterfly project, and second graders and kindergartners work together sewing an alphabet with each pair of children working together on a letter square. Fifth graders interact with younger children during lunch or recess. This community of students extends all the way up to the alumni. One student said, "The alumni are not just donors, they are people you know because you've worked and connected with them." Every two years, former Riverdalians return to conduct workshops and talk to the students about their professions.

Riverdale's new Middle School, officially opened in fall 2005, serves grade six, seven and eight. It is housed in a completely renovated and restored Hackett Hall and is connected it to Mow Hall via a second floor bridge to the new Student Center that features a beautiful dining hall, multipurpose rooms and more. Beloved history teacher and Riverdale veteran, Milton Sipp, heads the Middle Division and works with faculty, many of whom teach across a wide range of ages. There are student deans, home base teachers, and grade-level coordinators.

Middle School students gather most mornings for an all-school meeting, which can sometimes be a full length assembly. Sixth and seventh grade students have home base teachers who meet with them at the beginning and end of each day and accompany them to lunch. There's an emphasis on interdisciplinary work, study habits and in-depth topical studies and a full range of arts courses, intramural sports for sixth graders, and interschoolastic sports for seventh and eighth graders.

The Upper School consists of grades ninth through twelfth; the two largest points of entry are sixth and ninth. The Upper School is structured but not rigid. There are many required courses, but by eleventh and twelfth grades over forty electives are available, including: Masterpieces of Western Literature, American Government, Non-Western Religions, African-American Literature, Native American Literature, Molecular Biology and Race and Class in New York City. Math is "ability grouped" in the Upper School: Students with aptitude in this area move at an accelerated pace and those who need more reinforcement get it. There are honors sections in math and language. No class ranking is made. The curriculum is challenging and rigorous, however, students are supportive of each other and there is not an abundance of cut-throat competition. "It doesn't matter what anybody else gets as long as you did your best" is the message. And one student talked about "growth in grades": As the work got harder, her grades improved.

In Fall 2007, Riverdale underwent a NYSAIS (New York State Association of Independent Schools) evaluation. RCS was reaccreditated, and in its official report the NYSAIS Visiting Committee stated that many aspects of the school impressed them. "The vitality of RCS's academic program; outstanding, dynamic, creative teaching; diversity; and the balance of academics, arts, activities, and athletics. Students are friendly and confident and display a strong sense of community. Riverdale students are outstanding examples of civility, which is a reflection of the care offered by the faculty and staff," states the NYSAIS report.

It's very difficult to fall through the cracks at RCS because there is a strong support network of people and programs. Advisors (for groups of ten or twelve) meet regularly. There is easy access to faculty, whose schedules are posted and some of whom stay for the entire long day even if they finish early.

Seniors are required to take a year-long interdisciplinary course called I.L.S. or Integrated Liberal Studies. Introduced into the curriculum in 1980, I.L.S. surveys the cultural history of the West from the perspectives of four disciplines: literature, philosophy, the history of science and the history of music and art. The course culminates in a final oral examination and is a hallmark of the RCS experience.

Students help students in several ways. Eleventh and twelfth graders are selected, as an honor, and trained to act as peer counselors to seventh graders, dealing with academic and social issues under the Peer Advisory Leadership (PAL) program.

Mr. Satish Joshi, Director of Community Arts and Artist in Residence, has been inspiring students for many years. Graduating seniors leave farewell messages to him painted on the walls of the art room: "Satish, you know me. That in itself is a great thing. I ❤ you." and "Thanks for the best homeroom ever." Riverdale's art and literary magazine *Impressions* has repeatedly won the award of the National Council of Teachers of English, one of the highest awards for excellence in student literary magazines.

Backpacks are dropped casually in the halls. Seniors can leave the campus when they are not scheduled for classes or other obligations. (These are privileges, not rights, and can be revoked for bad behavior.) Each year a Senior Leadership Conference is held at a camp or conference center at which seniors explore their own leadership role in school; teachers conduct workshops on the college application process and on coping with senior-year demands. Class officers are elected, and seniors get a sense of solidarity as a class. The weekend launches them in their role as leaders of the Upper School. The student government has three representatives from each grade.

The junior class is pushing for more privileges: RCS juniors can't leave campus until April of junior year. (At Horace Mann and Fieldston students can leave in ninth grade.) But one student maintained that having to stick around campus contributes to the feeling of community. Each year the senior class parents give a gift to the school.

Though sequestered from many of the ills of urban life, RCS students are concerned about the wider world. At the recent One World Day, students explored a wide range of cultural and world issues in a series of workshops on such topics as women's rights in developing countries and other interesting current issues.

Frank Hackett's "spirit of internationalism" is translated into respect for differences between people. Relationships between groups at RCS are good. One tenth grader told me: "It's not too cliquey; everyone knows what they like to do and no one gets in anyone else's way." In athletics, "Everyone works together on the field."

There are over thirty-eight clubs, and new ones are added each year. They include the successful Mock Trial Club, S.C.C. (Students of Color Committee), Film Club, Environmental Club, Amnesty International, Model Congress and Community Service. An activity period for clubs is scheduled during the school day, so that students can find time to engage in extracurricular interests.

School spirit at RCS is manifested through athletic competition in the Ivy Prep League. Riverdale's athletic center houses an Olympic-size pool and a full-size gym and fitness center where many trophies are on display. There are sixteen junior varsity and varsity sports teams including a swim team, football team, golf team and a strong fencing team. Riverdale's football team achieved sports fame in the sixties when Frank Bertino coached Riverdale to seventeen undefeated seasons. Horace Mann alumni wince when they remember how future pro player Calvin Hill led RCS to a winning streak of fifty-one games. Today, the annual "Buzzell" basketball game in February against arch-rival Horace Mann draws a crowd. The game was named for a Horace Mann student who died and the proceeds are donated to charity.

One Riverdale student, who plans to be a litigator, describes RCS as "a healthy, fun environment that promotes community feeling. If you work hard and apply yourself, you'll really succeed and help is always there if you need it."

Popular College Choices   Brown, University of Pennsylvania, Harvard, Princeton, Duke, Yale, Vanderbilt, Washington University, Boston University, Johns Hopkins, Tufts, Cornell, Columbia, Barnard, Williams

Traditions   Spring Carnival, Winter and Spring Concerts, Book Fair, Buzzell games, Talent Show, Children Helping Children (charity outreach program), C.A.R.E. program (Children Aware of Riverdale Ethics), Homecoming Day, Career Day, One World Day, Fifth, Eighth and Twelfth Grade Graduation Ceremonies, Reunion and cocktail parties by decade for Alumni

Publications   Lower School literary publication: *The Rivulet*
Middle School literary magazine: *Crossroads*
Upper School newspaper: *The Riverdale Review* (since 1916)
Literary magazine: *Impressions* (winner of several national awards for excellence)
Alumni magazine: *Quad*
Yearbook: *The Riverdalian*
Photography journal: *Exposures*

Community Service Requirement   None

Hangouts   Dino's Pizza, Riverdale Diner, Bagel Corner, RCS cafeteria (with a view of trees and fields) and library

Rodeph Sholom School

Nursery Division
(2 and 3 year olds)
7 West 83rd Street
New York, NY 10024
(646) 438-8510
website: www.rodephsholomschool.org

Early Childhood/Elementary Division
(Grades Pre-Kindergarten–1st)
10 West 84th Street
New York, NY 10024
(212) 362-8769

Elementary/Middle School
(Grades 2–4)
168 West 79th Street
New York, NY 10024
(212) 362-0037

Coed
Nursery–8th grade
Accessible at 7 West 83rd Street and 168 West 79th Street
Not accessible at 10 West 84th Street

Mr. Paul Druzinsky, Head of School
Ms. Erin Korn, Director of Admissions

Birthday Cutoff   Children must be 2.6 years old by September 1
for the 2s program
Children must be 3 years old by September 1 for the 3s program
Children must be 5 years old by September 1 for kindergarten

Enrollment   Total enrollment: 660
Nursery enrollment: approximately 150
Lower and Upper Elementary enrollment: approximately 350
Middle School enrollment: approximately 150
Average graduating class size: 35-40

Tuition Range 2009-2010 $10,810 to $33,540, nursery 2s through
8th grade

Temple membership is included in the tuition; lunch is provided for students in grades 2 through 8
Financial aid available beginning in kindergarten

After-School Program   for Nursery through 6th graders; weekdays until 5:00 P.M.; a variety of creative, recreational and educational activities for an additional charge

Summer Program   Rodeph Sholom Summer Camp from late June through mid-August; an additional payment is required

———

Founded in 1958 as a nursery school; the Elementary Division was added in 1970 and the Middle School in 2000. The Rodeph Sholom School is a Reform Jewish day school affiliated with the reform synagogue, Congregation Rodeph Sholom. It is the only Reform Jewish day school to serve students from nursery through eighth grade. The Nursery Division is housed in the temple building on West 83rd Street. Pre-kindergarten through first grade are housed in a modern building on West 84th Street, connected via a courtyard to the 83rd Street building. Elementary and Middle School Divisions meet in fully renovated brownstones on West 79th Street which house two gyms—one gym is state-of-the-art with bleachers, three libraries (two are fully computerized and linked to the Internet), two computer labs, four science labs, two art studios, many classrooms have "Smartboards," and a cafeteria. In view of allergies the school is completely nut-free.

Getting in: Parents should call in the fall for an application and to reserve a place in a group tour. ERB or ISEE testing results, (depending on the entry level), a school report, and individual or group interviews with the child are required for admission to kindergarten and above. "We are looking for students who can meet the demands of our challenging and enriched academic environment," says the Admissions Director.

Parents: It's a mix of executives, artists, lawyers, academics, physicians and so on. A parent who has been at the school for several years points out that as the school has expanded, the parents have evolved from a group of West Siders to those with more polish and considerably more money: "Formerly the parents were psychologists, painters, a social worker—your basic West Side shleppers. Now they're media executives, managing directors, executive editors; people who golf." One parent said, "We have kept our child in Rodeph Sholom from nursery through the grades because it provides top-notch academic

365

preparation without the personal competitiveness we see at many other schools. It's a warm community and the administration welcomes parental involvement. The sports and visual arts programs are great and the kids place into a variety of private and public high schools."

An active PA organizes several annual fund-raisers including the book fair (open to the neighborhood), and the Spring Benefit. The PA also sponsors dialogue meetings throughout the year; recent topics include: computers, Jewish studies, and neighborhood safety. The PA frequently purchases blocks of tickets to sporting events and Broadway shows.

Program: The Rodeph Sholom School provides a challenging yet supportive environment firmly rooted in Jewish values. The school believes "the higher you place the bar, the higher the children will reach." Although there are three divisions (Nursery, Elementary, and Middle School) there is interaction between older and younger students.

The school has three libraries, four modern science labs, a multimedia room with HD video and surround sound, a large gym, and ample outdoor space for recess, and a Kosher-style cafeteria. Most classrooms in the lower divisions are filled with children's artwork, creative writing, poems and graphs. Younger children play outdoors in the courtyard daily, children in kindergarten go to Central Park every day. Jewish Studies are woven into the curriculum and each Shabbat (Friday) a different child's parent/guest is invited to participate in nursery and Pre-K classes.

The school's approach to teaching is a balance of traditional/ instructional and discovery-based methods. Literary instruction begins in Pre-K. By first grade students write, edit and publish their own books. Math, social studies, handwriting, writer's workshop, Hebrew and Jewish studies are taught in the classroom. Students leave their classrooms for special instruction in Jewish Studies and Hebrew, science, computer, library, art, music and physical education.

Beginning in Pre-K, computers equipped with Internet access are used in all classrooms at RS. The technology curriculum includes: keyboarding, graphics, spreadsheets, database management, telecommunications, Internet, e-mail and desktop publishing. At 79th Street, at least four classrooms have "Smartboards."

The science curriculum focuses on problem solving skills in Life, Physical or Earth Sciences. Fourth graders focus on the earth, compare states of matter, analyze weather patterns, find earthquake foci, and hone mapping skills. Fifth graders study ecology and evolution, and seventh graders cover in-depth units on the human body.

The integrated curriculum is driven by social studies. Prekindergartners focus on "Me and My Family." Kindergartners study citizenship and their community. In first grade, the social studies curriculum expands to The Neighborhood and the Market. First graders learn how fruit is grown, transported and sold; they take field trips to various neighborhood and open-air Greenmarkets in the city; they create their own market in the school lobby and sell produce to students, faculty, and parents; and they donate their profits to a charity of their choice. Second graders study New York City. Third graders cover core themes of social studies including history, geography, economics and government. Fourth graders survey the four regions of the United States in depth.

In the Middle School, fifth grade focuses on the leadership and sacrifices required to turn the colonies into an independent nation with a democratic government. The year ends with an in-depth study of the Civil War. In sixth grade, students begin a two-year study of world history beginning with the ancient world and ending with Asia and the Americas. Eighth graders return to a study of the United States including units on Industrialization, and other watershed events with a special emphasis on the World Wars and the Holocaust.

The Jewish Studies curriculum includes music, art, dance and theatre projects in the Hebrew language, Shabbat, teaching of the Torah portion, holidays and festivals, charitable deeds, Israel, and Jewish history, life and traditions. Beginning in first grade, Hebrew is taught using a combination of phonics and whole language techniques, including reading, writing, conversation and music. A yearly musical Midrash Hour, with music and lyrics written by students and music teachers features a central Jewish theme.

Music is taught by two full-time instructors utilizing Orff instruments, Dalcroze Eurhythmy for movement and Kodaly Training for singing. All second through eighth graders have the opportunity to further their private instrumental studies. This after-school miniconservatory features faculty made up of New York City's finest professional musicians and offers lessons on nearly all band and orchestral instruments. Students in this program also play in one or more of the school's eight performing ensembles; the program culminates with an annual spring concert.

As you walk the halls you notice that art is an important part of the Rodeph Shalom experience. The school has two fully equipped art studios. Three full-time art instructors give formal instruction, as well as helping classroom teachers integrate art projects into the regular curriculum. Students use the resources of nearby museums, including the Metropolitan, Natural History and Children's Museums. Starting in seventh grade, students choose an area of the arts as their major. If they choose to major in the visual arts, they have art classes twice a week. Students who are especially talented in the visual arts and who are focusing on attending an art school may take a portfolio class.

Field trips and overnight trips include Broadway shows, Lincoln Center performances, the Tenement Museum, Asia Society, the Jewish Environment Program Teva and Bear Mountain. Longer trips include visits to Washington, D.C., the Deep South and Israel.

Elementary and Middle School students have physical education three times a week at one of the school's two modern gymnasiums. There are four full-time coaches on staff. Students participate in a wide range of sports including, soccer, basketball, baseball, gymnastics, hockey, softball, and track and field.

There is a "no-cut" policy for athletes. The Middle School has its own teams. Many extracurricular activities take place during the school day and play an important role in the life of the school. The RS team, the "Future Problem Solvers," takes part in an international academic competition in which students brainstorm, research, and write solutions to current world issues. It has been recognized as New York State Champions for over a decade. Middle School has its own student council.

Parents say that Rodeph Sholom provides a well-rounded education. One father told me, "They do a great job of combining Jewish identity with a solid academic grounding. It's a first rate education without any pretensions, the kids work hard because the school makes it fun."

Popular Secondary School Choices   Brearley, Bronx Science, Chapin, Riverdale, Horace Mann, Collegiate, Nightingale, Columbia Prep, Spence, Fieldston, Dalton, Abraham Joshua Heschel, Trevor Day, Fiorello LaGuardia High School of Music, Art and the Performing Arts, Stuyvesant, Trinity

Traditions   Jewish Holiday Celebrations (Purim Carnival, lunch in the Sukkah, Passover Seders, etc.), Science Week, 1st Grade Fruit Market, 2nd Grade Model Neighborhoods of NY, Midrash Hour, Teva Environmental Trip

Publications   The Rodeph Sholom *Sun*
The Rodeph Sholom PTA Newsletter: *Worth Menschoning*
Graduation Yearbook

The Rudolf Steiner School

Lower School
15 East 79th Street
New York, NY 10075
(212) 535-2130 (main number)
(212) 327-1457 (admissions), fax (212) 744-4497
Upper School
15 East 78th Street
New York, NY 10075
(212) 879-1101 (main number)
website: www.steiner.edu

Coed
Nursery–12th grade
Not accessible

Ms. Rallou Hamshaw, College Speaker
Ms. Irene Mantel, Director of Admissions, 2s–6th grade
Ms. Julia Hays '73, Director of Admissions, 7th–12th grades

Birthday Cutoff   September 1

Enrollment   Total enrollment: 350
2s places: 24
3s places: 25
4s and 5s places: 20
Graduating class size: approximately 20–25

Grades   Semester system
Letter grades begin in 7th grade
Departmentalization begins in 7th grade

Tuition Range 2009–2010 $21,000 to $30,350, nursery 2s–12th grade
Lunch is included through 2nd grade and is optional thereafter
for an additional payment; organic produce and milk and vegetarian alternatives served daily

Financial Aid/Scholarship   A fair portion of the student body
receive some form of aid

Endowment   N/A

After-School Program Extended Day for Grades K 5s through 3rd grade Monday–Friday, 3–5:45 P.M.
A variety of activities for an additional payment, availability depends on enrollment

Summer Program A 2-week June Days Camp is offered for children in preschool through grade 3 for an additional charge
A 3-week June Music Program is offered for children in grades 4 through 8 for an additional charge
Both summer programs are open to students from outside the Rudolf Steiner community

---

The Rudolf Steiner School in New York City (established 1928) is part of an international community of schools (180 in the U.S., 900 worldwide) that integrate intellectual and artistic development. Rudolf Steiner (1861–1925), was an Austrian scientist, philosopher, artist and educator. The lower school is housed in a beautiful McKim, Mead & White mansion just off Fifth Avenue; a sweeping marble staircase graces the foyer. At the heart of Steiner's Waldorf philosophy is the belief that education is an artistic process. There is a holistic approach to learning. "Innovative teaching methods work to develop clarity in thought, balance in feeling, and conscience and initiative in action." Steiner provides an education that balances individual development with a sense of social responsibility. There is even an emphasis on the "spiritual" side of children's growth—not religious, but focused on developing imagination, compassion, and ethical principles.

Getting in: "The Rudolf Steiner School isn't looking for any one type of child," I was told. ISEE scores are required in grades six and above, along with two years of recent class records. The school's philosophy dictates that they teach to a broad spectrum of styles and abilities within each class and students come from varied economic and cultural backgrounds. Because of increased interest in Waldorf education and the competitive private school admissions climate, Rudolf Steiner maintains a wait list for admission.

Parents should call in early September for dates of fall open houses and to receive an admissions packet. Parents may tour the school without applying but must reserve space in advance. Children applying for preschool, kindergarten, and first grade are interviewed in small groups. Students applying to second grade and up might be interviewed in a small group or individually. A parent interview is scheduled separately.

Parents: Parents are very involved in the life of the school and the Waldorf method depends on a certain level of parent support. An eclectic group of parents—business types and artists—animates the lobby at drop-off and pick-up times. Parents run the annual Fall Fair, worth attending if you're interested in the school, as it showcases Waldorf education. The Parents Association has two co-presidents, and there is an eight-member Parent Council elected by the parent body, which meets monthly. There are evening parent study groups, and parent education forums throughout the year.

Program: The Waldorf method is based on the belief that children pass through three basic stages of cognitive development, and the curriculum is designed to engage the abilities of the growing child at each of these stages. In preschool this is accomplished through creative guided play; in elementary school through the imaginative and artistic presentation of material by the class teacher; and in high school through challenging the student's awakening capacity for independent thought. What's different about the Waldorf method is not so much the content—there is an in-depth curriculum—as in how and when they are taught. Parents say once you see it in action you will "fall in love with the school."

The preschool is a perfect fit for those who like natural materials and loathe plastic primary-colored toys. It has a timeless feeling: there are wooden blocks and toys; shells and stones; colorful cloths and soft dolls. The children model beeswax (a favorite Waldorf material), paint with watercolors, bake bread and make soup every week. They also play in Central Park every day, weather permitting, and end every morning with a story.

Don't think it is not academic—there's lots of learning going on: songs, stories and nursery rhymes expose children to the world of words; watching marionette shows and participating in dramatic play strengthen the power of memory and the imagination. Counting games and rhythmic activities build a foundation for arithmetic and number skills, and so on.

Beginning in first grade, reading and math are taught with the aim of developing each child's pictorial imagination. Foreign languages—Spanish and German—are introduced. Each morning includes a "main lesson block" in one subject area, which is studied in-depth for approximately four weeks. Instead of textbooks, all students write and illustrate their own "main lesson books." (These are beautiful and impressive.) "The curriculum is designed as a unity and its subjects are introduced and developed in a sequence that mirrors the inner development of the growing child." Academic subjects such as English, math and foreign languages are scheduled for several weekly periods. Afternoons are reserved for additional academic work and for drama/movement, gym, music, or crafts.

In accordance with the Waldorf method, teachers stay with their class for several grades; a teacher might stay with his or her students from first all the way though eighth grade! Needless to say, students develop lasting relationships with their teachers. One parent said, "The Waldorf teachers are intellectual as well as artistic and they have amazing respect for the children."

The high school academic program prepares students for college; it cultivates artistic expression, promotes academic excellence and develops practical skills. At this point new students join those who have come up from the elementary school. Each class has its own faculty advisor who coordinates class activities, monitors the students' academic and personal progress, and serves as a liaison between the school and home. Students say that the social life is lively and warm.

Many students participate in sports; there are teams in soccer, volleyball, basketball, softball and track. Teams are open to all students and compete in the Independent School Athletic League, and also against other Waldorf Schools.

For more than twenty years, Steiner has maintained a very active exchange program with European Waldorf Schools. Tenth grade students who are strong academically are encouraged to participate. Students have gone to exchange programs in Germany, Spain, France, Switzerland, and Austria.

At the Hawthorne Valley Farm, a biodynamic and organic dairy and vegetable farm in upstate New York, with which the school has a close association, students examine the ecological implications of farming through visits to the farm and guest lectures.

Popular College Choices   Amherst, Barnard, Brown, Boston University, Columbia University, CUNY, Maryland Institute College of Art, Middlebury, Oberlin, University of Chicago, The Rhode Island School of Design, New England Conservatory, Skidmore, Sarah Lawrence College, Swarthmore, Smith, Tulane, Vassar, Wesleyan, Wellesley

Traditions   Annual Fall Fair and Spring Auction, all-school seasonal and holiday festivals, concerts, annual book fair, grandparents and special friends day, 5th grade Olympics, class plays grades 1–12, 6th grade farm trip, 7th grade outward bound trip, 8th and 12th grade class trip of their choice, end of the year class picnics, alumni reunions

Publications   Monthly bulletin for the entire school community
Upper School literary magazine: *The Key*
Student newspaper: *15 East*
Annual alumni news magazine
Student yearbook

Community Service   20 hours per year for students grades 8 through 11, 12th grade has a 3-week internship of their choice

Hangouts   The Nectar Coffee Shop, Viand Coffee Shop, Central Park

Saint Ann's School

129 Pierrepont Street
Brooklyn Heights, NY 11201
(718) 522-1660
e-mail: admin@saintannsny.org
website: www.saintannsny.org

Coed
3s–12th grade
Not accessible

New Head of School to be announced before the end of 2010
Ms. Linda Kaufman, Associate Head of School
Mr. James Busby, Assistant Head of School
Ms. Diana Lomask, Director of Admission

Uniform   None

Birthday Cutoff   None specified; readiness is stressed

Enrollment   Total enrollment: 1,089
Preschool total enrollment: 60
Preschool places: 28
Kindergarten total enrollment: 60
Kindergarten places: 30
1st Grade total: 80
1st grade places: 20
9th grade total enrollment: 80
9th grade places: 5–10
Graduating class size: approximately 80

Grades   Semester system
No letter grades are given throughout the school; standardized tests are given each year to fifth and eighth grade students and the results are reported to parents
Departmentalization begins in 4th grade

Tuition Range 2009–2010 $21,750 to $28,100, Preschool through 12th grade
No additional fees
A tuition refund plan and a monthly payment plan are available; accessible by subway or car

Financial Aid/Scholarship   21.6% of the student body receive some form of aid

Endowment $3.3 million

Diversity   22% children of color
Saint Ann's enrolls Prep for Prep students, as well as students from a variety of scholarship programs

Homework   1st grade: none
2nd: ½ an hour
3rd and 4th: 1 hour
5th and 6th: 1½ hours
7th and 8th: 2 hours
9th–12th: 3–4 hours
The guideline is 20 minutes per class, but there is usually more

After-School Program   Open to current or new Saint Ann's students only
Kindergarten through 6th grade: 3:00 to 5:30 P.M. (6 P.M. if necessary)
Creative activities, computer, games, sports, study, art, theatre, music, and so on; an additional payment is required

Summer Program   Open to current or new Saint Ann's students (preschool through 8th grade); Six-week program that begins at the end of classes and continues through the end of July, offering creative activities, sports and field trips
Three-week gymnastics program
Soccer Program for grades 2–6
Two week science program for grades 6–8
Basketball Program for grades 2–6
Arts Program for grades 2–6

———

Saint Ann's School was founded with approximately sixty children in 1965 under the aegis of St. Ann's Episcopal Church. The rector of the church envisioned a school for gifted children, "with uniforms and a healthy dose of religion." Founding Headmaster Stanley Bosworth (known to all simply as Stanley), a former French teacher at the progressive (now-defunct) Walden School, was only thirty-five years old when he came to

Saint Ann's. He came with his own vision: "It was my vow all those years ago that this particular school would somehow provide 10 percent of our nation's poets." It was Stanley's vision that prevailed.

In 1981, Saint Ann's was chartered by the New York State Board of Regents; in 1982 Saint Ann's was formally disaffiliated from the church. The sixties are long gone, Stanley's retired and Larry Weiss, formerly the Head of Horace Mann's Upper Division, has taken the reins, but one thing still remains at Saint Ann's, the philosophy that no student approaches the school without stars in his or her eyes.

Dr. Weiss has made Saint Ann's less "insular." By that he means he has worked to build relationships with other private schools in the area and with the neighborhood as well. Dr. Weiss teaches a first year Chinese language course and a seminar on contemporary China.

Saint Ann's is a school where gym is called "Recreational Arts," where there are no grades, no class rankings and no rigid curriculum. Saint Ann's has produced award-winning playwrights as well as a Westinghouse Scholar. A parent said, "The unconventional tone of the school gives these kids a shared bond and a respect for the unconventional in life . . . these kids are not afraid to break the mold." Saint Ann's is an academically rigorous school for very bright children. The arts are considered of equal importance with the traditionally defined academic courses.

Located in Brooklyn Heights, the school attracts many local families. Approximately one-quarter of the students come from Manhattan. Some years ago, the school renovated the basement of The Bosworth building (the main building) and added a gym, a lecture room and an art gallery, plus five additional classrooms. More recently, the two-story dining room was redesigned to create two balcony rooms which are used both as additional dining space. The Farber Building, for first through third grade students, affords more space for middle and high school students, and in spring 2009 the school purchased a second brownstone adjacent to The Rubin Building, extending the campus on Pierrepont Street.

Getting in: The brochure/viewbook states: "We admit the talented." Saint Ann's students must be self-motivated and have the ability and maturity necessary to handle freedom and rigorous academic requirements. They use a "holistic approach" when it comes to admissions. The admissions process is an eclectic one that considers both achievement and glimmers of special talent. Candidate profiles are cross-checked with ERB scores where appropriate. In addition to testing and interviewing the applicant, the admissions director will observe a child in his or her nursery school on occasion. Parents of applicants to the lower grades are interviewed with special concern for receptivity to the values of humanism and the arts. The admissions director provides parents with an opportunity to offer insights and/or additional information about their child that might help in making a decision. The appropriate division head also interviews middle and high school applicants. Parents say that there is little of the "admissions anxiety" found at the Manhattan schools because "kids at Saint Ann's don't get their sense of self-worth from outshining others; there is very little glitter or glitz." Another parent said, "The atmosphere was informal and friendly." Saint Ann's maintains a wait list but there is not much movement on it.

Saint Ann's is not a member of ISAAGNY (Independent Schools Admissions Association of Greater New York) but does adhere to the same admissions notification and parent-reply dates as the other independent schools. The school's midwinter break is scheduled in February, a week before that of the public schools. Spring break is scheduled to coincide with Easter and Passover.

The typical Saint Ann's student is "bright, arty, concerned for others and confident." Is there a self-consciousness about being gifted? A parent says, "It has the effect of creating among the children a sense of community and specialness that overrides all other differences including ethnic background, family income and gender."

Although admittedly it is more of an accomplishment to make an award-winning scholar out of a mediocre student, Saint Ann's is nonetheless remarkably good at encouraging bright children to realize their potential fully. A mother told me, "All of my children's special talents—repeat, all of them—were nurtured, developed and tested in the very loving laboratory of Saint Ann's." One parent told me that her son's first grade teacher recognized that he had a talent for art. "She was so enthusiastic and encouraging that it brought out more than his ability to draw and paint—it also developed his interest in art history and a strong sense of himself." In college he majored in a different subject, but he was on the staff of the humor magazine, and art will be a lifelong interest.

Aside from the excitement of teaching exceptionally able students, teachers say Saint Ann's is a great place to work because of the freedom and flexibility: "Teachers get to teach exactly what they want to teach within the context of a loosely defined curriculum." In the Lower School most teachers have a special talent or interest; they are painters or writers, for example, "and the administration encourages these interests." A significant portion of the student body is made up of the children of faculty, approximately 100-105. The middle and high school teachers are selected not because they have a master's in education but because they have an expertise in an intellectual and/or creative area: The theater teachers are often playwrights and actors, the English teachers are writers and so on. Many of the teachers are young and "There is an enormous energy, excitement and commitment."

Parents: With respect to the parent body, one parent said she never felt that her bank account, background or lifestyle made a difference at Saint Ann's: "If I didn't fit in, I never noticed." One parent said, "Saint Ann's isn't interested in the parents; when you drop off your child, he becomes a Saint Ann's child." Consequently, there is no Parents Association. Parent events at the school include, Parents Night at school, cocktail parties, dance concerts, two middle school and high school productions each year, voice recitals and instrumental concerts. There is a welcoming party for new parents at the school. Alumni continue to be devoted to the school as evidenced by their participation in fund-raising publications and special events. Currently over 40 members of the faculty are alumni and, there are 112 children of alumni presently enrolled in the school. *The Saint Ann's Times* reports on news of over two thousand alumni.

Program: Lower School at Saint Ann's is composed of grades kindergarten through third. Separation is handled gently. Parents say: "They are unbelievably sensitive." A parent can stay in the classroom if necessary. Kindergartners come for a playtime in the spring and begin with half/class half/day for the first day of school in the fall. The Head of the Lower School, Gabrielle Howard, is outstanding; she has been at Saint Ann's since 1973, initially as a teacher. Cathy Fuerst is the Head of the Preschool. She has served as a Lower School master teacher for eleven years, as an assistant to the Director of Development, and as Coordinator of the Lower School after-school program.

Classes are identified by teachers' names. In a kindergarten class of twenty children there is a master teacher and an assistant. Students in the Lower School address teachers by their first names.

The viewbook says, "Reading is central." Writing, math, science, art, music and dance round out the rest of the Lower School schedule. Reading is taught with eclectic methods—"any way the child needs"—including phonics. By the end of first grade about 95 percent of the children are reading. A former Lower School teacher told me that "many first graders are reading Beverly Cleary or Roald Dahl, but some are still on Mack and Tap. But by the end of the first year most are on a second grade reading level." "Parents must be aware of any learning difficulties their child is having," advises one parent. There are several learning specialists at Saint Ann's who work with the division heads to identifying and remediating learning issues.

Parents say, "You have to get the daily and weekly information from your child but the school will let you know if your child isn't working up to his potential." The anecdotal reports are extensive and informative.

Since the student body is a narrowly selected group of very bright children, the academic atmosphere at Saint Ann's is not one of cutthroat competition. "It's very nurturing and informal; kids are allowed to be who they are." For instance, parents say, a first grader can take a sixth grade math class and not feel out of place. (In fact, a first grader once did take sixth grade math; a teacher accompanied him to the class and stayed with him.) And of course there is no competition for grades because there aren't any. (On longer research papers students might receive a "good" or a "check", in addition to extensive comments.)

In the Preschool and Lower School, students leave their classrooms for "specialties" in art, music, dance and recreational arts. Kindergartners also leave the classroom for dance. Beginning in second grade, students leave their homeroom class for math and in third grade for science and computer. Third grade is the last year of the classroom-based program; there are still blocks in the classroom. Formal instruction in computer begins in third grade. Third graders learn to type, use Hypercard, and even some programming. One Lower School group studying Greek mythology wrote an epic poem seventy pages long. Most Lower School classes produce their own play or musical each year.

Middle School at Saint Ann's is equivalent to grades four through eight. It is up to the teacher whether or not students use their first or last names. Full departmentalization begins in the first year of Middle School (fourth grade), which requires a lot of maturity. As a former Lower School teacher said, "There's a lot of choice for a ten year old."

Each fourth grader also has a locker with a lock.

The viewbook says that "subject achievement and aptitude define placement, particularly in math and language groups. The makeup of English and history classes is largely determined by age." Sixth graders learn the structure of language and an introduction to Latin. Formal language instruction begins in the seventh grade, and students can choose from Latin, Greek, French, Spanish, Chinese and Japanese. Science is part of the curriculum each year. Middle Schoolers take five years of science. All sixth and seventh grade students take a class in health issues.

One parent said, "My fourth grader is learning what I learned in college. In our conversations she talks about Greek and Norse myths and Latin."

The arts are considered academic subjects at Saint Ann's. The Middle School has its own literary magazine. Middle Schoolers perform in mixed-age plays and musicals; recent productions include *The Comedy of Errors*

379

and Roald Dahl's, *The Witches*. A parent told me that when her son was in fifth grade, his theater teacher, an off-Broadway director (the kind that Saint Ann's delights in hiring), sparked his interest in performing and he eventually was selected as a member of a well-known theater troupe.

Athletics are popular at Saint Ann's. Upper middle school students may join interscholastic teams in softball, soccer; baseball, basketball, fencing, gymnastics, track and field, and volleyball. In addition to the regular sports program, classes are offered in badminton, bocce, indoor climbing, Ultimate Frisbee, fitness, jump rope, exercise, karate, yoga, and Inward Bound (adventure training). There is plenty of school spirit exhibited at sports events. Saint Ann's has several gymnasiums and uses nearby parks for playing fields.

Milk, fruit, etc., are provided free of charge; as well as hot lunch from first grade through the middle of eighth grade. Lunch is available for high school students for an additional charge.

The High School at Saint Ann's is composed of grades nine through twelve. There is a tremendous amount of freedom and choice in the High School at Saint Ann's so students must be self-motivated.

The teachers in the High School—all "masters" in their disciplines—"love what they do and they communicate it to the students." The viewbook describes the High School curriculum as "adventurous." The ambiance at Saint Ann's is informal and the curriculum rigorous. Parents say the school stresses "Latin, writing, reading, theater and playwriting." The school has a commitment to Western civilization and respect for the Western canon. (In this way it's not so different from a "traditional" school like Trinity.)

Saint Ann's was one of the first private schools to offer Chinese language studies at the middle and high school levels. Now in its 25th year, the program begins in seventh grade and includes six years of the language. There are opportunities for summer study in Beijing. In addition to Chinese, Japanese language is offered to eight graders through high school students.

One English class I observed was discussing Nabokov's *Lolita*. Some of the students had their feet up on their desks, others were sprawled or supine yet the conversation was electric. In a classroom nearby, a young attractive Spanish teacher gave her student a high five for a correct answer. History classes often have seminars on current events. Also singled out for praise were Ruth Chapman, an art history/English teacher, and Angelo Belfatto, an art teacher elected graduation speaker by the class of 2000. "It's worth insisting that your child take one of his classes just to read the evaluations he writes—you will not believe anyone could be so articulate about your child," said a parent.

Extracurricular activities keep Saint Ann's open seven days a week. Over the weekend the school may be used for play rehearsals, sports and yearbook meetings. There is a playwriting class for high school students and one for middle school students and a playwriting festival each spring. Nancy Fales Garrett's playwriting course is so good that nearly every year a play by a Saint Ann's student is accepted for production at The Young Playwright's Festival at Playwright Horizon's annual off-Broadway run in the fall. Students can work on photography or literary magazines.

Both middle and high school students with a scientific bent can participate in the independent science research program in addition to the broad range of science courses offered. And several each year are selected for the Science Honors Program at Columbia University, and junior and senior math teams compete in the New York Interscholastic Math League.

High school students travel, study and work abroad. Visits to museums in New York City, inaugurations in Washington, D.C., and model congresses at universities in the northeast corridor complement in-class curricula. There is an exchange program with a high school affiliated with Fudan University in Shanghai.

A parent of two Saint Ann's students recounts: "My son had four years that were so spectacular in every way that college was a bit of a let down." Saint Ann's students are encouraged to strive for awards and honors (Saint Ann's produces numerous National Merit Scholarship Finalists and AP scholars), and these accomplishments are conspicuously listed in the *Saint Ann's Times* each year.

Technology: The Director of Institutional Technology supplies an overview of the present and future role of computers at Saint Ann's, maintains the school-wide network, coordinates computing activities among the various departments. The Director of Institutional technology also runs the Computer Resource Center located in The Bosworth Building—a fully-equipped lab where teachers can bring classes to do Internet-based research and use programs such as Adobe Creative Suite and various interactive math, science and language programs. "We've attempted to make computers available and useful to all of our students and staff, from the third grade to the twelfth, and from the Head of School to the kitchen staff." Thus the Saint Ann's population is largely computer-literate. The Computer Center, with three classrooms, is used for third through twelfth grade computing classes as well as high school robotics classes. It is equipped with 50 computers, two servers and a wireless network.

The Annie Bosworth library (for middle and high school students) and the Lower School Library are fully computerized with Internet access. The school has a T1 high speed connection to the Internet in place and all students and staff have e-mail addresses and can create their own web pages if they wish.

All six science labs have wireless Internet access and projector setup. They have data acquisition instruments that enable students to conduct experiments and collect data in real time. The students are able to analyze the data on the spot as part of the lab.

The math department makes use of computers as well. Students have published math papers on the school website. Classes from fourth grade through high school visits the Resource Center to use graphic applications of materials they are studying in class.

Ever aware of the arts, Saint Ann's has a multimedia computer lab in one of the music rooms, and the high school film classes and digital photography classes make use of digital editing software.

Saint Ann's students apply to and are accepted at a broad spectrum of colleges including the top Ivy League universities. A parent said, "The school devotes enormous energy to getting the students into the best schools—that means the best school for the child, not necessarily the parent."

Graduation is held in the Church of Saint Ann and the Holy Trinity. Caps and gowns are not worn but *Pomp and Circumstance* is played. According to tradition, the President of the Board of Trustees and the Head of School speak, as well as a member of the faculty. The Head of the High School awards the diplomas. There are five student presentations that can be in any medium.

Popular College Choices   Columbia, Princeton, Brown, Oberlin, Amherst, Bard, University of Chicago, University of Michigan, Wesleyan, Yale, NYU, Vassar

Traditions   Fun Run, Senior Cruise, Grandparents Day

Publications   Middle School literary magazine and High School literary magazine
Photography or art magazine
Publications on a variety of subjects including: art, humor, nonfiction
Development office publication
Saint Ann's Times and *Postscript*

Community Service Requirement   None; however, the service program is very active involving students at every level; middle and high school students volunteer in the Brooklyn D.A.'s Office, the Brooklyn Heights Synagogue Shelter, Legal Outreach, and at P.S. 8

Hangout   On the red stairs and in front of school

St. Bernard's School

4 East 98th Street
New York, NY 10029-6598
(212) 289-2878, fax (212) 410-6628
website: www.stbernards.org

All boys
K–9th grade
Accessible

Mr. Stuart H. Johnson, III, Headmaster
Heidi R. Gore, Co-Director of Admissions
Anne S. Nordeman, Co-Director of Admissions

Birthday Cut-Off   None

Uniform   Kindergarten: Monday–Friday: students are required to wear khaki-colored trousers or shorts and St. Bernard's shirts; sneakers are worn to school; Grades I–IX: Monday–Thursday: navy blazers must be worn to and from school, Grades IV–IX polo, or oxford shirts or turtlenecks, khaki-colored trousers or shorts, sneakers for athletics only; starting in Grade III athletic clothing is provided by the school; Fridays: blazers, ties and oxford shirts required

Enrollment   Total enrollment: 383
Kindergarten places: approximately 45

Grades   Kindergarten: Written reports in February and June; parents have a teacher conference in November
Grades I–III: detailed anecdotal reports in December and June
Parent conference in March
Grades IV–IX: Midterm reports in October; end of term reports in December, March and June

Tuition Range 2009–2010 $33,270, Kindergarten through 9th grade
Lunch, books, supplies, physical education and tuition refund plan are included

Financial Aid/Scholarship   20% of the student body received some form of aid

Endowment   N/A; reputed to be large

Diversity   Minority students represent 22% of the student body; the school enrolls students from Prep for Prep, A Better Chance, The Oliver Program, Early Steps, Summer on the Hill

Homework   Begins gently in the Junior School; (K–III); Grade I: Students read aloud to parents for twenty minutes each night
Grades II and III: reading and math assignments, finish work not completed in school, study spelling words, approximately 20–40 minutes
Middle and Upper School: regular homework in each subject, some homework can be completed in study periods, teachers are available for help, during a prep time, which is held at the end of the day

After-School Program   St. Bernard's boys in Junior School can participate in the Nightingale-Bamford Hobbyhorse after-school program; a wide variety of creative activities are offered
Afterschool sports at St. B are available; the coaching staff supervises intramural games, including soccer, basketball, baseball, softball, lacrosse, and a tennis program for Grades II–IX
The Carpentry Club is available to boys in Grades II, III, V and VI

Summer Program   Summer sports camp from mid-June through mid-August

---

St. Bernard's School was named after the rue St. Bernard, a street in Belgium, not after a breed of dog. It is pronounced with the accent on the first syllable. Founded by John C. Jenkins, a young Englishman and Cambridge graduate, in 1904, St. Bernard's has always had an affinity for English traditions. It unselfconsciously calls its alumni Old Boys. But St. Bernard's is a kinder and gentler place than its British counterparts. Parents say there is a family feeling here combined with a crispness of attitude, with fun. A parent said "There's enough leeway so that the boys can be boyish."

Stuart Johnson, a Yale man, formerly a member of the St. Bernard's faculty who had also taught at Groton, was thirty-two when he was appointed to his post as headmaster. Mr. Johnson is described as "unpretentious, caring, witty and a bright and stylish writer" and it is said that he "writes wonderful messages in bulletins and follows the traditions set forth by the other heads." "He goes out of his way to know everyone," said a parent. "He even came to a lacrosse game in Greenvale!" Manners are very important; Mr. Johnson shakes each boy's hand each morning.

Getting in: Parents are advised to call for an application and brochure in September or October of the year before the child will enter kindergarten. St. Bernard's does not require any application fee. Readiness is what is important. Boys in this year's kindergarten have birthdays spanning the entire year, including some younger boys with summer birthdays.

After the application is received by the school, they will call you to arrange a parent tour as well as a separate time for your child's interview. The tour, usually for two families at a time, is given by one of the co-directors of admissions and lasts about an hour and a half. Leave plenty of time for the tour because it is very thorough. After visiting parents meet privately with Mr. Johnson; questions are welcomed. The co-directors visit as many nursery schools as possible to see the boys in their current setting. All boys have a thirty minute interview at St. Bernard's. You are told not to prepare your son for the individual interview. It is a formal evaluation but the boys usually enjoy themselves (thirty minutes of undivided attention!) Reading material is provided for those parents who are able to concentrate. There is a strong sibling and legacy policy.

For the upper grades, applicants are considered on a rolling basis, space permitting. Current transcripts, and ERB test results are required in addition to interviews.

Parents: A lot of Old Boys send their sons to St. Bernard's. Parents say the parent body is composed in part of "families with good values." Certainly the tone of the parent body is "understated," families of all faiths are comfortable here.

Many parents who are prominent editors, writers or journalists send their sons to St. B's because of the school's emphasis on literacy. The beautifully written brochure says one of the basic premises at St. B's is "a regard for the beauty and power of English—in reading, writing, speaking, listening."

Class cocktail parties are held in the fall or winter and different families take turns as hosts. All parents are members of the Parents Association. It sponsors events such as the Book Fair, The Great Skate, an annual benefit, and a Raffle. The PA also publishes a newsletter, and all parents are required to walk on the school's safety patrol. On Parents' Night in the fall, mothers and fathers gather and are addressed by the headmaster and then meet the teachers. There is a special visiting day for grandparents in the spring.

Program: Traditions are an integral part of life at St. Bernard's, and parents say the boys—and Old Boys—look forward to many of them. A school-wide assembly is held on Fridays. At assembly a hymn is sung, announcements are made and there is a program. Each boy gains experience in public speaking beginning in grade I. Each boy recites a poem or performs in a play at assembly. Topics at assembly range widely.

There is a tradition at St. Bernard's involving an alligator given to the neatest class. At Friday assemblies the alligator is presented by one class to another with some original poetry or a song.

On your tour you will see desks arranged in traditional rows with the teacher at the front of the class speaking to the students. You might hear a student reciting a poem, or a nine year old reciting his multiplication tables, but don't be misled; although there is plenty of structure, there is flexibility and creativity within each classroom. Boys may stand upon their chairs, work on the floor in groups, sit in a circle and read aloud. "The combination of bright kids and unusual teachers makes St. Bernard's unique. The real beauty of St. Bernard's is its teachers," says Mr. Johnson. There is little turnover in staff at St. B, there are some eccentrics and there's a big age range. One parent described her sons' teachers as "warm, kind and intellectual." Some teachers give the boys nicknames." Another parent said: "There are kids whose fathers had the same teachers, they are all well remembered, some revered, for generations." From fourth grade up all homeroom teachers are men.

A major expansion of the building is complete. The renovations include: a state-of-the-art gymnasium, science wing with new labs, a teaching theatre, two kindergarten classrooms with separate play-deck, and a carpentry room.

Junior School at St. B's is grades K–III. Grade I boys are divided into two reading groups with much fluidity between them. Boys must read aloud to their parents, homework is never unreasonable, but there is a certain amount expected every night.

There are reading specialists and math specialists on the staff of the special learning department. There is concern for the individual child. One mother spoke about the progress her son made in grade I: "It's a caring environment and they keep a close watch.

A typical grade I schedule: The day begins with an assembly in the gym and goes on to art, gym, library, science, spelling, phonics, reading, math, recess, lunch, physical education, work-time/ crafts and dismissal. The curriculum is well rounded, parents say, and there is time for physical activity every day, either on the outdoor play deck or in the fields of Central Park just a block away. There is at least one computer in every classroom, in addition to a large new computer lab, and the science labs for grades kindergarten through IX are very well equipped. The school-wide computer network supports a Windows-based system; boys have access to the Internet and other reference materials.

Third graders do a lot of written work. They study Greek mythology "and are very devoted to it," a parent said. Awards for best and most-improved handwriting are given in each class.

Music begins in kindergarten. Tryouts for the St. Bernard's singing group begin in fourth grade. Rehearsals are held twice a week before school. At performances, boys wear special ties and trousers. Art is hands on, with an academic approach and every homeroom performs at an Assembly.

The Middle School is grades IV through VI. Fourth graders have a meeting before the school year begins to discuss the transition to Middle School.

The Garrett McClung Prize is a special award given in grade V for achievement. Six prizes are given out at the end of grade VI.

The Upper School consists of grades VII through IX. Special events during these years include the annual eighth grade Shakespeare production. The play varies from year to year (in recent years it has been *The Tempest* and *The Taming of the Shrew*), and St. Bernard's boys play all roles. Another sixth grade tradition is a visit to Civil War battlefields in Virginia. There is an eighth grade debating society, an Upper School public speaking contest, and a Model Congress elective.

In grade VII *To Kill a Mockingbird* is read along with the Classics in the upper grades. Parents say the boys are very well prepared for the ongoing schools because of St. B's emphasis on reading and writing.

The student council is composed of elected members from grades IV through IX. The council meets each trimester and each class elects its own president, vice president and secretary. The entire council meets with the headmaster.

The entire school benefits from the handsomely renovated Jenkins Library, in which an oil painting of the stern-faced founder overlooks the stacks. There are shelves of O.E.D.'s (Oxford English

Dictionaries) and study carrels for the older boys as well as CD-roms and other research tools. A separate section of the library is reserved for the younger boys so that they do not disturb the concentration of the older boys.

Intramural sports competition begins in grade III. Ninety percent of boys from grade V through grade IX play on at least one team each year. There are varsity and junior varsity Red and White teams in all sports. St. Bernard's teams excel in soccer, lacrosse, and baseball.

Values are stressed throughout St. Bernard's and there is a code of conduct. There are essay and composition prizes and a public speaking prize. At the final assembly numerous awards and prizes are given out; one of the highest awards is the Payne Whitney Honor Cup.

Consistent with the belief that "a good heart is finally more valuable than a well-stocked, well-trained head," food drives are held at Thanksgiving, Christmas and Passover/Easter. In addition, each class does a project or community service work. Older boys visit the elderly at the Florence Nightingale Nursing Home or decorate the cafeteria or other common areas of the home for the holidays; the St. B's singing group performs or just visits informally. Other community service opportunities include the Environment Club (which has donated to a school in rural Ecuador), a recycling program, and bake sales for charities. There is usually a student-led response to a major disaster: For hurricane and earthquake victims, a well-decorated jar for contributions will be placed in the lobby and a check sent to a relief fund.

St. Bernard's imparts a palpable enthusiasm for learning, and the techniques for mastering any subject. One parent said what surprised her the most about St. Bernard's was its warmth.

About one third of the graduates go to boarding school and the rest transfer to independent day schools in the area, most after eighth, some after ninth grade.

Traditions   St. Bernard's book of school songs, Friday assemblies, eighth grade Shakespeare play, sixth grade trip (Gettysburg), eighth grade trip (Ecuador), ninth grade trip (Paris), fifth grade animal report, passing of the alligator, Science and Technology Fair, Book Fair, Sports Day, Parents' Evening, Father's Dinner, Junior Old Boys' Lunch, Old Boys' Dinner, Grandparents' Visiting Day, Spring Concert, Christmas Carols

Publications   Yearbook: *The Keg*
Literary magazine: *The Budget*

Parents Association Publication: *St. Bernard's Gazette*
Alumni Bulletin: *St. Bernard's School*

Community Service Requirement   No specific requirement but each boy must perform community service in a number of ways available through various programs within the school. There are also many opportunities to serve the local community: Yorkville Common Pantry, the Florence Nightingale Nursing Home, New York City Audubon Society, The Environment Club

Popular Secondary School Choices   A variety of New York City's private and public schools as well as many New England boarding schools including, Trinity, Riverdale, Horace Mann, Dalton, Columbia Prep, Stuyvesant High School, St. Paul's, Andover, Exeter, Deerfield, Choate, Loomis-Chaffee, Hotchkiss, Groton

Saint David's School

12 East 89th Street
New York, NY 10128
(212) 369-0058, fax (212) 289-2796
website: www.saintdavidschool.org

All boys
Pre-Kindergarten–8th grade
Accessible (3 elevators)

Dr. P. David O'Halloran, Headmaster
Ms. Julie Sykes, Director of Admissions

Uniform   Grades pre-kindergarten through omega (Kindergarten): collared or turtleneck shirts only, no jacket required, sneakers are allowed
Grades 1–8: tie and jacket (jacket can be any color); Bermuda shorts allowed in September and May, no sneakers

Birthday Cutoff   Children entering Pre-kindergarten must be 4 by September 1
Children entering Kindergarten must be 5 by September 1
Children entering 1st grade must be 6 by September 1

Enrollment   Total enrollment: 400
Pre-kindergarten places: 16
Kindergarten places: 55
Graduating class size: approximately 40

Grades   Trimester system
Pre-kindergarten and Kindergarten have three written reports and two parent/teacher conferences each year
First through Eighth Grades have three written reports and one parent/teacher conferences each year
Letter grades begin in 4th grade
Departmentalization begins in 4th grade
Final exams begin in 7th grade

Tuition Range 2009–2010 $22,265 to $33,400, Pre-kindergarten through 8th grade
The cost for lunch, books, and athletics is included in the tuition

There is a 8-month tuition payment plan available to parents
A 10 percent discount is given on the tuition of the second child of parents with three or more children in the school; there is a discount of 25 percent for the third child and 50 percent for the fourth and additional children

Financial Aid/Scholarship   Approximately 8% of the student body receives some form of financial aid

Endowment   Approximately $22 million

Diversity   17% children of color
Prep for Prep students enrolled

Homework   1st: 20-30 minutes
2nd: 45 minutes
3rd: 1 hour
4th and 5th: 1½ hours
6th: 1½–2 hours
7th and 8th: 2–2½ hours Parent/teacher conferences are held mid-year as well as in the fall for preprimary families; detailed descriptive reports are sent to parents three times a year

After-School Program   The Saint David's after-school program is open to Saint David's boys in kindergarten through eighth grade; an additional payment is required; The program runs Monday through Thursday until 5:30 P.M.; various activities including sports, art, Robotics, Italian, Chinese, comedy and chess; St. David's also has a popular hockey program for boys in Kindergarten through eighth grade

Summer Program   A June Program for boys in kindergarten through fifth grade the last two weeks of June; Monday through Friday, 9:00 A.M. to 3:00 P.M.; an additional payment is required; a variety of sports, arts and crafts, and model-making; most are held in Central Park and the 94th Street Sports Center; a spring break mini-camp is also offered during the first week of spring vacation

———

Although Saint David's School, founded in 1951, is relatively young, it is interesting to note that the school has more traditions than most of the long-established East Side boys' schools founded at the turn of the century. The school building, originally three private homes designed by Delano and Aldrich in 1919, retains much of the beauty, warmth and architectural detail of the period. Additionally, the school has a multi-level, well-equipped, 16,300 square-foot athletic center located at the Sports Center, 215 East 94th Street. Saint David's is a Catholic school for boys but the Saint David's community is inclusive; about forty percent of the boys practice other religions, and the catalog states that Saint David's "is a family school in every sense of the word." Parents say Saint David's "offers a balance of academics, arts and athletics with a spiritual component." Saint David's is known for an emphasis on literature, languages, history and art." The school is framed by the classical notion of balance in all things, particularly, scholarship, athletics, aesthetics and spirituality.

Saint David's was founded by lay Catholics and, according to the mission statement, Saint David's remains grounded in the traditions of that faith. The school remains committed to the teachings of the Church. Saint David's students are taught "to respect and learn from all religious traditions, to prize diversity and to develop the spiritual and ethical values necessary for successful moral decision making." One parent described Saint David's as a place where "the school and teachers work to develop boys who will be able to think critically about what life presents them with, and they do that by providing the boys with a foundation of ethical and moral instruction." One parent who is not Catholic (approximately half the school is non-Catholic), and who recently relocated to New York City with her family from another country said she chose this school for her son because, considering the language and cultural differences, she felt Saint David's would provide "a challenging but nurturing academic environment with less pressure than at some other schools." Another parent said she chose Saint David's for "its heart, soul and mind."

Getting in: Applications should be filed by December 1st. After the application is filed (there is a $60 fee), tour and interview dates are scheduled. Individual tours of the school are given by parent tour guides. Applicants for grades Pre-kindergarten and Kindergarten are interviewed in small groups while applicants for grades one through seventh have a one-on-one interview with a teacher. Applicants for grades four through seven spend a day in a classroom. The admissions office reports that a diverse group of boys is chosen from a variety of nursery schools; approximately eighteen schools are represented in a class of forty-five. Every effort is made to give prospective parents a personal, relaxed and comprehensive application experience.

Parents: The parent body at Saint David's is described by a parent: "There is wealth but parents are far from ostentatious." Parents do dress well, and many wear suits to school events, but are typically far more casual at drop-off and pick-up. An annual dinner dance is held in the winter, which always includes a successful auction. Parents mingle more informally at class cocktail parties, morning coffees, school performances, sporting events, and the Annual Family Skating at Wollman Rink. There is a strong Parent Association and many opportunities for parents to be involved at the school.

Program: Saint David's has had remarkably few heads of school in its history; David Hume was headmaster for thirty-seven years. In July 1992, Dr. Donald Maiocco became the school's fourth headmaster and retired in June 2004. On July 1st, 2004, the school welcomed Dr. P. David O'Halloran as the school's fifth headmaster. A native Australian, Dr. O'Halloran came to Saint David's after a ten-year tenure at Allen-Stevenson and a stint as Headmaster of the Hilltop Country Day School in New Jersey. Dr. O'Halloran greets every boy by name as they enter the school every morning. Parents, faculty and students appreciate his open-door policy. In his five years, he has over seen the expansion of art, music, science spaces, spearheaded a new curriculum and has been a proponent of increased faculty compensation.

Saint David's mission is "to provide the finest education available within the best traditions of the Church." The Catholic religion is an important part of the Saint David's experience. Boys attend morning chapel, religious classes, Mass (five times a year, third grade and up, held at the Church of Saint Thomas More). Preparation for First Communion and Confirmation are offered. Religion classes are ungraded and other faiths are also explored during the course of the year. The brochure states that "students of all faiths are encouraged to draw on their own religious traditions."

The chapel is a small wood-paneled room with beautifully-restored stained glass windows. First and second graders attend chapel once a week for Bible stories. Third through eighth graders begin each day with chapel, at which hymns are sung and faculty members relate a story, personal or otherwise, that reflects a particular moral or ethical lesson. These "chapel talks" can be humorous, serious, spiritual or just enlightening, and range from an account of a close call with bears on a hiking trip to an explanation of the Book of Kells, an English teacher's description of the significance of the Jewish holidays, or a well-loved member of the kitchen staff singing spirituals.

Saint David's calendar lists five fêtes de l'écoles or celebration days such as Founder's Day. Each day is marked by a special program. On Saint David's Day, new members of the school community bite a leek to symbolize their becoming a son or daughter of Saint David's.

Lunch is served family style; teacher's sit at the head of each table and food is passed. Much attention and effort goes into the planning of healthy, balanced meals using local produce where possible. Ethnic lunch celebrations explore different cultures through food, music, videos, and questions and answers. Minding table manners and engaging in appropriate meal-time conversation are expected.

The school added 6,000 square feet by renovating an adjacent apartment building owned by the school. The new and renovated space includes a music suite, an additional art room, a math lab, and state-of-the-art science labs. The school also provides housing for many faculty members in this building.

Lower School is composed of pre-kindergarten through third grade. There is one pre-kindergarten class of approximately sixteen students and three kindergarten classes of seventeen students each, including an OMEGA kindergarten class which serves a useful purpose for boys who may be young or need more time before first grade. The Lower School offers a structured program; basic skills are emphasized and reading and math are taught in small formal groups according to ability. There is no grading in the Lower School, but homework is introduced in first grade. Formal reading instruction also begins in this year with small group instruction. Math lab manipulatives, fundamental math skills and concepts are introduced, reinforced, and mastered for math instruction. Math is also tracked or grouped by ability.

A wonderful Lower School tradition is the armband ceremony, held monthly to recognize boys for anything from academic excellence to being a good friend or helping a teacher. Community service is another integral part of Lower School at Saint David's. Boys collect winter clothing and holiday gifts for Graham-Windham Family Services and contribute to City Harvest food collections. There are weekly classes in science, music, art, pottery, woodworking and technology. Lower School has its own dedicated cozy library that offers classic works as well as newly published volumes. Traditions permeate school life at Saint David's starting in Lower School. First grade boys put on an annual Christmas pageant; second graders perform a play about the founding of America and participate in the annual Turkey run; third graders build gingerbread houses with their fathers and invite the Spence girls for a concert. Trips to the Brooklyn museum of Science, the Cloisters, the Metropolitan Museum, Ellis Island, The Tenement Museum and The Rose Center augment the curriculum. Sixth grades enjoy team-building activities on their overnight trip to Ramapo, seventh graders go on an annual week-long trip to Cape Cod in October and are led on explorations by instructors from the Cape Cod Museum of Natural History. Eighth grade boys study Renaissance art and architecture on their Italian Study Tour.

Lower School boys have a midmorning break for recess, juice and cookies. They change for sports every day and participate in a daily sports period where they learn skills, sportsmanship and teamwork. The intramural sports program starts in third grade. The Player of the Week program recognizes outstanding performances.

There is no Middle School at Saint David's: Grades four through eight are considered part of the Upper School. Letter grades begin in fourth grade. Upper School boys are taught to develop critical reading skills in the context of a traditional curriculum, some modern literature is read, but the focus remains on the Classics. Writing skills are stressed; boys learn how to write creatively and analytically. In science, students investigate the structure of atoms and human anatomy along with the scientific process. History at Saint David's takes the boys through a journey from Ancient Egypt, the Renaissance to the war in Vietnam as well as present world conflicts. In math, conceptual understanding and computational accuracy receive equal emphasis, students are taught to apply their knowledge to real-life situations. There's an honors math program for boys in seventh and eighth grades and an annual Math Bowl that pits Pythagoreans against Newtonians. Foreign languages include, Latin, French and Spanish; all fifth and sixth graders are required to take Latin which becomes an elective in seventh and eighth grade. Most boys choose between French or Spanish in sixth grade and a pilot program that began in September 2009 introduces Spanish to boys in kindergarten.

The eighth grade Humanities course is an interdisciplinary course that combines history, art history, research skills and writing and is one of the hallmarks of senior year. The course includes three major projects—a long essay, a power point presentation and an artistic interpretation of an artist or architect. Additionally, trips near and far are blended into the program, spanning a ten-day study tour of Rome,

Florence and Assisi to visits to the Metropolitan Museum. Although there is a decided emphasis on the Classics, the faculty always finds a way to weave the achievements of women, the experiences of different cultures, music, art and current events into the program.

Drama and music are popular—fifth graders perform musicals such as *Oliver Twist* and *The Pirates of Penzance*; sixth graders perform *Godspell* and *Joseph and the Amazing Technicolor Dreamcoat*, and many others. Seventh graders perform a Greek tragedy that ties into the history curriculum. Public speaking goes beyond the stage. Boys learn to recite poetry, make science presentations and generally learn to speak well on their feet. All boys are required to play a variety of musical instruments in fourth and fifth grade, many choose to continue with further music instruction and have appeared on stage at Carnegie Hall and The New York Philharmonic.

Interaction between the grades is important at Saint David's. On the first day of school, eighth grade boys escort the new kindergarten boys to their classrooms establishing an important connection. Fifth graders host a Halloween party for third graders, eighth graders read to Lower School boys during "early morning club," and fourth graders mentor third graders through the transition to Upper School.

Study skills are emphasized throughout all grade levels. The Saint David's Academic Planner is introduced in second grade to teach boys how to plan and organize their time, work and materials. A Homework Workshop is held for fourth grade parents as their sons enter Upper School. Note-taking, writing, spelling, editing, and test taking skills are discussed, developed and honed. Upper School boys have many long-term projects that foster healthy time management skills.

The athletic program enjoys the spectacular 94th Street Sports Center where boys play basketball, wrestle, play floor hockey, and workout. For soccer, baseball, track and lacrosse the boys use local parks. Competition against other boy's schools in the Independent School League begins in fifth grade; seventh and eight graders try out for varsity teams. Although being competitive is an obvious goal, having fun playing sports embodies the true spirit of Saint David's sports program.

Extracurricular activities for Upper School boys include, the literary magazine *(The Canticle)*, the yearbook, Junior Varsity and Varsity sports teams, the school orchestra, Chamber Singers and student government. At the end of their eight-year-plus years at Saint David's, boys have painted Greek vases and dissected sheep's hearts, studied Latin and created their own websites. The school brochure asserts,

"A boy who graduates from Saint David's . . . is the sum of early skill development and more mature analytical thinking, of gentle reminders to live by the Golden Rule and the Headmaster's call 'to be good men.'"

A June graduation takes place at the Church of St. Thomas More in a nonreligious ceremony (boys wear ties and jackets). Awards are given in athletics, music, art and academic areas. The ceremony is followed by a reception at Saint David's. A festive, more casual graduation party is held at the 94th Street Sports Center in mid-May.

Popular Secondary School Choices   Saint David's graduates attend a variety of independent day and boarding schools, including Riverdale, Regis, Collegiate, Poly Prep, Horace Mann, Fieldston, Dalton, Trinity, Choate, Hotchkiss, Deerfield, St. Paul's, Lawrenceville, Taft, Kent, St. Andrew's

Traditions   Morning "chapel talks", class plays, Math Bowl, History Bowl, weekly poetry recitation in Lower School, St. David's armbands, second grade Turkey Run, Player of the Week, fêtes de l'écoles, all-school Christmas concert, fifth grade Native American presentation, eighth grade art history lectures and ARCO project and eighth grade modern art interpretation, Annual Dinner/Dance and Auction, faculty/parent athletic contests, annual alumni soccer match, alumni Christmas party

Publications   *Saint David's Magazine*
Literary magazine: *The Canticle*
Lower School literary magazine
Yearbook Alumni publication: *Generations*

Hangouts   Green Tree Deli, 3 Guys Coffee Shop

Saint Hilda's & Saint Hugh's

619 West 114th Street
New York, N.Y. 10025
(212) 932-1980 FAX (212) 531-0102
website: www.sthildas.org

Coed
Beginners (2-year-olds)-8th grade
Accessible

Ms. Virginia Connor, Head of School
Ms. Kate Symonds, Director of Admissions

Birthday Cutoff September 1

Enrollment Total enrollment 380
Beginners program places: 20
Nursery places: 10
Kindergarten places: 5-10
Graduating class size: approximately 30-35

Financial Aid/Scholarship $1.7 million; approximately 25% of the student body receives some form of aid

Endowment $3.8 million

Tuition Range 2009-2010 $8,000 to 33,000, 2s (2 days) through 8th grade all fees included, except for optional lunch for grades 4 through 8 for $900

After-School Program St. Hilda's & St. Hugh's after-school program is open to enrolled children; a variety of creative and recreational activities from 3 to 6:30 P.M.; an additional payment is required

Summer Program Summer camps in June and July for an additional charge

———

St. Hilda's & St. Hugh's is a coed Episcopal day school founded in 1950 by the Reverend Mother Ruth of the Community of the Holy Spirit, an Episcopal religious order for women. The school is staffed by an entirely lay faculty. The school is traditional without being stuffy and academics are rigorous. There is a uniform/dress code for students. In grades one through eight and faculty are addressed formally as "Mr. Smith," and "Miss Jones." The entire community attends the daily chapel service where in addition to prayer, various topics are discussed. "St. Hilda's is very clear about its identity as an Episcopal School," explains one parent.

The school has undergone several renovations. Facilities include a greenhouse, three state-of-the-art science labs, three acoustically engineered music studios, art studios with a kiln, etching press and wood shop, a 6,000 square-foot play deck, a two room technology center, regulation size gym, library and an indoor play space with climbing equipment.

Getting in: Parents must complete an application before touring the school. Both parents are expected to tour the school. After the tour, the child is interviewed for about one hour for lower grades or up to a full day for older applicants. ERBs are required for kindergarten and above.

Parents: The parent body is a metropolitan mix, and although families of all faiths are welcome, the school is Episcopal. According to a parent, "the atmosphere is warm and cohesive," and that the single overarching quality that "most St. Hilda's & St. High's parents have in common is integrity." The Parents Association, known as the PA, is open to all parents in fact every parent is automatically a member of the PA. The PA links the parents to school life through workshops, fundraisers and coordinates a variety of other school initiatives. Parents volunteer for a myriad of activities including decorating the school for the Family Hoedown, setting up and working at the Annual Holiday Party, assisting in the Thanksgiving Food Chain, and more.

Program: The school has three divisions, the Lower Division is for Beginners through third graders; the Middle School is for fourth through sixth grades, and the Upper Division is for students in grades seven and eight. The curriculum is developmentally appropriate but highly structured. In the early years, children learn to socialize, observe nature, and have weekly art projects. As children move into the Nursery and Kindergarten grades, the program includes classroom jobs, an introduction to a second language, art, movement, music, library, shapes, colors, field trips, self-portraits, formal science study and a unit on dinosaurs and classic tales. In Lower School, grades 1 through 3, formal reading instruction begins in earnest using a traditional phonics-based program and appropriate literature. Additionally, students learn organizational skills, writing, math, technology, social studies second languages, the arts and daily physical education classes along with field trips throughout the New York City area that tie into the third grade year-long study of New York City area.

Middle School, grades four through six, and Upper School, grades seven and eight, mark the gradual transition from assisted learning to independent learning. By sixth grade subjects are fully departmentalized. Interdisciplinary projects cover pre-colonial America, U.S. geography and parables in scripture. Readings include, *The Phantom Tollbooth, The Giver, The Devil's Arithmetic* and *Bud, Not Buddy*. History covers Ancient Greece, Africa, Egypt India and Mesopotamia. By Upper School students are reading *To Kill a Mockingbird, The Odyssey, Fahrenheit 451*, taking pre-chemistry, physics and algebra using graphing calculators. French, Spanish or Mandarin is required from Nursery on; Latin is required in seventh and eighth grades.

A variety of interscholastic sports teams are offered including soccer, volleyball, cross-country, basketball, track and field, softball and baseball.

St. Hilda's & St. Hugh's has a sister school in Chengalpattu, India. As part of a post-tsunami outreach effort, the school shares materials and human resources with their companion school that serves children ages 3 to 14. The new school, named CSI St. Hilda's & St. Hugh's Matriculation School, was funded by school resources and provides a cross-continental experience for all. Approximately 85 percent of CSI's population is Dalit, formerly known as the untouchables or oppressed. These children were previously denied access to education, making the alliance especially rewarding and relevant.

Parents say that although the workload and homework get pretty heavy at St Hilda's, "It's worth all the work. The bottom line," explains one parent "is that my daughter is thriving. She is interested in her class work, fond of her classmates, and loves her school."

Popular Secondary School Choices   Brearley, Bronx Science, Chapin, Collegiate, Groton, Episcopal High School (Va.), Lawrenceville, Miss Porter's, Nightingale-Bamford, Pomfret, Regis, Stuyvesant High School, St. Andrew's, Trinity

Traditions   Annual Holiday Party and Cultural Celebrations such as Kwanzaa, Hanukah, Math Night, Art Fair, Gym Show, Gospel Celebration, Family Hoedown, Christmas Pageant, Spring Production, Teacher's Appreciation Breakfast, Dad's Chorus

Publications   *Viewbook* and Annual Report
School News
Parent Involvement Guide

Community Service Requirement   In addition to the companion school, CSI in India, there are school-wide service opportunities including celebrating various patron saints, human rights letter-writing project, planting and harvesting herbs for a local soup kitchen, a "Nets for Life" project to fight the spread of malaria in Africa, a Thanksgiving food chain for a local soup pantry: student form a human chain to stock the pantry; monthly clothing and supplies drives

Saint Luke's School

487 Hudson Street
New York, NY 10014
(212) 924-5960, fax (212) 924-1352
website: www.stlukeschool.org

Coed
Junior kindergarten–8th grade
Not accessible

Mr. Bart Baldwin, Head of School
Ms. Carole J. Everett, Director of Admissions and Financial Aid

Birthday Cutoff   Children entering junior kindergarten must be 4 by September 1
Children entering Kindergarten must be 5 by September 1

Enrollment   Total enrollment: 205
Junior kindergarten places: 15-18
Kindergarten places: 10-15
Graduating class: approximately 20-24

Grades   The Lower School is on a semester system (grades junior kindergarten–4); there are two formal parent conferences (others arranged as needed), and two written reports that include checklists and comprehensive narratives
The Upper School (grades 5 through 8), is on a trimester system; there are three written reports that include letter grades and comprehensive comments, and two formal parent conferences
Letter grades begin in 5th grade
Departmentalization begins in 5th grade

Tuition Range 2009–2010 $27,750 to $30,525, junior kindergarten through 8th grade

Financial Aid/Scholarship   21% of the student body receives some form of aid; a tuition payment plan is available

Endowment $2 million

Diversity   33% students of color, 3 Prep for Prep students enrolled as of fall 2009, 7 Early Steps students enrolled as of fall 2009
St. Luke's enrolls students from a variety of diversity programs including Prep for Prep, Early Steps, Boy's Club and A Better Chance; There is an active Parents Association Diversity Committee that holds monthly meetings and a Faculty Diversity Coordinator, along with a Diversity Coordinator

Homework   Begins gently with the expectation that parents of junior kindergarten and kindergarten children will read with their child for at least 30 minutes every evening; written assignments begin in 1st grade; with a 10-minute assignment at least once a week; 2nd and 3rd grades approximately 20-30 minutes per night
4th grade: 45 minutes–1 hour per night
5th and 6th grades: 1½ hours per night
7th and 8th grades: approximately 2 hours per night

After-School Program   St. Luke's After-School Program/Extended Day: Monday–Friday, from 2:30 P.M. until 6 P.M.; a series of very popular enrichment classes and supervised study; a variety of creative and recreational activities; an additional fee is required, but financial aid is available; varsity intramural sports teams for Upper School students

St. Luke's School was founded in 1945 and retains its affiliation with the Episcopal Church. The program is ecumenical but there is chapel from one to three times a week, depending on the grade, at the Church of St. Luke's in the Fields, a landmark building dating from 1822, rebuilt in 1985. Mondays are for silent meditation. Approximately fifty per cent of the students go to the altar for a non-denominational blessing or communion. The approach to religion is multicultural and inclusive, and religious education encourages understanding and acceptance of all faiths, and appreciation of culture, traditions, and beliefs of all people.

Notwithstanding, St. Luke's is an Episcopal day school, "for children of all faiths that educates the mind, body and spirit," explains the Director of Admissions. Located on an historic garden block in the West Village, the school is easily accessible from a variety of locations outside the neighborhood because of its convenient proximity to public transportation.

Spacious classrooms face the tranquil garden, a two-acre enclosed tree-lined campus nestled in a bustling West Village neighborhood. All classrooms are afforded good light and little street noise. The school which has been updated and renovated over the years has a library/media center, gymnasium, art, studio, auditorium, music, computer and foreign language rooms, a science lab, and a cafeteria that serves a hot lunch and organic produce, and a large playground. Sports teams use the school gym, Pier 40, and other nearby fields.

Getting in: Interviews are required for parents and children, and applicants must submit the results of ERB testing. Applications are due by December 1st, but will be accepted on a rolling basis after the deadline if there is an opening in a grade.

Parents: There is a very active Parents Association. Especially active is the Parent Diversity Committee and the Outreach Committee that does community service and has adopted a school in Binge, South Africa. PA meetings are usually held after morning drop-off, but there is an occasional evening meeting with child-care provided. Parent volunteers help with fundraisers, chaperone class field trips, volunteer in the library, and orchestrate grade-wide phone and e-mail chains as well as special events such as the Halloween and Family Dances.

Program: The school is traditional and structured but a relaxed atmosphere permeates the environment. The program prides itself on being balanced, challenging, while offering a variety of educational approaches and plenty of individual attention. St. Luke's has no formal dress code—dress is casual.

Interdisciplinary teaching is strong. The school is divided into two divisions: Lower School is composed of junior kindergarten through fourth grade; Upper School is fifth through eighth grades. Cooperative learning and small group instruction are a hallmark of the program. Technology is thoughtfully integrated in all disciplines, and an integrated drama program has been added in recent years.

Upper School students learn strong academic and study skills, and are required to complete courses in English, history, math, social studies, foreign language, science, art, music, religious studies, physical education, library and technology. Group work and cooperative study continue with research assignments in many disciplines. Foreign language starts in junior kindergarten with French. The students continue with French until Grade 5 when they can choose to continue with French or switch to Spanish. An Upper School outdoor education program includes a three-day trip to Camp Mason, near the Delaware Water Gap.

Popular High School Choices   A mix of public and independent day and boarding schools, including, Berkeley-Carroll, Brearley, Browning, Concord Academy, Convent of the Sacred Heart, Dalton, Friends, Kent, Fiorello LaGuardia High School of Music, Art and the Performing Arts, Loyola, Marymount, Middlesex Academy, Miss Porter's, Nightingale-Bamford, Packer Collegiate, Peddie, Poly Prep, Regis, Riverdale, Saint Ann's, Spence, Stuyvesant High School, Trinity

Traditions   Human Rights Day, Lessons and Carols, Jog-a-thon, Halloween Dance, AIDS Walk, Community Service to St. Clement's Food Pantry, Book Fair, Outdoor Education, Grade 8 Leadership Retreat, Choir and Band Concerts

Publications   Literary Magazine: *Portfolio*
Grade 5 Literary Newspaper: *Bookworms*
Lower School Literary Newspaper: *Wormlets*
Newsletter: *St. Luke's Times*

Hangouts   Lilac Chocolates, Angelique, Cowgirl Hall of Fame, The Hudson Diner, Rivoli Pizza, Milk and Cookies, the Water Park

The School at Columbia University

556 West 110th Street
New York, NY 10025
(212) 851-4215, fax (212) 851-4270
Admissions (212) 851-4216
website: www.theschool.columbia.edu

Coed
Kindergarten–8th grade
Accessible

Annette Raphel, Head of School
Kathryn Kaiser, Principal of the Primary Division
Kevin Fittinghoff, Principal of the Intermediate Division
Rekha Sharma Puri, Director of Admissions and Enrollment

Birthday Cutoff Children entering kindergarten must be 5 by December 31

Enrollment Total enrollment: approximately 500
Kindergarten places: approximately 60

Grades Trimester system; narrative reports with checklists, two in-depth parent/teacher conferences each year with an optional third conference at the end of the year; two detailed narrative report cards with checklists each year, letter grades begin in the Middle Division

Tuition 2009–2010 $29,000 Kindergarten through 8th grade

Fiancial Aid/Scholarship Columbia-affiliated families receive a 50% primary tuition scholarship benefit; additionally, non-affiliated Columbia families are awarded financial aid on the basis of demonstrated need; recently, Columbia awarded $5 million in financial aid to The School

Endowment Supported by the endowment and resources of Columbia University

Diversity The student body is highly diverse and reflects the population of the neighborhood and community

After-School Program A variety of programs, over 80 classes, Monday through Friday from 3:30 P.M. to 5:30 P.M.; financial aid is available

Summer Program Educational support services by invitation only

---

What started as The School Search Service at Columbia University for the children of Columbia's faculty has evolved into The School at Columbia University. The School, as it's simply called, has a decade under its belt and is going strong. It focuses not only on attracting top faculty, but also on fostering diversity (one of the citys most diverse), education and community outreach.

The School serves some of the children of Columbia's faculty along with children from the Upper West Side (only from in Districts 3 and 5), selected through a random lottery.

The goal is to have a roughly 50/50 mix of children from Columbia families and children from the neighborhood. This is because the mission of The School is to serve as a recruitment and retention strategy for University faculty, to build community within the University and between the University and the neighborhood, and to serve as a resource and development lab for the New York City public schools. To build bridges to the neighborhood and produce materials and methodologies for the public schools, the demographics for The School have to be similar to those of a neighborhood public school.

Spearheaded by Dr. Gardner Dunnan who was Headmaster at Dalton for 23 years, The School's current Head, Annette Raphel and hails from Massachusetts as a top administrator, and is a winner of the Presidential Mathematics Award and has guided the school's first three graduating classes.

The School boasts the latest in technology—there are plasma screen TVs everywhere, even in the lobby—in a brand new 72,000 square-foot, five and a half floor facility. The School's building is adjacent to and connected through a common stairwell to a portion of Columbia's residential housing, making it ultra-convenient for some to get to school.

The School follows in a long line of other Columbia spin-off schools such as The Barnard School (now Horace Mann Lower Division) and the Horace Mann School (from Teacher's College), The Speyer School and The Lincoln School (no longer extant).

Unlike any other private school in the city, The School has the privilege of making use of the University's expansive facilities including, Butler Library, Dodge Physical Fitness Center, Baker Field, art studios, laboratories, fields, and the Earth Institute. In addition, University faculty members are regularly involved in the programs of The School.

Getting in: Applications, or, "Inquiry Forms'" for families who both affiliated and not affiliated with Columbia University are available on-line and in hard copy at The School's lobby beginning September 1st. Application or "Inquiry" deadline is October 30th. Late applications are considered, depending on availability. The School holds an admissions lottery for applications in early November. Lottery forms are available on The School's website and at The School. There is no application fee and ERBs are not required, but evaluations from prior schools or programs are.

Although places are not guaranteed, every West Side family should enter the lottery. It's a no brainer; if you win an application you don't have to apply, and if you do, it's an option. Of the approximately 1,000 families in the lottery, The School admits a total of 30 to 40 children for kindergarten, and another 10 for grades one through seven. The School only interviews about fifty or so families from the lottery, so once you get an application you have a high probability of being offered a place.

"We make ourselves available for anyone who needs help with the process," explains Rekha Sharma Puri, The School's Director of Admissions and Enrollment. "The team here is dedicated to ensuring that all families understand our mission, culture and program. A hands-on approach with many personal interactions is crucial to the way we operate—we are truly humbled by the overwhelming interest in our school."

Parents and children are interviewed separately on the same visit. On occasion, additional evaluations are requested and needed, The School will fund the cost. Admissions priority is given to siblings enrolled at The School.

Parents: Roughly one-third of all class parents have Columbia e-mail addresses, the rest are a mix. No fancy Fifth or Park Avenue cocktail parties here, but one on Central Park West may well occur.

The common goals of The School's PA are, of course, to raise money and plan events, and are an extremely inclusive group of dedicated parents. It works on community outreach and building relationships among The School and its neighbors. Showy dinners and splashy auctions are out, expect potluck dinners, collaborative curriculum breakfasts as well as other events that are low-key, warm and comfortable.

"These are parents who have already made the commitment to diversity," remarks one parent. "Play dates are easy, and so are the friendships," the parent says. "Almost all families live in the immediate area; friendships form along the lines of their interests."

The PA is in full gear. It publishes a newsletter, and has held a few events like a recent Q&A informational meeting. The School's Head also publishes a weekly newsletter that highlights recent research in educational practices. All parents are invited to share their areas of expertise and Columbia professors pitch in on a regular basis, from directing scenes in Shakespearean plays to lecturing on the electoral college.

Program: The School is a supportive, first rate learning environment, with a student/teacher ratio of approximately five to one; the focus is on the students. One parent raves, "They know my child, they know what books he likes to read, and they know he likes history so they brought in some history books." Other parents praise teachers, too. "The faculty is extraordinary, experienced teachers that are responsive."

The School offers eleven subject areas to all children: educational technology, literacy/English, performing arts-music, science, social studies, social and emotional learning, Spanish, visual arts, wellness. Teachers work together to create integrated units, which culminate in single projects. Seventh grade math students use their research skills, writing and math skills for The School's Great Mathematics Project that culminates in a grand exposition in which younger children grill the older ones on their areas of study. In first grade, students read stories that inspire dances they choreograph and perform on sets they make in art. A poetry assembly brings together older students with their younger buddies to listen to pod-casts in Spanish. In addition, teachers incorporate student interests into their lessons, and encourage students to problem-solve creatively and collaboratively.

Many members of the faculty take classes at Columbia and Teachers College free of charge; many hold graduate degrees. They present at educational conferences, consult, and on occasion, publish. Parents seem pleased with the faculty, and have consistently given them high ratings on school surveys.

For some subjects, like dance, special teachers are arranged, often with a portfolio of skills. For its dance program, The School has a contract with Steps on Broadway, a dance company that trains four-year-olds to seventy-four year olds.

The creative, experimental and interdisciplinary program boasts a

Child Study Team that evaluates and supports every child. Classrooms, called "pods," are common spaces that form the nucleus of each classroom. In kindergarten through fourth grade, children learn math, science, culture and society, communication arts and technology, fine arts, wellness and fitness. In fifth through eighth grades, specific academic subjects, science and technology, math, humanities, fine arts, and wellness and fitness are often sequenced to provide a deeper understanding.

The latest in technology is omnipotent at The School—no black boards here—white boards and Smartboards only. Moreover, there is a complete commitment to technology. Digital technology, multimedia materials and their applications, wireless connections and laptops are available, almost one for every student.

As a research and development center for the larger University, The School has a Center for Integrated Learning and Teaching (CILT) that sponsors and participates in research projects related to many aspects of a kindergarten through eighth grade program. Recently, CILT developed two experimental software programs that are currently in use. There's also plenty of professional development for faculty, including University sponsored research and academic collaborations, workshops and conferences.

Popular Secondary School Choices A variety of public and private schools including Bronx Science, Beacon, Fiorellco La Guardia High School of Music, Art and the Performing Arts, Bard II, Stuyvesant High School, Brooklyn Latin, School of the Future, Riverdale, Calhoun, Fieldston, Trinity, Horace Mann, Dalton, Columbia Prep

Traditions Welcome Dinner, Buddies, Family Science Celebration, Geography Bee, Penny Harvest, Curriculum Share, Book Fair, Field Day, Talent Show, All-School Curriculum Night

Publications *The Lion's Share* (weekly)
The Columbia Cub (monthly)
Blue Prints (yearbook)
assorted school blogs

Community Service Requirement Community service is a popular pastime at The School; a recent graduating class raised enough money to fund their class trip by encouraging parents to pledge money for each hour of service performed at various agencies

The Solomon Schechter School of Manhattan

50 East 87th Street
(corner of Madison Avenue)
New York, N.Y. 10128
(212) 427-9500
website: www.sssm.org
e-mail: sssm2@aol.com

Lower Elementary Division
Kindergarten–1st grade
50 East 87th Street (corner of Madsion Avenue)
New York, N.Y. 10128
(212) 427-9500 ext 18

Upper Elementary and Middle School
Grades 2nd–8th grade
15 West 86th Street
(between Central Park West and Columbus Avenues)
New York, N.Y. 10024
(212) 427-9500 ext 10

Coed
Wheelchair accessible

Dr. Steven C. Lorch, Head
Yeal Even-Moratt, Head of the Lower Elementary School
Benjamin Mann, Head of Middle School
Gary Pretsfelder, Head of the Upper Elementary School
Rabbi Laurie Katz Braun, Director of Admissions

Uniform   K–5: Boys: navy or gray slacks, blue shirt (white on Fridays), navy sweater with crest
Girls: navy jumper or skirt or slacks, white blouse, navy sweater with crest
6–8: Boys: khaki or navy slacks or corduroys, blue or white button down, turtlenecks or polo shirt, and navy sweater with crest
Girls: khaki or navy slacks, corduroys or skirt, blue or white button down, turtleneck or polo shirt, navy sweater with crest

Birthday Cutoff   Children applying for kindergarten must turn 5 years old by October 31st; developmental readiness is the main consideration

411

Enrollment   Total enrollment: 139
  Kindergarten places: 20

Grades   Detailed anecdotal reports for kindergarten; grades 1–8 receive detailed anecdotal reports with checklists as well as a portfolio assessment for grades 3–8

Tuition Range 2009–2010 $29,500 to $29,950 Kindergarten through 8th grade; (Tuition is based upon a sliding scale depending on parents' ability to pay)

Endowment   N/A

Financial Aid/Scholarship   55%

Diversity   8% students of color

After-School Program   Interscholastic sports teams in soccer, basketball; other activities include, Chess Club, Avaiation Club, Yoga Club and Yearbook

––––––––

The Solomon Schechter School of Manhattan opened its doors in 1994 with a kindergarten class of 14 students, housed at Park Avenue Synagogue, under its current head of school, Dr. Steven Lorch. In September 2001, the school expanded and added a second location, on West 86th Street, at the Society for the Advancement of Judaism, for it's middle and upper grades, and continues to grow. A Pre-kindergarten program is being developed, and another expansion at 100th Street and Columbus Avenue will open in September 2010.

The school is composed of three divisions: Lower Elementary for grades kindergarten through 1st grade; Upper Elementary for grades 2-5; and Middle School for grades 6-8.

The Lower School now has eight grades and enrollment is strong. The Solomon Schechter School is one of a network of over 70 Solomon Schechter schools throughout the United States and Canada, the first of which was established in 1951. Among these sister schools is the Solomon Schechter High School of New York, with which the school collaborates on a number of joint community initiatives. The two schools are separate entities, though there have been discussions from time to time about possible future affiliation.

The Solomon Schechter School of Manhattan was conceived in 1994 as an initiative of the United Synagogue of Conservative Judaism and the rabbis of the nine Conservative synagogues in Manhattan. During its formative period, a group of dedicated parents and community leaders came together to develop the school's mission and character. Elie Wiesel serves as Honorary Chairman of the Board of Trustees, Dr. Samuel Klagsbrun as Chairman of the Education Committee. Dr. Klagsbrun says that at the school "children learn to participate fully in modern society and contribute to our general culture while feeling completely at home in the Jewish world." The aim was to "establish a Jewish day school . . . where students will be given a rich understanding of their Jewish heritage, a fluent command of the Hebrew language, and a passion for Jewish learning. The goal is to nurture culturally aware, compassionate, and socially responsible individuals who will constitute the future leadership of the American Jewish Community."

Recently, Solomon Schechter became fully-accredited, by NAIS, NYSAIS, ISAAGNY, and the New York Board of Regents, among other organizations.

The mission of the school is to develop "Textpeople," "People who find meaning in the world through confident, active, skilled learning—Torah, scientific discovery, the arts, worldly experience and knowledge of every kind—both for its own sake and for the pursuit of truth."

Getting in: Parents must fill out an application and schedule a tour. Tours are available in the fall and spring. Applications are available beginning in September. Kindergarten applicants are required to submit a complete application along with the application fee, the confidential previous school or program information form, and the results of the Early Childhood Admissions Exam, administered by the ERB. Children entering kindergarten are interviewed in playgroups. When possible, nursery school visits are made. Older applicants for grades 1-7 are asked to submit a completed application with fee, previous school forms, and standardized test results, and the ISEE for upper grades. Applicants must also spend a half-day at school; parents for all grades are asked to meet with the Head of School.

Parents: One parent described the social mix as "An eclectic group who are down-to-earth and 'heimish,' " and diverse geographically and religiously (although all the children are Jewish). Parents help out in the office, go on field trips and volunteer in the classroom.

The PA sponsors brunches, an annual kosher food tasting evening, an Education Night and an annual retreat. All parents are members of the PA and invited to attend meetings.

Program: The Head of the Elementary and Middle School, Dr. Steven Lorch, who has degrees from Harvard and Columbia, has previously been the head of three other Jewish schools in North America, Australia and in Israel. According to Dr. Lorch, there are two language objectives for the kindergarten year: 1) that every child will read and write in English by the end of the year; and 2) every child will become proficient in Hebrew. "To achieve these objectives the classroom has to truly be an enriched bilingual environment."

The classroom teachers are bilingual (English/Hebrew) and work with the Early Childhood Director to design the curriculum. The classroom emphasizes experiential or active learning. There are early childhood materials, including blocks, as well as computers in the classroom. The classes often break into smaller groups for math activities, block building, computers, and so on.

A main feature of the program is an interdisciplinary (or thematic) approach to learning. Topics of study are chosen by the students, kindergarten through second grade, on the basis of their interests and each topic is then investigated from a variety of perspectives: social studies, Jewish tradition, the arts, science, literature, mathematics, writing: all contribute to a rich and textured understanding of the topic at hand.

The school's main educational philosophy is simple: "to help children learn to use their minds well." To this end, the program provides for various important learning experiences. Creative and guided play is serious business, along with challenging and constructive activities. Teachers are readily available and know the children well. Good manners and respect are important.

Reading is taught by combining elements of both Whole Language and phonics. Children use manipulative materials when learning math and sciences. Children are instructed by specialists in music and physical education twice a week. There is daily physical exercise, either on the outdoor play roof or in nearby Central Park.

Children are introduced to Jewish life through the Jewish Studies curriculum and Hebrew is taught using the natural method of language study. Religion plays a central role in the life of the school; however the Jewish observances by families run the gamut. Prayer, activities related to holidays, the observance of dietary laws and acts of kindness (charity) are stressed. Girls are offered full egalitarian privileges and participation.

Jewish issues and religious thought play a central role in the life of the school. Students study math, science, history, English, Bible, rabbinical thought, Hebrew and French or Spanish. Extracurricular courses and activities include the Bridges to Brotherhood, Blacks and Jews in Dialogue, Investment Club, City Lights (which brings students to special High Five! Performances), Solomon Society (student government), choir, drama, studio art, theater production arts, newspaper, yearbook, web design, festival and daily prayer planning committees. There are interscholastic sports programs offered in cross-country, soccer, volleyball, basketball and softball. Most of the school's Jewish rituals and holiday celebrations are entirely planned and carried out by the students in consultation with the school's rabbi.

Traditions   Monday and Thursday prayer in the Chapel (parents are welcome), Friday friendship circles, Kabbalat Shabbat, Siddur ceremonies, Family Shabbaton retreat, tzedakah (charity) roundtables, (Middle School presentations), annual concerts. Fourth and fifth grade environmental educational retreats (Teva), 7th grade study trip to Washington, D.C., 8th grade study tour of Israel

Publications   Weekly newsletter: *Daf Kesher*
Yearbook: *Lev Ha'inyan*

The Spence School

Lower School
(Grades K–4)
56 East 93rd Street

Middle and Upper Schools
(Grades 5–12)
22 East 91st Street
New York, NY 10128-0657
(212) 289-5940, fax (212) 289-6025
website: www.spenceschool.org

All girls
Kindergarten–Grade 12
Accessible

Ms. Ellanor Brizendine, Head of School
Ms. Alice Shedlin, Director of Admissions

Uniform   Grades kindergarten–4: plaid jumper and white shirt, solid-color stockings, tights, socks
Grades 5–8: navy blue skirt, navy blue pants and white shirt
Grades 9–12: solid gray skirt or gray slacks, any shirt that has sleeves and covers midriff; no leg warmers, leggings or long underwear, low-heeled shoes only
Uniform is not required on Fridays
After fall trimester, seniors may petition to cease wearing their uniforms
Before the start of school uniform fittings are held at Spence
Gym outfits are given to the girls free of charge

Birthday Cutoff   Girls entering kindergarten must be 5 by August 31

Enrollment   Total enrollment: 621
Kindergarten places: approximately 52
Graduating class size: approximately 40

Grades   Semester system in Lower School
Trimester system in Middle/Upper Schools
Grades kindergarten–4: checklist (skill acquired, developing skill, needs support, exhibits strength, marked improvement)

416

Grades 5–8: letter grades begin in Grade 7, detailed anecdotal reports plus a checklist
Grades 9–12: letter grades and detailed reports
Departmentalization begins in Grade 6
First final exam in Grade 6

Tuition Range 2009–2010 $34,500 Kindergarten–Grade 12
Additional fees: Parents Association dues $75

Financial Aid/Scholarship Approximately 19% of the entire student body receives some form of tuition assistance, 26% in the Upper School
Financial aid accounts for 15% of the operating budget

Endowment $85 million (as of January 2009)

Diversity 29% students of color; 26% in the Upper School
Spence enrolls Prep for Prep students, ABC (A Better Chance) students, TEAK students, Early Steps students, and Oliver Program students
Cultural Awareness For Everyone (CAFÉ),
The Afro-Latino Alliance
Jewish Culture Club
Asia F.O.C.U.S, Spence Women's Action Network (SWAN)

Homework Kindergarten: none
Grade 1 and: approximately 10–20 minutes
Grades 3 and 4: 30–45 minutes
Grade 5: 1 hour–1½ hours, plus reading assignments
Grade 6: 20–30 minutes per subject per night plus reading assignments
Grades 7 and 8: approximately 2½–3 hrs per night
Grades 9 through 12: approximately 3–4 hrs per night

After-School Program Second Act After-School Program: coed, open to students from other schools; a variety of creative and enrichment activities for an additional charge; Monday–Thursday from 3:00–6:00 P.M., Friday from 2:00 to 4:30 P.M.
Middle School: interscholastic sports program
Upper School: varsity teams
Some club meetings and choir, drama and dance rehearsals for

grades 5–12 are held after school; choruses rehearse during school periods except for select choir and glee club

Summer Program   Second Act June Program for students in grades K–4; there is an additional charge

Jump Start: a Grade 9 one-week program for new Grade nine students

Early Start: a foreign language orientation program for new Middle School students Camp Spence: a two-week day camp for girls entering Kindergarten through Grade 4.

The Spence School, founded in 1892 as Miss Spence's School for Girls, is housed in elegant buildings on East 91st Street and East 93rd Street and offers a well-rounded, rigorous academic program, strong in performing arts, the sciences, visual arts and foreign language studies. Spence artfully combines the traditional and innovative; it was one of the first independent schools to use the computer in the lower grades, and multicultural perspectives add excitement and relevance to the traditional core of studies.

"Relevance" is a key concept at Spence. Spence's mission, "to educate girls and young women to the highest academic and personal standards necessary for responsible, effective citizenship," is summed up in the school motto: "Non Scholae Sed Vitae Discimus: Not For School But For Life We Learn." Spence is committed to a diverse, academically talented student body. One parent said, "It's very fast paced; you need to have a child who can handle that."

In 1998, Head of School Mrs. Edes Gilbert retired; she was the last of a generation of Grand Dames who governed prestigious Manhattan girls' schools. The current Head of School, Ellanor "Bodie" Brizendrine, is the 14th Head the school has seen, and the fit seems to be a good one. Having served as a Head of School at Marin Academy and as a former Dean, English teacher and Interim Head of Bryn Mawr, she brings a special brand of maturity and sensitivity to women's education to Spence.

Recently, Spence successfully completed a ten-year NYSAIS evaluation for reaccredidation. The Visiting Committee found the Spence traditions of rigor and inquiry, as well as its concern for meeting the challenges of diversity and the demands of a rapidly changing world to be strong. Also, the role of women is highly valued, and inextricably entwined with all aspects of the life of the school.

Since 2008, Spence has had a complete website with interactive calendars, photo galleries, information on faculty, staff and curriculum plus. Additionally, Spence recently purchased an adjacent brownstone on East 90th Street, and plans to renovate are in the works.

Getting in: Spence is one of the few very selective schools where parents can have an individual tour and interview before they even apply. Admissions personnel told me, "No letters of recommendation, please." What are they looking for? "We are offering a place to a girl who will take full advantage of everything a Spence education has to offer." One parent was very impressed by the Upper School student who led her tour: "She was so open, obviously not scripted, and she answered all our questions, which indicated to me that Spence is proud of what it does, and the girls are not afraid to talk about it." Parents are given a card with the name of the young woman who led their tour so that they can contact her through the admissions office if they have any additional questions. Once the application is made, parents applying for kindergarten are given an appointment for their daughter's interview. In the Lower School, this takes place with a small group of other girls at the school. In the Upper and Middle Schools, the appointment is individual. Spence has a wait list.

One mother told me that there is no typical Spence girl: "What distinguishes Spence from the other girls' schools is that there is no norm here. The girls are individuals and all are enthusiastic about learning."

Parents: A parent described the parent body at Spence as dominated by two groups: "Those with well-worn, polished shoes (old money), and those with brand-new Jimmy Choo's (new money)." Another parent described the parent body as "some families who don't live on their salaries—attorneys, investment bankers, independent entrepreneurs." But the Upper School is more diverse. Many prominent Jewish families feel comfortable at Spence and the school's diversity has increased too. "But," says one parent, "ascension through the ranks of Spence's Parents Association requires a certain amount of social skill and savvy." Parents play an essential role in the school's community; monthly meetings are open to all parents. There are over 25 committees with volunteer opportunities, such as sponsoring class meetings and evening lectures, fund-raising events, and annual traditions such as the Book Fair and the Halloween party. Class cocktail parties or suppers are held at Spence.

Program: Two teachers are assigned to each kindergarten section and the class frequently breaks into small groups. Teachers integrate a variety of subjects into each day's lessons, frequently presenting academic material. There is a resource center for students who need support. A parent said, "Teachers reinforce learning through writing, speaking, observation, drawing." Classes write and illustrate their own books.

In kindergarten, students learn social studies, math, language arts, science, art, dance, physical education, and music based on the Kodaly approach. They also participate in computer and library programs.

Computer classes are part of the curriculum in all divisions of the school. Alumnae from the late seventies remember an emphasis on computer even then. In grades kindergarten through fifth, LOGO, a computer graphics language, is taught. Keyboarding and word processing are taught in third grade. The Lower School has its own computer lab with Macintosh computers. There is a fully equipped Lower School science lab and two science teachers whose sole responsibility is to work with kindergartners through fourth graders. One computer science course is required in the Upper School.

In addition to academic subjects, Grade 1 students take courses in art, music, and physical education. Art, dance and drama teachers are working professionals. In the spacious art room I saw highly individualized stick puppets and masks. Throughout the social studies curriculum, the brochure states, there is a "special emphasis on the role of women in history and focus on the rich diversity of cultures," and social studies is coordinated with language arts, music and art.

Grade 2 is introduced to chess with a semester devoted to learning the intricacies of the game. The Spence Grade 6 Chess Team took home a highly coveted trophy from the U.S. Chess Federation National K-12 Championship held in Orlando. One year, for an integrated Grade 2 unit on baseball, a parent told me, "For English they read the biography of Jackie Robinson, for art they studied baseball murals and created their own, in history they examined integration and baseball and in gym, they learned the essence of the game—they played it!"

Grade 3 participates in an immigrant project; they study a person or family from another country. They also study the history of New York and take many field trips to places such as Phillipsburg Manor, Ellis Island, The Museum of the City of New York and the Natural History Museum.

"Simulations" enrich Grades 4 and 5 social studies curriculum. Art is incorporated into these simulations as well as research and writing skills. Grade 4 works extensively with maps, globes and terrain models to aid their learning of the geography and history of the United States. In science, they explore oceans and rivers as a way of understanding the ecosystem in coordination with the geography lesson in social studies. Math explores more complex methods and critical thinking. Grade 4 explores math concepts through computer programming, LOGO, and students learn to articulate their knowledge of mathematic reasoning through writing and discussion.

Foreign language begins in third grade, with a choice between French and Spanish. One parent said games and songs are used to teach language in the early years. An optional second language can be elected in seventh grade.

Health education starts early and covers a variety of topics from nutrition to body image and anatomy to peer and family relationships. As part of the social and emotional learning curriculum, the fifth grade participates in the prepare/personal safety program. More important, parents say that self-confidence, self-esteem and leadership are constantly reinforced in the girls: "They are always supporting the girls in their choices and decisions," "The girls are self-confident from beginning to end."

Drama, dance and music are part of the curriculum in each grade. Kindergartners perform at the Holiday Pageant in December. Fourth graders perform a ballet. Lower School senior chorus is for third and fourth graders. The Grade 6 chorus, a Middle School chorus and Glee Club are open to all. The Select Choir (which travels abroad) and three chamber ensembles in the Upper School are open by audition. There is an instrumental music program for grades one through twelve, and private lessons at Spence are in great demand.

The dance program is extensive: folk, jazz, ballet, in addition to physical education classes. One mother of a lower school student said of her daughter's dance performance: "They were in unison doing these routines; we were all stunned." The Middle and Upper School dance company performs at Symphony Space each year.

All girls gain experience with public speaking. One parent said her daughter, who is normally reluctant to perform on stage, got up in front of the Lower School to read her own poem: "She never would have had the confidence if she hadn't been at Spence." The other girls were supportive. "There was no competitiveness. All the girls' poems were great."

To mark the transition from Lower School, Middle Schoolers (Grades 5 through 8) have their own two floors, and their own uniform. The head of the Middle School told me "there is a real esprit de corps in Middle School; it has its own identity." Middle Schoolers have their own student council. Grade 6 is fully departmentalized and letter grades begin in Grade 7.

Art continues to be integrated into the curriculum with the Visual Arts program beginning in Grade 5.

In Grade 8 students read *Jane Eyre, Romeo and Juliet,* and *The House on Mango Street* and a selection of poetry and American short stories. In history, both Western and non-Western cultures are explored, and students hone their research methods. The Middle School teaches students the skills they need to write about demanding texts.

The Middle School fields teams in basketball, softball, soccer, volleyball, track and field and swimming. These teams participate in interscholastic competition.

Middle Schoolers participate in community service projects through the Community Service Club for Grades 6 through 12 and volunteer in the Lower School. Middle Schoolers have the opportunity to perform in the annual Eighth Grade Play. Annual dances for Grades 7 and 8 graders provide opportunities to socialize with the opposite sex.

If you go straight through Spence from kindergarten to twelfth grade you are known as a "survivor." Attrition typically occurs after eighth grade when some girls go to boarding schools or, occasionally, to a coed day school. According to a survivor, "The work builds up in eighth and ninth grades and then increases again in tenth and eleventh, but if you're good at budgeting your time you don't notice."

The Upper School at Spence consists of Grade 9 through 12. The Upper School is academically rigorous. Students who enter at Grade 9 are required to ease their transition by attending the summer Jump-Start Program, an orientation program that is free of charge. Girls with a problem subject can go to the Resource Center. "If necessary," says a student, "teachers will even look over your notes with you." Classes are kept small, about twelve to fifteen students. The average course load is five to six full credit courses. In addition to the usual core subjects, computer science, performing arts, speech and health are Upper School requirements, as are four years of foreign language or three of one language and two of another. Spence does not stress the AP program, but offers AP courses in French and studio art.

Many electives are offered to juniors and seniors and material covered is often as sophisticated as college level course work. Some electives include Conflicts in the Middle East, Astronomy, Native American Literature, Computer Programming and Robotics. Students are required to take two years of lab science; most choose to take another advanced-level science course. The Middle and Upper School science labs are completely renovated. A chemistry lab, a dedicated Middle School lab and a prep room for setting up experiments before class have been added. The physics lab has also been expanded. Senior Seminar and independent study are also available.

Students say that a friendly teacher-student relationship at Spence makes their school unique. One reason for this is that teachers in the Middle and Upper Schools must teach a range of grades and as a result get to know the girls as they mature. Teachers also act as advisors to their students both as homeroom teachers and as faculty advisors to student-led clubs.

According to the brochure, in English a "special emphasis is placed on a cross-cultural study of literature so that students are exposed to a range of material outside the Western tradition that enriches their understanding of other cultures." An elective course in world literature is required. Senior Seminar and/or independent study are also available.

Clara Spence, visionary educator and founder of The Spence School, believed in a broad curriculum to meet the interests of the students. Today, many courses at Spence are developed based upon student interest or faculty initiative. Reflecting increased student interest, the history elective program in the Upper School includes Conflicts in the Middle East, Latin America: From Conquest to Independence, as well as Indian History and Japanese History. In a thoughtful course called African-American Literature, students are introduced to the writings of the men and women who shaped contemporary black American culture: DuBois, Hurston, King, Baldwin, Malcolm X and others.

Students with proficiency in the arts can take advanced course work in studio art, photography and the performing arts.

Spence has wonderful opportunities for foreign language study abroad including Adventures in Real Communication, open to tenth through twelfth graders, who can take a one- or two-month program in France, Spain or Latin America. There is the School Year Abroad option for eleventh and twelfth graders, the Swiss Semester in Zermatt for tenth graders, the San Patricio Exchange in Madrid for tenth or eleventh graders and for ninth graders, a one- or two-month spring program in Evreux, France. For those who prefer an experience closer to home, participation in the Maine Coast Semester in Chewonki, Maine, study at the Mountain School in Vermont in association with Milton Academy or the Island School Program in the Caribbean are offered.

An eleventh grader told me that after school most girls either do homework, participate in school clubs or go out with their boyfriends, who pick them up at school. "Athletics are popular, chorus is fabulous and so is the choral master. Attendance at dance concerts and Glee Club events is good," she said.

Ninth and tenth graders have privileges; they can leave school if they have parental permission. Eleventh and twelfth graders can simply sign out. Ninth and tenth graders share "the Pit," a lounge area contiguous with the ninth and tenth grade lockers. There are junior and senior lounges that are carefully and thoughtfully located on the same floor as the College Counselor, the Registrar and the Upper School Dean. Senior privileges include not wearing their uniform in spring of senior year, coming in late on Fridays (if they don't have a class) and being allowed to use the elevators. "You'd think they'd never used an elevator before. They stop at every floor," says one parent.

There is an Upper School student council. One student council event is Color or Theme Days: Themes are picked, such as Western Day or Come As You Are Day, and the faculty dress up too. The Upper School student council is currently grappling with weightier issues such as reconsidering the school uniform and establishing an honor code.

There are numerous opportunities for faculty-led and student-led extracurricular participation at Spence. Faculty-led activities include dramatic productions, dance company, athletic teams and chorus, while student-led activities include drama club, Amnesty International, French club and Spanish club. Because of the size and unique nature of its community, many students have the opportunity to assume a leadership position in a club or activity by the time they graduate.

Commencement is held at the Church of the Heavenly Rest. Awards are given out at the Athletic Awards Banquet for athletic achievement and sportsmanship. The White Blazer Award is given to a student who is well respected in the athletic community, demonstrating determination, sportsmanship, cooperation, dedication and leadership. At Final Assembly external academic awards, such as National Merit Scholarships, are announced, but graduates no longer have the traditional Spence prizes for special academic achievements bestowed upon them. It is thought this will discourage excessive competition, according to the school. But one junior mentioned that "they didn't acknowledge the good work that everybody did."

When asked what embodies the spirit of Spence, Head of School, Bodie Brizzendine, replied: "Students are encouraged to dig deep and ask questions, understanding that learning is a life-long process, day to day, " echoing the school's motto, "Not for school, but for life we learn."

Popular College Choices   Columbia, Cornell, Princeton, Harvard, Dartmouth, University of Pennsylvania, New York University, Wesleyan, Brown, Duke, Yale, Amherst, Boston University, Emory, Washington University, George Washington, Trinity, Tufts

Traditions   Opening Assembly, Lower School Halloween party, Lower School New Parents' Dinner, Lower School Field Day, Fall Play, Spring Reading, Spring Play, Grade 8 Play, Grade 8 trip, Skating Party, Middle School Sing-Off Competition, Middle School picnic, Lower School Holiday Program, Grade 6 and 7 Event, Grandparents' and Special Friends Day, Bias Awareness Conference, Mini Olympics, Mini Olympics, The Bridge, Dance Concert at Symphony Space, Lower, Middle and Upper School Choral Concert, Book Fair, Spence Boutique, Student Council 91st Street Fair, Grade 10 trip to Washington, D.C. Black Rock Consortium trips

Publications   Newspaper: *The Spence Voice*
Literary arts magazine: *Fingerprints*
Yearbook: *Threshold*
Newsletter on current political issues: *SPARK*
Lower School magazine: *Inspiration*
Head's Newsletter: *Vantage Points*

Community Service Requirement   Spence has a Director of Outreach and Public Purpose, a position created in 2008 that coordinates community service and outreach endeavors for the school community; virtually every student participates in some form of community service throughout their years at Spence

Hangouts   Corner Bakery Yura on 92nd Street, junior lounge, senior lounge

425

The Studio School

117 West 95th Street
New York, NY 10025
(212) 678-2416
website: www.studioschoolnyc.org
e-mail: jtarpley@studioschoolnyc.org

Coed
Nursery (18 mos)–8th grade
Accessible

Ms. Janet C. Rotter, Head of School
Ms. Jennifer K. Tarpley, Director of Admissions

Birthday Cutoff   Children entering nursery must be 18 months by the start of school; Children entering kindergarten must be 5 by August 31

Enrollment   Total enrollment: approximately 120
Nursery places (18 months–2½ years): 14
Early childhood places (3- and 4-year olds): approximately 15
Kindergarten and up: 5 to 6 places, as available, in upper grades

Grades   Trimester system
Parents receive in-depth progress reports about their child's development plus parent/teacher conferences three time a year; in the classroom written curriculum reports are presented to parents at the end of each trimester

Tuition Range 2009–2010 $7,174 to $28,875, Nursery through 8th grade
All fees are included

Financial Aid/Scholarship   20% of the student body receives some form of aid

Endowment   None

Homework   Begins at age six and is a discrete part of the curriculum, viewed as independent study that is worked on jointly by the teaher and student; grading begins in the middle elementary classes

After-School Program Clubhouse, an informal, family-style, extended day program for children ages 4 and up, is available each day until 5:45 P.M. for an additional payment; children of mixed ages participate in planned group activities and individual pursuits; formal enrichment classes, called Explorations, are offered for children ages 5 and up in chess, improvisational theater, ceramics, dance, sports, model airplane, and more; also for an additional fee

Summer Program Summer Camp for children ages 2- to 14-years-old from mid-June through the end of July; a variety of creative and recreational activities for an additional payment

---

The Studio School was founded in 1971 by Robert and Dolores Welber as a "one room schoolhouse" in Greenwich Village. Three years later Janet Rotter, a graduate of Bank Street, came to Studio as an assistant teacher. She is currently Head of the School, as she has been for the past twenty-five years.

The Studio School moved to the Upper West Side in the late 1970s to expand its enrollment and provide more space for the early-childhood and elementary divisions. Today, the school has a brand-new building, the result of a massive capital project that claimed the space of three former brownstones on West 95th Street. The new facility has a welcoming reception area and lobby, many large, sunny, bright, well-equipped classrooms, a new library, a music room, an art room, dance studios, a gym, greenhouse, lounges, community space, a science lab and offices. The Studio School has always emphasized a sound traditional curriculum combined with a developmental approach incorporating each child's social and emotional growth. The school has a neighborhood feeling and parent involvement is welcome.

Getting in: Parents can attend an open house/tour before applying. The school offers two open houses in the fall, starting in October. At the open houses, parents have the opportunity to ask questions and talk with teachers about the program. Tours are held every week in the fall, and also begin in October. Parents are given a tour of the building and can see children in their classrooms. They also receive information on programs and curriculum. After a completed application has been sent in, the Director of Admissions will call to schedule an interview and a visit for the child. Children five and under are interviewed in small groups with parents. Older children spend time in a classroom. ERB testing is requested for applicants to third grade and above.

Parents: Studio offers a very diverse yet an incredibly close-knit community. "We all speak the same language here," observes one parent. The school holds a number of meetings and conferences throughout the year. In monthly Group Curriculum meetings, parents have the opportunity to learn about their child's curriculum and ask questions of teachers and staff. There's also a Parent Connection program by means of which current parents smooth the way for new ones. Parent participation is both valued and encouraged at every level, and especially appreciated in fund-raising.

Program: One of the founding principles of The Studio School is that children of all ages can learn from each other; the school uses cross-age and cross-grade grouping. Students are organized by age in mixed age groupings like 8s and 9s, instead of third and fourth grades, with sixteen children per class. There is a teacher and an assistant in each classroom through second grade. Class groupings are carefully evaluated and reassembled each year. All areas of every classroom are well-organized and developmentally appropriate. There are plenty of cubbies, hooks and shelves for each student's personal items and learning materials, books, puzzles and more.

"The Studio School's approach blends recognizing child development practices with a working knowledge of how children learn," says Ms. Rotter. "We are out-of-the-box, we have all kinds of kids, and focus on fostering an emotionally connective student-teacher relationship and creating a curriculum that will inspire students to pursue knowledge for its own sake. We take elements from many philosophies." At Studio, creativity and academics go hand-in-hand, "We are not a mold," concludes Ms. Rotter.

Attention is paid to all aspects of the emotional, intellectual, physical, and social life of the students. One parent explains her daughter's experiences, "The teacher is very aware of my child's attitude towards her work. They work with her on the development of self-discipline, organization and self-evaluation in addition to teaching the curriculum—the mixed grades, Morning Group and the Gatherings class that cuts across all grades have been so important to her developing her ability to express herself, her thoughts, and her needs."

The block room is used by all groups through six-and-seven-year olds. After "walking and exploring" the neighborhood, younger children will recreate in blocks what they have seen. After a recent trip to the Brooklyn Bridge, the older children spent a week recreating it with blocks as a part of an in-depth study of the bridge.

Studio has a paper-making factory for third and fourth graders that recycles paper. Another unique aspect of The Studio School curriculum is the Kitchen Science class. Each day, a team of students, ages four to fourteen, prepares a hot lunch under supervision of a chef and the Kitchen Science teacher and serves it to the entire school. As part of the class, the Kitchen Science team studies healthy nutrition and conducts basic culinary experiments, such as the solution of solids in liquids, i.e. oil and water and more. The program also features a Multicultural Festival, in which parents work with the Kitchen Science team to prepare lunches that reflect various cultural traditions. The school's kitchen is its heart, and the school will find something for every child to eat in addition to learning about table manners, and how food is prepared. Lunch is served daily, family style, menus are in Spanish and English.

Reading is taught using a variety of teaching methods including Whole Language, sight words, basal readers, and phonics. Children are also read to every day. There is a cozy carpeted Early Childhood library where elementary and middle school students have weekly library and research classes.

Reading and writing at Studio are inseparable and students have both subjects every day. Children ages six and older have Thinking and Writing classes in which they learn how to think and process ideas and discover their own voice. In addition, elementary students have Library Discovery classes each week where they learn to read and write in various genres, such as poetry, fables, myths, short stories, folktales, biographies, autobiographies, essays and plays in developmentally appropriate ways.

Besides English class, middle school students study the English language in-depth, in such classes as Verbatim, where they learn about the history of English words and share individual research about other languages with one another, "What do you mean?" is a class where students earn the rules of grammar and create games designed to help them remember these rules through practice and play. Computers are also used for research.

Math is taught sequentially, helping students move from the concrete to the abstract, from block building to algebra. Students of all ages use manipulative materials, such as rods, geoboards, and base ten blocks, designed to further deepen their understanding of concepts and relationships. While the school emphasizes accuracy in computation, it also seeks to ensure that students can use different approaches to solve problems and to think for themselves.

Studio's One World curriculum integrates social studies with science. Designed by Ms. Rotter, the One World class helps children gain perspective on the past and present and explore their relationship to the larger world and what it means to live in a global community. Studying subjects in tandem, students are inspired to make insightful and original connections between subjects and concepts.

Spanish is taught throughout the school. Instruction begins with singing in Spanish in the early years and progresses to more formal instruction. French and Latin are offered for older students. Independent study programs are available in other languages, such as Japanese and Chinese.

The arts program permeates the entire school. The youngest children play with clay, crayons, paper and paints and singing and music are part of their daily lives at school. Older students participate in the school's chorus, work with Orff instruments, recorders, and learn to read music and study its history and theory. Studio Players is a weekly class where middle school students write and perform their own plays, and develop their skills in, and appreciation of, the dramatic arts. A highlight of the year for the community is the students' annual production. Students work with other media in the visual arts and mediums, such as paint, clay (the school has its own kiln), charcoal, and photography.

For physical education, toddlers and early childhood students play in the brand-new indoor gym that is lined with student artwork, on climbing equipment and the outside yard with hollow blocks, and elementary students, ages five and older, go to Central Park every day—weather permitting—and have dance class once a week. Middle school students jog around the reservoir, take calisthenics, play tennis, yoga, and compete on sports teams in soccer, basketball and baseball.

In Reach Out class middle school students learn more about community service and ways that they can promote change in real life situations. The program requires students to engage in projects outside of school. Projects are discussed between teachers and students and chosen at the beginning of the school year. Participation extends throughout middle school culminating with the completion of an independent community project before graduating. At graduation, students deliver individual speeches before receiving their diplomas.

Popular Secondary School Choices Graduates attend various independent schools including: Saint Ann's School, Brooklyn

Friends, Elisabeth Irwin, Ethical Culture/Fieldston, Friends, Horace Mann, Trevor Day, York Prep and various public schools like Beacon, Bronx Science, Stuyvesant, Millennium, Brooklyn Tech and School of the Future

Traditions   Welcome Back Evening, Student Sponsored Halloween Party, Holiday Bake Sale, Thanksgiving Feast, Ice Skating/ Winter Picnic, Multicultural Festival, Auction/Gala, Middle School Spring Play, Family Picnic, All School Graduation Party

Publications   Studio School Newsletter *Studio Scripts*
Learning and curricula elements *Inscape*
Literary journal of the graduating class's creative work *Silhouettes*

The Town School

540 East 76th Street
New York, NY 10021
(212) 288-4383
website: www.thetownschool.org

Coed
Nursery–8th grade
Accessible

Mr. Christopher Marblo, Head of School
Ms. Natasha Sahadi, Director of Admissions

Uniform   None for nursery and kindergarten divisions
Lower and Upper School girls: plaid kilt or navy jumper or navy and tan skirt; solid-colored collared or turtleneck shirt in the colors of the plaid; girls may wear solid navy, gray or tan pants except on Fridays; sweaters, socks, leggings and tights may be worn in the colors of the plaid
Lower and Upper School boys: solid navy, gray or tan pants; solid-colored, collared or turtleneck shirt in the colors of the plaid
Friday is dress-up day for assembly: Girls wear skirts, boys wear navy jacket, white or blue shirt and tie
The first Tuesday of each month is a non-uniform day: Denim and sweat clothes may be worn

Birthday Cutoff   Children entering nursery school must be 3 by September 1
Children entering kindergarten must be 5 by September 1

Enrollment   Total enrollment: 405
Nursery places: approximately 34
Kindergarten places: approximately 26–32
8th grade graduating class: approximately 38-40

Grades   Trimester system
Letter and effort grades are given in the Upper School beginning in 6th grade
Departmentalization begins in 5th grade

Tuition Range 2009–2010 $19,000 to $32,400, nursery–8th grade
Tuition includes lunch, trips
A tuition refund plan, extended payment plan and accident plan are available

Financial Aid/Scholarship   Approximately 14% of the student body receive some form of financial aid

Endowment   Approximately $23 million

Diversity   Approximately 32% of the student body is diverse

Homework   Because of the long school day, homework in the early years is kept to a minimum:
Kindergarten: occasionally
1st grade—HomeLinks twice a week
2nd: beginning in the second half of the year, about 15 minutes
3rd and 4th: 45 minutes–1 hour
4th, 5th and 6th: 1 hour–1½ hours
7th 8th: 2–3 hours

After-School Program   The Town School After-School Programs are Postscript and Clubhouse
Junior Postscript Program: for pre-K and kindergarten students, Monday through Thursday, 2:45–4:00 P.M., Friday, 12:30–1:30 P.M., a variety of creative and recreational activities; a fee is required
Postscript Program: for grades 1–6, Monday through Thursday 3:45–5:00 P.M., Friday, 1:00–2:30 P.M., with extended day option until 6:00 P.M.; activities include: fencing, basketball, computer, photography, woodworking, gymnastics, arts and crafts, CATS tennis, theatre; a fee is required
Clubhouse Program: a multi-aged option with rotating choices daily, beginning at 12:00 until 6:00 P.M.
Intramural sports program
Interscholastic athletic competition for grades 5–8

Summer Program   Summersault program for ages 3–9, open to children from the community, an additional payment is required

---

The Town School is a coed elementary school that ends with eighth grade. It overlooks the East River on quiet East 76th Street, opposite John Jay Park. The Town School emphasizes warmth and is sensitive to the developmental needs of young children. A traditional core of academic skills is taught using an innovative curriculum. The

1936 school brochure description of Town was accurate then and now: "Progressive but not radical . . . its object is to create an environment in which the child may develop the best that is in him and give him a thorough understanding of every subject he studies." Expectations are high but this is not a pressure-cooker environment. Because of the focus on the elementary grades, parents say there is an intimacy that provides an opportunity for leadership and the development of self-confidence. Students leave Town well prepared and well rounded.

Founded in 1913 by Miss Hazel Hyde and originally known as "Miss Hyde's School," The Town School acquired its present name in 1936 during the era of the town car and town house. The school motto roughly translates as "Be joyful in the pursuit of knowledge." Former head of school Fred Calder describes the committed faculty and administrators at Town School as "a group of people who [still] believe that the education of young children begins and ends with warmth, humor and good sense." Miss Hyde was known for attracting exceptional faculty who were very involved in running the school. To this day, the teachers at The Town School retain their influence through the "corporation" (known as "the members"), who serve as an advisory group to the Head.

Town School parents almost all agree that there is an emphasis on the process of learning rather than the rote accumulation of facts. Parents say, "Children learn how to think, and they learn that it's OK to be wrong or to fail."

In 1985 The Town School sold air rights to Glick Development Affiliates for $7 million. Some of this windfall went toward a capital improvement and maintenance fund, some toward the school's sizeable endowment and a portion went into renovation and addition of facilities, including two new science labs for Lower and Upper School students, a darkroom and a technology lab. Town students have use of their own auditorium, as well as a full-size gym. The school is uncluttered, clean and carpeted (no echoing hallways here). It's easy to see why children are comfortable here.

Getting in: There are no essay questions on the application. Parents may tour the school before they apply for their child. Many tour guides are members of the faculty, are very knowledgeable and don't mind answering numerous questions. At a later date, parents bring their kindergarten applicant in for a small group interview while the parents meet with the director of admissions.

Parents: The parent body at Town is relatively low-key. Says one parent, "These aren't all parents who went to private schools themselves." The Parents Association was founded in 1951. There is a monthly newsletter to inform parents about activities and meetings. Curriculum evenings and parent education seminars keep parents apprised of what's going on in the world of education and at Town (a recent panel discussed gender issues in elementary education). Head of School Marblo realizes that "parents [today] particularly need to discuss the challenges they face with their children." Activities for Town families include the Welcome Back Festival in the fall in Central Park, Science Night, the Book Fair, a theater performance at each grade level and the Spring Benefit. One mother described the events she attended: "Everyone came, there were nice feelings, nothing was hyped up, just a wonderful, warm environment."

Program: Kindergartners have a fairly long day, from 8:15 A.M. until 2:30 P.M. Monday through Thursday and until noon on Fridays. First through eighth graders eat hot lunch at school; pre-kindergartners and kindergartners bring their own lunches. There are two kindergarten classrooms, each with two teachers. (All of the nursery and kindergarten division head teachers have a master's in Early Childhood Education.) In addition to the teachers, there are three language arts specialists and a school psychologist. The kindergarten rooms are situated at opposite ends of a short carpeted hallway where, during activity time, children from each class can play and socialize. Each kindergarten classroom has a block area, wood shop, listening corner, two computers, lots of pets and their own bathroom and kitchen. When I visited, the children were busily working in small groups, some with clay or wood, some painting.

The Town School has traditionally celebrated the arts, and art is integrated into the curriculum at every level. Kindergarten through fourth grade visit the Lower School art studio once a week. Self-portraits and still lifes in the style of Matisse, as well as other artists, are often on display. There is a kiln for firing clay. Students frequently visit museums, and visiting artists come in to share their art, music, or drama expertise.

Music and movement classes begin in the youngest nursery classes when both are taught simultaneously. Students learn to play various instruments, dance, play games, and get ready for the Lower School program. Lower School students learn through the Orff approach. Children learn to combine speaking and singing skills, play percussion instruments in the context of literature and other themes. Additionally, third and fourth graders study the violin. Each grade produces a musical play that integrates what they are learning in social studies. Children perform at assemblies as well as outside of school at community events. The Lower School Chorus, The Upper School Band, and the Upper School Percussion Ensemble and String Ensemble also perform regularly. Upper school students continue with formal dance and music instruction and performing arts skills. The annual eighth grade musical is a much anticipated full-scale production.

Unique to The Town School is the community based curriculum, used in kindergarten and developed by Town School teachers. It revolves around a year long study of how the neighborhood community mirrors the school community. It integrates language arts, science, math and the arts into a comprehensive educational program using field trips as the core to build skills in observing, collecting and recording information.

The language arts program is literature based and by first grade students are writing in response journals daily. Invented spelling is used, but spelling skills are taught in second grade. First graders move out of the classroom for science in the Lower School science lab, library, gym, dance, music, art and Spanish.

All grades have computers in their classrooms. By third grade students use the technology lab (which is equipped with PCs) where they learn keyboarding skills and word processing. Students learn to use software related to the language arts, math and social studies. By fifth grade students take a unit of math in the technology lab, writing workshop, and Internet research in science, social studies and foreign language.

Fourth graders study their own family unit, write letters to relatives, study their own country (countries) of origin and use this as a basis to learn about other immigrating groups. A book-publishing party is held in the spring. A multicultural curriculum is in place. The first grade examined the Cinderella myth from the perspective of different cultures, including Chinese and Egyptian. Assemblies often feature multicultural performers. Irish step dancers performed at one assembly and invited the students to come onstage and participate.

In math, using the University of Chicago Math Program, children learn to reason logically, see mathematical patterns and relationships, and understand the presence of math in everyday life. Manipulatives, math games and literature are woven into the curriculum to develop abstract mathematical thinking while reinforcing computational concepts. The Lower School science lab features scaled-down versions of the familiar black tables and stools; the curriculum stresses the process of inquiry. For instance, second graders studying the Northeast woodlands create a nature mural; each child researches a forest animal to add to the mural. Fifth graders studying oceanography use The Voyage of the Mimi, a computer companion program. There are numerous trips to reinforce laboratory learning: Third and fourth grade students travel to a working farm; fifth and sixth graders go to Camp Sloane, an environmental center in upstate New York. Seventh and eighth graders go to Blairstown, New Jersey, for an Outward Bound-type program.

Parents say that The Town School really "honors individual learning styles." Educators recognize that some children function better with lots of background noise and others appreciate a more quiet setting. (Outside the second grade classroom there is an inviting bench with pillows, perfect for quiet reading, and there are other nooks and crannies for small group activities.) Throughout the Lower School there is no tracking; collaborative units are used instead. Students might have a group lesson and then divide into smaller groups.

There is also recognition that children learn at different rates. One tour guide explained: "They journey from first through fourth grades at their own rate, but by fourth grade they are all at the same place." The learning specialists at Town move into the classrooms, avoiding the stigma to certain children of being "pulled out" for remedial help.

Students use the full-size gym, one of four playroofs or John Jay Park playground, a wonderful resource right across the street. From kindergarten through fourth grade coed cooperative games and skills are stressed. In fifth grade, intramural competition begins. There is a full-size gym, and Upper Schoolers have two double periods a week for sports at Randall's Island. They have a very fine basketball, soccer, softball, and baseball programs. In the Upper School all students can participate in a variety of single-sex interscholastic sports. Parents say Town is a great place for girls who are interested in sports.

The Upper School at Town is composed of fifth through eighth grades. As in the Lower School, desks in the upper grades are grouped for collaborative learning. But fifth grade is an important transition year with new responsibilities and expectations. The fifth grade day is fully departmentalized, yet a nurturing homeroom structure provides age-appropriate support. Students choose between either French or Spanish in fifth grade. Latin instruction begins in seventh grade. Support is provided: A learning specialist who is devoted to fourth and fifth grade help students acclimate for Upper School. Fifth through eighth graders take a "Lifeskills" program taught by a team including the school psychologist, the director of diversity, and the school nurse that covers social decision making, diversity, sexuality, education, and substance abuse.

The social studies curriculum in the Upper School compares different cultures during the same time period or with the same theme. Fifth grade studies ancient Egypt, Greece and India; sixth grade studies Medieval Europe, Islamic Empires, and Feudal Japan.

Seventh grade focuses on The Age of Discovery and Exploration and Pre-colonial America. The eighth grade studies U.S. democracy from early America through the Civil Rights Movement.

Readings in English focus on the classics and are often related to social studies within a spiral curriculum. Science continues to be experiential. The science lab is networked with the computer lab. Collaborative science projects require tremendous research and culminate in a science fair. Town School graduates place well in advanced science and math in the ongoing schools. Each year a number of students are accepted at Stuyvesant High School (one of the specialized New York City public high schools.)

Students have the opportunity to perform in class plays and in musicals. Fifth to eighth graders have an intensive trimester of art, music and dramatic arts. The eighth grade performs in a play as a graduation year culminating activity. Upper School students can participate in a variety of clubs, including various publications, environmental club, "mathletes," and diversity. Student photographers help provide photographs for the yearbook.

Town School students have the opportunity to assume positions of leadership. The student senate is an elected body with co-presidents, co-vice president and class representatives. The senate plans assemblies and organizes social events and community service activities. The Town School has relationships with many community organizations, including The Ronald McDonald House, Project Cicero, and City Harvest Food drives, book drives, and bake sales which are often organized by students. There is an in-house recycling program and Town is a member of the Green Schools Alliance.

Eighth grade is an important and exciting year at The Town School. There are many opportunities to be role models for the entire school and especially to younger Buddy Classes, including leading the Student Senate, planning assemblies and special events. The eighth grade musical is the culmination of years of musical training and performance. At graduation the William Lee Younger, Jr. Educational Award is given to "the student who flourished at Town [and] developed into an individual of fine character and dedication to excellence."

Discussion about ninth grade placement begins in the spring of seventh grade. A Placement Director and the Upper School Head work and support individual families. Many Town School graduates return to talk about their high schools. All eighth graders take a "Decisions" course, a learning experience that strengthens and prepares each student for high school.

A parent who has sent two children to Town says, "They care for each child as an individual and work with them until the children find something good in themselves. Kids admire kids with different strengths, and they cheer for each other. Although expectations for academic achievement are high, they care equally about the emotional and social development of each child." A parent says, "My child is known and understood as a whole person." Most Town School graduates choose to go on to the coed day and boarding schools. (Two different Town grads I know were graduation speakers for their high schools, one from Trinity, the other from Dalton, who was also the Student Senate President.) A number also go to the specialized public high schools each year. The close-knit feeling at Town persists after graduation. Parents say: "There is a strong feeling of community. Students go back to school to visit their teachers."

Popular Secondary School Choices   Trinity, Dalton, Horace Mann, Fieldston, Columbia Prep, Riverdale, Spence, Brearley, Nightingale and Stuyvesant High School, Bronx Science, Poly Prep

Traditions   Fall Welcome Back Picnic, Book Fair, Spring Benefit, parenting lecture series, class trips for grades 3–8, 4th grade musical, annual 8th grade musical, alumni/ae reunions

Publications   Alumni/ae News: *Currents*
Annual report
Yearbook
Newspaper
The Town School Family News (monthly)
Literary magazine *Pen and Ink*
The Cry of the Wolf
Eighth grade short story collection

Community Service Requirement   Community service begins in the nursery program; every class has a buddy class in another division; the student senate organizes community service projects, often in conjunction with the Yorkville Common Pantry; during winter trimester, 5th–8th graders participate in a community service period once a week, going to a nearby soup kitchen and serving lunch to the homeless and so on; 8th graders also work with second grade students at P.S. 36 every Friday after school

Hangouts   Bagels & Co., John Jay Park

Trevor Day School

Lower School
Early Childhood Division
(Nursery–Kindergarten)
11 East 89th Street
(212) 426-3300
Elementary School
(1st–5th grade)
4 East 90th Street
New York, NY 10128
(212) 426-3350
fax (212) 410-6507
e-mail: LSAdmissions@trevor.org

Upper School
(6th–12th Grade)
1 West 88th Street
New York, NY 10024
(212) 426-3360
fax (212) 873-8520
e-mail: USAdmissions@trevor.org
website: www.trevor.org

Coed
Nursery–12th grade
Accessible (Both Campuses)

Mrs. Pamela J. Clarke, Head of School
Ms. Araina Jewell, Director of Admissions, Lower School
Mr. Christopher Seeley, Director of Admissions, Upper School

Uniform Published dress code that emphasizes appropriate attire

Birthday Cutoff September 1

Enrollment Total enrollment: 785
Nursery places: 20
Kindergarten places: 45
Graduating class size: approx. 60

Grades Semester system with a trimester system in high school
Extensive written reports plus family conferences twice a year for

Nursery through 12
Letter grades begin in 9th grade
Full departmentalization by 5th grade
First final exam in 6th grade

Tuition Range 2009–2010 $23,300 to $33,000, Nursery–12th grade
No additional fees.
Families purchase laptops in 5th and 9th grades

Financial Aid/Scholarship   Approximately 20% of the students receive some form of financial aid totaling $3.1 million
Percentage of financial award extends to the Afterschool program and to laptop purchase

Endowment $10 million

Diversity   Approximately 18 percent students of color
Students come from Early Steps, The Oliver Program, A Better Chance, TEAK, and Prep for Prep

Homework   Kindergarten–1st: parent/child reading for 30 minutes
2nd: 30 minutes (reading, and 15 minutes of math and spelling practice)
3rd: 1 hour
4th: 1 ½ hours
5th and 6th: 1 ½–2 hours
6th–8th: 2–2 ½ hours
9th–12th: Up to 4 hours
(An additional 30 minutes of reading is expected each night for all grades)

After-School Program   Available for Pre-kindergarten through 12th grade for an additional fee, includes music conservatory, recreational activities and athletics with numerous team sports offered in the Upper School

Summer Program   All programs require an additional payment
June Camp (ages 5-10), Trevor Day Students only (9 A.M.–3 P.M.)
Summerday Camp: for 3–6 year olds; 5 weeks, 9 A.M.–12 P.M. for 3 year olds; 9 A.M.–2 P.M. for 4 year olds, and 9 A.M.–3 P.M. for 5- and 6-year olds

Trevor Day School, previously known as "The Day School," was founded as a nursery school in 1930 under the aegis of the Church of the Heavenly Rest. In 1971, The Day School, having grown into a primary school, became independent of the church. The Rector of the church continues to serve ex-officio on the board of trustees, but Trevor Day School has no religious affiliation. Over a decade ago, the school took the last name of long-standing board member, Paul Trevor, who had made many significant contributions to the school.

In 1991 Trevor Day School expanded further by acquiring the old Walden-Lincoln school building on West 88th Street and creating a high school division (grades nine through twelve). In 1992, the school connected its Early Childhood Division located on East 89th Street to its East 90th Street Elementary Division. Today, Trevor Day School is divided into the Lower School and the Upper School. The Lower School has two divisions: Early Childhood, (Nursery through Kindergarten) and Elementary, (Grades One through Five). The Upper School, located at 1 West 88th Street, consists of the Middle School (grades Six through Eight) and the High School (grades Nine through Twelve).

Trevor Day School offers an eclectic blend of the old and the new. There is an elegant marble staircase in the limestone lobby of the East Side building suggesting that this is a staid traditional school, but don't be misled. Trevor Day School has incorporated many innovative features into a curriculum that stresses active learning: Common Rooms, Miniterms, family conferences and a policy of no letter grades until ninth grade.

The school's mission statement emphasizes cooperation and collaboration rather than competition as a motivational device.

Getting in: Trevor Day School offers information evenings and tours. Do call and ask for these dates. The application and other materials are all available to submit online by email. Once parents have applied, they come to the school twice, once for a parent tour and once with their child. Kindergarten visits are held on Saturdays to help ease the stress for worrying parents. Children applying for kindergarten are met in the lobby of the 89th Street building and go upstairs for choice time and to work at a table with age-appropriate materials. At the same time, parents have an opportunity to ask questions of a panel of administrators, faculty, parents and Upper School students. One parent who said that she barely survived the admissions process in general, commented that "Trevor was wonderful at handling the shy, quiet child, both through admissions and in the classroom."

On a separate date parents are taken on a tour of the school and then meet with a member of the admissions staff for about thirty minutes. Parent representatives and admissions staff lead the small tour groups and they are very informative as well as candid. Nursery applicants are not separated from their parents, but are engaged by a teacher while the parents talk to members of the admissions staff. Recommendations are optional. Trevor families come from all over— the East and West sides, downtown, and the boroughs.

Families applying to the Upper School, grades six through twelve, are scheduled for tours and interviews in the fall and early winter. Small group tours for parents and students are either preceded or followed by an individual interview for each student and his parents. Parent admission representatives lead middle school tours, members of the student admissions committee lead high school tours.

Parents: Parents describe the parent body at Trevor Day as a "mixed but cohesive group of East Siders, West Siders, Jews, WASPs and families of color. But the parents, along with the students, teachers and administrators, all share a strong enthusiasm for the school." All parents are automatically members of the Parents Association, which sponsors community-building activities, such as the two-week-long program "Everybody Reads at Trevor Day School," and runs several fundraising events including the very popular Auction and Fall Festival.

Program: Trevor Day School is composed of four divisions, Early Childhood, Elementary, Middle and High Schools. The Early Childhood Division consists of Nursery, Pre-kindergarten and kindergarten. The Nursery program runs from 8:30 A.M. to 1:00 P.M., five days a week. Pre-kindergarten ends at 2 P.M., Monday through Friday (3 P.M. after February). The kindergarten day at Trevor Day School runs from 8:40 A.M. to 3:00 P.M., Monday through Thursday, and until 2:00 on Friday. There are five kindergarten classes, each with about sixteen children, a head teacher and an assistant teacher. My guide told me that "the homeroom is an extension of the home." The smallish square classrooms are neat, well-equipped, clean and carpeted and each has its own bathroom and a locker for each child. Pre-kindergarten and kindergarten students visit the library weekly, where parent volunteers read to children and help them select books. Spanish is introduced in Nursery. Pre-kindergartners and kindergartners visit the well-equipped art and music studios twice a week in half groups; they participate in physical education and roof time (on the padded playroof), daily, in half groups and as a class, and there are specialists in physical education, Spanish, music and art. Lower School students go to a well-equipped art room staffed by two full-time teachers. Their expressive and very individual work is permanently displayed throughout the 89th Street building as part of a school-wide Art Show.

Parents say Kindergarten at Trevor Day School is "academic" but nurturing and "takes into account the varying rates of development of the children." Along with traditional skills the children gain a sense of security. "The development of self-esteem is important," say parents. "They know each child is cut from a different cloth." The curriculum is structured but not too much so. In Pre-kindergarten and Kindergarten the classes split into half groups for traditional academics, including reading and math Pre-kindergartners and Kindergartners begin working with math manipulatives and playing math games, using big books, practicing letter sounds, writing in their journals using approximate spelling and developing handwriting skills.

The Elementary Division consists of Grades One through Five. Hot lunch is offered starting in Grade One. Classroom life in this division is informal but the day is structured. The school believes that children should feel free to make mistakes: "We'd rather have a child take chances, do something daring." In order to free children from the constraints of working for grades, there are no letter or number grades until Ninth Grade. Students in nursery through Eighth Grade receive narrative reports, with extensive checklists, sometimes as long as three to four typed pages, and also receive regular feedback from teachers. Family conferences starting in Pre-kindergarten and continuing through the high school are a feature unique to Trevor Day School. Students participate in the Family Conference whose goal is to emphasize the idea that the students share the responsibility for their own education. Teachers and parents remain in close contact throughout the year.

There are four homerooms in the first and second grades with two teachers in each class of about sixteen children. There are several computers in each first grade classroom. By third grade students are divided into four large homerooms with about twelve students and one teacher. All three grades—first, second and third—have separate classes in art, music, computer, library and physical education. There are Common Rooms, considered the nucleus of the learning community—a place where students can do homework, use computers, play chess or learn independently or with the guidance of a teacher—for the fourth and fifth grade students as well as for Middle and Upper schoolers. Parents say there is more social interaction with the entire grade during the early years because groups are mixed, not tracked. One parent said of a new student, "He was so happy at Trevor Day School that he wanted to spend weekends there!"

Reading and math groups might be as small as four to eight

children. Third grade uses literature and word processing as part of the writing experience while the children continue to practice their handwriting in workbooks. During math some of the class used Cuisenaire rods, some were doing math with numbers on a Smartboard and some were working with manipulatives or playing math games. The students in all four groups were actively engaged. The Investigation Colloquium Method is used to teach science, emphasizing "child-directed exploration and interpretation." First graders study the science of Central Park; second graders, life cycles (which includes plants and mealworms); third graders, environmental science; fourth and fifth grade students use a science lab and work collaboratively.

The computer program at Trevor Day School begins in the Kindergarten; all of the Lower School classrooms have computers and Smartboards, and about fifty-percent of Upper School classrooms have Smartboards. Third and fourth grade have a mobile laptop lab and wireless classrooms while fifth grade students have their own laptops. In the mid-nineties, Trevor Day School became the first private school in Manhattan to join the Microsoft/Anytime Anywhere Learning program. All students in Grades Five through Twelve use laptops for inquiry and learning. (Families purchase them outright; a payment plan is available.) Students generally take them for granted. The goal of this program is for the computer to become a "transparent" tool, like paper and pencil. "I use the laptop in every class," said a seventh grader. "In English, to write essays and take notes on classroom reading, in history, foreign language and science to take notes and do homework, in math for writing assignments and graphing."

Social studies topics begin with community and interdependency, and students learn early on an awareness and respect for difference. Topics broaden from a study of family history to units on immigration and ethnic diversity in New York City and the history of Manhattan Island. The third grade studies the Hudson River and the populations that inhabited its shores. Fourth graders begin a two-year sequence in American history.

Music and movement are an integral part of the curriculum. Music study begins with the Orff, Kodaly and Dalcroze methods and students start learning to play recorders in third grade. Grades four and five are partially departmentalized. The homeroom teacher, who is also a subject teacher, serves as advisor to approximately thirteen children. Students make use of a central Common Room with glass-fronted classrooms on the perimeter. There are two Common Room periods a week as well as a daily quiet reading period.

The Miniterm is first introduced in grades four and five. This is a three-week period during which students take both academic electives and classes that launch students beyond the traditional subjects. Sometimes, Miniterm is devoted to an original musical, a production that relates to "the lives and experiences of the students, using material taken from various literary sources as well as the students' own work." Music and dance from other cultures are often incorporated. Throughout the year there are opportunities for students to gain confidence in public speaking and to participate in plays. A parent said, "Nobody is ever excluded. Everyone is in the plays, and no one is made to feel inferior."

Fifth graders begin Interscholastic sports. Parents praise the art program, which stresses each child's individual expression, as well as the attainment of skills. According to the head of the Lower School art department, "Children need to be who they are. If one is an artist, he is given a lot of credit for becoming an artist." From an early age, Trevor Day School students learn to use and maintain a variety of art materials from a central supply area. By fourth grade they are working on projects in various media, including drawing, painting, collage, 3-D paper, ceramics and printmaking. Starting in Middle School, students can do film, video production, stained glass, and computer animation, graphics and photography in the school darkroom. A new video lab provides movie-making for students in grade six through twelve.

The Middle School is composed of grades six through eight. The Middle School Common Room is the center of student and teacher activity. The Common Room is designed to promote communication between students and teachers. It often lends itself to very academic and intellectual conversations that ultimately end up being an extension of the classroom. The teacher's desks line the room and students use the center of the room to work during discretionary periods. The homeroom/advisor system changes somewhat in the Middle School. Nine to ten students, (a mix of students from grades six seven and eight), share an advisor and meet together at the start of each day. The advisor actively supports each student's intellectual and social growth, acting as an advocate and academic counselor as well as the primary contact for both family and school. In addition, each student meets individually each week with an academic advisor. There are no grades in the Middle School, but students do self-assessment and continue, when they meet individually with their advisor each week, to receive feedback in the form of "accountability reports." These reflect not only the content and quality of the student's weekly course work, but also the student's emerging understanding as well as critical thinking skills. Students and parents also receive detailed narrative reports three times a year.

The Middle School has its own three-week-long Miniterm. During this exciting term, English, math, and world language, classes continue and students take academic electives in the morning and rehearse for a gala musical in the afternoon, take short courses and participate in special arts offerings. Students are involved in all aspects of putting on this full-scale production. Miniterm reinforces community spirit at Trevor Day School, with everyone working toward a common goal in different capacities. Health education is introduced during Miniterm, which includes an AIDS curriculum.

The teaching of English in the Middle School is literature based. Students write, edit and produce finished drafts. Much time is spent on the mechanics of grammar and vocabulary building. Group discussion and collaborative learning activities dominate the classroom experience. In sixth grade students are assigned "considerable homework in reading and writing." Seventh graders focus on essay writing, critical thinking and oral expression. Eighth graders engage in "formal literary analysis of classic adult literature" while continuing to improve their essay-writing skills.

World language study, that begins in Lower School with Spanish, continues in sixth grade with either a choice of French or Spanish.

The Middle School history curriculum begins with geography in sixth grade which lays the foundation for World History in seventh and eighth grades.

Science in the Middle School utilizes a laboratory format. Emphasis is on the scientific method. By the end of eighth grade, all students have covered the basics of biology, physical science and chemistry.

In mathematics, critical thinking, problem solving and competency are stressed. All eighth graders take Algebra I.

Participation in the arts is not optional at Trevor Day School. All sixth graders take a rotational Arts Workshop series, sampling the arts available to seventh and eighth graders. Electives include Video Workshop, Designing for Illustration and Photography, ceramics and stained-glass making.

Middle Schoolers may select from vocal or instrumental electives in music. There is a Middle School chorus and a number of smaller, elective singing groups. Students interested in dance can participate in Choreolab, which meets after school and puts on an annual student dance concert.

Community service is a vital part of the Middle School. There are numerous food, toy and clothing drives. Seventh and eighth graders may volunteer to serve either in the Trevor Day School Community, or outside of school.

Grade levels focus on themes such as cooperation, collaboration and leadership on a number of alternative education opportunities off campus.

Physical education is required four times a week. After school there is a range of intramural and interscholastic sports. Parents say that no child is ever cut from a team. If you show up and participate, then you are considered a member of the team. But a participant in the physical education programs says, "We deemphasize competition in gym until 3:00 P.M. and then we don't like to lose." Between 70 and 80 percent of the Middle and High School students participate in afterschool sports programs.

The High School is composed of grades nine through twelve. The High School building has a working theatre, music rooms, a dance studio, a full-size basketball court, darkrooms, ceramics studio and an videostudio. The High School library has 15,000 volumes, a microfiche and is computerized. Trevor Day School renovated its science floor and updated the science program.

The High School includes a student-faculty center that serves as an extension of the formal classroom. It functions as a meeting space for teachers and students, and like the entire school, has access to a wireless network. Every student has a laptop.

Twenty-two credits are required for graduation. This includes three math, three science, three language, four English, three history and nine trimesters of the Arts. Students complete the three-year science requirement in an innovative science program that offers a coordinated course of biology, chemistry and physics each year for three years. At the end of three years, students have completed the equivalent of a year in each of the three subjects. Advanced courses in computer science, World language, English, history, mathematics and the sciences are offered. Letter grades are introduced in ninth grade and are sent home three times a year with written reports. All High School students are requested to complete eighty hours of community service over their four years. Students in Grades Five through Twelve play or practice every afternoon on Interscholastic sports teams.

Highlights from the English curriculum include: Asian-American Literature, Rites of Passage, 19th and 20th Century Literature, Romantic Poetry, African American Literature, Irish Literature, Tennessee Williams and his Contemporaries, Hemingway and His Circle, Jane Austen and the Romantic Novel, The Playwright-Poet, Philosophical Literature, Images of Women, Gender and Shakespeare, The Art of the Short Story, Baseball and Literature, British & American Drama Since 1950, Marquez and his Contemporaries, etc.

Ethical Foundations is a one-year program that is required for all ninth grade students. The three-part course covers health, nutrition and wellness, human sexuality, social justice and ethical decision making.

Trevor Day School students participate in their graduation; many seniors give thoughtful talks. The strong sense of community at Trevor Day School persists after graduation. A parent of two alumnae says, "There's a warmth among the children, a camaraderie that continues even though some go on to different schools. They're still friends."

Cynthia E. Bing, former president of the Board of Trustees, describes the school's unique approach: "There is an adult presence that is not obtrusive. Students are encouraged to take the initiative but there are plenty of adults around to help them make [wise] decisions." Parents and alumni say that the emphasis on independent learning and time management pays off in college.

Popular College Choices   Bard, Bates, Carleton, Carnegie Mellon, Columbia, Connecticut College, Cornell, Emory, Johns Hopkins, Middlebury, NYU, Oberlin, Princeton, Sarah Lawrence, Skidmore, Smith, Tufts, University of Michigan, University of Chicago, University of Pennsylvania, Washington University, Vassar, Wesleyan and Yale

Traditions   Fall auction/dinner, head of school's fund-raising party, class parties, Fall Festival, parent workshops, Friday assemblies, potluck dinners, High School Conference Day, Miniterm musical productions, Music Conservatory student recitals, All School Skate at Wollman Rink, Choreolab dance production, High School Choir at Mets Game

Publications   *Yearbook*
Newspaper: *The Dragon*
Magazine: *Trevor*
Student literary magazine

Community Service Requirement   80 hours—20 hours per year in high school; many activities for grades one through eight; community service at Trevor is a recommendation rather than a requirement

Hangout   Common Room and High School Center (open and supervised until 6:00)

449

Trinity School

139 West 91st Street
New York, NY 10024
(212) 873-1650
website: www.trinityschoolnyc.org

Coed
Kindergarten–12th grade
Partially accessible

Mr. John Allman, Headmaster
Ms. Jennifer Levine, Director of Admissions, Kindergarten–4th
Grade
Ms. Jan Burton, Director of Admissions, Grades 5 through 12

Uniform   Lower School: For boys, white or navy long or short sleeve Trinity polo-style shirt or turtleneck, khaki or navy chinos or corduroy pants, tan or navy walking shorts may be worn in warm weather, no jeans or gym shorts; white or navy or Trinity sweater or sweatshirt; tied shoes or sneakers; for girls, white or navy turtleneck, white or navy long or short sleeve Trinity polo-style shirt; tan or navy pants, shorts may be worn in the warm weather, no jeans or gym shorts; Trinity navy or white sweaters or Trinity sweatshirts; shoes or sneakers, appropriate leg wear; Middle School (Grades 5 through 8): no jeans, short skirts or shorts permitted; skirts or slacks and neat collared, solid color shirts are preferred; hats cannot be worn in class; Upper School (Grades 9 through 12): jeans and sneakers may be worn; clothing must be neat, clean and socially appropriate

Birthday Cutoff   Children entering kindergarten must be 5 by September 1

Enrollment   Total enrollment: 984
Kindergarten places: approximately 60
Graduating class size: approximately 110

Grades   Semester system; Trimester system in Middle School
Kindergarten–5th grade: detailed anecdotal reports and checklists
Departmentalization begins in 5th grade
Letter grades begin in 6th grade
First final exam is offered in 7th grade

Tuition Range 2009–2010 $31,725 to $32,820, Kindergarten through 12th grade Additional fees: approximately $1,655 for lunch; cost of trips may range from $100 in the Lower School to $800 in the Upper School; $25 accident insurance required $400 for graduation expenses

Financial Aid/Scholarship Approximately $4 million available 18% of the student body receives financial assistance

Endowment Approximately $50 million

Diversity Approximately 55 Prep for Prep students enrolled (The Prep for Prep program is housed at Trinity School); 36 Early Steps students
Trinity School has a Black Affairs Club, Women's Caucus, Jewish Affairs, Gay-Straight Alliance, Asian-American Alliance and a Diversity Leadership Coalition

Homework Kindergarten: None
1st grade: minimal, beginning in second half of 1st grade
2nd: 15–20 minutes (some homework given Monday is due on Friday); nightly silent reading
3rd: 30–45 minutes (spelling quizzes and tests)
4th: 45 minutes–1 hour
5th and 6th: 1–2 hours
7th and 8th: 2–3 hours
9th–12th: 40 minutes per subject, approximately 3–4 hours

After-School Program K–6: After-school program for an additional fee, a variety of creative and recreational activities
Some clubs meet after school
Intramural sports for 7th and 8th graders
Interscholastic sports in the Ivy Preparatory League (boys) and the Independent School Athletic Association (girls)
Extended day program

Summer Program June and July Program
Trinity Day Camp: a variety of creative and recreational activities, including swimming; Trinity students have priority in enrollment and there is usually a wait list; camp and admissions have no connection; an additional payment is required

Trinity School was founded in 1709 when William Huddleston, a lawyer, clerk of Trinity Church, and schoolmaster, first received a grant from the Society for the Propagation of the Gospel, an Anglican missionary organization, to teach poor children in the parish of Trinity Church. Trinity was the first public charity school in New York City, and was originally located in Trinity Church at the head of Wall Street. While Collegiate claims to be the oldest school, Trinity claims to be the oldest continually operated school in Manhattan, as it remained open throughout the British occupation of New York City during the Revolutionary War. Trinity was a coed school until the mid-nineteenth century. Currently celebrating its three hundredth anniversary, Trinity is its extremely proud of its heritage—not only has Trinity moved around town quite a bit over its 300 years, and expanded beyond its founder's dream—the school remains as it was since its inception 300 years ago one of the city's best and finest schools, delivering a competitive, rigorous, thoughtful, comprehensive program. As the school grew, the city withdrew its support from charity schools. Trinity then reincorporated as a private boys' school, eventually moving uptown alongside the town houses of the well-to-do on Manhattan's Upper West Side. At this time Trinity modeled itself on the English public—our private—schools like Harrow, Eton, Westminster and Winchester. Trinity was a single-sex traditional school until the sixties. One alumnus said that "the Kennedy days marked the fall of the 'preppie' era at Trinity."

Beginning with the Upper School in the seventies, Trinity School again became coed, and by the late eighties was coed throughout. Trinity is a traditional school with "West Side" style; this is the key to the school's popularity. Many dualities are present in Trinity: highly selective admissions but generous financial aid; a diverse student body, with an emphasis on classical education—the school's motto is *Labore et Virtue*—all bound by a respect for Trinity's traditions; a Protestant ethos amid the mostly Jewish and Hispanic residents of the Upper West Side.

In July 2009, John Allman assumed the reigns as Trinity's twenty-ninth Headmaster. He came from St John's, a private school in Houston. Mr. Allman brings to Trinity an expertise in English and coaching as well as his wife, Michele, and their three sons.

The Headmaster and trustees are committed to diversity at Trinity. Trinity's annual report recently boasted that Trinity has a "truly diverse" lower school: "Our goal is a school population that reflects our city's." Approximately one-third of the students in the Lower School are children of color. The Parents Association has its own Diversity Committee to support this commitment, and meetings have been held with parents to discuss their concerns and also to encourage them to help with recruitment of children from diverse backgrounds. Trinity's Multicultural Coordinator works across divisions, with students, parents, and faculty. Each division has its own diversity team as well. Parents publish a diversity newsletter for all families and a bi-annual Multicultural Festival.

Despite the name Trinity, compulsory weekly chapel and the presence of an Episcopalian chaplain, Trinity School's chapel is non-denominational; all religions are welcomed and celebrated. The school strives to be extremely inclusive; the school is popular with Jewish families. Scheduled holidays include Rosh Hashanah, Yom Kippur, Hindu and Muslim holidays, Christmas, Passover and Good Friday. There is the traditional all-school Christmas chapel with a candlelit procession, a holiday fair and a Lower School Christmas program, and also a Chanukah chapel. Beginning in first grade all Lower School students attend chapel once a week and often sing as a group in chapel. There is a Lunar New Year chapel, and recently the Lower School introduced the Islamic Call to Prayer in chapel. The chapel program is interfaith, and one parent said the religious component is not as prominent as the ethical and moral aspects. For example, on Valentine's Day her child's class read their own work aloud, and one child read a story about being friends forever. Chapel speakers in the Upper School might include a senior faculty member or a protester from Tiananmen Square. Chapel provides opportunities for the entire community to participate in skits and stories with yearly themes such as "community," "friendship," and "sources of joy." All students take introductory religion courses in fifth and sixth grade. Eleventh and twelfth graders can choose among eight electives, including "Morals and Exemplars" and "Faith and Doubt in Literature," to fulfill their one-semester religion requirement.

Getting in: There are two or three open houses in the fall. Parents of kindergarten applicants are advised to send in their completed application along with the $60 application fee as soon as possible to be granted an interview at the school. A wait list for interviews has been maintained in recent years. Kindergarten tours are extensive and are given by Lower School parent volunteers; interviews are on different days. Children take a short tour of the library. Parents meet with an admissions officer while the child goes with another admissions officer or teacher to a nearby office and then everyone regroups after about half an hour so ask your important questions quickly. Your four-year-old may have questions of his/her own (most likely "Can we go home now?") but this is to be expected. There is a small play area for children should parents wish to spend additional time in conversation. Don't send your child to Trinity to be coddled. A parent said, "Trinity is a tough, no-nonsense school, but they really care about the kids."

Trinity requests a recent photograph of your child, so have some good wallet-size pictures ready. Do not cancel your interview appointment with Trinity unless your child really is ill, but, the Director of Admissions says, "If you need to, the office will try hard to reschedule your appointments." Even so, the demand for kindergarten places is so high at Trinity that there exists the chance that you might not get another appointment time. According to one nursery school director, "They like to see both parents." Once admissions decisions have been made, Trinity has an active wait list, and there is a strong sibling policy.

Although occasionally places are available in other grades the main entry point after kindergarten is ninth grade. Each family is interviewed individually and has a student guide for the tour of the Upper School. Interviews begin in late September and end in mid-January. There are open houses in the fall, and throughout the process there are opportunities to meet and talk with faculty members. After a candidate has been accepted, he or she visits classes.

Parents: The style at Trinity is both traditional and informal. "It's a very relaxed atmosphere for a traditional school," one parent said. There is no typical parent. This is definitely not a celebrity school although there are more than a few. There is a multicultural mix along with a fair share of East and West Side powerhouses. Many East Side parents said the one thing they would change is that they would move Trinity to the East Side of Manhattan. One parent said the school is financially mixed. There is money, but "by and large it's low-key." School dinners are held in the Trinity cafeteria. Parents Association meetings are scheduled so that all parents can attend, and there are meetings between the Parents Association and the Trustees. Parents of entering kindergarten students attend a May reception and ninth grade parents attend dinner parties at parents' homes.

Separation is handled gently. The kindergarten schedule is staggered in the beginning, and parents walk children up the stairs to their classroom. After a few weeks parents say goodbye at the bottom of the steps and the students go up by themselves. They shake hands with the teacher at the end of the day. Lower School Principal Rosemary Milliman greets the children each morning. Parents say Milliman is always asking parents for input on how to improve the school. Lower School parents are kept informed about school and classroom events by the LS weekly newsletter, *The Tuesday Newsday*.

Program: There are three kindergartens with two teachers each, approximately twenty students in each class. The children go out of their classrooms for music, gym, swimming (on the premises) and art. There is swimming, gym or turf time daily and many play areas for kindergartners with age appropriate equipment. In first grade the three kindergartens split into four smaller classes with approximately fifteen children in each; each class has a head teacher and an assistant. Parents say that this is a great advantage academically: "Students receive a lot of individual attention—they are really focused on developing important reading and math skills early." The approach to teaching reading is eclectic, with a multi-disciplinary approach. "We use many approaches to accommodate different learning styles," teachers and the principal attest. The Writing Workshop includes creative writing and reading stories aloud. Trinity seeks to instill a love for reading with programs such as D.E.A.R. (Drop Everything and Read). Kindergartners deliver their own *Sunny Day Newspaper* weekly. The marvelous and recently renovated Lower School library at Trinity is inhabited by larger-than-life stuffed figures from children's classics: *Clifford the Big Red Dog* and some of Maurice Sendak's *Wild Things*.

By second grade, expectations are greater. One parent said she was afraid to go out and leave her second grader with the babysitter because he wouldn't be able to do his homework. New material is never introduced in homework assignments. Reading and math groups are formed according to ability. Foreign language (French or Spanish) is introduced in third grade. Formal computer instruction in the computer lab begins in kindergarten. At many points in the Lower School the curriculum is integrated. For example, second graders study Native Americans of the Eastern Woodlands in social studies, and in music they present a festival of Native American song, story and dance for parents.

There is support for different learning styles, and a staff of specialists works with the homeroom teachers. At Special Services Night parents meet the team of specialists who provide remedial instruction. As in many independent schools, some tutoring is initiated by the parents. A breakfast was held with the school psychologist and parents to discuss academic pressure but a consensus was not reached. "Some parents think there is too much pressure and some think there is too little, depending on how their child is doing," I was told. While academic achievement is appreciated in the Lower School, one parent said, "You don't have to be brilliant to be happy at Trinity. There is a spectrum of intelligence." One mother whose daughter is struggling with the academics, but bubbling with enthusiasm for Trinity nonetheless, was told by her child, "I'm really learning a lot this year!"

One of the highlights of the tour is the Lower School science room, which looks like a Woods Hole laboratory with aquatic life tanks around the room and charts, specimens and waders hanging on the walls. Howard Warren, Lower School science head, oversees a hands-on science program. Warren received a Governor's Environmental Study Citation for his memorable beach cleanup with third graders (who do a unit on the environment). Warren takes the fourth graders wading into Jamaica Bay to collect specimens, which they bring back and put into the tanks, study and release at the end of the school year.

Music is an area of strength at Trinity. Twice weekly, beginning in kindergarten, students use the Orff, Kodaly and Dalcroze methods to learn rhythm and singing skills. Every class performs music, ranging from psalms sung in chapel to rap songs about the fifty states. The Adventures in Strings Program gives fourth graders the option of studying violin or cello and continues through fifth and sixth grades. There is a Lower School and Middle School orchestra and many singing groups, including, The Tunes.

Trinity reorganized and consolidated the lower Middle (grades five and six) and upper Middle Schools (grades seven and eight) into one Middle School serving grades five through eight. The Middle School is housed in its own bright, renovated wing and features a Middle School technology resource center. The school now has two full size gymnasiums. Departmentalization begins in Middle School. Modern language instruction, begun in the Lower School, continues in grades five through eight. Latin instruction begins in grade 6. Students who need reinforcement take a curriculum support course in which they meet with a learning specialist in small groups. Middle Schoolers participate in the Pythagorean Contest.

Middle School at Trinity offers a solid, rigorous, core curriculum, along with elective courses and a myriad of leadership, service and athletic opportunities. Academically, the program requires at least five basic courses in English, history, math, science and a choice of French, Spanish, Classical Latin, or classes in the learning center. In athletics, Middle Schoolers choose between almost a dozen different sports including athletic clubs (interscholastic or intramural sports competition). During Middle School students make the leap to greater academic and personal independence. There are Chalk Talks born out of the Project Charlie anti-drug program in Middle School that focuses on life skills, health education, and adolescent development. There are two computer labs for middle school and technology, appropriate guidelines stressed, and computers and networks are provided free of service to students. Middle School arts offers sculpture, ceramics, drawing and printmaking, collage, painting, digital photography, several choral groups, musical theater, jazz ensemble, drama, orchestra and more. There are dress-down days, but students are asked to maintain a certain level of decorum.

The Upper School at Trinity is composed of the ninth through twelfth grades. After the architectural grandeur of the Lower School, Trinity's Upper School (Hawley Wing) with its cinderblock walls and bustling corridors has the feeling of a suburban public school. There are no bells in the Upper School. The Upper School library has many electronic databases, and students can work in carrels or on computers. Computers are networked throughout the entire school.

Approximately fifty percent of ninth grade students are new to Trinity. Trinity is a popular high school choice for students at the single-sex schools who want a city coed day school. To ease the transition into high school and integration of new students into the class, ninth graders have an orientation trip with senior leaders and faculty, and continue to meet once a week during the school year with their senior leader groups.

Contact between students in the three divisions occurs formally at all-school events several times a year. Currently, twice a week, ten to fifteen seniors eat lunch with kindergarten students, other seniors help fourth graders put on plays about Greek myths, several juniors and seniors work with Lower and Middle School students on math enrichment, and Upper and Middle School students meet in programs like Kids Helping Kids to discuss social issues. The Black Affairs Club meets with and mentors children of color in the Lower School.

The graduation requirements at Trinity are similar to those at the other rigorous high schools. Students take a minimum of five or six academic courses in grade nine. In grades ten through twelve, they must take a minimum of four, but almost all students take more. Seniors may choose from a variety of electives, including Journalism, and A World Elsewhere. English is required but seniors choose from seven different options each semester. About seventy percent of the seniors are enrolled in advanced science. A new interdisciplinary course taught by teachers of chemistry and religion is offered in ninth grade.

Some classrooms are set up in traditional rows or seminar style with oak lectern desks, but in English, history, modern languages and religion, the desks are arranged in a circle or the tables in a rectangle to promote discussion.

Although Trinity maintains its traditional emphasis on the Classics and the study of Latin and Greek, *Labore et Virtue,* the school's motto, stands for hard work and moral excellence. There is much praise among alumni for the excellence of Trinity's Latin program. The study of DWAMs (Dead White Ancient Males) really comes alive at Trinity. Advanced reading in elegiac poetry and Ovid's *The Art of Love*, a provocative and satirical portrait of love in ancient Rome, is offered. Advanced students can participate in The Latin Epic, in which students read a book of the *Aeneid* in a tutorial and later take part in a public examination by college professors. In addition to Latin and Greek, students can continue study in French or Spanish. The English department strongly recommends that Upper School students read five books over the summer. Ninth graders begin the year with a six-week Writing Workshop to perfect their essay-writing skills. Eleventh and twelfth grade English electives offer different courses each semester. After a solid grounding in modern European and American history, seniors can choose from the following electives (these vary from year to year): Retreat from Liberalism, Mass Consumption, Leisure, and Culture in the United States, U.S. History, 1968-2004, and Globalization and its Discontents.

Honors courses exist only in mathematics and modern languages. Science requirements are biology plus one year of another laboratory science. Science electives include Psychology, Marine Biology, Cutting-Edge Issues in Biology and Chemistry I and II, and advanced courses in biology, chemistry and physics.

High school students can do advanced independent work in addition to the required four academic subjects. Advanced work is graded pass/fail and doesn't count as a credit toward graduation. Seniors, however, may enroll in an independent study in a specific discipline such as chemistry or studio art, but they must also take four other courses. Seniors receive a letter grade for their independent study program.

The arts and theatre programs at Trinity are extensive. Theatre at Trinity is exciting. Every year there is a major musical production and a Cabaret. I saw a rehearsal for *Fiddler on the Roof* in the chapel;

another year it was *Carousel*. The Theater IV play production course allows students to direct any one-act play of their choice. These spring productions are very well attended.

Adjoining visual arts and ceramics studios are large and bright. Students make good use of New York City's museums. There is room for individual initiative in the arts at Trinity. When they're not studying, students can relax in the Swamp (a seating area off the main lobby) or on the other side of the lobby. There is a no-smoking zone around the school. Students can leave campus as early as the second half of ninth grade.

Four representatives from each grade serve in the student senate (grades nine through twelve). The senate recently voted to install a Snapple or soda-vending machine but this was not permitted. Homecoming, run by the student senate, takes place at varsity and junior varsity games in the winter. The senate runs a daily breakfast cart.

There are over two-dozen clubs, such as, Green School Alliance, Film Makers Club, and Jewish Affairs Club, with over 200 members.

The athletic program at Trinity is wide ranging and strong. Some teams hold two-hour morning practice sessions. Games are held after school and some are well attended. Soccer, lacrosse, basketball, and swimming are a few of Trinity's best teams, but although some students may say "this is definitely not a rah-rah school," everyone was excited when the Varsity Boy's Basketball Team captured a recent NYSAAIS Class "C" New York State Championship for the second time in three years and the fourth time in school history.

At graduation, awards are bestowed upon Trinity seniors, in recognition of excellence in nearly every area. The three students with the highest grade point averages in each grade receive the a Hawley Prizes. Important non-academic awards include prize for community service and the Annelle Fitzpatrick Award for gentleness of spirit. On Prize Day in May, all academic departments announce the students in grades nine through twelve, who are recipients of endowed prizes, including four prizes that have been given annually since 1890—the Eaton Prize for Classics, the Alumni Prize in English, the Rector's Prize in Religion, and the Eaton Prize for Senior Mathematics. At a formal induction ceremony in the spring, students with outstanding academic records are elected to the Cum Laude Society, the high school equivalent of Phi Beta Kappa. There are some students who compete for these prizes, but the real source of competition, one alumnus comments, is college placement.

Graduation exercises, complete with academic gown, are held in a church at 96th and Central Park West. A Baccalaureate service, planned by the seniors, is held the night before graduation at Trinity Church, the original site of the school, near Wall Street. By tradition, the graduation speaker is the parent of a senior.

Popular College Choices Yale, Harvard, Brown, Princeton, University of Pennsylvania, Cornell, Wesleyan, Stanford

Traditions Holiday Fair, Spring Benefit, Latin Epic, Reunion Weekend, Cabaret, Theater IV productions, senior and first grade Halloween Costume parade, Multicultural Fair

Publications Yearbook: The Bruner
Literary magazine: *Columbus*
Newspaper: *Trinity Times*
Middle School Literary magazines: *Ink and Ink Jr.*
Middle School newspaper: *In the Middle*
Photography journal: *Malinconico*
Trinity School magazine: *Trinity Per Saecula* (Trinity through the Ages)
French Literary Magazine: *Correspondences*
Spanish Literary Magazine

Community Service Requirement Trinity has a mandatory Middle School community service requirement; themes include the environment and helping children; there is no community service requirement for High School, but most Trinity students participate in at least one community service activity; in Lower School, an entire grade will do projects together; the Student Volunteer Service Organization (SVSO), born in the sixties, along with the The Chaplain's Office, continues to coordinate a range of student volunteer activities, such as Santa's helpers, the Thanksgiving program for senior citizens, You Gotta Have Park and the March of Dimes Walkathon

Hangouts The Swamp (a small seating area in the rear of the Upper School lobby), the Food Zone (seating in the lobby where students can eat), the McDonald's at 91st and Columbus

United Nations International School

24–50 Franklin D. Roosevelt Drive
New York, NY 10010
(212) 584-3071, fax (212) 685-5023
website: www.unis.org
e-mail: admissions@unis.org

Coed
Kindergarten–12th grade
Accessible

Mr. Stuart Walker, Director
Mrs. Amelia Tattew, Director of Admissions

Birthday Cutoff Children entering kindergarten must be 5 by August 31

Enrollment Total enrollment: 1,541
Kindergarten places: 85
Graduating class size: Approximately 115

Grades Semester system
Number grades begin in 7th grade
Full departmentalization by 7th grade

Tuition Range 2009–2010 $22,900 to 25,450, Kindergarten through 12th grade, additional fee for new parents, $1,500 per family

Financial Aid/Scholarship 8.2% of the student body receive some form of financial aid; $762,573 has been awarded

Endowment $13,287,949

Diversity Students at UNIS come from over 120 countries.

After-School Program Open to UNIS students only
A variety of creative and recreational activities from 3:00 P.M. until 6:00 P.M.; an additional payment is required
Varsity and junior varsity teams

Summer Program UNIS offers a comprehensive variety of creative and recreational summer programs for children ages 4 to 14; an additional payment is required

461

UNIS is housed in a modern, spacious building overlooking the East River. A large garden forms the tranquil core of the building. For younger students, the school has a fully equipped, multi-level playground. UNIS was founded in 1947 by a group of United Nations parents to provide their children with an international curriculum and to inspire in its students the spirit and ideals of the UN. Today, UNIS is open to all New York City families. Students at UNIS represent over one hundred and twenty countries; the faculty and staff represent over sixty-six different nationalities.

UNIS Manhattan is organized into three schools: the Junior School is for kindergarten through fourth grade students, the Middle School is composed of fifth through eighth grade, and the High School, Tutorial House is for ninth through twelfth grade students. There is also a kindergarten through eighth grade campus in Queens. Each school has its principal and staff, who insure a smooth transition from school to school. Mr. Stuart Walker is the Director. Mr. Walker is an Australian and was formerly head of the Blue Mountains Grammar School in Australia.

Getting in: UNIS offers spring and fall tours (led by current parents) for prospective applicants; students in fifth grade and above are welcome to accompany their parents on the tour. Once an application has been filed, the school will contact parents to set up an interview date and parents can also tour at this time. Children applying to kindergarten through fourth grade are observed in an informal play group of four or five, while at the same time, their parents meet as a group (approximately twenty families) for a Q and A session with the school principal and admissions staff. All students are required to submit results of ERB testing. Teacher recommendations are required unless the student's school report includes comprehensive teacher's comments; personal recommendations are welcome but not required. The school is sensitive to applicants from other cultures and countries and is familiar with all of the different national systems. Each year space is held for children of incoming U.N. diplomats. Approximately fifty-four percent of parents are affiliated with the U.N.

Program: The curriculum is designed to provide for direct interaction by the children with the world around them. The children are encouraged to think for themselves, while working cooperatively in small groups. In the Junior School, academics are stressed in an integrated program that includes music, art, French, Spanish, science and computer science taught by specialists. Creativity is encouraged.

UNIS recognizes that the Middle School years are critical ones for social, emotional and intellectual growth. The curriculum builds upon the basics learned in previous years, adding new subjects and additional language options. In English, Middle School students read world poetry and explore works of literature from many countries and cultures. UNIS places high value on the teaching of modern languages. French and Spanish are offered from kindergarten on, and beginning in seventh grade eight languages are taught by native speakers with beginning, intermediate and advanced classes available. English as a Second Language is a separate course.

The curriculum of the Tutorial House (high school) balances electives and required subjects. In Grade 10 students can pursue a special talent or interest, whether it be math, science, languages, writing, the humanities, music or art. In Grades 11 and 12, all UNIS students participate in International Baccalaurate classes; approximately eighty-five percent of UNIS students are enrolled as IB diploma candidates. Students who earn the IB diploma usually qualify for advanced standing of up to one year at many American colleges. Seventy-five percent of graduates choose to attend colleges in North America.

UNIS has a well articulated computer studies program. Technology is integrated into classroom instruction in many different subject areas. I saw computers in all of the classrooms and there are four computer labs. The school is networked, connecting all classrooms and bridging the Manhattan and Queens campuses. The school is connected to the Internet through a T1 line.

There are numerous opportunities for leadership throughout the school. Students can be elected to Student Council as early as Grade 2. Members of the Student Councils of all four schools meet periodically with their principal and with the director to discuss issues of concern.

The UNIS athletic program includes twelve varsity and four junior varsity teams.

The annual UNIS/UN conference is an exciting annual event. This conference is held in the UN's General Assembly Hall and requires months of planning and research by UNIS students and students from the more than fifty participating schools from around the world.

Popular College Choices   Bard, Barnard, Boston College, Brown, Columbia, Cornell, Dartmouth, Duke, University of Edinburgh,

Fordham, George Washington, Harvard, McGill, New York University, MIT, University of Pennsylvania, Princeton, University of St. Andrews, Stanford, Syracuse, University of Toronto

Traditions   United Nations Day, Winter and Spring Concerts, UNIS/UN Conference, Theater Workshop, Science Weekend, Math Weekend, Sports Day, Sports Banquet, Ski Weekend, International Book and Craft Festival, Outdoor Environmental Education Trips, Overseas Language Immersion Trips, 3 Annual Tutorial House Dances

Publications   Yearbook
Upper School Newspaper: *UNIS Verse*
Literary Magazine: *Avenue X Magazine*
Annual UNIS/UN Conference Working Paper

Community Service Requirement   An important aspect of student life is community service, either in-house or at an approved public service agency in the metropolitan area

Village Community School

272-278 West 10th Street
New York, NY 10014
(212) 691-5146
website: www.ncsnyc.org

Coed
Kindergarten–8th grade
Accessible

Eve Kleger, Director
Judy Calixto, Director of Admissions

Birthday Cutoff Children entering kindergarten must be 5 by December 31

Enrollment Total enrollment: 330
Kindergarten places: 40
Graduating class size: Approximately 40

Grades Students are in mixed-age groups in the Lower School and move into groups that span one-year by 6th grade when departmentalization begins; standardized tests begin for 8-year-olds and continue through the Upper School; there are parent-teacher conferences twice a year along with detailed narrative reports and checklists

Tuition Range 2009–2010 $32,000, Kindergarten through 8th grade; lunch fees are included in the tuition

Financial Aid/Scholarship 22% to 25% of the student body receive some form of financial aid

Endowment $2 million

Diversity VCS enrolls students from Prep for Prep and Early Steps, has a Diversity Statement that underscores the mission of the school and Faculty Diversity Search programs; there is a full-time Diversity Director who coordinates a variety of diversity groups for students and parents

After-School Program After School at VCS are offered daily Monday–Friday 3:15 P.M. to 4:45 P.M.; classes and activities include sports, arts and crafts, music, theatre, dance, computer, woodshop, and yoga; an additional payment is required
A drop-in play group is available from 3:00 P.M. until 6 P.M. for an hourly fee, billable at the end of each month; Intramural sports are offered to Upper School students including soccer, volleyball, basketball and softball

Summer Program VCS has a two-week summer camp in June, including hiking and basketball camp options; an additional payment is required

---

Village Community School was founded in 1970 by a small group of parents and educators who wanted to create a new school for children in grades kindergarten through 8th grade in the West Village. VCS's original historic Victorian structure, with its high ceilings, wide stairwells, and a newer sky-lit library was originally a public school one hundred years ago and spans the entire block of West 10th Street between Washington and Greenwich Streets. Today, the building has been seamlessly joined with a modern addition that was completed in 2003. The five story facility houses spacious, sunny classrooms, a large outdoor play area, a free-standing woodshop, naturally lit art and music rooms, a state-of-the-art computer lab, three science centers, a sky-lit library, a roof-top play area, gym, auditorium and a modern kitchen and lunchroom.

Getting in: Parents can call after Labor Day to request an admissions packet and schedule a tour. VCS encourages touring before applying. Once an application is received, they are contacted by a member of the admissions office and two separate appointments are made—a group interview for the child with four other applicants, another for the parents with a member of the school's administration. Each visit lasts about 30-40 minutes. Children applying for second grade and above are invited to spend half-a-day visiting the school with a group of their peers. VCS requires ERB testing for all applicants.

Parents: The majority of parents live in the neighborhood, although some hail from surrounding neighborhoods as well as from New Jersey because of the nearby Christopher Street PATH station. VCS engenders a close-knit, diverse community. Parent involvement is highly valued, needed, and strong. Parents serve in a variety of ways ranging from class parent to chairing an event to serving as a Council board member. Parents meet informally several times each month with the Head of School for Coffee and Conversation. Breakfasts with division heads are offered several times a year as well. There are numerous opportunities for parent information sessions on a variety of subjects including, internet safety, nutrition, social studies in children and diversity.

Program: There are two divisions: The Lower School is composed of grades kindergarten through five. The Upper School is composed of grades six through eight. VCS offers a coherent curriculum, yet allows for teachers and students to pursue topics of interest as they arise.

VCS has a friendly, relaxed atmosphere but the curriculum is highly structured. Basic skills—reading, writing and math are taught from the beginning along with intellectual and artistic subjects. Much attention is paid to social and emotional development. Lower School students take art, music, woodshop and library as well as physical education. Parents say that in the Lower School VCS is very nurturing; but in the upper grades the expectations are more demanding. Critical and abstract thinking are stressed. A foreign language is introduced in the Upper School and the program is fully departmentalized. Latin, Spanish and Mandarin are offered.

Students have choices each semester among a variety of electives including many areas of the arts, theater, music, dance, film, and other arts-related interests. Special class activities include weekly Upper School Community Meetings, an Outdoor Education Trip and an Activity Day as well as grade-level dances. There is physical education daily and athletic teams in various sports.

Individual attention is paid to each student approaching the high school admissions process. Starting in seventh grade, families are guided through the array of options and the application process.

Popular Secondary School Choices   VCS graduates attend a variety of city high schools including the specialized public schools, NYC independent schools and boarding schools including, Berkeley Carroll, Calhoun, Collegiate, Columbia Prep, Dalton, Elisabeth Irwin, Fieldston, Abraham Joseph Heschel, Horace Mann, Marymount, Packer Collegiate, Riverdale, St. Ann's, Trinity, Andover, Hotchkiss; popular public schools include, Beacon, Bronx Science, Brooklyn Tech, Stuyvesant, Fiorello La Guardia High School of

Music, Art and the Performing Arts, High School of American Studies at Lehman College

Traditions   Fall Festival Upper School Trip, Book Fair, Benefit Auction, School Plays, Holiday and Spring Concerts, End-of-Year Picnic

Community Service Requirement   VCS has a Community Service Committee which helps coordinate student and parent organized events such as a Penny Harvest, canned food drive, coat drive, Green-Day Up, recycling drive; the committee also serves as a resource for parents and teachers

York Preparatory School

40 West 68th Street
New York, NY 10023
(212) 362-0400
www.yorkprep.org

Coed
Grades 6–12
Accessible (elevator)

Mr. Ronald P. Stewart, Headmaster
Mr. Chris Durnford, Principal
Ms. Elizabeth Norton, Director of Enrollment
Ms. Lisa Smith and Ms. Jacqueline Leber, Director of Admissions

Uniform   There is a dress code; students wear a York Prep polo shirt in white or navy and khaki slacks and/or skirts, Monday through Thursday; Friday is casual dress day

Birthday Cutoff   None

Enrollment   Total enrollment: 345
6th grade places: 30
9th grade places: 20–30
Average graduating class size: 60

Grades   Semester system
Numerical grades begin in grade 6
Grades and progress updates are reported weekly to parents and students via an open on-line grading book; students receive quarter grades four times a year

Tuition Range 2009–2010 $33,200 to $33,900, 6th–12th grades
Additional fees: for books, activities, and student insurance, $1,800

Financial Aid/Scholarship   Approximately 25% of the school receive some form of aid
$800,000 in financial aid was distributed in 2009–2010

Endowment   None

Diversity   York Prep admits Prep for Prep students

After-School Program Jump Start; Scholars Program; varsity, junior varsity and middle school team competition in the Inter-school League and other leagues in volleyball, soccer, track, base-ball, softball, basketball, cross country and tennis;
An active intramural program in fencing, lacrosse, golf, swim-ming, tennis, volleyball and basketball
Academic clubs meet after school
for all subject areas; all teachers keep office hours until 4P.M.;
Extracurricular club activities include: ballroom dance, book club, chess and backgammon, community service, environmental club, fashion club, first aid, ski club, drama, literary magazine, school newspaper, photography and animation, psychology club, Model UN, Radius Club, rock band, set building, student government, WYRK, yearbook

Summer Program An academic enrichment program is offered from mid-June–July for an additional charge for York Prep stu-dents. Students can take advancement classes or make-up work in a tutorial environment; Week-long sports and study skills camps are held in August

---

York Prep was founded in 1969 by its present Headmaster Ronald Stewart and his wife Jayme Stewart. In 1997 the school moved from its former location on East 85th Street into its current home on the Upper West Side, a handsome seven-story granite building originally designed as a college, formerly occupied by the Hebrew Union College. Having completed a "boiler to roof" renovation, the school, crisply painted in yellow and blue, reflects the can-do optimism and leadership exuded by the Oxford-educated headmaster, Ronald Stewart, and his wife, Jayme Stewart, who has been Director of College Guidance since the school's inception. Together the Stewart's oversee every aspect of the school which operates free of the politics of a board of trustees.

Liv Tyler and Kelly Klein are two of the school's glamorous grads; so is James de la Vega, a graffiti artist (recently profiled in *The New York Times*), who grew up in El Barrio and studied art at Cornell.

When you enter the school, a regulation sized basketball court serves as the backdrop to the reception desk. Two uniformed security guards stand nearby. On closer inspection one turns out to be a statue. York Prep values both athletics and a sense of humor, both great advantages when managing adolescents, as the Stewarts, who have three grown children, know well. The school believes that if you put children in a situation where they have to work hard, they can be successful. Participation in athletics and other extracurricular activities is encouraged here. A parent told me: "It's a very nurturing school, the teachers are great; it's the perfect alternative to one of the real high-powered schools; an excellent private school education."

The schoolhouse has two modern science laboratories, a library/media center (with beautiful Shaker-style windows), three technology centers, performance and art studios, and a sprung hardwood floor gymnasium with weight and locker room facilities. The classrooms are light and airy, carpeted and climate controlled. The classrooms are equipped with state-of-the-art technology including Smartboards, wireless access, and laptop equipped science, music and animation materials. Students and staff have e-mail addresses, and all staff members have voicemail. In addition, all classrooms are linked to the school's in-house television station, WYRK, which gives students interested in television, broadcasting, journalism, and production, the opportunity to showcase their talents.

Getting in: Open houses for parents are offered regularly, September through January, by the Headmaster and the Admissions Department. Applicants and their parents are offered a private interview with the Associate Director of Admissions and the applicant is invited to spend a day visiting classes.

Program: Headmaster Stewart believes that a student must be offered a real opportunity for success, and that is a major factor in student motivation. York Prep's curriculum provides a strong foundation in the traditional core subjects of a liberal arts education. For a small school, it offers an impressive range of courses with electives in most fields for study. For qualified students, AP courses are available.

York Prep's academic system of support and challenge has helped many students rediscover the thrill and joy of learning. Beginning in sixth grade, students are tracked by homogeneous ability groups according to subject in classes averaging 15 students. These tracks are fluid; students whose skills improve will move into the next track enabling students to experience success while always being challenged to work beyond their "comfort level." Each student's program is constantly evaluated for proper placement within the tracking system to ensure the right balance of challenge and support is maintained in all subject areas.

"York Prep's system of academic support has helped many students who've been 'over-faced' [at other schools] rediscover the thrill of learning," says Stewart. For gifted students, York Prep provides the challenge of its top track honors courses and a Scholars Program. The Scholars Program meets two mornings a week, during which students take advanced seminars in subjects such as philosophy and math matrixes. The three year program culminates after a formal Scholar's Thesis with students earning a diploma with Honors. Seniors and eleventh graders who qualify are eligible to take courses at Columbia University and New York University.

The school has always provided academic support and accommodation for gifted students with different learning styles and educational needs. The Jump Start program is an individualized and intensive program that works to strengthen reading comprehension and writing skills. This program also imparts organizational and study skills. It was created to help students develop independence not only with day-to-day tasks but also with respect to long range goals. There is an additional fee for the Jump Start program.

Communication between parents and the school is weekly. York Prep uses Edline, a password-secured on-line website that provides current grades, homework, and class news every Friday.

A wide range of sports is offered at York and the full trophy cases are proof of their success. Art offerings vary from digital photography, art for portfolio and animation classes to music and drama productions. Clubs vary from debate to ballroom dance and from broadcasting journalism on York Prep's station to boatbuilding. Students can choose from competitive or non-competitive basketball, softball, soccer, swimming, track, tennis, cross-country track, aerobics, gymnastic, golf and weight training and trips such as ski weekends or to Washington, D.C., Europe or Canada. The range of clubs and activities changes each year according to student interest. Wherever there is student interest, there is an activity.

York Prep students volunteer their time at more than 150 non-profit organizations, including the American Red Cross, the ASPCA, the Central Park Conservancy, the Legal Aid Society, and so on. Many students surpass the required hours of the Community Service Program.

Stewart says, "Each child needs a feeling that he can do something well—whether it's athletics or something else. We tell them 'you pick it, we'll support you.' " This philosophy is carried all the way through to graduation. York Prep is very successful at college placement thanks to the expertise of Jayme Stewart, author of *How to Get Into the College of Your Choice* (William Morrow & Co., 1991). Ms. Stewart works with each student individually to find the right match for college. Her thoroughness and tenacity as a student advocate pay off as students enroll in their top choice schools.

Popular College Choices Barnard, Bentley, Clark, Cornell, Boston University, George Washington, Hobart, New York University, Skidmore, SUNY, Syracuse, University of Michigan, University of Rhode Island, University of Vermont

Publications Literary Magazine: *Genesis*
Yearbook: *The Legend*
Newspaper *The Paw*

Community Service Requirement 100 hours over 4 years

NEW AND ADDITIONAL SCHOOLS

Several new schools have opened recently, usually with preschool, kindergarten and elementary grades, some with the intention of adding upper grades. As it is yet unclear how to fully evaluate them, they are simply listed to indicate their availability. Other schools, that have a much longer history, but which from their relative size, geographic location, or mission statements would appeal to a limited group of Manhattan parents are also simply listed, as are some schools which are all jewish or catholic, etc., or unwilling or unable to furnish information about their programs.

Academy of St. Joseph
coed
(Grades Nursery 3s and expanding
to 8th grade)
111 Washington Place
New York, NY 10014
Tel (212) 243-5420
website:
www.academyofsaintjoseph.org
Total enrollment: 25
Tuition 2009-2010: $11,800 to
$19,800

Beekman School
(Grades 9–12)
220 East 50th Street
New York, NY 10022
Tel (212) 755-6666
Fax (212) 888-6085
website: www.beekmanschool.org
Total enrollment: approximately 97
Tuition 2009-20010: $28,500

Beth Jacob Parochial School
(Orthodox Jewish, Grades
Kindergarten–8)
142 Broome Street
New York, NY 10002
Tel (212) 473-4500
Fax (212) 460-5317
no website
Total enrollment: 130
Tuition 2009-2010: N/A

The Blue School
(Nursery 2s through 5th grade)
432 Lafayette, Mezzanine (mailing
address, administrative offices)
New York, NY 10003
1 Avenue B, corner of Houston and
Avenue B (main location)
New York, NY 10009
Tel (646) 602-7066 (main number)
Tel (212) 228-6341 ext 16
(admissions for all programs)
Fax (212) 260-3824
website: www.theblueschool.org
email: info@theblueschool.org
Total enrollment: Approximately
100
Tuition 2010-2011: $4,400 to
$28,400

The British International School
(Nursery 3s through 8th grade)
20 Waterside Plaza
New York, NY 10010
Tel (212) 481-2700
Fax (212) 481-8263
website:
www.britishinternationalschoolny.org
email: info@bis-ny.org
Total enrollment:189
Tuition 2009-2010: $32,800

Brooklyn Free School
(Ages 5 to 16 years-old)
120 16th Street
Brooklyn, NY 11215
Tel (718) 499-2707
website:
www.brooklynfreeschool.org
email:
contact@brooklynfreeschool.org
Total enrollment: Approximately 60
Tuition: A sliding scale

**The Cathedral School of the
Holy Trinity**
(Grades Nursery–8)
319 East 74th Street
New York, NY 10021
website: www.cathedralschoolny.org
email: info@cathedralschoolny.org
Tel (212) 249-2840
Fax (212) 249-2847
Total enrollment: 130
Tuition 2009–2010: $9,500–$10,500

**Ecole Internationale de New
York**
(Ages Nursery to 5th grade)
111 East 22nd Street
New York, NY 10010
Tel (646) 410-2238
website: www.einy.org
email: Jeremy@einy.org
Total enrollment: Approximately 40
Tuition 2009-2010: $22,500 plus
additional fees: one-time enrollment
$2,000 and lunch $990

Frederick Douglass Academy
(Grades 6–12)
2581 Adam Clayton Powell
Boulevard
New York, NY 10039
Tel (212) 491-4107
Fax (212) 491-4414
website: www.FDA1.com
Total enrollment: approximately
1100
Tuition: N/A

The Kew-Forest School
(Grades Kindergarten-12)
119-17 Union Turnpike
Forest Hills, New York 11375
Tel (718) 268-4667
Fax (718) 268-9121
website: www.kewforest.org
Total enrollment: approximately 360
Tuition: N/A

King's Academy
(Grades Nursery–12)
2341 Third Avenue
New York, NY 10035
Tel (212) 348-7380
Fax (212) 348-0515
Total enrollment: approximately 100
Tuition 2009-2010: Between $375
to $425/month

Manhattan Christian Academy
(Grades Pre-kindergarten–8)
401 West 205th Street
New York, NY 10040
Tel (212) 567-5521
Fax (212) 567-2815
website: www.mcanyc.org
Total enrollment: 280
Tuition 2009-2010: $3,800 to $4,300

Manhattan Day School
(Grades Nursery–8)
310 West 75th Street
New York, NY 10023
Tel (212) 376-6800
Fax (212) 376-6388
website: www.mymds.web.org
Tuition: N/A
Total enrollment: 450

Manhattan Free School
(Ages 5–18 years)
215 East 6th Street
New York, NY 10003
website:
www.manhattanfreeschool.org

Mestivta Timereth Jerusalem
(Orthodox Jewish, Grades
Kindergarten–12)
145 East Broadway
New York, NY 10002
Tel (212) 964-2830
Fax (212) 349-5213
no website
Total enrollment: approximately 150
Tuition 2009-2010: Approximately
$6,000

Northeastern Academy
(Grades 9–12)
532 West 215th Street
New York, NY 10034
Tel (212) 569-4800
Fax (212) 569-6145
Total enrollment: approximately 177
Tuition 2009-2010: $5,396

**Saint Spyridon Greek Parochial
School**
(Greek Orthodox, Grades Pre-
kindergarten–8)
120 Wadsworth Avenue
New York, NY 10033
Tel (212) 795-6870
Fax (212) 795-6871
Total enrollment: 300
Tuition: N/A

Saint Thomas Choir School
(Boarding for boys only, Grades
4–8)
202 West 58th Street
New York, NY 10019
Tel (212) 247-3311
Fax (212) 247-3393
website: www.choirschool.org
Total enrollment: 40
Tuition: 2009-2010: $11,000
boarding included

Yeshiva Rabbi S.R. Hirsch
(Orthodox Jewish, Grades
Nursery–12)
85–93 Bennett Avenue
New York, NY 10033
Tel (212) 568-6200
Fax (212) 928-4422
Total enrollment: approximately 500
Tuition: N/A

Speyer Legacy School
211 West 61st Street, 6th floor
New York, NY 10023
Tel (212) 581-4000
website:
www.speyerlegacyschool.org
email: info@speyerlegacyschool.org
Total enrollment: approximately 35
and growing
Tuition 2009-2010: $28,500

**Yeshiva University High School
for Boys**
(Orthodox Jewish, Grades 9–12)
2540 Amsterdam Avenue
New York, NY 10033
Tel (212) 960-5337
Fax (212) 960-0027
website: www.yuhsb.org
Total enrollment: 325
Tuition: N/A

RESOURCES FOR CHILDREN WITH LEARNING DISABILITIES

When parents are first told that their child has been diagnosed with a learning disability they are heartbroken. They feel as if they've done something wrong that might have caused or contributed to their child's disability. Then they start shaking the family tree for any relatives who might have had a learning problem—was it your brother, grandmother, aunt or cousin who had so much trouble in school? Parents start to think that their child is the only one struggling and then they worry about the erosion of their child's self-esteem. Learning disabilities are diagnosed in children with a wide range of IQ's; very bright children can have LD's that aren't diagnosed until later in their schooling because they came up with ingenious strategies to compensate for their deficiency. Skilled educators will usually see red flags early on, in pre-kindergarten or earlier. Most primary schools have early intervention specialists on staff, including speech therapists. Keep in mind that individual schools have different timetables for developmental skills. With a wide age range within classrooms, children will be at different points of development throughout their school years.

If you are concerned about a "developmental lag" at any point, don't be afraid to ask the teacher if she thinks you should have your child evaluated; if her answer isn't satisfactory, go to the division head or guidance counselor with your concerns. If you're still not sure why your child isn't doing grade level work the first order of business is to get a psycho-educational evaluation (see also section on Advisors, Testers and Test Preparation, p. 34) to determine exactly what the problem is and what you can do about it. This guide, The Parents League, and the organizations listed below can refer you to a qualified tester. Word of mouth may also be a good way to find one. The best bet is to find a tester who is also trained in neurology and is a licensed psychologist. The test is long and is usually given in two-hour segments, morning and afternoon, over a couple of days. Reports are detailed and sophisticated.

The best grades for testing children are: kindergarten or first grade (an important year for acquiring learning skills), fourth grade (skills are consolidated and more independent learning is expected); seventh grade (so you can better assess high school options), tenth grade (because now is the time to make critical high school decisions, like qualifying for extended time on SATs.) Medication is sometimes prescribed for children with related attention disorders to help them focus, settle down, and get to work.

Reevaluate and retest every three to four years. Your child's school should be apprised of any testing you do outside, and provided with the results so they can best work with your child. Remember this is a partnership. A representative at The Parent's League who has run numerous parent workshops and seminars on learning disabilities offers a comforting thought, "If a child is completely evaluated and a learning disability has been identified, there is often a sense of relief and it is much easier to set a course of remediation." Once the right type of intervention and programming are in place, learning often becomes enjoyable again.

Schools for children with learning disabilities are small in size and highly structured. Classes in a therapeutic setting vary in size from six to twelve students per class with an assistant as well as additional sessions with various specialists who work with students one-on-one. Often, these schools will have mixed-age groupings of students because many learning disabled children learn at different rates that don't correlate with their ages. These programs really work and are worth all the time and money that you will invest. Many children who attend a specialized school are mainstreamed back into a regular educational environment, often the goal of many of these schools. Students who stay in their present schools may require extensive and costly tutoring after school. Don't expect your child's private school to provide all the services he'll need, but most schools will provide study skills programs and extended time for tests and exams. Keep your chin up and take heart, many children with learning disabilities have gone on to wonderful colleges, (including the Ivy League) and have successful careers.

Here are some of the schools in the New York City area that educate children with learning disabilities, and/or psychological, social, behavioral or emotional issues. With the exception of the Parkside School, most of the schools listed below are very similar. The Parents League can also provide a listing of schools for children with developmental and learning disabilities. There are many success stories out there and here are some of their alma maters:

Aaron Academy
42 East 30th Street
New York, NY 10016
Tel (212) 867-5443
Fax (212) 867-5379
www.aaronacad.org

Coed
Grades 6–12
Current Enrollment: 60

Aaron School
309 East 45th Street
New York, NY 10017
Tel (212) 867-9594
Fax (212) 867-9864

Coed
Ages: 5–10/11 years
Total Enrollment: 118

The Churchill School and Center
301 East 29th Street
New York, NY 10016
Tel (212) 722-0610
website: www.churchillschool.com

Coed
Ages: Kindergarten–12th grade
Total enrollment: approximately 400
Tuition: none

An outreach center for services and programs for children and adolescents with attention and/or learning problems. The Churchill School serves children who have average to above average cognitive ability whose learning in a mainstream classroom is compromised by a learning disability. This may be a language processing or reading disability, perceptual and/or motor weakness or attention issues. Churchill cannot meet the needs of students with primary emotional and social issues. Students with dyslexia, a reading disability, Attention Deficit Disorder with Hyper-Activity (ADHD), respond to the multisensory small group instruction at Churchill. The high school opened in 2004 and offers a Regents' Curriculum and more. Admissions and additional information are available on the school's website.

The Gateway School of New York
211 West 61st Street, 6th Floor
New York, NY 10023
Tel (212) 777-5966
Fax (212) 777-5794
website: www.gatewayschool.org

Coed
Ages: 5–13 years-old
Total enrollment: 112
Tuition 2009-2010: $43,600 to $46,750, ages 5-13 years-old

When Gateway was founded in 1965, it was one of the first schools in New York City to work exclusively with children who had learning disabilities. The aim of The Gateway School is to remediate and mainstream children who have moderate to severe learning disabilities.

The Gillen Brewer School
410 East 92nd Street
New York, NY 10128
Tel (212) 831-3667
Fax (212) 831-5254

Coed
Ages: 3–10 years-old
Total enrollment: 86
Tuition: N/A

The Gillen Brewer School started as an early childhood program and evaluation site, and now extends up through second grade. Parents are very pleased with the school. The program serves children who have a wide variety of learning issues and developmental delays.

The Mary McDowell Center for Learning
20 Bergen Street
Brooklyn, NY 11201
Tel (718) 625-3939
Fax (718) 625-1456
website: www.marymcdowell.org

Coed
Ages: 5–10 years-old
Total enrollment: 247
Tuition: N/A

The Mary McDowell Center for Learning educates children with developmental delays and learning disabilities. A good resource for families who live in Brooklyn.

The Parkside School
48 West 74th Street
New York, NY 10023
Tel (212) 721-8888
Fax (212) 721-1547

Coed
Ages: 5–10 years
Total enrollment: 80
Tuition 2009-2010: $36,500

The Parkside School's program serves children who have a wide range of language-based learning difficulties. The school offers a well-designed comprehensive array of academic and other support services. This very supportive program offers a highly structured, multisensory curriculum that inspires children and makes learning fun.

Rebecca School
40 East 30th Street
New York, NY 10016
Tel (212) 810-4120
Fax (212) 810-4121
www.rebeccaschool.org

Coed
Ages 4–18

Robert Louis Stevenson School
(Serves children with learning disabilities and Attention Deficit Disorders, Grades 8–12)
24 West 74th Street
New York, NY 10023
Tel (212) 787–6400
Fax (212) 873-1872
website: www.stevenson.school.org
Total enrollment: 58
Tuition 2009-2010: $45,000

Stephen Gaynor School
148 West 90th Street
New York, NY 10024
Tel (212) 787-7070

Fax (212) 787-3312
website: www.stephengaynor.org

Coed
Ages: 5–14 years-old
Total enrollment: 193
Tuition 2009-2010: $43,000

The oldest school in New York City, (founded in 1962) for children who have dyslexia, ADD, visual spatial and/or non-verbal learning disabilities. Stephen Gaynor is highly respected in the community and does an excellent job of mainstreaming children who have a wide spectrum of special needs.

West End Day School
255 West 71st Street
New York, NY 10023
Tel (212) 873-5708
Fax (212) 873-2345
website: www.westenddayschool.org

Coed
Ages: 5–12/13 years-old
Total enrollment: 45
Tuition: N/A

According to Carrie Catapano, Head of School, West End Day is "a school for bright academically inclined children who are not being served well in a mainstream setting." The staff works closely with each family to develop a highly individualized program.

Windward School
Windward Avenue
White Plains, NY 10605
Tel (914) 949-6968
Fax (914) 949-8220
website: www.windwardny.org

Coed
Grades: 1st–9th
Total enrollment: 553
Tuition 2009-2010: $41,000

Windward is located in Southern Westchester, and offers a multisensory program for children with language-based disabilities and average to superior IQs. Windward's staff is extremely skilled at remediating children to achieve their full potential and then mainstreaming them.

Winston Preparatory School
126 West 17th Street
New York, NY 10011
Tel (646) 638-2705
Fax (646) 638-2706
website: www.mail.winstonprep.edu

Coed
Grades: 6th–12th grades
Total enrollment: 220
Tuition: N/A

Winston Prep is an individualized program for junior and senior high school students who have learning differences. The goal of Winston's program is designed to maximize independence and self-reliance. Class size is about 12, and every student has one-to-one instruction, called Focus, in English and math daily. Athletic and other extracurricular activities are available after school. Winston sends the majority of its students on to college. Teachers are trained in a variety of methods, and are knowledgeable about how to teach children with learning issues.

The Learning Resource Center at Columbia Grammar and Preparatory School
5 West 93rd Street
New York, NY 10025
(212) 749-6200
website: www.cgps.org

Coed
Grades: Kindergarten–12th (the school goes from Pre-K–12)
Tuition 2009-2010: $33,040 to $34,990, Pre-K through 12th grade

This is not a school for severely learning-disabled children. The program is designed for high achieving students who need extra support. CGPS's Learning Resource Center is well established, organized and structured. According to the school it "will provide some degree of professional skills and remediation on a temporary basis." Roughly, ten or more well-trained professionals staff the Learning Center, and enrollment is limited to only approximately forty students school-wide (The school has about 1,000 students.) There is an additional cost for any student in the Learning Center, (see entry *supra* p. 186).

Lindamood Bell New York Learning Center
110 East 55th Street, 5th Floor
New York, NY 10022
Tel (212) 644-0650 or (800) 300-1818
website: www.lindamoodbell.com
Coed

A supplemental program for students with a variety of learning issues.
Rates and enrollments vary.

The Smith School
131 West 86th Street
New York, NY 10024
Tel (212) 879-6354
website: www.smithschool.net

Coed
Grades 7-12
Total enrollment: 50-60
Tuition 2009-2010: $27,000 to 30,500, 7th through 12th grade

For the last decade the Smith School, founded by its current Director,
Karen Smith, has mainstreamed students with a variety of LDs and developmental disabilities into well-functioning students who are ready to take
advantage of a four-year academic, liberal arts college experience. Small
class size and individualized attention foster superb study and organizational skills combined with a solid core curriculum ensure success for
every student. There is a community service requirement of 10 hours each
semester, after-school and summer programs are available for an additional fee. Graduates attend a wide variety of colleges and universities.

The Quest Program at The Dwight School
291 Central Park West
New York, NY 10024
(212) 724-2146 ext. 212

Coed
Grades: Nursery through 12th

Dwight is also not a school for children with learning disabilities.
However, the school has a small program (approximately fifteen per-

486

cent of the student body is enrolled) for students who have minor learning difficulties and need extra support in the classroom. The Quest Program is set up so students do not have to go to a tutor every day and can still participate in a full college preparatory curriculum. The Quest Program has an upper and lower division and resembles in a way the Parisian system with lots of mnemonics, repetitive learning and drills. The program is flexible enough so that students who need help in one subject area can get it, without compromising their schedules, it also serves students with a range of abilities. Parents are kept apprised of their children's test results in reading and writing. The additional fee for the program averages approximately $15,000 per year, depending on the amount of sessions needed. (*supra,* p. 220)

A complete listing of educational resources in the New York City area for children with learning disabilities can be obtained from:

The National Center for Learning Disabilities, 381 Park Avenue South, Suite 1401, New York, NY 10016-8806, (212) 545-7510 or 1-(888) 575-7373 ext 210, website: www.LD.org

NCLD is a voluntary, not-for-profit organization founded in 1977 by Carrie Rozelle. NCLD operates a national information and referral service and is the nation's only central, computerized resource clearinghouse committed solely to the issues of LD.

The Learning Disabilities Association of New York City Telephone Referral Service: Weekdays from 9 a.m. to 5 p.m., (212) 645-6730, FAX (212) 924-8896, website: www.LDANYC.com.
This nonprofit organization is an affiliate of the Learning Disabilities Association of America. Trained counselors will explain how to recognize symptoms, and offer referrals to community based agencies in the New York City area. The Learning Disabilities Association also provides printed material and conducts workshops.

The International Dyslexia Association, 71 West 23rd Street, Suite 1527, New York, NY 10010, (212) 691-1930, Fax (212) 633-1620, website: www.nybida.org
This is the New York branch of the International Dyslexia Association, which advocates a multisensory approach for teaching children with dyslexia. A non-profit organization dedicated to children and families with special needs. They offer a free telephone referral service to parents looking for information on testing, schools, trained remediators, psychologists and other professionals. The International Dyslexia

Association also sponsors an annual two-day conference on a topic of interest to parents, a conference for teenagers and parent support groups. A yearly membership is available.

The Parents League of New York, Inc., 115 East 82nd Street, New York, NY 10028, (212) 737-7385, website: www.parentsleague.org
The Parents League sponsors a workshop and provides information and referrals about learning disabilities to member parents. The Parents League offers counseling from particularly knowledgeable experts in learning disabilities about which schools specialize in which type of LD.

Resources for Children with Special Needs, 116 East 16th Street, 5th floor, New York, NY 10003, (212) 677-4650, Fax (212) 254-4070, website: www.resourcesnyc.org, e-mail address: info@resourcesnyc.org

Resources for Children is a nonprofit information, referral, advocacy, training and support center for programs and services for children (from birth to age twenty-one) with learning, developmental, emotional or physical disabilities. Resources for Children publishes a family support guide listing camps and summer programs for children with special needs.

Advocates for Children of New York, Inc., 151 West 30th Street, 5th floor, New York, NY 10001, (212) 947-9779, Fax (212) 947-9790, website: www.advocatesforchildren.org

Advocates for Children works to protect and extend the rights of children with learning and/or developmental disabilities in public schools.

National Dissemination Center for Children with Disabilities, 1825 Connecticut Avenue NW, Suite 700, Washington, D.C. 20013-1492, (800) 695-0285, website: www.nichcy.org

A Parent's Guide to Special Education in New York City and the Metropolitan Area, Laurie Dubos and Jana Fromer, Teacher's College, Columbia University Press. 2006.

This is the most complete guide to special education in the area. It is thorough, detailed and informative—an invaluable resource for any parent with a child with learning disabilities or other special needs looking for a school in the New York City area.

Also see the New York City Department of Education's website, www.schools.nyc.gov for special education public school programs.

PUBLIC SCHOOL OPTIONS

Many parents agonize over the choice of public or private school education for their children. If sending their children to private school would be a tremendous financial burden on families already stretched to their limits, it is very important not to add additional pressures. Parents should resist societal pressure and use common sense to make the right decisions for their family. Children might be better off with a parent who is accessible, rather than one who is working 24/7 to make tuition payments. Select public schools offer a top-notch education at a rock bottom price and parents who get involved in their child's school can really make a difference.

The public schools have experienced a revitalization as a result of a number of factors: more families are making the decision to raise their children in the city, and the cost of a private school education is well beyond the reach of many families.

The New York City public school system, the largest in the nation, offers a truly diverse student body, enrichment programs for gifted students, magnet/option programs*, bilingual immersion programs, collaborations with the city's major cultural institutions, corporate grants. Whatever is new and exciting in education is happening in New York City's public schools. Be aware that there is tremendous variation among individual schools in terms of philosophy, physical plant, magnet grants, enrichment programs, extracurricular activities and parent involvement. There are traditional schools as well as smaller "option" schools and charter schools. Much has changed an continues to change since Chancellor Joel Klein has taken the reins at the Department of Education.

The two questions parents ask most often concern class size and safety in the public elementary schools. For grades kindergarten through third grade, class size is "limited" to twenty-five students but can go to twenty-eight or more in some schools. For grades four through six, the maximum class size is generally thirty-two, but can go beyond that. Student-teacher ratios vary from school to school because some schools have student teachers and parents often pay for

*Option or alternative schools are schools of choice that are at the forefront of the educational reform movement. They are small, director-managed schools with a clear guiding vision and specific philosophical, thematic and curricular commitments. Although they are located in regular school buildings, they are autonomous. Staff, parents and students elect to attend these schools. Admission is by application or lottery, which often can be obtained from the schools. Parents must contact each school since application requirements and notification dates vary from program to program.

extra para-professionals to staff classrooms. Regional and district superintendents say "there are fair, firm and consistent rules of discipline in effect at all the elementary schools. Every elementary school should have a guard in front who requests identification from visitors. The standard time to visit and/or preregister for the public school in your catchment area or zone (immediate neighborhood) is during the fall the year before your child will be attending school. See the NYC Department of Education website, infra.

How to Begin Finding Out About New York City Public Schools

1. **The New York City Department of Education's website:** www.schools.nyc.gov; this website is very well-designed, easy to navigate, and provides the most current and accurate information about the city's public schools including a continuum of special education and charter schools.
2. **Center For Educational Innovation/The Public Education Association (CEI/PEA),** 28 West 44th Street, Suite 300 New York, NY 10036, (212) 868-1640, website: www.cei-pea.org, Walter O'Brien, Network Team Leader, email: wobrien@cei-pea.org. This one hundred year old organization which merged with CEI in 1999, is an advocate for high quality schools for all of New York City's public school children. The CEI/PEA's Education Information Center provides timely and useful information to parents and the public about public schools.
3. **The Manhattan White Pages**
   In the front of the telephone book is a section called Government Pages, you will find a listing of all the Manhattan public schools, elementary through high schools.
4. **www.insideschools.org** is a website with information about many public schools. The website is based at Advocates For Children, a Manhattan non-profit organization.
5. **New York City's Best Public Elementary Schools, New York City's Best Middle Schools,** and **New York City's Best Public High Schools,** all by Clara Hemphill, **et al.**

Before calling the elementary school or middle school directly to request a tour, check the Department of Education's website for each school's admissions or enrollment procedures and materials. Many schools' applications or enrollment forms can be filled out on-line and sent in electronically. Representatives of the Parents Association usually conduct school tours and can answer many of your preliminary questions. A school might have an excellent reputation but you should see the school with your own eyes and let the principal/teachers describe the school's philosophy to you. Some alternative/option schools require a parent tour before application.

Students who live within a zone, or regional district, often, but not always, have first priority for enrollment in neighborhood elementary schools, followed by students who live outside the zone but within the district. Students may also attend a school outside their zone providing they qualify and space is available. Parents must contact the district office of the desired school for variance information.

Free busing on a Department of Education School bus to a school outside the student's zone is no longer provided; although busing is provided for students attending a gifted and talented school within the student's district. Students may obtain a bus pass for New York City buses.

PROGRAMS FOR GIFTED AND TALENTED STUDENTS

Tracking (ability grouping) within grades at the elementary level, an educational practice familiar to many baby boomers, has fallen out of favor these days. However, many parents still prefer their "bright" children to be with other children of similar ability. In the past, many middle-class families made financial sacrifices to send their children to prestigious private schools where they would receive an enriched educational program. The burgeoning gifted and talented programs (also known G&T programs) within the New York City public schools are an attempt to lure white, middle class parents back to public education. Much like the private schools, most of the G&T programs require parents to apply on behalf of their children one year prior to the year of enrollment. Some of the public G&T programs will only accept students who score above a certain percentile on a standardized test or I.Q. test. The Stanford-Binet V, for instance, is used in District 2, and is part of a screening process (which includes an interview with the child) at some schools. New York City public school G&T programs fill up quickly and waiting lists are maintained. All of these programs are free of charge.

Many of the programs for talented and gifted students are contained within the public elementary and middle schools. A few programs are housed separately. The gifted and talented programs are not all alike—there are different models and different approaches—parents are advised to check their websites.

Testing

Testing must usually be done the year of application at an approved testing site and by an approved tester. The results are shared with the parents and sent to the program. The usual fee ranges from at least $250 and often accommodation can be made for families who are in need.

The Programs

The programs highlighted below are only a few of the most sought after elementary, middle and high school programs for gifted and talented students available in Manhattan public schools. For information on G&T or alternative programs in your zone, check the Department of Education's website and keep in mind that the birthday cutoff for public schools is December 31.

The Hunter College Campus Schools:
Both Hunter College Elementary School (website: hces.hunter.cuny.edu) and Hunter College High School (website: www.hchs.hunter.cuny.edu) are located at 71 East 94th Street (94th and Park), New York, NY 10128 (212) 860-1267, Kindergarten admissions (212) 860-1401, High School admissions (212) 860-1261.

Hunter College Elementary School, better known as, Hunter Elementary is administered through Hunter College of the City University of New York. The school is tuition free and serves as a laboratory for the study of education of gifted children. You must apply for your child one year in advance of enrollment—apply to kindergarten the year your child is four. Application deadlines are usually around mid-November. Parents can apply directly via the website by downloading admissions materials. Admissions to kindergarten are open only to Manhattan residents. There are no sibling or legacy policies. Getting a child into Hunter Elementary is as prestigious, if not more prestigious, as gaining admission to a top-tier private school. Once parents have applied for kindergarten, they enter the first round of selection—taking the Stanford-Binet V test. Parents receive a list of Hunter approved testers who administer the test for $275. Progression to round two is based on the Sum of Scaled Scores. The qualifying score changes each year based on the current pool of applicants, although it has not dropped below the 97th percentile (or between 142-148 on the Stanford-Binet V) in recent years. Approximately 200 of the roughly 2,000 children who test for Hunter Elementary are invited for the second round of admissions which consists of an on-site assessment, (children come in groups of nine or ten), a simulated preschool class that is taught by a master teacher. While in the class the children are observed by three child psychologists while anxious parents wait in the library. Only 50 children are accepted each year for kindergarten, 25 girls, 25 boys; Hunter maintains an active wait list of 24 children, also equal numbers of girls and boys—your child needs to be both lucky and smart. Reply dates are mid-February.

Hunter College High School, Website: www.hchs.hunter.cuny.edu (212) 860-1267 information, (212) 860-1261 for admissions.

At sixth grade, students from all five boroughs can apply to Hunter for seventh grade, the only point of entry to Hunter High School. Applicants to seventh grade are tested in sixth grade. Parents are advised to visit the website (see above) where all admissions information is posted and they can apply directly on-line. Entrance is based solely on performance on the Hunter entrance exam taken in the sixth grade. Each year there are approximately 2,000 applicants for 164 places. In order to qualify to sit for the entrance exam, student must meet the eligibility criteria for scores on the fifth grade NY-state wide exams. The cut-off score changes from year to year, but is always well within the top 10 percent; in 2009, the qualifying scores were 712 on the ELA portion and 734 on the math. Students outside Department of Education schools can qualify by scoring in the 90th percentile or above on the standardized tests used at their schools. Students who, for some reason, have no fifth grade scores can take a pre-qualifying exam at Hunter for a fee. Students who qualify can apply directly to take the exam, providing official copies of their scores from their schools. The entrance exam is given every year on the first Friday in January. Applications are due by mid-December, there is a $65 fee, no checks or cash, money orders only.

The Anderson Program, Public School 334, 100 West 77th Street, New York, NY 10024, (212) 595-7193 website: www.ps334anderson.org

The Anderson Program accepts applications from all five boroughs for kindergarten through eighth grade. Admissions procedures for kindergarten through fifth grade are available on the Department of Education's website (www.schools.nyc.org) under G&T programs. There are three kindergarten and first grade classes, the rest of the grades each have two classes per grade. Applications can be downloaded from the website. There are also additional in-house tests required for middle school, grades six and seven.

NEST (New Explorations in Science Technology and Math). 111 Columbia Street, New York, NY 10002, Tel (212) 677-5190, website: www.schools.nyc.gov, enter NEST

NEST serves children from kindergarten through 12th grade. Lower school consists of grades kindergarten through fifth, middle school is 6 through eight, and high school is grade 9 through 12. Call or check the school's website for admissions materials and procedures the fall before you plan to enroll.

Delta Honors Program at Booker T. Washington Middle School, MS 54, 103 West 107th Street, New York, NY 10025, (212) 678-5855, Grade 6 through 8, Department of Education website: www.schools.nyc.gov, enter Delta Honors Program.

This honors program housed inside a dreary public school building sends approximately eighty percent of its students onto all the best private and public schools. Founded in 1986, Delta Honors students are admitted on the basis of test results, teacher recommendations, and an interview. Parents must register for tours and check the website or call for specific admissions procedures and materials. Most accepted students score at least in the 90th percentile or higher on the ELA and math tests, and must live in the district. The program is broad, thoughtful and interdisciplinary and even though the facility may seem scary to some parents, the quality of the program makes up for whatever else is lacking.

New York City Laboratory School for Gifted Education (Lower Lab), PS 77, 1700 Third Avenue (between 95th and 96th Streets), New York, NY 10128, (212) 427-2798, Fax (212) 423-0634

The Lab School "operates on the premise that gifted education need not be elitist." The Lab School serves kindergarten through fifth grades. For students across District 2, Lower Lab shares space with PS 196, a zoned elementary school. Expansion plans to add additional classrooms at both PS 77 and PS 196 are a hot topic among members of the PTA, who given the resources would expand city-wide. The current total enrollment is 343 students; students who are admitted to Lower Lab School participate in the citywide G&T process by taking the OLSAT and the BSRA standardized tests. Parents of children who qualify then rank their school choices and are selected accordingly; see the Department of Education's website (www.schools.nyc.gov), enter Lower Lab School for specific admissions procedures and materials. Lower Lab offers a strong core curriculum taught through a variety of approaches, plus a variety of academic and extracurricular activities that encourage students to problem solve and excel in many ways. Students in Lower Lab must apply to the Upper Lab School as they would to any other G&T middle school program as admission to Upper Lab is not automatic.

New York City Laboratory School for Collaborative Studies (Upper Lab School), 333 West 17th Street, New York, NY 10011 (212) 691-6119, Fax (212) 691-6219, website: www.nyclabschool.org or the Department of Education's website www.schools.nyc.gov and enter NYC Lab School for Collaborative Studies.

The Upper Lab consists of grades six through twelve. Total enrollment is approximately 950. The Upper Lab School is rigorous and academic, but non-traditional; emphasis is put on collaborative and interactive approaches to learning combined with team teaching. The Middle School has consistently scored in the top five in reading and math scores in the city. The majority of students come from District 2, but a small number are accepted from out of the district. Applications should be filed by mid-December of the year prior to enrollment. The largest point of entry is at sixth grade. Sixth and seventh graders are required to take a teacher-designed math problem solving test and a teacher-designed essay test; both are administered at the Upper Lab School. Ninth grade is the second largest point of entry. Eighth graders test for ninth grade making the high school even more competitive. Applicants for ninth grade should check specific admissions details on the Department of Education's website. Applicants must have both solid scores and their academic background should include at least one year of Spanish. "We look at grades and courses." Advanced Placement and other college courses are offered in the eleventh and twelfth grades and internships are available in eleventh. Students can take college level courses at area universities including NYU, Borough of Manhattan Community College, Hunter and Parson's School of Design, The New School, and Rockefeller University.

THE PUBLIC HIGH SCHOOLS
The Specialized High Schools

There are nine specialized high schools; eight of them require the Specialized High School Admissions Test (SHSAT) and/or an audition. The nine specialized high schools are Bronx High School of Science, Brooklyn Latin, Brooklyn Technical High School, High School for Mathematics, Science and Engineering at the City College High School, High School of American Studies at Lehman College, Queens High School for the Sciences at York College, Staten Island Technical High School, Stuyvesant High School and LaGuardia High School of Music and Art and Performing Arts. Three of the four specialized high schools mentioned in this guide, Stuyvesant High School, Bronx High School of Science and Brooklyn Technical High School, known as "the science schools," emphasize mathematics and science studies, the fourth, LaGuardia High School of Music and Art and Performing Arts, emphasizes academics and professional expertise in the arts. Recently, approximately 10,000 students were offered spaces at one of NYC's specialized high schools. The New York State Education Law requires a written examination for admission to the science schools. The three science schools are different from one another; check their websites for specific admissions information, procedures and expanded information.

The general timetable for admissions to the specialized high schools is similar to that of many private schools.

THE SPECIALIZED HIGH SCHOOL INSTITUTE
345 Chambers Street
New York, NY 10282
(212) 312-4800 EXT 1012
fax: (212) 312-4815

Founded in 1995 as The Math/Science Institute, and recently renamed The Specialized High School Institute, this is a unique program that has expanded to other boroughs in addition to its original location at Stuyvesant High School. SHSI is not run by or affiliated with Stuyvesant, rather it is its own 18-month preparatory program designed to groom able middle school students from diverse backgrounds for admission to one of the three specialized science high schools. Participating students attend various parochial, public and independent private schools. Housed at Stuyvesant High School, the program has expanded. Recommendation to the program must be made by the student's current school principal or guidance counselor. SHSI has summer sessions and various programs. In addition to test preparation, students take various courses in literature, writing, math, science and research skills.

Bronx High School of Science

75 West 205th Street, Bronx, New York, NY 10468, Tel (718) 817-7700, website: www.bxscience.edu.

Total enrollment: approximately 3,000 students. Students come to Bronx Science from every borough. The Bronx Science yellow school bus can be seen travelling up and down Manhattan's avenues. The school population is approximately 40% of Asian descent. Bronx Science students have opportunities for independent research. There is a Holocaust Study Center and Museum, many foreign languages are offered, and there are partnerships with The Bronx Zoo, Columbia University, and so on. The handbook says, "Bronx Science is the nation's all time leader in the Westinghouse Science Talent Search." The school has five alumni Nobel Laureates. Extracurricular activities include over 60 clubs, numerous school publications, orchestral and vocal music programs, and 30 athletic teams; a nationally acclaimed speech and debate team; mock trial, and a full-scale theatrical production each year.

Brooklyn Technical High School

29 Fort Greene Place (South Elliot Place at DeKalb Avenue), Brooklyn, NY 11217, Tel (718) 804-6400, website: www.bths.edu.

Total enrollment: approximately 4,000 students. The student body is diverse. The brochure states that Brooklyn Tech excels in the areas of engineering, math and science and computer science. During ninth and tenth grades students take an academic core of studies and are introduced to engineering, computer science and lab science through hands-on experiences in well-equipped laboratories. At the end of sophomore year, students select a major area of concentration which they begin in eleventh grade. All tech students are prepared to follow any course of study at the college level, but are particularly well versed in their major area. Brooklyn Tech has over 100 clubs and fields varsity and junior varsity teams in handball, fencing, football, swimming, baseball, soccer and basketball. Brooklyn Tech has affiliations with The Manhattan Theater Club, Polytechnic University, The Brooklyn Philharmonic, Chemical Bank, and Junior Achievement.

Stuyvesant High School

345 Chambers Street, New York, NY 10282, (212) 312-4800, website: www.stuy.edu

Total enrollment: approximately 3,300 students. Stuyvesant High School occupies a high-tech building in lower Manhattan. In addition to advanced courses in mathematics and the sciences, students can select from a wide range of electives. Advanced Placement classes in biology, chemistry, physics, foreign language, mathematics, English and social studies are offered. Stuyvesant's extracurricular offerings are broad. There are over 100 clubs, a symphony orchestra, dance band, choral and ensemble groups, thirty-two athletic teams, fifteen student publications and an active student government. The school has an Olympic-size swimming pool.

Fiorello H. LaGuardia High School of Music and Art and Performing Arts

108 Amsterdam Avenue, New York, NY 10023, (212) 496-0700, website: www.laguardiahighschool.org

Total enrollment: approximately 2,600. LaGuardia is the high school featured in the movie *Fame*. It is the only public high school in the world that offers a complete academic program along with professional-level training in the arts. Because of the dual nature of the program, LaGuardia students can expect to put in very long days. Admission to this high school is based on an individual audition in dance, drama, instrumental music, vocal music, technology or art. Only New York City residents are eligible. The handbook describes what is needed for the audition.

OTHER
RESOURCES

1. **The National Association of Independent Schools (NAIS),** Office of Public Information, 1620 L. Street NW, Suite 1100 Washington, D.C. 20036, (202) 973-9700, website: nais.org. The website has a database of over 1,500 schools and other information.

   NAIS is an organization to which accredited independent schools may apply for membership. The primary function of NAIS is to serve its over 1,400 member schools. NAIS does not accredit independent schools but does issue guidelines, chart trends, sponsor workshops and publish information on issues relevant to the independent school community from diversity to boarding schools. Many of these publications are available on the school's websites.

   Parents who are interested in learning more about boarding schools can call The Association of Boarding Schools (TABS), 95 W Pack Square, Ste 201, Ashville, N.C. 28801, Answer Line, (828) 258-5354, website: www.boardingschools.com. TABS has over 300 member schools and has a fabulous website loaded with information and an entertaining video.

2. **Educational Testing Service (ETS),** Rosedale Road, Princeton N.J., 08541, (609) 921-9000, website: www.ets.org.

   The Educational Testing Service publishes informational pamphlets on many issues related to independent schools.

3. **Reading Reform Foundation of New York,** 333 West 57th Street, Suite 1L, New York, NY 10019, (212) 307-7320, website: www.readingreform.org.

   The Reading Reform Foundation of New York, founded in 1981 by a group of reading specialists and interested citizens, is a non-profit literacy organization based on the belief that almost every child, regardless of social and economic background, can learn to read, write and spell if taught by effective methods (with an emphasis on the use of phonics). Reading Reform Foundation offers graduate level courses, periodically throughout the year in the teaching of reading, writing and spelling, and sends skilled teaching consultants into public schools throughout the city to work with classroom teachers.

4. **The Council for Spiritual and Ethical Education,** PO Box 19807, Portland, Oregon 97280, Tel (503) 232-1531 or 1-(800) 298-4599, website: www.csee.org.

   The Council for Spiritual and Ethical Education (CSEE) is a nondenominational organization composed of approximately 450 member schools the majority of which are secular coed day and boarding schools located all over North America.

CSEE is independent of any religious body and does not impose any one point of view. According to the website, "CSEE offers resources and educational opportunities to independent schools for state-of-the-art programs in moral development, ethical leadership, growth of spirit, and instruction about our world's religious traditions." CSEE conducts workshops, and hosts events and conferences on values and ethics.

CSEE has been actively promoting community service in schools for many years and sponsors conferences that feature community service workshops.

Some New York City Independent Schools that are Members of CSEE: see website for a complete listing.

The Allen-Stevenson School	Marymount School of New York
The Browning School	The Nightingale-Bamford School
The Buckley School	The Packer Collegiate Institute
The Caedmon School	Saint David's School
The Cathedral School	St. Hilda's & St.Hugh's School
Collegiate School	St. Luke's School
Convent of the Sacred Heart	The Spence School
Grace Church School	The Town School
Horace Mann School	Trinity School

5. **The Catholic Center,** Office of Superintendent of Schools, Education Department, 1011 First Avenue (between 55th and 56th) (18th floor), New York, NY 10022, (212) 371-1000

    For a small fee, The Catholic Center will mail its complete directory of elementary and secondary schools.

6. **The National Coalition of Girls' Schools,** Suzanne Beck, Executive Director, 50 Leonard Street, Suite C, Belmont, Massachusetts 02478, (617) 489-0013, website: www.ncgs.org

    The National Coalition of Girls' Schools has over 110 member schools in North America (both public and private). Its members share a commitment to the values and advantages of an all-girl's education. They conduct research, gather data, and sponsor forums for leading girls' and womens' groups; NCGS publications, including: *Choosing a Girls' School* (a directory of girls' schools), *Raising Confident, Competent Daughters,* and *What Every Girl in School Needs to Know,* and *Girls and Technology,* are available by mail order.

7. **American Association of University Women (AAUW),** 1111

Sixteenth Street N.W., Washington, D.C. 20036, 1-(800) 326-AAUW (2289) (membership information and to locate a local branch of AAUW). For a copy of *How Schools Shortchange Girls* and *Separated by Sex: A Critical Look at Single-Sex Education for Girls,* call or check the website. Members' Help Line 1-(800) 326-2289.

In 1992 the AAUW Educational Foundation released the report *How Schools Shortchange Girls* which challenged myths about the education of girls in the public schools and uncovered disturbing evidence of new barriers to their learning. In March 1998 the AAUW released a report that finds separating by sex is not the solution to gender inequity. *Separated by Sex: A Critical Look at Single-Sex Education for Girls* is controversial and well worth reading. Recently, AAUW published *Tech-savvy: Educating Girls in the New Computer Age.* The AAUW has been working toward eliminating the educational, financial and legal barriers faced by women and girls for over 130 years. Parents can request free of charge useful guides for assessing gender bias in their children's schools—the *School Assessment Guide* and *Growing Smart: What Works for Girls in School.*

8. **The Association of Teachers in Independent Schools in New York City and Vicinity, Inc.** (ATIS), P.O. Box 1385, Gracie Station, New York, N.Y. 10028, website: www.atisnyc.org.

    ATIS was found in 1914 to ensure that teachers in private schools were properly paid and protected. Today the incorporated, non-profit organization continues its support of educational professionalism and increased opportunities for private-school teachers. Check the website for specific events, conferences and additional information.

9. **New York Interschool Association Inc.,** 378 West End Avenue, Suite 706, New York, N.Y. 10024, Tel (212) 501-0031, Ms. Cathy Cramer, Executive Director, email: ccramer@interschool.org, website: www.interschool.org. Founded in 1971, Interschool is a close consortium of eight elite Manhattan private schools that participate in a variety of activities, such as faculty and administrative resource sharing, professional development, and selected academic and cultural activities with one another. The eight member schools: Brearley, Browning, Chapin, Dalton, Nightingale-Bamford, Spence, Collegiate and Trinity. In addition, there are approximately 30 or more associated private schools in the New York area.

10. **The Interschool Faculty Diversity Search,** (212) 501-0031, website: www.interschool.org, see Faculty Diversity Search.

    The Search is an organization whose purpose is to enlarge the pool of talented candidates of color for faculty and administrative positions in participating schools. Although the Search is administered by New York Interschool (a consortium of eight Manhattan independent schools), but many more schools (over 30) participate.

11. **The Guild of New York Independent Schools,** Rev. Stephen Katsouros, Present Chair, The Loyola School, Tel (212) 288-3522.

    The guild is an informal association of approximately fifty-two heads of school (from schools located in all five boroughs) who meet approximately twice a year at various clubs around the city, and may meet elsewhere as well, to discuss common concerns and issues within the independent school community and to coordinate their calendars (vacation schedules, opening and closing dates). They do not discuss tuitions. The guild does not provide information to parents about individual schools and the chair rotates every few years. "It's a support system, and it is simply helpful for heads of schools to meet," remarks one former chair.

12. **NYC-Parents in Action Inc.,** P.O. Box 287451, Yorkville Station, New York, NY 10128, (212) 987-9629, website: www.parentsinaction.org

    NYC-Parents In Action, Inc. is a nonprofit, voluntary organization incorporated in 1979 as a parenting education program in response to growing alcohol, marijuana and other drug use among minors and their parents. Rumors circulate that certain schools have more drug and/or alcohol abuse than others. The truth is that a portion of the student body at all the New York City independent high schools (and boarding schools) does experiment with alcohol, drugs and/or sex. NYC-PIA provides information, parent education, seminars and workshops and provides trained facilitators for parent-organized discussion groups. The Parent Representative program provides a link to the parent body within the independent schools. NYC-PIA publishes a newsletter. In cooperation with the Parents' League, NYC-PIA sponsors Teen Scene—a candid discussion of teen life in the city by a panel composed of students from various independent and boarding schools.

13. **New York State Education Office of Non-Public Schools,** New York State Education Department, Non-public School

Services Team, Room 481 Education Building Annex, 89 Washington Avenue, Albany, New York 12234, Tel (518) 474-3879, website: www.emsc.nysed.gov/nonpub

New York State Education Office of Information, Reporting and Technology Services, (a division of the State Education Office that compiles statistical information), Room 863, Education Building Annex, 89 Washington Avenue, Albany, New York 12234, Tel (518) 474-7965, website: www.emsc.nysed.gov/irts

All data is available on the website or often can be obtained more easily from a school's brochure or directly from a school.

ACCREDITING ORGANIZATIONS

The New York State Board of Regents authorizes both the New York State Association of Independent Schools and the Middle States Association to accredit schools. According to the National Association of Independent Schools, "Accreditation is a process of peer evaluation that certifies that schools meet certain generally accepted standards of educational quality defined by an independent entity." Each of the independent schools sets forth its accreditation in one or more of its school publications. Tradition determines which organization accredits the school. NYSAIS deals primarily with the independent schools in New York State, whereas Middle States accredits many independent as well as public schools in the Middle Atlantic states. Note: NYSAIS and Middle States do not provide parents with information about specific schools—do not call them to find out which school is the best for your child.

How does it work? Both NYSAIS and Middle States evaluate a school based on its philosophy (or mission) and how well the school puts its philosophy into practice—is the school doing what it says it does? This evaluation process takes place every ten years or so. The first step in the reaccreditation process is a year-long self-study. Next, the school is evaluated by a team of recognized evaluators, which often includes heads of other independent schools. The evaluating team makes recommendations for improvement, and the school is requested to provide an action plan for implementing these changes. Accreditation is granted if the self-study, evaluation and planning reports reveal that the school meets the standards for accreditation. Accreditation is granted for a period of ten years. After approximately eight and a half years, the school begins another self-study and the cycle is renewed.

1. **New York State Association of Independent Schools (NYSAIS),** 12 Jay Street, Schenectady, NY, 12305 (518) 346-5662, website: www.nysais.org, email: webmaster@nysais.org, Executive Director: Mark W. Lauria, Ph.D.

   NYSAIS is a voluntary association of approximately 170 independent nursery, elementary, middle and secondary schools in New York State whose enrollment is about 60,000 students. NYSAIS publishes a useful pamphlet entitled *Choosing a School: A Guide for Parents.* One of its main activities is advocacy for independent education.

2. **The Middle States Association of Colleges and Schools,** 3624 Market Street, 2nd Floor Annex, Philadelphia, PA 19104, (215) 662-5600 or 5610

   The Middle States Association established standards that are administered by the three accreditation authorities under the auspices of the Middle States Association: the Commission on Elementary Schools, the Commission on Secondary Schools and the Commission on Higher Education. The Middle States Association is a nonprofit organization established in 1887 to set standards for American education. Middle States publishes information on school standards and the accreditation process.

3. **New York State Board of Regents, New York State Education Department,** Meryl H. Tisch, Chancellor, Milton L. Cofield, Vice Chancellor, website: www.regents.nysd.gov.

   According to the Regents website, Regents' responsibilities include the general supervision of all educational activities within New York State as well as presiding over The State University of New York (SUNY) and the New York State Education Department.

Index of Schools and Programs

Family Guide Website Index

Claremont Preparatory School, www.claremontprep.org
Collegiate School, www.collegiateschool.org
Columbia Grammar andPreparatory School, www.cgps.org
Convent of the Sacred Heart, www.cshnyc.org
Corlears School, www.corlearsschool.org
Council for Spritual and Ethical Education, The, www.csee.org
Dalton School, www.dalton.org
Delta Honors Program, schools.nyc.gov, search Delta Honors Program
Dwight School, The, www.dwight.edu
Doctor Topher Collier, www.DrTopherCollier.com
Early Steps, www.earlysteps.org
Ecole Internationale de New York, www.einy.org
Education First, www.nycedu1st.com
Educational Records Bureau, The, www.erb.org
Educational Testing Service, www.ets.org
Ethical Culture Fieldston School, The, www.ecfs.org
Family School, The, www.familyschools.org
Fiorello H. LaGuardia High School of Music and Performing Arts,
    www.laguardiahighschool.org
Frederick Douglass Academy, www.FDA1.com
Friends Seminary, www.friendsseminary.org
Gateway School of New York, The, www.gatewayschool.org
Geneva School, The, www.genevaschool.net
Grace Church School, www.gcschool.org
Greenberg Educational Group Inc., www.greenbergeducationalgroup.com
Hewitt School,The, www.hewittschool.org
Horace Mann School, www.horacemann.org
Howard Greene & Associates, www.howardgreeneassociates.com
Hunter College Elementary School, hces.hunter.cuny.edu
Hunter College High School, www.hchs.hunter.cuny.edu
Independent Educational Consultants Association, The, www.iecaonline.com
Inspirica, www.inspirica.com
Interactive Math Tutor, www.interativemathtutor.com
International Dyslexia Association, The, www.nybida.org
Interschool Faculty Diversity Search, The, www.interschool.org
Kew-Forest School, The, www.kewforest.org
Knickerbocker Greys, The, www.knickerbockergrey.org
La Scuola D'Italia G. Marconi, www.lascuoladitalia.org
Learning Disabilities Association of New York, The, www.LDANYC.com
Learning and Resource Center at Colubia Grammar and Preparatory School,
    The, www.cpgs.org
Lindamood Bell New York Learning Center, www.lindamoodbell.com
Little Red School House and Elisabeth Irwin High School, www.lrei.org
Lower Lab School, www.schools.nyc.gov, enter Lower Lab School

Loyola School, www.loyola-nyc.org
Lycee Francais de New York, www.lfny.org
Lyceum Kennedy, www.lyceumkennedy.org
Mandell School, www.mandellschool.org
Manhattan Country School, www.manhattancountryschool.org
Manhattan Day School, www.mdweb.org
Manhattan Free School, The, www.manhattanfreeschool.org
Manhattan Private School Advisors, www.privateschooladvisors.com
Mary McDowell Center for Learning, The, www.marymcdowell.org
Marymount School of New York, www.mrymount.K12.ny.us
Metropolitan Montessori School, www.mmsny.org
Montessori School of New York International, The,
      www.montessorischoolny.com
National Association of Independent Schools, The, www.nais.org
National Center for Learning Disabilities, The, www.LD.org
National Coalition of Girls' Schools, The, www.ncgs.org
National Dissemination Center for Children With Disabilities, www.nichny.org
NEST, www.schools.nyc.gov
New York City Department of Education, schools.nyc.gov
New York State Association of Independent Schools, www.nysais.org
New York State Board of Regents, www.regents.nysd.gov
New York State Education Office of Information, Reporting and Technology
      Services, www.emsc.nysed.gov/irts
New York State Education Office of Non-Public Schools,
      www.emsc.nysed.gov/nonpub
New York Interschool Association Inc., www.interschool.org
Nightingale-Bamford School, The, www.nightingale.org
NYC-Parents in Action Inc., www.parentsinaction.org
NYU Child Study Center, www.aboutourkids.org
Overqualified LLC, www.overqualifiedtutoring.com
Packer Collegiate Institute, The,www.packer.edu
Parents League of New York, Inc., The, www.parentsleague.org
Philosophy Day School, www.philosophyday.org
Prep for Prep, www.prepforprep.org
Poly Prep Country Day School, www.polyprep.org
Professional Children's School, www.pcs-nyc.org
Rabbi Arthur Schneier Park East Day School, www.parkeastdayschool.org
Ramaz, www.ramaz.org
Reading Reform Foundation of New York, www.readingreform.org
Rebecca School, www.rebeccaschool.org
Regis High School, www.regis-nyc.org
Resources for Children with Special Needs, www.resourcesnyc.org
Riverdale Country School, The, www.riverdale.edu
Robert Louis Stevenson School, www.stevenson.school.org

Rodeph Sholom School, www.rodephsholomschool.org
Rudolf Steiner School, The, www.steiner.edu
Saint Ann's School, www.saintannsny.org
St. Bernard's School, www.stbernards.org
Saint David's School,www.saintdavidschool.org
Saint Hilda's & Saint Hugh's, www.sthildas.org
Saint Luke's School, www.stlukesschool.org
Saint Thomas Choir School, www.choirschool.org
School at Columbia University, The, www.theschool.columbia.edu
School Consultants on Private Education (SCOPE), www.summerscope.com
Schoolhouse Tutors, www.schoolhousetutors.com
School Search, NYC, www.schoolsearchnyc.com
Schools & You, www.schoolsandyou.com
Smart City Kids, www.smartcitykids.com
Smith School, The, www.smithschool.net
Solomon Schechter School of Manhattan, The, www.sssm.org
Spence School, The, www.spenceschool.org
Speyer Legacy School, www.speyerlegacyschool.org
Stephen Gaynor School, www.stephengaynor.org
Studio School, The, www.studioschoolnyc.org
Stuyvesant High School, www.stuy.edu
SuperTrans NY Inc., www.supertrans-ny.com
TEAK Fellowship, The, www.teakfellowship.org
Testing for Kindergarten, www.testingforkindergarten.com
Town School, The, www.thetownschoool.org
Trevor Day School, www.trevor.org
Trinity School, www.trinityschoolnyc.org
United Nations International School, www.unis.org
Upper Lab School, www.nyclabschool.org
Victoria Goldman, www.VictoriaGoldman.net
Village Community School, www.vcsnyc.org
West End Day School, www.westenddayschool.org
Windward School, www.windwardny.org
Winston Preparatory School, www.mail.winstonprep.edu
Yeshiva University High School for Boys, www.yuhsb.org
York Preparatory School, www.yorkprep.org